AF712534

Legal Research Methods in a Modern World: A Coursebook

Also by Henrik Spang-Hanssen:

Cyberspace & International Law on Jurisdiction
1. ed. 2004
ISBN 978-87-574-0890-4

Public International Computer Network Law Issues
1. ed. 2006
ISBN 978-87-574-1486-8

J. Paul Lomio
Henrik Spang-Hanssen &
George D. Wilson

Legal Research Methods in a Modern World: A Coursebook

DJØF Publishing
2011

J. Paul Lomio, Henrik S. Spang-Hanssen & George D. Wilson
Legal Research Methods in a Modern World: A Coursebook
Third edition

© 2011 by DJØF Publishing
Jurist- og Økonomforbundets Forlag

DJØF Publishing is a company of the
Association of Danish Lawyers and Economists

All rights reserved.
No parts of this publication may be reproduced,
stored in a retrieval system, or transmitted in
any form and by any means – electronic, mechanical,
photocopying, recording or otherwise – without the
prior written permission of the publisher.

Cover: Tor Morisse
Print & Binding: Toptryk Grafisk, Gråsten

Printed in Denmark 2011
ISBN 978-87-574-2467-6

Sold and distributed in Scandinavia by:
DJØF Publishing
Copenhagen Denmark
Email: forlag@djoef.dk
www.djoef-forlag.dk

Sold and distributed in North America by:
International Specialized Book Services (ISBS)
Portland, OR 97213, USA
Email: orders@isbs.com
www.isbs.com

Sold in all other countries by:
The Oxford Publicity Partnership Ltd
Towcester NN12 6BT, UK
www.oppuk.co.uk

Distributed in all other Contries by:
Marston Book Services
Abingdon, Oxon, OX14 4YN, UK
Email: trade.orders@marston.co.uk
www.marston.co.uk

The reason "why judges and lawyers should divert … to the principles and decisions of foreign and international law … is globalization. No institution of government can afford any longer to ignore the rest of the world."

Former U.S. Supreme Court Associate Justice Sandra Day O'Connor, Southern Center for International Studies, Atlanta , Georgia, 28 October 2003

The greatest consequence of globalization is that there aren't any purely national solutions to global challenges.

Angela Merkel
German First Chancellor
(Time Magazine, 11 January 2010)

Lawyers today need to be educated more broadly if they are to serve their clients and society well.

Stanford Law School Dean Larry Kramer

Legal education has changed little over the past century. Yet the challenges today's lawyers must meet are wholly new and different. Lawyers can contribute creative and effective solutions if we prepare them to do so … with innovative interdisciplinary and international programs, expanded clinical education, and a deepened, nonpartisan commitment to public service.

John L. Hennessy, Stanford University President

It has become more and more obvious that an international operating lawyer cannot rely anymore on his knowledge of the national system only. He must be trained in comparative legal methodology and open minded to legal solutions of other jurisdictions. …Consequently, the national legal education systems have to adapt to this new generation of lawyers who are not anymore only concentrated on the[ir] own jurisdiction[s] but are global players on the international legal market.

Universiteit Maastricht, The Future of Legal Education (June 2007)

Comparative Legal Studies [should] indeed inspire students to learn more about and rethink the biases of their own cultural and legal education.

Günter Frankenberg, Critical Comparisons: Re-Thinking Comparative Law, 26 Harvard International Law Journal 411, 412 (Spring 1985)

The interest in comparative studies in American law schools is a response to the increasing relevance of foreign law to the concerns of lawyers and their clients on a shrunken, interdependent globe. Both as professionals and as leaders in the public and private sectors, lawyers in the West participate in a continual institutional reconstruction of the relevant world. Now that their relevant world embraces both the common law and the civil law … a familiarity with other people's law is indispensable to an adequate legal education.

Mauro Cappelletti, Preface to J. Merryman & D. Clark, Comparative Law: Western European and Latin American Legal Systems (Indianapolis: Bobbs-Merrill 1978), at vii

[The] common-law lawyer and [civil-law lawyer] each [has] assumed the modes of thought in which he had been trained to be fundamental and universal … [leading to] horrible examples of legal provincialism….

Roscoe Pound, The Place of Comparative Law in the American Law School Curriculum, 8 Tulane Law Review 161, 167 (Feb. 1934)

The case-study method paints a wrong picture of the legal profession for law students because of its reliance on using appellate cases to teach legal thoughts or reasoning based on the Langdell (Socratic) method.

Professor Douglas A. Berman, Ohio State University, ABA Journal (July 2007), at page 44

Tomorrow's lawyers will be plucking increasingly valuable data from exponentially-growing fields of information, working with colleagues and clients spanning the globe, and establishing automated systems to leverage scarce legal resources more efficiently.
Law plays a foundational role in American society and increasingly in articulating our global community.

Gene Koo, New Skills, New Learning, at page 24

The global economy is becoming more interconnected, so thinking how to teach comparative and international law becomes more and more important every year.

Columbia Dean David Schizer, The National Law Journal (September 10, 2007)

A comparatist should not limit to the staid and dry juxtaposition of the regulations of one legal system with those of another, with little or no critical analysis; as such, comparatists do not compare, they contrast. What is required is analysis.

Werner F. Menski, Comparative Law In A Global Context (2007)

Preface

First edition - It is nearly impossible for foreign students, scholars and lawyers/jurists, on visits of some months to either an American university or other research institution, to learn how to do legal research effectively on U.S. material. One has to have experienced American society and, moreover, the U.S. legal research environment, for quite some time to be able to truly understand the way American legal research is conducted.

The same can be said about Americans visiting Europe and its different legal families.[1]

This book is an attempt to outline usefully the basic research methods in the United States (overall common-law) and in Europe (overall civil-law). In addition, it tries to point out the salient issues the "visiting" scholar in particular should remember.

The two chapters on European Union resources (Chapter 4) and public international resources (Chapter 5) were deemed by the authors to be pertinent in the context of earlier chapters on U.S. and European sources and legal methods. The subsequent, shorter chapters on legal families (Chapter 6) and on comparative law (Chapter 7) also seemed appropriate.

We have tried to make the content of this book proportionate to the amount of lecture material that would ordinarily be provided in a course on legal research methods.

The process of writing the book has been a collaborative effort between Paul Lomio and Henrik Stakemann Spang-Hanssen. The former took responsibility for Chapter 2. The latter composed the bulk of the draft manuscript and assumed responsibility for Chapters 3-7. The authors have reviewed and discussed each other's contributions.

[1] The American law graduate will likewise find that at least two years is necessary for studying abroad in Europe effectively, and that "the first year is likely to be wasted." Max Rheinstein, *Comparative Law – Its Functions, Methods and Usages*, 22 ARK. L. REV. 415, 424 (Fall 1968). The organization of legal studies in Europe is "so different" from what it is in the U.S. that "an American student is likely to be lost unless he is individually guided." *Idem.* at 424-25.

The authors devoted special attention to Sections 2.1. and 3.1. from the perspective of their national legal systems, so as to make sure the different "cultures" in the U.S. and Europe are emphasized for the book's readers.

We anticipate receiving many suggestions for improvement and we hope, in turn, to be able to bring out improved later editions of the book.

We are extremely grateful to George D. Wilson, reference librarian, attorney-at-law and lecturer in law at Stanford Law School, for his invaluable comments on and contributions to the manuscript and for his careful proofreading. Also, we would like to thank Alba Holgado at the Robert Crown Law Library for her expert help in making the front-page and several graphics/tables.

If this book will help prevent even just a few students, scholars and lawyers/jurists from making the most common mistakes, our goal will have been fulfilled.

In addition, we hope it will assist students around the world who participate in such activities as the annual Philip C. Jessup International Law Moot Court Competition in Washington D.C. (arranged by the International Law Student Association (ILSA)), who have gained access to Westlaw and LexisNexis databases for international legal materials but who still must gain understanding of how these databases work. To such individuals especially, [3rd ed.: section 5.3, Chapter 11, and Appendix 2 & 5] should be of help

We would like to emphasize that in this book we use the term "law" in the sense it is used in the U.S. (covering the broad body of judicial decisions, legislative enactments, and administrative/executive regulations/rules) and not as in Civil Law countries, where the term is mostly only regarded as the law made by parliaments. For the latter meaning, we generally use the terms "act" or "statute."

Because the URLs of websites often change, we have chosen only to give references to main/home webpages. Pinpoint URLs can be found at our special website for the book at [now] <**www.hssph.net/legalrm**>, which will be kept current updated from time to time. As Chapter 2 points out, currency is an obsession with the American lawyer.

Citations in footnotes have generally been made on the basis of the American legal citations system. The bibliography in the appendix has been constructed in accordance with the European system, including full spelling of American law reviews. As this book does not deal with case law decisions in detail, it does not contain a case list.

Robert Crown Law Library, Stanford University, September 2007

J. Paul Lomio & Henrik Stakemann Spang-Hanssen

****

Preface to **Second edition** - This second edition is primarily an update of Chapter 4 due to the expected changes in the European Union caused by the Lisbon Treaty of December 2007.

Some errors in the first edition have been corrected.

Tips and notes in grey shadings have been included in chapters 1, 3-7.

I would like to thank Professor and Library Director Lee F. Peoples, Oklahoma City University, very much for his suggestion to make a "manual" for teaching European Civil Law. A first draft was published in March 2008 with approval of Professor Peoples and made available through a link from the book's corresponding website. A new version of this document is attached to this second edition as an Addendum of the book (without copyright for DJØF).[2]

As my co-author has unfortunately been too much burdened with other tasks, a real revised edition must come later.

The updates – with few exceptions - have been made in chapters of which I am the sole author and I have the full responsibility for any faults made in this second edition.

Because the book's paragraphs are written with justified alignment, text sometimes will occur with large spaces between words in connection with a longer URL for a website. But I have chosen not to cut the (true) URL, which

[2] This "manual" can also be found as "The Modern Law School's *Uriaspost* - the Post of Danger" at <http://ssrn.com/abstract_id=1102293> (where it may also have been updated from the text printed in this book).

would be the only way to eliminate such large space.

I am extremely grateful to George D. Wilson for his once again careful proofreading.

Great thanks also go to Alba Holgado at the Robert Crown Law Library for her expert help in making several graphics.

Also, it should be noted that websites are often changed, and thus we have chosen not to give pinpoint references to websites' URLs in the book, but rather to announce them at this book's corresponding website at <www.hssph.net/legalrm>, which will be kept updated from time to time.

Leland Stanford Junior University, August 2008

Henrik Stakemann Spang-Hanssen

****

Preface to current edition – This edition is expanded and revised to a large extent from previous editions; hence, the new title **Legal Research Methods in the Modern World**. Chapters have been reshuffled so the book should correspond more to the curriculum/syllabus for courses on legal research methods in foreign law / finding resources in foreign law and/or how to study foreign law. In this respect, new chapters (e.g., on Russia and China and on researching foreign law) have been included. To help American teachers in this respect, syllabuses have been included for some chapters, see the Appendix. For the same reason, we have at the end of each chapter made a bibliography ("Further Reading") and removed the full alphabetic bibliography to the book's corresponding website at <**www.hssph.net/legalrm**>. The Appendix portion on renumbering/equivalences tables of E.U. treaties from previous editions has been removed – for lack of space – to <**www.hssph.net/legalrm/Research_book_2-Edition_Appendix_4.pdf**> at our special website for the book. Furthermore, previous chapters 2 (U.S. – now chapter 5) and 4 (E.U. – now chapter 9) have been updated to respond to more current facts and circumstances. In the case of American legal research, the book explains the impacts of recent, significant developments, such as the introduction of Bloomberg Law, WestlawNext and the revolutionary Law.gov movement.

Like previous editions, Henrik Stakemann Spang-Hanssen has done the overall editing, layout and the Index for the full manuscript. Great thanks go again to Alba Holgado at the Robert Crown Law Library for her expert help in making several graphics.

The process of writing this edition has been a collaborative effort between J. Paul Lomio, George D. Wilson and Henrik Stakemann Spang-Hanssen. Messrs. Lomio and Wilson took primary responsibility for Chapter 5 (U.S.). Spang-Hanssen assumed responsibility for all other Chapters. The authors have reviewed and discussed each other's contributions. The authors again devoted special attention to make sure the different legal "cultures" in the U.S. and Europe are emphasized for the book's readers.

We intend to update our special website for the book, now at <**www.hssph.net/legalrm**>, more frequently.

Leland Stanford Junior University, January 2011

Paul Lomio
Henrik Stakemann Spang-Hanssen
George D. Wilson

We have received many fine suggestions for improvements, for which we are extremely grateful, as to revision of the first edition – which truly was only the authors' first attempt to construct an initial, simple "bridge across the Atlantic Ocean" – and we still hope to receive more comments and suggestions, which will also be highly appreciated and should be sent to:

Paul Lomio: plomio@stanford.edu and/or
George D. Wilson gwilson@stanford.edu and/or
Henrik Stakemann Spang-Hanssen: hssph@yahoo.com

About the Authors

J. Paul Lomio is Library Director and Lecturer in Law at Stanford Law School. He holds both a U.S. Juris Doctor degree and an LL.M. degree in Law and Marine Affairs as well as a Masters of Library and Information Science. He was admitted to the Washington State Bar Association and was a member of the Gonzaga Law Review and has published several law review articles. He taught Resources in the Law at San Jose State University (SJSU) for ten years and currently teaches Advanced Legal Research at Stanford Law School (SLS). He was appointed to the Law Librarians Advisory Committee for the California Office of Administrative Law, served a three-year term on the Association of American Law Schools Committee on Libraries and Technology and is a member of the Electronic Court Filing Task Force for the United States District Court, Northern District of California. He currently serves as a member of the West Academic Advisory Board. He has received several distinguished awards, including the Marshall D. O'Neill Award for "exceptional and enduring support of Stanford University's Research Enterprise." See: <www.law.stanford.edu/library>.

Henrik Stakemann Spang-Hanssen is a Danish Supreme Court Attorney-at-law. Since 1998, he has worked as an independent senior researcher and been Lecturer in Law, residing mostly in the United States. He holds masters degrees in law from Copenhagen University in Denmark and Santa Clara University in California. He has clerked for the Chief Justice of the Supreme Court of Denmark. He has taught courses/seminars for law students, paralegals, and attorneys. He practiced law in his own law firm for over 15 years and worked as an external District Attorney in Appeals Courts in Denmark. He has been an elected member of the Attorney Disciplinary Board for the Copenhagen District. He has served as chairperson of a special committee on debt-collecting businesses and been a member of the Danish Law Society's committee concerning foreclosure auctions, debt-collecting businesses, bankruptcies and moratoria. He has several times served as a judge at the international final rounds of the Phillip C. Jessup International Law Moot Court Competition in Washington, D.C. He is a member of The American branch of the International Law Association (ABILA), The American Society of International Law (ASIL) and an associate member of the American Bar Association. In addition, he has written (in Danish) the two fundamental books used by the Danish Law Society (Denmark's bar association) and the Danish Attorney Disciplinary Board – "Advokatnævnet" (chaired by a Justice of the Supreme Court of Denmark) - and three books (in English) on issues of public international law and cyberspace. He is regarded by many as an expert on the intersection of public international law and public international computer networks. See: <www.hssph.net>.

George D. Wilson is Reference Librarian, and has been a Lecturer in Law, at SLS. He holds a U.S. Juris Doctor degree (from Georgetown University Law Center) as well as a Masters of Library and Information Science degree (from SJSU). He is a member (inactive) of the bars of California, Colorado, the District of Columbia and Maryland, and is admitted to practice before various U.S. federal courts. He has practiced law in California and Washington, DC. He has taught Advanced Legal Research and Foreign and International Legal Research at SLS. He has authored/co-authored or edited/co-edited a number of publications. He is a member of several professional associations/societies. See: <http://stanford.edu/~gwilson/>.

All authors have taught university courses on legal research.

Summary Table of Contents

Table of Contents

CHAPTER 1

Introduction

To the non-American reader: Please take notice on vital information given in footnotes in this book –as an American reader would do (In other US-works it might be in end-notes.

1.1. Why one cannot use his/her own legal methods on foreign material

The organization of legal studies in Europe is "so different" from what it is in the U.S. that "an American student is likely to be lost unless he is individually guided."[1] The same can be said about Civil Lawyers searching for American material.

In this respect should not be forgotten, that the greatest consequence of globalization is that there aren't any purely national solutions to global challenges[2] and that the reason why [todays] judges and lawyers should divert to the principles and decisions of foreign and international law is globalization. No institution of government can afford any longer to ignore the rest of the world.[3] Thus, Lawyers today need to be educated more broadly if they are to serve their clients and society well.[4]

A basic requirement to do this, is knowing how to find and do research in foreign countries' legal material. In this respect should be noted that Civil Law is today the dominant legal tradition in:[5]

[1] The American law graduate will find that at least two years is necessary for studying abroad in Europe effectively, and that "the first year is likely to be wasted, "Max Rheinstein, *Comparative Law – Its Functions, Methods and Usages*, 22 ARK. L. REV. 415, 424-25 (Fall 1968).

[2] Angela Merkel, German First Chancellor, TIME MAGAZINE, 11 January 2010.

[3] Former Associate Justice of the U.S. Supreme Court Sandra Day O'Connor, *Southern Center for International Studies, Atlanta , Georgia*, 28 October 2003.

[4] Stanford Law School Dean Larry Kramer.

[5] See Chapter 2 on legal families.

- Continental Europe, including Russia
- All of Central and South America
- Many parts of Africa
- Many parts of Asia
- American State of Louisiana
- American Territory of Puerto Rico
- Canadian Province of Quebec
- Israel

1.2. Overview of division of "sources-of-law" in different areas

As the term "sources of law" is ambiguous and can be misunderstood, in this book we have divided the term into: (a) "law-source(s)" and (b) "law-foundation-sources".[6]

We reformulate "sources of law" to "*law-sources*,"[7] which is something (such as a constitution, treaty, statute, or custom) that provides authority for legislation and for judicial decisions. This is the normal American understanding in a legal research course. The term will be used for the remainder of this book, except in Chapter 5 (on US legal research methods). Thus, it deals with the concepts of governmental institutions that formulate legal rules and the published manifestations of the law.[8]

We also reformulate "sources of law" to "*law-foundation-sources*" (only with a plural "s"), and by that we mean the science / knowledge on/of jurisprudence / origins of legal concepts and ideas.[9] This a highly particular, scientific term, for what a jurist considers regarding what should and what should not be allowed to be a source of law.[10] For example, should "custom" or "legal cultural tradition" be allowed to be a "source of law"? This subject

[6] Together these terms cover the Latin term "*fons juris*", see BLACK'S LAW DICTIONARY (9th ed.) (St. Paul, Minnesota: West, 2009) ,p. 1523 & John William Salmond, JURISPRUDENCE (7th ed.)(London: Sweet & Maxwell, 1928), p. 164, available at the Internet Archive at <http://www.archive.org/stream/jurisprudence00salmuoft/jurisprudence00salmuoft_djvu.txt> [herinafter SALMOND].

[7] The Danish terms are a "retskilde" and "retskildetyper"

[8] Roy M. Mersky, Donald J. Dunn & J. Myron Jacobstein, FUNDAMENTALS OF LEGAL RESEARCH 1-2 (8th ed.)(University casebook series)(New York, N.Y.: Foundation Press, 2002) [hereinafter MERSKY].

[9] *Idem.*

[10] The Danish term "retskilde"

matter is covered in a basic, first-year, university course in Civil Law countries.[11] The concept is sometimes even in the U.S. called "sources of law" and deals with what a source of law is, what it should be, and how it arises; how to make interpretations of legal texts; how to use a source or sources of law; and whether there exists any governing hierarchy.[12]

1.2.1. Chart on Law-Sources in Public International Law

The division of law-sources in public international law is listed in Article 38 of the Statute for the International Court of Justices and on that basis the following overview table can be made:

Primary Sources (Ranked)	Jus Cogens[13]			
	International Treaties – establishing rule expressly recognized by the [involved] States	International Custom - as evidence of a general practice accepted as law	The General Principles of law recognized by civilized nations	The practice of international organizations, most notably that of the United Nations, as it appears in the resolutions of the Security Council and the General Assembly
Soft law[14]	Judicial decisions	The most highly qualified juristic writings		

Table 1: Overview of Law-Sources in Public International Law

1.2.2. Chart on Law-Sources in the United States

The division of law-sources in United States law can be listed as indicated in the following table:

[11] The Danish term for the university course is termed "Retskildelære."

[12] SALMOND *supra* note 6 and MERSKY *supra* note 8.

[13] AKEHURST'S MODERN INTRODUCTION TO INTERNATIONAL LAW 56-60 (8th ed.) (by Peter Malanczuk)(New York ; London : Routledge, 2002) [hereinafter AKEHURST].

[14] *Idem*, at 54.

Primary Sources (Ranked)	Constitution of the United States (including Treaties)			
	Statutes	Regulations and administrative law decisions	Case law	
Secondary Sources (No ranking)	Encyclopedias	Hornbooks	Treatises	Articles in Law Reviews & Scholarship Networks
	American Law Reports	Restatements of Law (American Law Institute)	Legal Dictionaries	

Table 2: Overview of Law-Sources in the United States

1.2.3. Chart on Law-Sources in Civil Law

The division of law-sources in Civil Law countries can be listed as indicated in the following table:

Hard Law (Somewhat no ranking)	Judicial precepts: - Constitution - Acts, codes, statutes - Regulations or government decrees - Treaties - E.U. regulations & directives	Precedence cases	Customary law
Soft law (No ranking)	Preparatory work	Law commentaries	Statements by Parliamentary Ombudsman
	Legal literature describing already existing rules or law	Case law	

Table 3: Overview of Law-Sources in default Civil Law country

1.2.4. Chart on Law-Sources in European Union Law

The division of law-sources in the European Union law can be listed as indicated in the following table:

Hard Law (Ranked)	Treaty of European Union (TEU) & Treaty on the Functioning of the European Union (FTEU)		
	Regulations (general application & binding in all Member States)	Directives (Implementation into national laws – not necessary for all Member States)	Decisions (binding upon those to whom decision is addressed)
Soft law[15] (No ranking) (Some claim there are no "secondary sources" in the E.U.)	White & Green Papers	Law commentaries	Statements by Ombudsman
	Reports from Commission	E.U. Parliament documents/journals	Member States' Parliament documents/journals

Table 4: Overview of Law-Sources in the European Union

1.3. Short overview of differences between common law and Civil Law

The different approaches of Common Law and Civil Law once were described as follows: continental jurists "have attempted to go too far, to define and fix that which cannot, in the nature of things, be defined and fixed."[16] Indeed, "[t]hey seem to have forgotten

- that they wrote on a question which touched the comity of nations, and that that comity is, and ever must be, uncertain;
- that it must necessarily depend on a variety of circumstances which cannot be reduced to any certain rule;
- that no nation will suffer the laws of another to interfere with her own to the injury of her citizens;

[15] Soft law on E.U. "law" cannot be found in general but have to be searched through the particular E.U. Member State on which one wants to do research (see Research Tip 9.1 in Chapter 9).

[16] *Hilton v. Guyot*, 159 US 113, 144 (US 1895). The words are from U.S. Supreme Court Justice Joseph Story's treatise *Commentaries on the Conflict of Laws, Foreign and Domestic*, quoting Louisiana Supreme Court Justice Porter about the difficulty of applying the positive rules laid down by the European jurists .

- that whether they do or not must depend on the condition of the country in which the foreign law is sought to be enforced, the particular nature of her legislation, her policy, and the character of her institutions;
- that in the conflict of laws, it must often be a matter of doubt, which should prevail; and
- that, whenever a doubt does exist, the court, which decides, will prefer the laws of its own country to that of the stranger."[17]

However, it would certainly be wrong to make out that there was an unbridgeable opposition between Common Law's method of inductive problem-solving and Civil Law's method of systematic conceptualism.[18]

In Europe today, Civil Law and Common Law show several signs of convergence. In the United Kingdom, statutory law increasingly overrides common law traditions of judicial law-making, while on the continent, legal theory increasingly acknowledges the fact and necessity of judicial precedent and law-making. Important areas of the law are unified under international treaties. British judges faithfully implement European Union law that is based primarily on Civil Law notions. The Court of Justice of the E.U. creatively applies principles from both legal worlds. Nevertheless, despite refreshing Common Law input, the dominant legal culture of the European Union and the emerging *ius commune Europaeum*[19] remain very much in the Civil Law tradition.[20]

European scholars often criticize the way Americans do legal research. However, they seem to forget that it is a question of doing legal research in a country where there is a body of law that to a large extent is built on cases, which means one must compare different judges' opinions and decisions.

In addition, even if one can find a statutory provision, it is necessary to compare it with case law to see whether the latter has invalidated, or changed, or added to the statute's content - or vice versa [think "Shepardize or KeyCite" – see Chapter 5].

Thus, the European scholars who criticize American legal research methods seem not to understand the U.S. legal system..

[17] *Idem.*

[18] K. Zweigert & H.Kötz, INTRODUCTION TO COMPARATIVE LAW 33, 251 (3rd ed.)(Tony Weir trans., Clarendon Press, Oxford 1998).

[19] See Glossary in Appendix 1.

[20] Herbert Hausmaninger, THE AUSTRIAN LEGAL SYSTEM 320 (Vienna: Manzsche Verlags- und Universitätsbuchhandlung, 2003).

It appears to be the widely-followed rule in the United States that if one wants to make a legal point or advance a legal thesis and validate it, one must cite copiously to authoritative sources (with exact page references – "pinpoint citations") that support one's view;[21] compare Article 38(1)(d) in the Statute of the International Court of Justice ("ICJ Statute"), which in general means simply to cite either to case law or to other scholars' articles.[22]

It is arguably a phantom or a failure of Civil Law scholars to assert that any claimed idea (thesis) is of their own invention. In the modern context of the World Wide Web it is more than likely that someone somewhere else already has dealt with the same thing and opined on it in an article, law review, book or blog. Thus, to some extent, it is even unethical for Civil Law scholars not to cite to foreign publications and scholars and instead claim they are the inventors of an idea or thesis.

Furthermore, in literature on public international law it is common practice among the "most highly qualified publicists of the various nations" – a source itself in ICJ Statute 38(d)(1) – to cite and refer to other scholars in footnotes.

The aim of Chapter 5 of this book is to educate scholars outside the U.S. on how to do research on American legal material and how to then draw some useful comparisons and contrasts for analysis in order to gain at least a modicum of understanding. Chapter 5 also seeks to illuminate the vital differences between American and, for example, European continental legal research methods. If one is making comparison or reference to American material, one will have to use the American legal method; only then can one truly compare it with European material and concepts, using the continental legal method.

It is an often seen failure of European scholars, and a dreadful mistake, to cite an American case or statute or regulation at hand without doing proper Shepardizing or KeyCiting, that is, using a legal citatory to the present validity of the case or statute. Such check should be done just before printing or delivering articles or manuscripts to publishers. Otherwise, for example, a dissertation involving American material should be denied eligibility for a doctoral defense in Europe. The problem of validation is probably grounded

[21] The scholar has no other power than the one that comes from his capacity to persuade. Rodolfo Sacco, *Legal Formant:, A Dynamic Approach to Comparative Law* (Installment II of II), 39 AM. J. COMP. L 343, 349 (Spring 1991).

[22] European scholars should note that most U.S. professors appear to be of the opinion that if an article does not have at least 100 citations (including of the pinpoint variety), it is not worth publishing.

on the European scholar's lack of education in and knowledge of using by and large up-to-the-minute legal resources such as Westlaw and LexisNexis for cite checking rather than merely as library search tools.

It should be noted here in this discussion of Civil-Common Law differences, at least in passing, that the American State of Louisiana is a Civil Law state,[23] and that the State of California, for example, is described at times as a "statute" state because of the large number of acts passed by the California Legislature (and signed by the Governor).

As for the difference between American and European scholars' work, one should note that an American dissertation for a law-related doctoral degree (equivalent to a European PhD) may typically be a minimum of 500 hundred pages long, with myriad footnotes (pinpointing the page of each reference citation), a table of cases and also a bibliography. American legal scholars regard an article or book without large amounts of footnotes (and, again, specifying the page of each reference citation) as essentially without value. This is due to the widespread opinion that an author's point of view becomes stronger when he or she can make abundant reference to case law or other scholars of like opinion.

In Europe, the stepping stone for legal students and scholars is the text of the law in question. There is very little unwritten law; case law is overall without importance. Thus, the basic building block, and starting point for analysis, of the law in Europe is the wording of a particular paragraph of a statute (In Europe, the symbol "§" can be used for a paragraph, section, and even a single statute; in the United States the symbol "¶" is used solely for a paragraph, while the "§" is employed only for a section).

A European dissertation for a PhD will usually be no more than 300 pages long, with very few footnotes; but it will contain an appendix with a bibliography (without pinpointing of the pages of reference citations) and no case list.

Some European scholars regard extensive use of footnotes (with pinpoint

[23] *Reynolds v. Swain*, 13 La. 193 (Louisiana Supreme Court 1839). As to differences between Louisiana law and the law of other U.S. states, see Robert A. Pascal, *Louisiana Civil Law and Its Study*, 60 LA. L. REV. 1 (Fall 1999). The U.S. territory of Puerto Rico is also belonging to Civil Law category.

citations) as a kind of plague[24] and, moreover, as an expression or evidence of the author only having compiled other people's opinions and ideas without any personal contribution, ideas, and opinion. Therefore, European legal scholars should not be astonished why their works are often rejected for publication by American law reviews.

Chapter 5 is written as an American will present and write the subject. Furthermore, it is written to be used for American courses on legal research methods.

Other chapters are written as an European will present and write the subject matter.

Thus, this book provides the reader with different ways of presenting and writing. The different styles of Chapter 5 and the other chapters are intended to help illustrate the differences in styles of law-related literature between America and Europe.

Europeans (Civil Law lawyers) have to learn that information in footnotes in American legal literature is regarded as having great value and should be studied seriously.

Americans have to learn that in Europe cited literature and bibliographies should be studied to find articles or books of importance – and that they will generally not find exact page-references in footnotes.

The main reason for this difference is that in Europe publication costs are very high; thus, publishers want to limit the amount of words/pages and physical paper consumption.[25]

The two cultures may never find a common denominator, as neither American or European scholars appear ready to denounce their vown ways of doing legal

[24] U.K. Oxford Professor V. Lowe has used the following new approach: "I have largely eliminated footnote references that can be found quickly and easily with Google. More readers are likely to be within reach of the Internet than within reach of a good law library," Preface in Vaughan Lowe, INTERNATIONAL LAW (England: Oxford University Press, 2007)(an update of James Brierly's LAW OF NATIONS)

[25] The latter was not originally based on eco-culture reasons, but the use of cutting trees/wood for publication purposes has become a profound environmental concern in Europe.

scholarship, including how they use footnotes and make citations.

Thus, each culture have to learn to use each others way of doing things – and how to present their scholarly works on the other side of the bridge.

A rough overview comparison between Common Law and Civil Law thinking can be set forth as follows:

Common Law	Civil Law
The law is a gradual development from court decision to court decision	The law is the codification – nation by nation – of abstract rules
A decision is never made until it has to be made – and only concrete experience counts	Decisions are made in advance in the abstract and they systematize the applicable rules
All aspects of a unitary legal transaction should be dealt with in the same place in the legal system (e.g., "law of sale" should deal with both the question of delivery and the question of the change in ownership from a sales transaction)	Aspects of a unitary legal transaction are separated into their discrete parts (e.g., a separate law of sale and claim of ownership)
Lawyers look at things in concrete practice	Lawyers look at things in the abstract
The frame of mind is to prefer to proceed cautiously, on the basis of experience, from this case or that case to the next case, as justice in each case seems to require	The frame of mind seeks to refer everything back to supposed universals
The approach is not to try to deduce the decision for the case at hand from any universally formulated proposition	
The underlying approach is based on the surefooted Anglo-Saxon habit of dealing with things ad hoc as they arise	The underlying approach is one based on anticipating things by abstract universal formulas
The Common Law lawyer reasons from instances to principles	The Civil Law lawyer reasons from principles to instances
The Common Law lawyer puts his or her faith in precedents	The Civil Law lawyer puts his or her faith in syllogisms[26]
The Common Law lawyer asks aloud in the same situation: "What did we do last time?"	The Civil Law lawyer silently asks in each situation: "What should we do this time?"
The working rule of the Common-Law lawyer is solvitur ambulando[27]	The instinct of a Civil Law lawyer is to systematize

[26] A "syllogism" can be defined as: (1) a deductive scheme of a formal argument consisting of a major and a minor premise and a conclusion (as in "every virtue is laudable; kindness is a virtue; therefore kindness is laudable"); (2) a subtle, specious, or crafty argument; (3) deductive reasoning (MERRIAM-WEBSTER DICTIONARY ONLINE <www.m-w.com/>).

[27] Latin for: "It is solved by walking," that is, the problem is solved by a practical experiment.

The Common Law lawyer thinks concretely in terms of cases, the relationship of the parties, and "right and duties"	The Civil Law lawyer thinks abstractly in terms of institutions
Common Law lawyers feel their way gradually from case to case	The Civil Law system is conceived as being complete and free of gaps
Common Law lawyers are skeptical of every generalization	Civil-Law lawyers delight in the systematic
Common Law lawyers think in pictures	Civil Law lawyers operate with ideas that often take on a life of their own
Case law	Enacted law
The law is concrete and comes from courts	The law is abstract and comes from study
Judges are recruited from among great lawyers	Judges are recruited from among professors
Judges were previously private attorneys	Judges were previously government officials
There is no division into private and commercial law	The law is divided into private and commercial law

Table 5: Comparison between Common Law and Civil Law Thinking

1.4. How to use the material – US common law – Civil Law (not filling in gaps but making interpretations)

In Civil Law there is a distinction between "hard" (sometimes termed "binding") and "soft" law. This distinction is sometimes characterized as between "primary" and "secondary" sources of law; these terms will no doubt be confusing for American readers, as they have a totally different meaning under U.S. Common Law, in which case law is a "primary source."

Another point to be emphasized is that Civil Law judges do not fill in gaps in "the law" (in the U.S.: "making law"). They are restricted only to filling in gaps in a very limited number of areas, that is, to make "close" interpretations of statutory text, or in situations where a statute's text explicitly allows a court to fill in a defined "gap" in the statute or act.

Civil Law lawyers do not talk about branches of law. Instead, they talk about the hierarchy of law based on the learning from the basic "legal research-course" on "law-foundation-sources."[28]

Civil Law is made by parliament, not by the "government," which latter term is used totally differently in the U.S. The Civil Law term "legislation" refers only to acts by parliament and decrees/rules issued via delegation from

[28] See explanation above in section 1.2.

such acts.

1.4.1. Translations

European courts and governments will never rely on non-(officially) authorized translations. Thus, it should be carefully ascertained just who did the translating of a document. A translation made by the author of the original document will usually be accepted.

Machine translations should only be used for giving a foreign reader an idea of what written material contains. He/she should never regard machine translation as reliable.[29]

1.4.2. Interpretation

The aim of interpretation[30] is to find the legal purpose or meaning, which might be different from the immediate linguistic meaning.[31]

The following different, yet "classic," interpretation methods do not influence the determination of the meaning or use of a rule:

- The most important interpretation method is the *Lex Superior Principle* – a rule at a higher level in the hierarchy is to be preferred over a rule on a lower level, that is , a legal rule issued by a lower body has to comply with rules on a higher level.
- A consultative interpretation-rule for choice between rules at the same level is the *Lex Posterior Principle* – a newer statute comes before an older statute. However, there might be some reason why the older

[29] Sarah Yates, *I Need This in English*, 9 AALL SPECTRUM 8-11 (2004-05); Francisco Avalos, *Legal Translations: Some Tips* (Lecture delivered at National Language Resource Center, San Diego State University on July 24, 1998 at <www.law.arizona.edu/Library/research/guides/legal_translations.cfm?page=research>, Harold Somers, *Use of Machine Translation by Law Librarians A Reply to Yates*, 99 LAW LIBRARY JOURNAL, VOL. 99:3, 611-619 (2007), Amber Lee Smith, *Foreign Law in Translation: Problems and Sources*, Chapter 14 in INTRODUCTION TO FOREIGN LEGAL SYSTEMS pp 267-271.

[30] Interpretation, as applied to written law, is the art or process of discovering and expounding the intended signification of the language used, that is, the meaning which the authors of the law designed it to convey to others. Henry Campbell Black, HANDBOOK ON THE CONSTRUCTION AND INTERPRETATION OF THE LAWS 1 (1896).

[31] The American term "comparative interpretation" seems to have a different meaning, as the method of interpretation in the U.S. seeks to ascertain the meaning of a statute or other writing by comparing its several parts and also by comparing it as a whole with other like documents proceeding from the same source and referring to the same general subject. See BLACK'S LAW DICTIONARY (8th ed.) (St. Paul: West Publishing, 2004).

statute has not been revoked.

- Another consultative interpretation-rule is the *Lex Specialis Principle* – there is a preference for the rule that deals with specific issue(s) of society; thus, a distinct and specific rule comes before a statute of general content.

1.4.2.1. Interpretation in the United States

Justice Scalia: International decisions have no impact on US law. Thus, he does not recognize international or foreign law decisions as a primary source![32]

The general contemporary American view of statutory interpretation is that there is not a great deal to say about the subject. The American understanding of statutory interpretation still remains quite limited and a unified theory of statutory interpretation may be unattainable. The phrase "statutory interpretation" might refer to a variety of judicial actions with respect to statutes. Unfortunately, there is no consensus as to which of these judicial actions are covered by the phrase "statutory interpretation," and some commentators contrast that phrase with another – "statutory construction" – to which they assign a different meaning. Other writers treat the phrases as synonymous, each phrase referring to all these judicial actions.[33]

As for American interpretation, Stanford Law School Professor Jane Schacter[34] once listed the U.S. judicial resources for statutory interpretation as follows:

1. The statutory language.
2. Legislative history (including committee reports, statements and other in-formation in the Congressional Record, or other material generated in the legislative process through which the law was enacted).
3. Other statutes (state or federal), or other sections of the same statute at issue in the case.
4. Judicial opinions (including previous decisions by the U.S. Supreme

[32] See further footnote 37 below.

[33] Robert Weisberg, *The Calabresian Judicial Artist: Statutes And The New Legal Process*, 35 STAN. L REV. 213, footnote 1 (January 1983); Daniel A. Farber, *Statutory Interpretation and Legislative Supremacy*, 78 GEO. L. J. 281 (December 1989).

[34] Jane S. Schacter, *The Confounding Common Law Originalism in Recent Supreme Court Statutory Interpretation: Implications for the Legislative History Debate and Beyond*, 51 STAN. L. R. 1, 12, 48 (1998).

Court or other federal or state courts).

5. Canons of construction.
6. Administrative materials (including federal regulations or policy statements, letters or advisory opinions written by agency officials, and agency adjudicatory decisions).
7. Secondary sources (including law review and newspaper articles, treatises, other books, and policy reports).
8. Dictionaries (whether general or legal).
9. "Judicially-selected policy norms" (norms unified by being non-originalist and reflecting the Supreme Court Justices' own invocation of policy values that are grounded in neither the text of the statute nor the legislative history nor any other claim about intended legislative design).
10. Miscellaneous other sources (including, to a certain extent, amicus briefs filed with the Supreme Court).

U.S. statutory law is the dominant source of contemporary American law, and it is the form of law that lawyers are likely to confront most often in almost any area of practice.[35] However, the pattern or manner of statutory law's interpretation is disputed. Although using legislative history to help interpret unclear statutory language seems natural, the U.S. Supreme Court's actual use of legislative history is in decline.[36] Others view the primary object of all rules for interpreting statutes to be to ascertain exactly from the words of the statute the meaning that the legislature intended. This is because government by unexpressed intent is tyrannical and it is – and should be – the law that governs, not the intent of the lawgiver. Legislative history ought not to be used as an authoritative indication of a statute's meaning.[37]

For U.S. students who have not (yet) taken a course in statutory interpretation, the discussion on the following several pages should give an idea of what mindset a first year Civil Law student is put into by his legal research professor.

[35] Jane S. Schacter, Stanford Law School, *Introduction to Course: Statutory Interpretation.*

[36] Stephen Breyer, *On the Use of Legislative History in Interpretating Statutes*, 65 S. CAL. L. REV. 845, 846 & 848 (1992)

[37] Antonin Scalia, *A matter of interpretation: federal courts and the law: an essay* 17, 29 (Princeton: Princeton University Press, 1997). See Jane S. Schacter, *Accounting for Accountability in Dynamic Statutory Interpretation and Beyond – Issues in Legal Scholarship, Dynamic Statutory Interpretation* (Berkeley: Berkeley Electronic Press, 2002): Article 5 at <www.bepress.com/ils/iss3/art5 >. See also Daniel A. Farber, *Statutory Interpretation and Legislative Supremacy*, 78 GEO. L. J. 281 (December 1989).

As for interpretation in the U.S.,[38] it can be summarized from the venerable legal encyclopedia Corpus Juris Secundum (CJS)[39] as follows:[40]

"Common law," in its broadest and most general sense, is those rules or precepts of law in any country, or that body of its jurisprudence, which is of equal application in all places, as distinguished from local laws and rules. The references in the Seventh Amendment to the Constitution of the United States, to "suits at common law, where the value in controversy shall exceed twenty dollars" and "according to the rules of the common law" mean the common law of England, as distinct from equity, admiralty and maritime jurisprudence. A like provision in a state constitution may be taken to mean the common law as modified by legislative enactment. Generally, however, "English common law" is the lex non scripta or unwritten law which is that portion of the law of England which is based, not on legislative enactment, but on immemorial usage and the general consent of the people.[41] Decisions of a higher court, not turning on the application of statutes or constitutional principles, constitute the common law.[42]

[38] "An act of Congress ought never to be construed to violate the law of nations [that is, public international law] if any other possible construction remains." *Murray v. Charming Betsy,* 6 U.S. 64, 118, 2 Cranch 64, 2 L.Ed. 208 (U.S. Supreme Court, Feb. 1804). The reason why judges and lawyers should divert to the principles and decisions of foreign and international law is globalization. No institution of government can afford any longer to ignore the rest of the world. One-third of U.S. gross domestic products is internationally derived. We operate today under a large array of international agreements and organizations directly impacting judicial decision-making. Globalization also represent a greater awareness of, and access to, peoples and places far different from our own. The fates of nations are more closely intertwined than ever before, and we are more acutely aware of the connections. We are already seeing internationalization of legal relations in American courts, and should see it increasingly in the future. The U.S. Supreme Court has held for more than 200 years that Acts of Congress should be construed to be consistent with international law absent clear expression to the contrary, Former Associate Justice Supreme Court Justice of the U.S. Sandra Day O'Connor, *Southern Center for International Studies, Atlanta , Georgia, 28 October 2003*

[39] CORPUS JURIS SECUNDUM: COMPLETE RESTATEMENT OF THE ENTIRE AMERICAN LAW AS DEVELOPED BY ALL REPORTED CASES (St. Paul: Thomson/West Publishing, 1936-) (CJS) is an authoritative American legal encyclopedia that provides a clear statement of each area of law.

[40] See also, Norman J. Singer, ('Sutherland") STATUTES AND STATUTORY CONSTRUCTION (6th ed.) (St. Paul: West Group, 2006).

[41] 15A CORPUS JURIS SECUNDUM (CJS) Common Law 1.

[42] *Idem.* Common Law 3.

The rules or canons of statutory construction – also termed statutory interpretation are merely aids for ascertaining legislative intent. However, such rules may be used only to remove doubt, and are never to be used to create doubt.[43]

The construction of a statute is a question for the court, and not for the jury.[44]

The process of statutory interpretation involves a reasoned search for the intention of the legislature, which begins with an examination of the language of the statute itself. However, all reasonable means will be used to arrive at the legislative intent. The court cannot attribute to the legislature an intent which is not in any way expressed in the statute. It is not the function of the court to determine and announce what, in its judgment, the statute should provide, but to ascertain, if there is ambiguity in its terms, what it does provide.[45]

As a general rule of statutory construction, the spirit or intention of a statute prevails over the letter thereof.[46] However, in some jurisdictions, intent prevails over the letter of the law;[47] the spirit and intent of legislation prevails over a literal reading of its language,[48] and the courts are not controlled by the literal meaning of the language of the statute.[49] In other jurisdictions, when the words of a law in their application to an existing situation are clear and free from all ambiguity, the letter of the law may not be disregarded under the pretext of pursuing the spirit of the statute.[50]

As a general rule, the courts cannot supply omissions in a statute.[51]

The general rule of statutory construction that words should be construed according to their common and approved usage does not apply to technical words and phrases that generally are considered to have a peculiar meaning. (e.g. commercial, trade, or professional terms).[52]

[43] 82 CORPUS JURIS SECUNDUM (CJS) Statutes 306.

[44] *Idem.* Statutes 307.

[45] *Idem.* Statutes 315.

[46] *Idem.* Statutes 317.

[47] *Idem.* Statutes 317, footnote 41 (referring to California, Connecticut, Maryland, Mississippi, and New Jersey).

[48] *Idem.* Statutes 317, footnote 42 (referring to Florida, Georgia, and Hawaii).

[49] 82 CORPUS JURIS SECUNDUM (CJS) Statutes 317, footnote 43 (referring to California, Connecticut, Illinois, Maryland, Missouri, Nebraska, and New York).

[50] *Idem.* Statutes 317, footnote 44 (referring to North Dakota, Pennsylvania, Arizona, California, Nebraska, North Carolina, Oregon, and Washington).

[51] *Idem.* Statutes 320.

[52] *Idem.* Statutes 322.

The maxim "expressio unius est exclusio alterius," under which the mention of one thing in a statute implies the exclusion of another, is merely an auxiliary rule of statutory construction which is not universally applicable and not conclusive. It should be applied only as a means of discovering the legislative intent which is not otherwise manifest, and should never be permitted to defeat the plainly indicated purpose of the legislature.[53]

The courts are reluctant to construe the intent of the legislature based solely on punctuation and grammatical construction, and a statute's punctuation alone is not a reliable guide in discovering its meaning.[54]

As a general rule, every word in a statute is to be given force and effect, and the courts should avoid a construction making any word surplusage.[55]

The words "or" and "and" in a statute generally are not treated as interchangeable, but they may be so treated when necessary to effectuate the obvious intention of the legislature.[56]

The presence of a comma separating a modifying clause in a statute from the clause immediately preceding it is an indication that the modifying clause was intended to modify all the preceding clauses and not only the last antecedent one.[57]

Where a statute has first been enacted in a foreign language and afterward translated into English, its history will be considered in construing it. The English text of laws enacted in Louisiana since 1812 must prevail, but the original French text prevails over an erroneous English translation of earlier laws.[58]

In construing an ambiguous statute, a court generally may consider legislative debates and reports of committees or commissions as an aid to construction, however, such materials will not be considered where the language of the statute is plain and unambiguous.[59]

Statutes are to be construed in the context of the existing law, and as a part of a general and uniform system of jurisprudence.[60]

In case of ambiguity, statutes are to be construed with reference to the principles of the common law in force at the time of their passage, and stat-

[53] *Idem.* Statutes 323.
[54] *Idem.* Statutes 325.
[55] *Idem.* Statutes 327.
[56] *Idem.* Statutes 333.
[57] 82 CORPUS JURIS SECUNDUM (CJS) Statutes 331.
[58] *Idem.* Statutes 334.
[59] *Idem.* Statutes 341.
[60] *Idem.* Statutes 391.

utes are not to be interpreted as effecting any change in the common law beyond that which is clearly indicated.[61]

Where a statute is ambiguous, a court generally may consult analogous statutes to determine its meaning, but the provisions of dissimilar statutes are not persuasive.[62]

Statutes adopted at the same session of the legislature generally are not to be construed as inconsistent or in conflict if it is possible to construe them otherwise.[63]

Since the more recent statute is a later expression of the legislative intent, if there is an unreconcilable conflict between two statutes, the later enactment normally will control. In such a case, the newer statute may be regarded as creating an exception to, or qualification of, the prior statute. However, where there is no clear intention to the contrary, a specific statute will not be controlled or nullified by a general one, regardless of the priority of their enactment.[64]

General and specific statutes should be read together and harmonized, if possible. However, in the event of an irreconcilable conflict between them, the specific or special statute ordinarily will prevail over the general one. Where the general act is later, the special statute will be construed as remaining an exception to the terms of the general statute, unless the more specific statute is repealed expressly or by necessary implication.[65]

Where a statute that has been construed by the courts is reenacted in substantially the same terms, the legislature is presumed to have been familiar with the judicial construction of the prior statute and to have adopted that interpretation as a part of the later act, unless a contrary intent clearly appears, or the later statute expressly provides for a different construction. The general rule that a later statute will be interpreted in accordance with a judicial construction of a prior statute does not apply where the later statute is unambiguous.[66]

As a general rule, however, the adoption of a statute by reference is construed as an adoption of the law as it existed at the time the adopting statute was passed. Therefore, the adopting statute normally is not affected by any subsequent modification of the statute adopted unless an intention to the con-

[61] *Idem.* Statutes 350.
[62] *Idem.* Statutes 351.
[63] *Idem.* Statutes 353.
[64] 82 CORPUS JURIS SECUNDUM (CJS) Statutes 354.
[65] *Idem.* Statutes 355.
[66] *Idem.* Statutes 356.

trary is clearly manifested. On the other hand, where the legislative intent to do so clearly appears, the adopting statute will include subsequent modifications of the original act.[67]

When a statute is patterned after a statute of another jurisdiction, it is appropriate to consider interpretations of the statute in the jurisdiction from which it has been borrowed.[68]

Where a state statute is virtually a verbatim copy of a statute of a sister state, the interpretation of the statute by the courts of the state where the statute was originally adopted is persuasive.[69]

The courts of the adopting state are not bound to accept the construction placed on the statute by the courts of the state from which it was adopted, and they will not do so where it would be contrary to the spirit and policy of the laws of the adopting state, or where it is regarded as unsound in principle, and against the weight of authority. Moreover, such a construction will not be applied where it is plain that the legislature adopting it had a different intention. It is the construction of the statute which prevailed in the original state at the time of its adoption by the other state that is presumed to follow the statute, and subsequent decisions have no controlling effect on the adopting state. However, such decisions may be strongly persuasive.[70]

1.4.2.2. Interpretation in Civil Law

In Civil Law,[71] the main issue is interpretation of the (written) law; case law is hardly an issue.

The purpose of interpretation is to lay down the legal meaning of each source of law so that one can determine how each source of law contributes to the legal argument. Thus, it deals with the question of law-supplementing.[72]

Civil Law judges and scholars will use the classic interpretation methods mentioned in the beginning of section 1.4.2.

[67] *Idem.* Statutes 357.
[68] *Idem.* Statutes 358.
[69] *Idem.* Statutes 359.
[70] 82 CORPUS JURIS SECUNDUM (CJS) Statutes 360.
[71] A U.S. student should take a course on statutory interpretation before doing research on Civil Law as a major issue in civil law research is interpretation.
[72] The Danish term is "retsudfyldende", Joseph Lookofsky, *Precedent and the Law in Denmark* - Danish National Report at the XVIIth Conference of The International Academy of Comparative Law, Utrecht 2006, at <http://www.cisg.law.pace.edu/cisg/biblio/lookofsky15.html> (visited June 2007).

As for rules concerning the relationship between a citizen and the public ("the state"), where there are several useful rules at the same level, the rule that is in the citizen's interest or favor should be used.

No guideline exists where there is a conflict between an older specific rule and a newer but more general one – or lex posterior contra lex specialis. In such situations, reasonableness, preparatory work to a statute, and legislators' intentions can be considered.

As courts in Civil Law countries do not (generally) make law, court decisions have only limited value. In rare cases, a decision will provide a more general opinion or point of view on the legal rule(s) involved in the case.

In all European systems that recognize judge-made law, only "similar" cases have precedential potential, so the facts of a case are obviously important for purposes of "distinguishing" the case at bar from prior decisions.

The key prospective element of a given decision is the court's reasoning (premises), that is , that part which serves to explain and legitimize the precedent-setting court's result (the ratio decidendi – in the U.S. called the "holding").

However, in Europe some court decisions – even by the high or supreme courts – are written in such a way that the reader cannot determine the whole scope of a decision, because the premises are so briefly stated or formulated in such an oracle-like fashion that they provide no clear guidance beyond the decision in the given, concrete case.

1.4.2.3. Interpretation in International Law

The main task for any tribunal,[73] which is asked to apply or construe or interpret[74] a treaty, can be described in a single sentence: "the duty of giving ef-

[73] Whether an international court is obliged to fill in gaps, and to avoid pronouncing a *non liquet* ("[I]s a competent legal tribunal in the position to refuse a definite answer to a legal question (in terms of rights and duties of the parties concerned) on the basis of material gaps" in international law), is a matter of dispute. See AKEHURST *supra* note 12, at 50 & 349; Ige F. Dekker & Harry H.G. Post, *The Completeness of International Law and Hamlet's Dilemma, in* ON THE FOUNDATIONS AND SOURCES OF INTERNATIONAL LAW 8-30(2003, T.M.C. Asser Press, The Hague, Netherlands); Judge Rosalyn Higgin's separate opinion in *Advisory Opinion on the Legality of the Threat or Use of Nuclear Weapons* (United Nations)(International Court of Justice, Advisory opinion of 8 July 1996), 1996 I.C.J. 226, 934.

[74] On interpretation. OPPENHEIM'S INTERNATIONAL LAW 1266-1284 (9th Ed.)(Eds.: Sir Robert Jennings & Sir Arthur Watts) (London and New York: Longman 1996) [hereinafter OPPENHEIM]; IAN BROWNLIE, PRINCIPLES OF INTERNATIONAL LAW 631-638 (5th ed.)(Oxford Press, 2002).

fect to the expressed intention of the parties, that is, their intention as expressed in the words used by them in the light of the surrounding circumstances".[75]

Part III of the Convention on the Law of Treaties[76] contains specific rules for interpretation[77] (the rules are not regarded as codification of any customary law rule, but they are rules in practice used in diplomatic circles). A "General Rule of Interpretation" is given in Article 31:

> 1. A treaty shall be interpreted in good faith in accordance with the ordinary meaning to be given to the terms of the treaty in their context and in the light of its object and purpose.
> 2. The context for the purpose of the interpretation of a treaty shall comprise, in addition to the text, including its preamble and annexes: (a) any agreement relating to the treaty which was made between all the parties in connection with the conclusion of the treaty; (b) any instrument which was made by one or more parties in connection with the conclusion of the treaty and accepted by the other parties as an instrument related to the treaty.
> 3. There shall be taken into account, together with the context: (a) any subsequent agreement between the parties regarding the interpretation of the treaty or the application of its provisions; (b) any subsequent practice in the application of the treaty which establishes the agreement of the parties regarding its interpretation; (c) any relevant rules of international law applicable in the relations between the parties.
> 4. A special meaning shall be given to a term if it is established that the parties so intended.

[75] Lord Arnold Duncan McNair, THE LAW OF TREATIES 365 (Oxford Clarendon Press 1961). See also, Rudolf Bernhardt, *Interpretation in International Law, in* ENCYCLOPEDIA OF PUBLIC INTERNATIONAL LAW 1416-1426 (Rudolf Bernhardt (Ed.), Elsevier 1995) & OPPENHEIM *supra* note 74, at 1266-128 & 423.

[76] Articles 26-38 in the Vienna Convention on the Law of Treaties of 23 May 1969 (into force 27 January 1980), U.N.T.S. Vol. 1155 p. 331, also at <http://untreaty.un.org /ilc/texts/instruments/english/conventions/1_1_1969.pdf>. As of April 2007, the convention has been ratified by 108 States. The U.S. is not a party, but it signed the Convention on 24 April 1970.

[77] Treaty law is the daughter of customary international law. The interpretation of treaties takes place on the basis of customary international law and the validity of treaties is determined by customary law. Treaties per se are ineffective without the support of customary international law. There is the difference that the treaty norm remains in the form in which it is frozen into the treaty (until such time as the treaty is changed), whereas the customary norm having an independent existence of its own, can continue to develop. It is a critical advance in a situation when fast moving changes require more adaptability and flexibility in a rule of law, I.C.J. Judge C.G. Weeramantry, UNIVERSALISING INTERNATIONAL LAW 233 & 239 (Boston: Martinus Nijhoff Publishers, 2004).

Articles 32 gives supplementary means of interpretation, including using preparatory works[78] as supplementary sources:

> Recourse may be had to supplementary means of interpretation, including the preparatory work of the treaty and the circumstances of its conclusion, in order to confirm the meaning resulting from the application of article 31, or to determine the meaning when the interpretation according to article 31: (a) leaves the meaning ambiguous or obscure; or (b) leads to a result which is manifestly absurd or unreasonable.

The last the rule given in Section 3 of the Convention on the Law of Treaties, "Interpretation of Treaties," Article 33, deals with interpretation of treaties authenticated in two or more languages, Article 33:

> 1. When a treaty has been authenticated in two or more languages, the text is equally authoritative in each language, unless the treaty provides or the parties agree that, in case of divergence, a particular text shall prevail.
> 2. A version of the treaty in a language other than one of those in which the text was authenticated shall be considered an authentic text only if the treaty so provides or the parties so agree.
> 3. The terms of the treaty are presumed to have the same meaning in each authentic text.
> 4. Except where a particular text prevails in accordance with paragraph 1, when a comparison of the authentic texts discloses a difference of meaning which the application of articles 31 and 32 does not remove, the meaning which best reconciles the texts, having regard to the object and purpose of the treaty, shall be adopted.

1.4.2.4. Interpretation in European Union

Statutory interpretation in the European Union is statutory interpretation without a single, authoritative text and one cannot expect different language versions of the same act or treaty always to say exactly the same thing.[79]

The goal for the E.U. courts is to capture the essence of E.U. legislation.

As the E.U. is a multilanguage legal regime, translation is more than a metaphor – it is a basic fact about the entire structure of the law.

While the E.U. courts do not use the translation history, the courts use

[78] "Travaux Préparatoires," see further below.

[79] Geert van Calster, *The EU's Tower of Babel – The Interpretation of the European Court of Justice of Equally Authentic Texts Drafted in More Than One Official Language*, 17 (1997) YEARBOOK OF EUROPEAN LAW 369 (Oxford Press 1998).

comparison of the various versions of the law as an important tool.[80]

The E.U. courts looks not only at the versions written in the languages of the parties to the particular dispute before the court, but also at other versions. When a dispute is over which of two fully authentic versions of a law should prevail, the status of the statutory language is itself contested. The E.U. courts will typically not determine whether some versions reflect an error in translation. Thus, the courts will not make reference to the translation history.

The language of a statute provides privileged evidence of what the legislature intended.

European courts are more comfortable than American courts in putting the purpose of a statute ahead of the language in the service of effectuating the legislature's will.[81]

1.5. Global Legal Information Network

The Global Legal Information Network (GLIN)[82] is a public database of official texts of laws, regulations, judicial decisions, and other complementary legal sources contributed by governmental agencies and international organizations.

GLIN is a searchable online database containing the following categories of legal documents for jurisdictions spanning the globe:

- Laws
- Judicial Decisions
- Legislative Records
- Legal Literature

Most of the material in GLIN is freely accessible to the public and the system does not require a user ID or password for search purposes.

[80] *Meico-Fell v Hauptzollamt Darmstadt*, [1991] ECR I-5569 at paras 9-10 (European Court of Justice (Sixth Chamber) Case C-273/90 of 27 November 1991 (It appears from the context in which that provision was adopted that the expression...means...that interpretation is confirmed by an examination of the other language versions, which have a clear meaning).

[81] Lawrence M. Solan, *Statutory Interpretation in the EU: The Augustinian Approach*, BROOKLYN LAW SCHOOL, LEGAL STUDIES PAPER No. 78 page 10 (July 2007) - Available at SSRN: <http://ssrn.com/abstract=998167>.

[82] Global Legal Information Network (GLIN) at <www.glin.gov/search.action>.

1.6. Further Reading (updates at corresponding website)

The URL for the corresponding website is <www.hssph.net/legalrm> with a full alphabetic bibliography.

Subject guides on ASIL and Globalex and LLRX:

- <www.asil.org/erghome.cfm>
- <www.nyulawglobal.org/globalex/>
- <www.llrx.com/category/1050.

AKEHURST'S MODERN INTRODUCTION TO INTERNATIONAL LAW (8th Ed.) (By Peter Malanczuk)(New York ; London : Routledge, 2002);

Avalos, Francisco, *Legal Translations: Some Tips* (Lecture Delivered At National Language Re-Source Center, San Diego State University On July 24, 1998 at <www.law.arizona.edu/library/research/guides/legal_translations.cfm?page=research>

Bernhardt, Rudolf, *Interpretation in International Law,* in ENCYCLOPEDIA OF PUBLIC INTERNATIONAL LAW (Rudolf Bernhardt (Ed.), Elsevier 1995)

BLACK, HENRY CAMPBELL, HANDBOOK ON THE CONSTRUCTION AND INTERPRETATION OF THE LAWS (1896).

Breyer, Stephen, *On the Use of Legislative History in Interpretating Statutes*, 65 SOUTHERN CALIFORNIA LAW REVIEW 845 (1992)

BROWNLIE, IAN, PRINCIPLES OF INTERNATIONAL LAW (7th Ed.)(Oxford Press, 2008).

Calster, Geert van, *The EU's Tower Of Babel – The Interpretation Of The European Court of Justice of Equally Authentic Texts Drafted in More Than One Official Language*, 17 (1997) YEARBOOK OF EUROPEAN LAW 363 (Oxford Press 1998)

Corpus Juris Secundum: Complete Restatement of the Entire American Law as Developed by All Reported Cases (St. Paul: Thomson/West Publishing, 1936-)

Dekker, Ige F. & Harry H.G. Post, *The Completeness of International Law and Hamlet's Dilemma,* in ON THE FOUNDATIONS AND SOURCES OF INTERNATIONAL LAW (T.M.C. Asser Press, The Hague, Netherlands, 2003)

Farber, Daniel A., *Statutory Interpretation and Legislative Supremacy*, 78 GEORGETOWN LAW JOURNAL 281 (December 1989)

GUIDE TO INTERNATIONAL LEGAL RESEARCH (The George Washington International Law Review) (Newark, NJ : LexisNexis Matthew Bender, 2010)

Lookofsky, Joseph, *Precedent and the Law in Denmark - Danish National Report at the XVIIth Conference of The International Academy of Comparative Law*, Utrecht 2006, at <http://www.cisg.law.pace.edu/cisg/biblio/lookofsky15.html> (visited June 2007)

LOWE, VAUGHAN, INTERNATIONAL LAW (England: Oxford University Press, 2007)(an update of James Brierly's Law Of Nations)

MCCONVILLE, MIKE & WING HONG CHUI, RESEARCH METHODS FOR LAW (Edinburgh: Edinburgh University Press)

MCNAIR, LORD ARNOLD DUNCAN, THE LAW OF TREATIES 365 (Oxford Clarendon Press 1961).

MERSKY, ROY M. , DONALD J. DUNN & J. MYRON JACOBSTEIN, FUNDAMENTALS OF LEGAL RESEARCH (8th ed.)(University casebook series)(New York, N.Y.: Foundation Press, 2002)

OPPENHEIM'S INTERNATIONAL LAW (9th Ed.)(Eds.: Sir Robert Jennings & Sir Arthur Watts) (London And New York: Longman 1996)

Pascal, Robert A., *Louisiana Civil Law and its Study*, 60 LOUISIANA LAW REVIEW 1 (Fall 1999)

Rheinstein, Max, *Comparative Law – Its Functions, Methods and Usages*, 22 ARKANSAS. LAW REVIEW 415 (Fall 1968).

SALMOND, JOHN WILLIAM, JURISPRUDENCE (7th ed.)(London : Sweet & Maxwell, 1928), p. 164, available at the Internet Archive at

<http://www.archive.org/stream/jurisprudence00salmuoft/jurisprudence00salmuoft_djvu.txt> (visited Nov. 2001).

SCALIA, ANTONIN, A MATTER OF INTERPRETATION: FEDERAL COURTS AND THE LAW: AN ESSAY 17, 29 (Princeton: Princeton University Press, 1997).

Schacter, Jane S., *Accounting For Accountability In Dynamic Statutory Interpretation And Beyond – Issues In Legal Scholarship, Dynamic Statutory Interpretation* (Berkeley: Berkeley Electronic Press, 2002): Article 5 at <www.bepress.com/ils/iss3/art5>.

Schacter, Jane S., *The Confounding Common Law Originalism In Recent Supreme Court Statutory Interpretation: Implications for the Legislative History Debate and Beyond*, 51 STANFORD LAW REVIEW 1 (1998).

SINGER, NORMAN J. ('SUTHERLAND"), STATUTES AND STATUTORY CONSTRUCTION (6th Ed.) (St. Paul: West Group, 2006).

Smith, A.L., *Foreign Law in Translation: Problems and Resources* (Chapter 14) *i*n RICHARD DANNER, INTRODUCTION TO FOREIGN LEGAL SYSTEMS (New York: Oceana Publications, 1994)

Solan, Lawrence M., *Statutory Interpretation in the EU: The Augustinian Approach*, BROOKLYN LAW SCHOOL, LEGAL STUDIES PAPER NO. 78 Page 10 (July 2007) - Available at SSRN: <http://ssrn.com/abstract=998167>

Somers, Harold, *Use of Machine Translation by Law Librarians A Reply To Yates*, 99 LAW

LIBRARY JOURNAL, Vol. 99:3, 611-619 (2007),

WEERAMANTRY, C.G. , UNIVERSALISING INTERNATIONAL LAW (Boston: Martinus Nijhoff Publishers, 2004).

Weisberg, Robert, *The Calabresian Judicial Artist: Statutes and the New Legal Process*, 35 STAN. L REV. 213 (January 1983)

Yates, Sarah, *I Need This in English*, 9 AMERICAN ASSOCIATION LAW LIBRARIES SPECTRUM 8 (2004-05)

ZWEIGERT, K. & H.KÖTZ, INTRODUCTION TO COMPARATIVE LAW (3rd Ed.)(Tony Weir Trans., Clarendon Press, Oxford 1998)

CHAPTER 2

Legal Families

2.1. Introduction

The goal of this chapter is only to give a very broad overview of legal families.

As this book is aimed primarily at the teaching of courses on legal research methods, and as the time allotted for such courses is quite limited, comprehensive coverage of each of the legal families is not possible.

A famous book on the subject of the different legal families is K. Zweigert & H.Kötz, Introduction to Comparative Law (in English translation by Tony Weir).[1]

See also below Chapter 3 on the requirement for doing research in a foreign country.

When studying international law and doing comparative law one should be aware of which legal family the country's law being studied belongs to.

Research Tip #2.1

A country's "legal family" has, among other things, a great impact on the way the law and the legal system of that country must be interpretated.[2]

[1] K. Zweigert & H.Kötz, INTRODUCTION TO COMPARATIVE LAW 145 (3rd ed.)(Tony Weir trans., Clarendon Press, Oxford 1998) [hereinafter ZWEIGERT].

[2] It is a well-known fact that major law firms in London and elsewhere are increasingly seeking students with specialist, regionally-focused legal knowledge (including language and cultural skills) that will equip them for a lucrative globally-oriented legal career. Werner F. Menski, COMPARATIVE LAW IN A GLOBAL CONTEXT: THE LEGAL SYSTEMS OF ASIA AND AFRICA 29 (London: Platinium, 2000).

A legal system is an operating set of legal institutions, procedures, and rules, one for each state. National legal systems are frequently classified into families grouped pursuant to the basis of legal tradition, which is a set of deeply rooted, historically conditioned attitudes about the nature of law; about the role of law in the society and the polity; about the proper organization and operation of a legal system; and about the way law is or should be made, applied, studied, perfected, and taught. However, this does not mean that in each family there does not exist great diversity, not only in substantive rules of law, but also in their institutions and processes.[3]

In Civil Law countries, rules governing a single transaction may be placed in widely separated parts of a Civil Law country code, which is abstract in language, whereas the Anglo-American follows the view that all aspects of a unitary transaction should be dealt with in the same place in the system.[4]

The factors that are crucial for the style of a legal system, or legal family are:[5]

- Its historical background and development.
- Its predominant and characteristic mode of thought in legal matters.
- Especially distinctive institutions.
- The kind of legal sources it acknowledges and the way it handles them.
- Its ideology.

2.2. A suggested division into legal families

One such division is the following:[6]

- The *Romanistic Legal Family* (France, the Benelux countries,[7] Italy, Spain and Portugal[8]) - The *Code Civile*[9] of 1804 is the heart of private

[3] John Henry Merryman, THE CIVIL LAW TRADITION: AN INTRODUCTION TO THE LEGAL SYSTEMS OF WESTERN EUROPE AND LATIN AMERICA 1-2 (2nd ed.)(Stanford, California: Stanford University Press, 1985) [hereinafter MERRYMAN].

[4] ZWEIGERT *supra* note 1 at 145.

[5] ZWEIGERT *supra* note 1 at 68.

[6] ZWEIGERT *supra* note 1 at 64. Others have divided law into the following five families: Western Systems, Socialist Systems, Islamic law, Hindu law, and Chinese law. René David, *Traité élémentaire de droit civil comparé* 222 (1950). See also, MERRYMAN *supra* note 3 at 5. See also a "List of country legal systems" in Wikipedia at <http://en.wikipedia.org/wiki/List_of_country_legal_systems>, including countries that are based on both religious law and Civil law, respectively Common Law.

[7] Belgium, the Netherlands, and Luxembourg.

[8] ZWEIGERT *supra* note 1 at 104

law in France and the great model for the codes of private law of the whole Romanistic legal family. It is a felicitous blend of traditional legal institutions from the *droit écrit* of the South – influenced by Roman Law – and the *droit coutumier* of the North – influenced by the Germanic-Frankish customary law. It bears throughout the marks of its heritage of the pre-revolutionary law (*ancien droit*). There was never any serious discussion of a complete reception of Roman law into France – unlike Germany later on. From two royal ordinances in the 17th century came the basis for a division between private law in the narrow sense, and commercial law, which the Romanistic and Germanic legal families – except Switzerland and Italy – still recognize by having different codes, much to the surprise of Anglo-American lawyers. In France and Italy, the highest court in civil and criminal matters differs in characteristic respects from the comparable high or supreme courts of the Anglo-American and German legal families.[10] The French *Court of Cassation*[11] goes in for lapidary "whereas"-clauses. Legal studies in France are part of a general education.[12]

- The *Germanic Legal Family* (Germany, Austria, Croatia, Switzerland, Greece, Turkey, and South Korea) - The effects of Roman law were much greater in Germany than in France and much greater than in England. Germany consisted of many small principalities until 1871. As there was no common German private law, no common German courts system, and no common German fraternity of lawyers, Roman legal ideas and institutions were adopted wholesale in many parts of the country and for many areas of law.[13] The Superior German Court gives reasons which are wide-ranging and loaded with citations like a textbook, while - again - the French *Court of Cassation*[14] goes in for lapidary "whereas"-clauses. And, again, unlike

[9] Or "Code Napoléon" [Napoleonic Code] (originally called the Code civil des Français).

[10] ZWEIGERT *supra* note 1 at 74-80 & 120.

[11] The [Court of Cassation] is the main court of last resort in France. Besides this high or supreme court for judicial cases (civil justice or criminal justice), France has other high or supreme courts, for example the Conseil d'État (for administrative justice), and Conseil Constitutionnel (constitutional challenges).

[12] ZWEIGERT *supra* note 1 at 130-131.

[13] ZWEIGERT *supra* note 1 at 133-135.

[14] The [Court of Cassation] is the main court of last resort in France, excluding cases of administrative justice, which go before the Conseil d'État.

Germany, legal studies in France are part of a general education.[15]

- The *Anglo-American Legal Family* (England, and Wales, Northern Ireland, the Republic of Ireland, Scotland,[16] United States of America, Australia (both federal and individual states), New Zealand,[17] Canada (except Québec)) – The courts in the Anglo-American Legal Family can "make" law. In general, Common Law demands a study of its historical origins – "the life of law has been experience." Roman law has not influenced English law (while it has affected Scottish law). Codification has never been a great thing in English law (contrary to the United States). England has no constitution[18] (again, in contrast to the U.S.).
- The *Nordic Legal Family* (Denmark,[19] Finland,[20] Iceland,[21] Norway,[22] and Sweden[23])[24] – Nordic Legal Family law has few, if any, of

[15] ZWEIGERT *supra* note 1 at 130-131.

[16] Scotland is often said to use the Civil Law system, but in fact it has a unique system that combines elements of an uncodified Civil Law dating back to the Corpus Juris Civilis with an element of Common Law long predating the Treaty of Union with England in 1707. Scottish Common Law differs in that the use of precedents is subject to the courts seeking to discover the principle that justifies a law, rather than to search for an example as a precedent, and that the principles of natural justice and fairness have always formed a source of Scottish law. Other comparable pluralistic (or "mixed") legal systems operate in Quebec, Louisiana and South Africa.

[17] 1966 ENCYCLOPAEDIA OF NEW ZEALAND at <www.teara.govt.nz/1966/L/LegalSystem/SourcesOfLaw/en>.

[18] However, England has the so-called Magna Carta Libertatum" ("Great Charter of Freedoms") of 1215, which led to the rule of constitutional law today. It influenced many common law and other documents, such as the United States Constitution and Bill of Rights, and is considered one of the most important legal documents in the history of democracy.

[19] Rasmus H. Wandall, *Researching Danish Law* (July 2006) at <www.nyulawglobal.org/globalex/Denmark.htm>.

[20] Legal order – Finland at <http://ec.europa.eu/civiljustice/legal_order/legal_order_fin_en.htm>.

[21] Rán Tryggvadóttir & Thordis Ingadóttir, *Researching Icelandic Law* (2007) at <www.nyulawglobal.org/globalex/iceland.htm>.

[22] Hans Petter Graver, *The Approach to European Law in Norwegian Legal Doctrine,* in Peter Christian Müller-Graff & Erling Selvig, eds., EUROPEAN LAW IN THE GERMAN-NORWEGIAN CONTEXT: ORIGINS AND PERSPECTIVES (Berlin: Berliner Wissenschafts-Verlag GmbH, 2001) & at <www.arena.uio.no/publications/wp03_18.pdf>.

[23] Legal order – Sweden <http://ec.europa.eu/civiljustice/legal_order/legal_order_swe_en.htm>.

[24] Usually, Scandinavia is regarded as Denmark, Norway, and Sweden. The Nordic countries are the Scandinavian ones plus Iceland and Finland.

the "stylistic" hallmarks of the Common Law. Roman law has played a smaller role Scandinavian Legal Familyin the legal development of the Nordic countries than in Germany. The Nordic Legal Family's laws belong to the Civil Law, but form a special legal family, alongside the Romanistic and German legal families. The political and cultural ties between these countries have always been very close, partly based on the fact that they, for some hundred years, were unified. In the 17th century, the countries each promulgated comprehensive codes unifying private law, criminal law and procedural law.[25] In the 19th century, they began modernization of their codes, and introduced amendments in separate reforming laws. Further, unified laws between the countries began to arise. A tendency toward conceptualism and the construction of large-scale integrated theoretical systems has never really been followed. All the countries have a constitution and their royal families/presidents have real executive power, which power belongs to the government – a special independent branch pursuant to the countries' constitutions – along with the Parliament and the courts.

- The *Law in the Far East* (China, Japan) – Legal systems in the Far East differ fundamentally from the legal families dealt with in all western systems, where the important questions of social life should primarily be regulated by rules of objective law rather than simply by conventions or habits. Disputes are often resolved by techniques other than actions at law. Thus, in the Far East, informal means of dispute resolution are enormously important. However, China and Japan have over the decades of the 20th and 21st centuries moved in the direction of being part of the Romano-Germanic family of law, with some elements of American law.[26]
- Religious Legal Systems:[27]

[25] As for Denmark: The Danish absolute monarch King Christian V issued in 1683 "Danske Lov" ["Denmark's Code"] (at <http://bjoerna.dk/DanskeLov/index.htm>), which to a large extent was a codification of previous Danish law. The first code is Codex Holmiensis/Jyske Lov [Code of Jutland] of 1241, issued by King Valdemar II (nicknamed "Valdemar the Victorious" or "Valdemar the Conqueror"). See further, DITLEV TAMM, RETS HISTORIE 213 [Legal History: Denmark – Europe – Global Perspectives](2 Ed)(DJØF Publishing, 2009).

[26] HIROSHI ODA, JAPANESE LAW (Butterworths, 1992).

[27] The law of Israel is a mixed system of Common Law and Civil Law, British Mandate regulations, and, in personal matters, Jewish, Christian, and Muslim legal systems.

- *Islamic Law*: The Shariah or Islamic law is a complex of divinely revealed rules, which a faithful Muslim must observe if he/she seeks to perform the duties of his/her religion. It does not depend on the authority of any earthly law-giver and is already existing and formulated. Only a few of the statements in the Koran (the highest source of Islamic law) constitute rules of law capable of direct application. Thus, in many cases legal consequences are not specified. In addition, there is the Sunnah, i.e., the words, habits, practices, and approvals attributed to the prophet Muhammad or to his immediate disciples.[28]
- *Hindu Law* – It applies to all persons who are Hindu, that is, who accept the complex mass of religious, philosophical, and social ideas compendiously referred to as Hinduism. It does not require a person to believe in a god and embraces a great variety of cults and rituals. It lacks a clearly defined theological doctrine, but does offer certain basic convictions of a religious or philosophical order. The oldest "law-books" are the *smritis*, where *smriti* a Sanskrit word denoting the "remembered:" wisdom of the old priests and scholars.[29]

2.3. Further Reading (updates at corresponding website)

The URL for the corresponding website is <www.hssph.net/legalrm> with a full alphabetic bibliography.

See also below in Chapter 7, section 7.1.6.1. a list of some basic books for different European countries written in English by natives.

GLENDON, MARY ANN, PAOLO G. CAROZZA & COLIN B. PICKER, COMPARATIVE LEGAL TRADITIONS – IN A NUTSHELL (3 Ed))(Thomson/West, 2008)

INTRODUCTION TO FOREIGN LEGAL SYSTEMS (Edited by Richard A. Danner, Marie-Louise H. Bernal)(New York; London: Oceana Publications, 1994) [Including following legal systems: French, Mexican, Japanese, Chinese, Ghana, Nigerian]

MERRYMAN, JOHN HENRY, DAVID S. CLARK & JOHN OWEN HALEY, COMPARATIVE LAW: HISTORICAL DEVELOPMENT OF THE CIVIL LAW TRADITION IN EUROPE, LATIN AMERICA,

[28] ZWEIGERT *supra* note 1 at 303.
[29] ZWEIGERT *supra* note 1 at 313.

AND EAST ASIA (Matthew Bender & Co, 2009)

MERRYMAN, JOHN HENRY, THE CIVIL LAW TRADITION: AN INTRODUCTION TO THE LEGAL SYSTEMS OF WESTERN EUROPE AND LATIN AMERICA (2nd ed.)(Stanford, California: Stanford University Press, 1985)

ZWEIGERT, K. & H.KÖTZ, INTRODUCTION TO COMPARATIVE LAW (3rd Ed.)(Tony Weir Trans., Clarendon Press, Oxford 1998)

CHAPTER 3

Requirements for Studying Foreign Law

3.1. Introduction

Modern law schools have decided to teach their students law beyond their national borders and thus put American teachers in a somewhat awkward position as far as trying to teach the law (i.e., Civil Law) of, for example, a country in continental Europe.[1] The same can be said for non-Americans trying to teach law from the United States.

The organization of legal studies in Europe is "so different" from what it is in the U.S. that "an American student is likely to be lost unless he is individually guided." The American law graduate will find that at least two years is necessary for studying abroad in Europe effectively, and that "the first year is likely to be wasted."[2]

Civil Law is today the dominant legal tradition in:[3]

- Continental Europe & Russia
- All of Central and South America
- Many parts of Africa
- Many parts of Asia
- American State of Louisiana
- American Territory of Puerto Rico
- Canadian Province of Quebec
- Israel

[1] This chapter is a revised version of "The Modern Law Schools' Uriapost – the Post of Danger" by Henrik Spang-Hanssen (teacher's manual), available at <http://ssrn.com/abstract=1102293> (reprinted as the Addendum in Second edition).

[2] Max Rheinstein, *Comparative Law – Its Functions, Methods and Usages*, 22 ARK. L. REV. 415, 424-25 (Fall 1968).

[3] See further chapter 2 on legal families.

This chapter will, from a continental European (Civil Law) point of view, try to provide a guide to American teachers and students as to what one should keep in mind before deciding to and then teaching/studying legal research (or using a comparative method) for the law of a country on the European continent.

To a very large extent, this is the same drill for a European wanting to do research on the law of another European country. Thus, an American is not specially disadvantaged but may not, as the Europeans, have been brought up realizing the difficulties lying ahead – or anticipating the kind of shock that can be felt.

At this place should be noted that Continental Europe consists of 47 countries (27 are in the European Union), of which none uses English as its legal language. Thus, the E.U.'s homepage must use numerous language translations for its gateways as shown below (next page).

3.2. The First Heavy Task – Reading a Foreign language – Caveat as to Translations

To be able to figure out how to do legal research or study the law of a (foreign) European continental country first of all requires that one knows and can read the language of the particular country to be investigated. Europeans learn one to three foreign languages in school.

Thus, language skills are the first and most vital decision maker. If one cannot read the law of a foreign country, it may be next to impossible to do any decent legal research.

Tip #3.1

On the basis of the foreign languages you can read, decide on a country using that language as its official language for its law.

Language constitutes a very heavy barrier for studying the law of a (foreign) European continental country, as only a micro-percentage is ever translated into, for example, English.

- bg Портал на Европейския съюз
- cs Portál Evropské unie
- da Internetportalen til EU
- de Das Portal der Europäischen Union
- et Euroopa Liidu portaal
- el Η δικτυακή πύλη της Ευρωπαϊκής Ένωσης
- en Gateway to the European Union
- es El portal de la Unión Europea
- fr Le portail de l'Union européenne
- ga Tairseach an Aontais Eorpaigh
- it Il portale dell'Unione europea
- lv Eiropas Savienības portāls
- lt Europos Sajungos portalas
- hu Az Európai Unió portálja
- mt Il-portal tal-Unjoni Ewropea
- nl De portaalsite van de Europese Unie
- pl Portal Unii Europejskiej
- pt O portal da União Europeia
- ro Portalul Uniunii Europene
- sk Portál Európskej únie
- sl Portal Evropske unije
- fi Euroopan unionin portaali
- sv EU:s webbportal

Tip #3.2

As for the text of legislation and court decisions, et cetera, only use translation(s) made by officially authorized translators.

European courts and governments will never rely on non-authorized translations; thus, carefully check who did the translating.

It is wrong - and out of proper context - to teach legal research on the basis of non-authorized translations, as it gives students the impression they can always use such material.

Even for Member States of the European Union one can not expect, for example, the English version to be a true translation of the twenty-three other language-versions; each translation to a certain degree reflects the law of the country that uses that particular language.

Thus, an English version can differ from a Danish or Swedish version - and even though those two countries are said to belong to the same (Nordic) legal family, their versions will also differ. Therefore, even for E.U. law, one must not try to circumvent the law of a certain E.U. country by using the English version. It is necessary to pay attention to the particular E.U. (language) law version of the country to be investigated.

The European Union website "Translation and Drafting Aids in the European Union Languages" at <http://ec.europa.eu/translation/index_en.htm> contains links to the following Multilingual resources (see next page):

- E.U. Terminology
- Europa Glossary
- Eurovoc Thesaurus
- Acronyms & Abbreviations
- Drafting Guides
- Interinstitutional Style Guide
- Language Aids for E.U. Translations
- Europa Languages and Europe

Beyond knowing the language, a researcher also must know something about the history of the country, its culture and society. Without such background knowledge, it is nearly impossible to understand the basis for the country's law. The CIA World Factbook <www.cia.gov/library/publications/the-world-factbook/index.html> and Wikipedia.org both provide helpful initial information on different countries.

Tip #3.3

Choose the law of a country about which you know something as to its history, culture and society.

European Commission

Translation and drafting resources

ission > Translation resources

Translating EU texts made easier — links to resources

Stuck for a term in an EU language? Need background information on the EU and its member countries?
Here's our pick of links you may find useful (for every EU language).

Language resources and useful links

Online dictionaries, glossaries, national sites, ...

I translate into / draft in...

- Bulgarian
- Czech
- Danish
- Dutch
- English
- Estonian
- Finnish
- French
- German
- Greek
- Hungarian
- Irish
- Italian
- Latvian
- Lithuanian
- Maltese
- Polish
- Portuguese
- Romanian
- Slovak
- Slovenian
- Spanish
- Swedish

Guidelines for contractors

Material to help our contractors produce high-quality translations.

I translate into...

- Bulgarian
- Czech
- Danish
- Dutch
- English
- Estonian
- Finnish
- French
- German
- Greek
- Hungarian
- Irish
- Italian
- Latvian
- Lithuanian
- Maltese
- Polish
- Portuguese
- Romanian
- Slovak
- Slovenian
- Spanish
- Swedish

Language recognition

- Our Field guide to the main languages of Europe [456 KB] will help you identify which language a text is written in. You'll know whether *Ďakujeme vám za návštevu našej stránky* is Czech, Hungarian, Lithuanian — or something else.
- Language identifiers

Clear writing guide

- How to write clearly [2 MB] <> — European Commission booklet (all EU languages) [March 2010]

Special character sets

Need to type special characters or accents but can't find them on your keyboard? One solution is to copy & paste from here:

- Unicode special character sets (the Cyrillic, Greek and Latin sets cover characters from all EU official languages)

Languages, countries and currencies

- Language codes for EU languages (639-1)
- Country codes for EU countries (ISO 3166)
- Country names and currencies

3.3. The Second Heavy Task – Choosing a Foreign country to investigate

If one can read several foreign languages, one should determine which legal family one prefers to investigate. If one has previously researched a legal family, it will obviously not require as much preparation to investigate the law of another country belonging to the same legal family.

On the other hand, if one wants to get a broader view of the law of different continental European countries, it can be more productive to choose the law belonging to another legal family (provided that one can still read the language, and knows something of the history, culture, et cetera of that country).

One way of dividing countries into legal families (see Chapter 2) is:

- Romanistic Legal Family (France, the Benelux countries, Italy, Spain and Portugal)
- Germanic Legal Family (Germany, Austria, Croatia, Switzerland, Greece, Turkey, and South Korea)
- Nordic Legal Family (Denmark, Finland, Iceland, Norway, and Sweden)
- Anglo-American Legal Family (England, and Wales, Northern Ireland, United States of America, Australia, Canada (except Québec))
- Law in the Far East (China and Japan)
- Religious Legal Systems (A. Islamic law, B. Hindu law)

Tip #3.4

Choose a country whose law belongs to a legal family that one prefers (and knows something about).

In turning to a new legal family, it can naturally be helpful to do a little research into it and its cultural background, et cetera (see Chapter 2).

3.4. The Third Heavy Task – Knowing basic differences between civil and common law

If one is brought up with Common Law and wants to study Civil Law, one should at a very minimum learn by heart the content of the rough overview comparison between Common Law and Civil Law thinking given in the Introduction (Chapter One) above.

And, an American should - before investigation of any law of continental Europe - also have read section 7.1 in Chapter 7, and especially beware of the differences in terms mentioned in section 7.1.1.1.

> **Tip #3.5**
> Be fully aware of the difference between Common Law and Civil Law.
> Also, note that the same English words and terms can be used – and understood - differently in the U.S. and in continental Europe.

3.5. The Fourth Heavy Task – Knowing the investigated specific country's legal research method

Nearly every country in continental Europe has its own unique ways of doing legal research. Thus, one must study the chosen country's special methods, which can often best be achieved by reading a guide or textbook authored by a native.

Note that teaching legal research is quite different in the U.S. and in Europe, as the aims of the courses are different (see section 7.1.1 below).

> **Tip #3.6**
> Often, useful guides on how to do legal research in a certain country, written by natives, can be found in English; for example, at Globalex <www.nyulawglobal.org/globalex/>.

3.6. Comparative Method or Nothing

Because a pure comparison of legal systems does not have any value or purpose, one has to figure out a comparative method that will work when investigating two or more countries' legal systems. See further below in Chapter 4, especially section 4.3, about "A Plan" for making a comparative method.

Pure comparison is without value since the same words/terms can have different meanings or be used differently in the legal systems (and their societies/cultures). Furthermore, even the legal systems and institutions of closely situated/related European countries can present great differences. Hence, the crucial importance of developing a method to compare the chosen legal systems.

An alternative is to decide not to make any comparisons at all, and try to forget anything one has learned about one's own legal system. This is like starting out on an "adventure" into a foreign legal system with a totally fresh mind (akin to having learned to walk and then abandoned that form of locomotion to figure out how to fly or swim!).

Tip #3.7

Decide whether to develop a comparative method.
Or, alternatively, not to make any comparisons at all.

Thus, students/scholars have to know how to build a legal comparative method.

The word "comparison" should not be used.

3.7. "Getting into the Country"

When the above mentioned steps are taken, one is ready to begin the real task of investigating the law of the foreign country and its legal research methods.

The following will try to be a (further) manual for the topic of legal research, especially for Americans.

It will deal primarily with where to find the law, as any comprehensive introduction to a Civil Law country's specific "legal research methods" is beyond the scope of this book.

One should not forget that in continental Europe case law is, overall, not important. Thus, searching for or studying case law should be the very last item on the agenda – and only if there is time for it.

Tip #3.8
Teaching on how to find the law (in the U.S.: legal research) is not a normal course of study in Civil Law countries; it is rare that one will find texts or hornbooks similar to those in the U.S. In Civil Law countries, books on "legal research" will deal with just what is law (law-foundation-sources[4]) and how statutes are interpretated.

Thus, in Civil Law countries it is more or less all about statutes.

Tip #3.9
Do not waist time on the case law of Civil Law countries. Instead, spend time on acts and statutes - and their interpretation.

3.7.1. The Country's structure

A basic requirement for doing legal research on a particular country in continental Europe is to know:

- The Constitution – and thereby the structure between:
    - Parliament
    - Government (N.B., the term is used differently in the U.S.)
    - President / Majesty, and
    - Courts
- What the powers are for each of the above-mentioned institutions
- How statutes are interpretated
- How the country's law in its entirety is divided into parts[5]
- What is hard law and what is regarded as soft law

Some guidance can be found at the ECJ's (CVRIA) website on "European Union Law in Europe" (English version) at

<http://curia.europa.eu/jcms/jcms/j_6/>,

which gives information about:

- Library and documentation → Links → National and international case law → National case-law database (English) (French).
- Legal information of European Union Interest - Courts of th Member States of the European Union

[4] See Chapter 1, section 1.2 for the definition of "law-foundation-source."
[5] See Tip #7.4 above and Table 36.

- Booklet “State of the court systems as at 1 January 2007” offer the reader an overview of the courts and procedures of justice in Europe, describes the court systems of each of the 27 Member States of the European Union. In addition, it includes a diagrammatic presentation of the national courts and specific bibliographical references (in French) at <http://curia.europa.eu/jcms/jcms/Jo2_7231/>.
- Library and documentation → Links Member States:

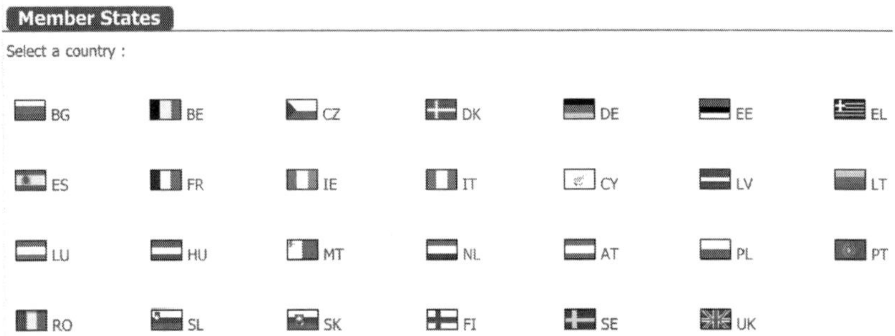

The legal order for several Member States of the E.U. is also given (English version) at

<http://ec.europa.eu/civiljustice/legal_order/legal_order_ec_en.htm>

illustrated next page (in an older version of August 2004 of the site).

Do not waist time on the issue of citation format, as in continental Europe there is no official pattern to citations (see section 7.1.8 below).

Moreover, Civil Law countries do not require Shepardizing (that is, using a legal citator to check the currency) of case law because judicial precedent is not important and because a newer statute on the same subject always will overrule an older one (see section 7.1.1 below).

No Civil Law countries have anything like the United States Code (U.S.C.) (see section 7.1.4).

The term “code” in continental Europe is used as a synonym for an act or a law.

3.7.1.1. Default scenario: Continental European Civil Law Country

The following facts can be regarded as the default scenario when doing research on a continental European Civil Law country.

It should give Americans some insight into how the continental European countries work in essence.

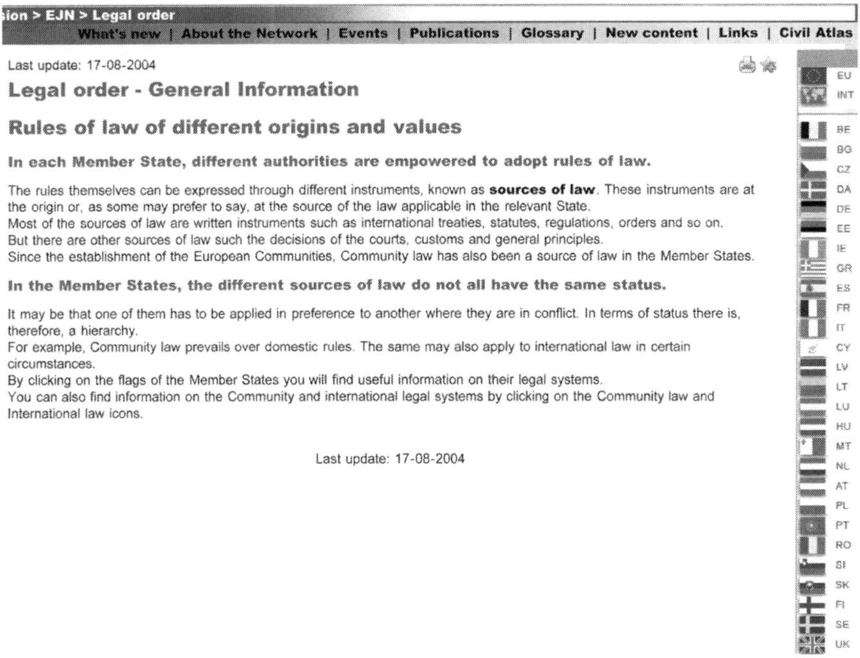

ion > EJN > Legal order

What's new | About the Network | Events | Publications | Glossary | New content | Links | Civil Atlas

Last update: 17-08-2004

Legal order - General Information

Rules of law of different origins and values

In each Member State, different authorities are empowered to adopt rules of law.

The rules themselves can be expressed through different instruments, known as **sources of law**. These instruments are at the origin or, as some may prefer to say, at the source of the law applicable in the relevant State.
Most of the sources of law are written instruments such as international treaties, statutes, regulations, orders and so on.
But there are other sources of law such the decisions of the courts, customs and general principles.
Since the establishment of the European Communities, Community law has also been a source of law in the Member States.

In the Member States, the different sources of law do not all have the same status.

It may be that one of them has to be applied in preference to another where they are in conflict. In terms of status there is, therefore, a hierarchy.
For example, Community law prevails over domestic rules. The same may also apply to international law in certain circumstances.
By clicking on the flags of the Member States you will find useful information on their legal systems.
You can also find information on the Community and international legal systems by clicking on the Community law and International law icons.

Last update: 17-08-2004

EU INT BE BG CZ DA DE EE IE GR ES FR IT CY LV LT LU HU MT NL AT PL PT RO SI SK FI SE UK

Based on the country's constitution, the power in the country is divided into the following three branches:

- The **Executive power**, which branch consists of:
    - The head of the country, who is a constitutional king/queen, which means he/she is not an absolute monarch – or a President
    - A government or cabinet led by a Prime Minister
- The Legislative power
- The Judicial power
- For Members of the European Union: the E.U. institutions have some impact on each country.

But basically, the E.U. only has the powers that each Member State has handed over to it directly (as most recently "updated" by the Lisbon Treaty of December 2007).

The **Legislative power** is in the Parliament, whose members are elected by a direct vote of the country's citizens. It is the only power to enact law/statutes. The Parliament can by a majority vote declare its mistrust in the government but cannot dissolve the government/cabinet. In such case of declared mistrust, a new government has to be composed, but new public elections will not be held unless the Prime Minister decides they should be.

Bills are introduced either by a Member of Parliament or by a cabinet minister. If an introduced bill obtains the support of a majority (normally 50 %) of the Members of Parliament it is then sent to a committee that studies the bill and makes recommendations. The bill – with suggested amendments – is thereafter read a second time in Parliament. If it continues to receive majority support, it will go to further negotiations in the committee, or go straight to a third and final vote in Parliament. If supported by a majority at this point, the bill in its final text will become law.

All bills and negotiations on the floor of Parliament will be printed in the Parliament's Records.

The statute or act that results will be signed by the responsible minister and the king/queen and enter into force either when published in the Official Journal or later, at a special date stated in its text.

The **Judicial power** cannot declare laws/statutes (made by Parliament) unconstitutional. Judges are appointed by the government and can only be removed through an impeachment process. Each judge has to retire at the age of 65.

The court system consists of district courts, appeal courts and a top or Supreme Court.

All court decisions can be appealed to a higher level court, but they can only be appealed once again upon permission of a special independent committee, whose members are appointed by Parliament.

Court decisions can not be remanded and returned to a lower court. The stare decisis doctrine is not used. The courts' task is to use – not make - the law and they can only interpret (fill in gaps) in a statute's text to a very small (and narrow) degree.

A commercial publisher will, upon subscription, publish those court decisions that the publisher's advisory board recommends should be published. Every citizen can, by paying a handling fee, obtain a copy of a decision from the court that issued the decision.

The **Government/Cabinet** is set up in the following way: After a four-year term – or after decision by the Prime Minister – a public election will be held with all seats of the Parliament on the ballot. All citizens have the right to vote, and an election/polling place cannot close before all citizens have had a chance to vote. Every vote has to be counted. A special commission of the country oversees the election.

After it has been established which persons have been elected to the Parliament and how many member seats each party has won, each party's leader will inform the king/queen as to whom the party suggests should lead the negotiations for drawing up a government/cabinet. After holding meetings, the person appointed by the king/queen as negotiator will announce which person he/she suggests should form the government/cabinet.

This latter person will then negotiate with others and decide what should be the political program for the government/cabinet and then seek to obtain the support of a majority of the elected Members of Parliament.

If majority support is achieved, the person will inform the king/queen that a government/cabinet has been set up and how the group of responsible individuals of the government/cabinet (the ministers) have distributed tasks/responsibilities between themselves. The king/queen will appoint the cabinet including the person chosen to be Prime Minister.

The ministers (in the U.S.: cabinet "secretaries") will thereafter initiate bills for Parliament and run their individual ministries. Often ministers are also elected members of the Parliament.

The ministers can issue decrees/rules pursuant to delegated powers given by Parliament through acts/statutes.

The police and prison system, and the administrative parts of the court system, fall under the Minister of Justice, who also (sometimes with Parliament's participation) issues court rules.

Cities, towns and local communities are run by elected mayors together with elected councils. They fall under the supervision of the government/cabinet (and Parliament).

3.7.1.2. In Civil Law skill at interpretation of statutory text is a requirement

Civil Law lawyers do not fill in gaps – like in Common Law – but interpretate the text of a statute or single subsection. See further Chapter 7, sections 7.2-7.3.

3.7.2. Online Searching

American students, who are taught about and how to use online legal databases such as Westlaw and LexisNexis, sometimes are not aware of databases on foreign law.

As for European Union law, information is often hard to find since the E.U. search-systems are not integrated into a convenient framework.

Legal research courses should alert students as to how to go about finding foreign law.

However, the main obstacle is language. If a student cannot read the foreign country's official language, then he/she can perform little if any research or study as to that Civil Law country. This is due to the fact that a Civil Law lawyer or student will begin searching for the act(s) or statute(s) that deal(s) with the particular issue surveyed; next read the text of such law; and thereafter search for commentary. Case decisions should only be searched if mentioned as important (a "precedent case") in the previously mentioned material. Beyond this, in Civil Law countries it is only to a small extent possible to search electronically for legal material; hence, the investigation has to be done "through" library shelves, which – depending on the library's collection - might not contain the investigated country's material. If online systems do exist, then it will again be necessary to be able to read the foreign country's language (and sometimes costly subscriptions are required).

3.7.3. Westlaw databases

Students should be aware of the special International Directory offered by Westlaw (in its "classic" format; the new Westlaw "Next" format is seemingly still undergoing development in terms of foreign and international resources). It gives access to some foreign information in English, but not much from continental Europe.

Also, see the list of some popular databases in Westlaw in Appendix 5.

And see the corresponding website for this book at

<www.hssph.net/legalrm>.

Westlaw's special overview site for European Union material is actually quite good and searching – when available – through Westlaw is often easier than through the E.U.'s own website.

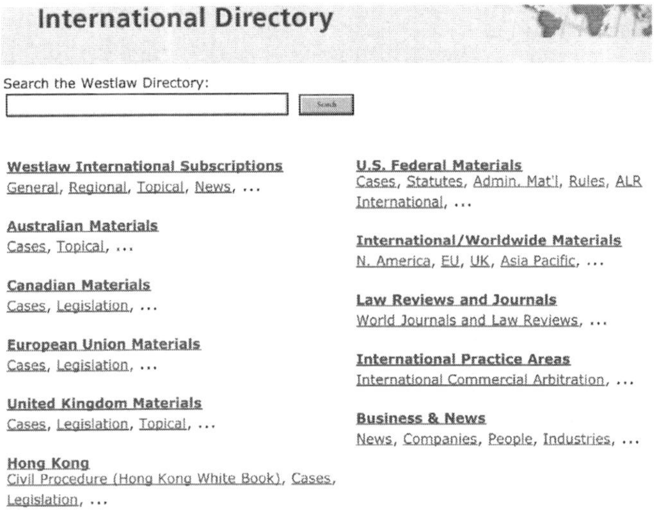
International Directory
Search the Westlaw Directory:
Westlaw International Subscriptions
General, Regional, Topical, News, ...
Australian Materials
Cases, Topical, ...
Canadian Materials
Cases, Legislation, ...
European Union Materials
Cases, Legislation, ...
United Kingdom Materials
Cases, Legislation, Topical, ...
Hong Kong
Civil Procedure (Hong Kong White Book), Cases, Legislation, ...
U.S. Federal Materials
Cases, Statutes, Admin. Mat'l, Rules, ALR International, ...
International/Worldwide Materials
N. America, EU, UK, Asia Pacific, ...
Law Reviews and Journals
World Journals and Law Reviews, ...
International Practice Areas
International Commercial Arbitration, ...
Business & News
News, Companies, People, Industries, ...

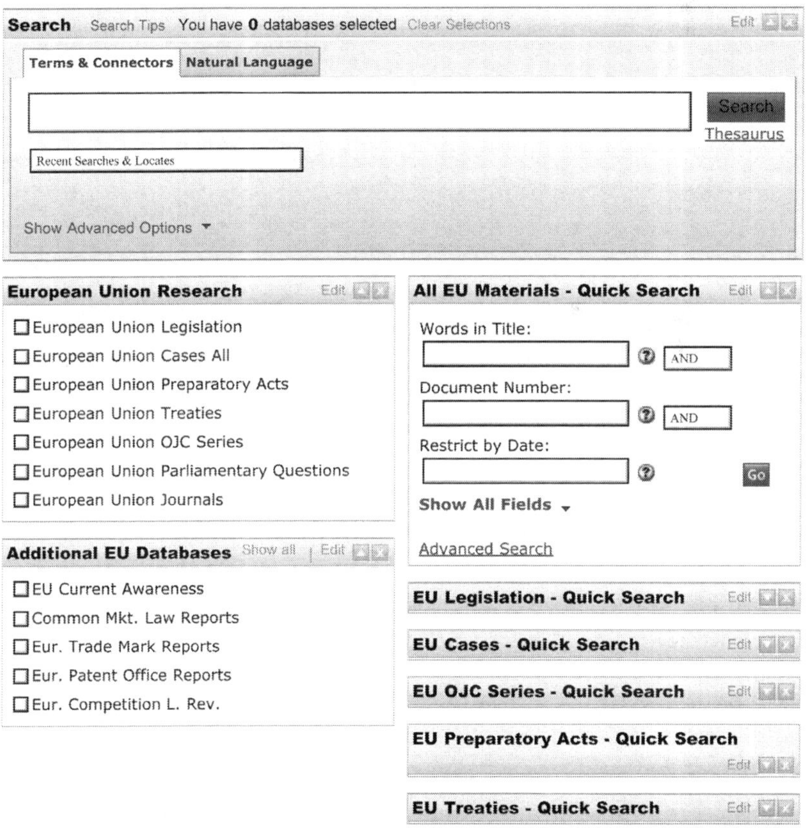
Search
Search Tips
You have 0 databases selected
Clear Selections
Edit
Terms & Connectors
Natural Language
Search
Thesaurus
Recent Searches & Locates
Show Advanced Options
European Union Research
European Union Legislation
European Union Cases All
European Union Preparatory Acts
European Union Treaties
European Union OJC Series
European Union Parliamentary Questions
European Union Journals
Additional EU Databases
Show all
EU Current Awareness
Common Mkt. Law Reports
Eur. Trade Mark Reports
Eur. Patent Office Reports
Eur. Competition L. Rev.
All EU Materials - Quick Search
Words in Title:
AND
Document Number:
AND
Restrict by Date:
Go
Show All Fields
Advanced Search
EU Legislation - Quick Search
EU Cases - Quick Search
EU OJC Series - Quick Search
EU Preparatory Acts - Quick Search
EU Treaties - Quick Search

3.8. Miscellaneous

Overall, it seems that teaching on Civil Law generally must remain quite superficial, as it is more than likely that a university's or other law library will not contain sufficient foreign legal source material to enable the legal research a native would do. Furthermore, for language reasons, students will not be able to perform legal research as a native would. Third, as the bases of Civil Law will be statutes, legal research in Civil Law countries will have to be done fundamentally differently from how it is done in the United States – concentrating on what statutes say and how they are to be interpreted.

Thus, courses on legal research of foreign Civil Law countries should focus on: what legal family the particular country belongs to; the institutions existing under the investigated country's constitution and their respective powers; which instruments (acts, rules, decrees, et cetera) each institution can issue; if possible, where the sources can be found in publications (in a library) and/or online; and studying a guide on legal research for the particular Civil Law country.

If an investigated country is a Member State of the European Union, it is obvious that the different E.U. institutions and the Union's different legal instruments (regulations, directives, et cetera) and how to find them, will influence/have an effect on the investigated country's law.

Beyond that, a course on legal research in Civil Law countries should include teaching of the general issues mentioned in Chapter 7, including the basic rules for interpretation (see section 7.3.3).

After some time teaching the basics on Civil Law, it may be appropriate to let students divide into groups and investigate one or several Civil Law countries' official websites and then culminate with either a paper or a presentation on what is the legal language of the investigated country(ies); how the particular Civil Law country(ies) work(s); what a legal research guide for the country(ies) communicate(s) about sources and interpretation(s), et ceterea; and where to find source material (in print or online).

3.9. Conclusion

Law schools that have chosen to offer cross-border law courses should appreciate the great efforts teachers in today's legal research classes will have to expend in preparation for such courses. And if they do not succeed to the degree students expect, law schools should still acknowledge that the teachers have been given a Uriaspost and be satisfied that they have at least survived the struggle.

The time may well have come when American law schools should realize that they need the assistance of scholars brought up in Civil Law countries[6] – just as European universities nowadays routinely invite or hire foreign continental European and American scholars to come and give lectures or advise students and colleagues on their native law. Arguably, today's law faculties should at least include one full time scholar brought up in a Civil Law country – or maybe even one from each legal family. Otherwise, it seems fair to conclude that the faculty cannot truly fulfill their modern "transnational" commitment to students.

3.10. Further Reading (updates at corresponding website)

> The URL for the corresponding website is <www.hssph.net/legalrm> with a full alphabetic bibliography.

Foreign Law Research at GlobaLex at <www.nyulawglobal.org/globalex/index.html#>

Guides on how to do legal research in a certain country, written by natives, can be found in English; for example, at Globalex <www.nyulawglobal.org/globalex/>.

International Legal Research Tutorial, Duke University at <www.law.duke.edu/ilrt/>

Of Maps, Stories, and Tapestries: Researching International and Domestic Law in the Age of Globalization (Chapter 1) in GUIDE TO INTERNATIONAL LEGAL RESEARCH (The George Washington International Law Review) (Newark, NJ : LexisNexis Matthew Bender, 2010)

People, Lee, *Strategies and Sources for International Legal Research*, 60 CONSUMER FINANCE LAW QUARTERLY REPORT 412

Price, M. Kathleen, *The Unambiguous Rightness of Meaning: The Search for Precision in Foreign, Comparative, and International Law Research* (Chapter 1) in ACCIDENTAL TOURIST ON THE NEW FRONTIER: AN INTRODUCTORY GUIDE TO GLOBAL LEGAL RESEARCH (Ed. Jeanne Rehberg & Radu D. Popa)(Littleton, Colo. : F.B. Rothman, 1998)

Rehberg, Jeanne, & Mirela Rozovschi, *Finding Foreign Law* (Chapter 4) in ACCIDENTAL TOURIST ON THE NEW FRONTIER: AN INTRODUCTORY GUIDE TO GLOBAL LEGAL RESEARCH (Ed. Jeanne Rehberg & Radu D. Popa)(Littleton, Colo. : F.B. Rothman, 1998)

Smith, A.L., *Foreign Law in Translation: Problems and Resources* (Chapter 14) *in* RICHARD DANNER, INTRODUCTION TO FOREIGN LEGAL SYSTEMS (New York: Oceana Publi-

[6] Such professors should, of course, be hired with the minimum condition that they assist the law schools' students in researching and writing papers concerning basic Civil Law legal methods.

cations, 1994)

Solum Lawrence, *Download it While it's Hot: Open Access and Legal Scholarship*, 10 LEWIS AND CLARK LAW REVIEW 841 (2006)

Top Ten Tips for Finding Foreign Law, University of Pittsburgh at

<www.law.pitt.edu/library/international/foreigntopten>

Volokh, Eugene, *Law Reviews, the Internet and Preventing and Correcting Errors*, 116 Yale Law Journal Pocket Part 4 (2006) at

<www.yalelawjournal.org/images/pdfs/57.pdf>

3.11. Various Exercises

Updated or new materials may be found at the book's corresponding website at <www.hssph.net/legalrm>.

3.11.1. Sample country datasheet

Choose a country in continental Europe, search the Internet and fill out the form below.

Country: ____________________________

Official Language: ____________________________

Belong to Legal Family: ____________________________

Word in English	Word in official language (for example in German: Verfassung = Constitution)	Official Website
Constitution		
Parliament		
Bills		
Parliament Reporter		
New law / acts		
Government		
President / Majesty		
Courts		
Supreme Court		
Case Reporter		
Legal Law Review / Journal		

3.11.2. Statutory interpretation example

In 1848, due to the many horse carriages in the cities and towns, the Parliament of Country A decided that the traffic direction should be on the right-hand side of the road. The rule became a statute in a new act named the Traffic Direction Act.

In 1920, a white paper on the traffic situation showed three quarters of the automobiles in Country A were produced and imported from the United Kingdom (where traffic stays to the left side of the road). Thus, these imported cars all had steering wheels on their right-hand side. Hence, the paper concluded that it would be safer if the traffic direction was changed to the left side of the road. This suggestion became a statute in the Road Act, which contains, among other things, rules on road conditions and snow clearance. However, by an inadvertent error, the statute in the Traffic Direction Act was not revoked.

Using the rules of interpretation, discuss which side – left or right - would be correct for traffic direction, and upon which rule the interpretation is based?

In 1970, Country A became a Member State of the European Union in which there already existed a Council Regulation on Traffic of 25 December 1968 stating that the driving direction in the European Union is the right-hand side of the road, as most cars in the Union have the steering wheel on their left side.

Using the rules of interpretation, discuss which side would be correct for traffic direction, and upon which rule the interpretation is based?

CHAPTER 4

Comparative Law Methods

As the future curriculum for American law schools – at least at Harvard,[1] Stanford[2] and Yale – will contain a requirement in each course to undertake comparison to other legal systems,[3] it seems appropriate for this book on legal research methods to contain a chapter on comparative law or more rightly termed, comparative (law) methods.[4] These must consist of detailed analysis as well as comparison. The process quite naturally requires study of some foreign law, after having studied the law of one's home country first.[5]

The usefulness of comparative legal study is beyond question.[6]

[1] The Harvard Law School announced not long ago that its first-year curriculum will reduce the number of hours spent on the traditional common-law courses and mix in three new classes: legislation and regulation, international and comparative legal studies, and problem-solving skills, ABA JOURNAL, July 2007, page 44.

[2] Stanford Law School will give law students access to the entire university and, for example, allow law students interested in intellectual property to take engineering and science classes. Law students might learn better negotiation skills at the business school or learn more nuances about the implications of a cross-border transaction by studying in the economics department. Dean Larry Kramer to ABA JOURNAL, July 2007, page 45.

[3] Compulsory jurisprudence comes too late in education and is too little. Alan Hunt, 6 *Jurisprudence, Philosophy and Legal Education – Against Foundationalism*, LEGAL STUDIES 292, 294 (November 1986).

[4] As comparative law methods deal with more than comparison, they are different from comparative jurisprudence. Consider the legal dictionary definition: "The study of the principles of legal science by the comparison of various systems of law." BLACK'S LAW DICTIONARY (8th ed.) (St. Paul: West Publishing, 2004).

[5] Max Rheinstein, *Comparative Law – Its Functions, Methods and Usages*, 22 ARK. L. REV. 415, 416 (1946) [hereinafter RHEINSTEIN].

[6] Günter Frankenberg, *Critical Comparisons: Re-Thinking Comparative Law*, 26 HARV. INT'L L. J. 411, 418 (1985) [hereinafter FRANKENBERG]. Comparative law is a tool of research and a tool of education, Otto Kahn-Freund, *On Uses and Misuses of Comparative Law*, 37 MOD. L. REV. 1 (1974) [hereinafter KAHN-FREUND II]. A man who knows no language except his own is far less able to appreciate its beauty and to understand its structure than he who can compare it with the languages of other nations,

Comparative legal analysis is also relevant in the E.U. framework, where comparison of different rules in the E.U. Member States often results in promulgation of rules in the form of an E.U. directive. The same applies for working out international conventions or treaties.[7]

As indicated previously, this book's primary aim is for use in teaching courses on legal research methods in the US and in Continental Europe, so this chapter should only be regarded as a very brief introduction to comparative law methods.

A famous European book (in English translation) is K. Zweigert & H.Kötz, Introduction to Comparative Law.[8] See also a number of well-regarded articles from other professors in the footnotes of this chapter.[9]

And see Chapter 3 above on the requirements for doing research in a foreign country.

4.1. Introduction – Not just comparison

There is no decisive definition of what comparative law or comparative (law) method is today.[10] However, comparative law is not simply a topic, but a method - or rather, it is the common name for a variety of methods of looking at law.

O. Kahn-Freund, *Comparative Law as an Academic Subject*, 82 THE LAW QUARTERLY REVIEW 40, 60 (1966) [hereinafter KAHN-FREUND I].

[7] Ruth Nielsen & Christina D. Tvarnø, RETSKILDER & RETSTEORIER [Source of Law & Legal Theories] 25 (1st Ed.) (Denmark, Copenhagen: Jurist- and Økonomforbundets Forlag [DJØF Publishing] 2005) [hereinafter TVARNØ] & K. Zweigert & H.Kötz, INTRODUCTION TO COMPARATIVE LAW 2 (3rd ed.) (Tony Weir trans., Clarendon Press, Oxford, 1998) [hereinafter ZWEIGERT].

[8] ZWEIGERT *supra* note 7 at 145.

[9] See also, THE OXFORD HANDBOOK OF COMPARATIVE LAW (Editor: Reiman & Zimmerman)(England: Oxford University Press 2007); Peter de Cruz, COMPARATIVE LAW IN A CHANGING WORLd (3rd ed)(London/New York: Cavendish 2007); COMPARATIVE LAW - A HANDBOOK (Editors: Örücü / David Nelken)(England, Oxford: Hart Publishing 2007); ELGAR ENCYCLOPEDIA OF COMPARATIVE LAW (Edited by Jan M. Smits)(Edward Elgar Publishing Limited, 2008); INTERNATIONAL ENCYCLOPEDIA OF COMPARATIVE LAW, Enclyclopedic Work Series (Edited by K. Zweigert and K. Drobnig)(The Hague: Martinus Nijhoff).

[10] Esin Örürü, *Unde Venit, Quo Tendit Comparative Law?, in* COMPARATIVE LAW IN THE 21ST CENTURY 1 (Andrew Harding and Esin Örürü (Ed.), Kluwer, 2002) [hereinafter ÖRÜRÜ].

Research Tip #4.1

"Comparison" is quite the buzzword currently in American law schools/universities.

But, it should be used – if at all – with great caution.

A pure comparison of legal systems does not have any value or purpose, one has to figure out a comparative method that will work when investigating two or more countries' legal systems.

Thus, students/scholars have to know how to build a legal comparative method.

Comparative law has two quite distinct roots: [11]

- Legislative comparative law – when foreign laws are invoked in the process of drafting new national laws or international conventions.[12] The comparative study of law can also take the form of a selective adoption of particular legal institutions or rules.[13]
- Scientific or theoretical comparative law – when the comparison of legal systems – or with other (for example, socicial or computer/technical) systems - is undertaken to improve one's legal knowledge.[14]

Comparative law offers the only way by which law can become interna-

[11] ZWEIGERT *supra* note 7 at 51.

[12] A systematic knowledge of the donor system will make a law reformer more efficient. On the European continent, codification or major legislative revision normally results in the type of comparative law studies that would delight the most learned professor of that subject in the universities. Such studies are usually conducted or commissioned by officials of a country's ministry of justice. The E. U. Commission staff has performed a function somewhat similar to that of a national ministry of justice. National law makers are increasingly compelled – by the operation of the E.U. – to take into account each other's systems. At the U.S. federal level, there are no institutional arrangements or procedures for regular recourse to foreign law in the executive departments, where most bills originate. The same is true in the U.S. congressional committees. Eric Stein, *Uses, Misuses – and Nonuses of Comparative Law*, 72 NW. U. L. REV. 198, 209, 210, 212 (1977-78).

[13] Rodolfo Sacco, Legal Formants, *A Dynamic Approach to Comparative Law* (Installment I of II), 39 AM. J. COMP. L. 1, 3 (1991) [hereinafter SACCO I].

[14] Comparative law remains a science as long as it acquires knowledge and regardless of whether or not the knowledge is put to any further use. SACCO I *supra* note 13 at 4 & 5.

tional[15] and consequently a science.[16] The increase in cross-border activity is expanding the use and utility of comparative law, which is moving from local/region-centric to global. The internationalization of transactions, the use of the Internet, and the increasing applicability of foreign law make comparative law an indispensable tool of the legal practitioner.[17]

On the European continent, legal unity began to disappear in the 18th century as national codes were put in the place of traditional Roman law.[18] The consequence was that lawyers concentrated exclusively on their own legislation, and stopped looking over the border. Comparative law "has to put an end to such narrow-mindedness."[19]

Comparative analysis is proper and relevant both where national rules already exist in a country, which is the starting point for the comparison with foreign law, as well as in situations where there is no existing rule in the "stepping stone country" and where foreign law thus is used as inspiration.[20] However, comparisons can also be made between different rules in a single legal system.[21] Comparison follows from a knowledge of the phenomena to

[15] Comparative law dissolves unconsidered national prejudices, and helps to fathom the different societies and cultures of the world and to further international understanding. ZWEIGERT *supra* note 7 at 16-25.

[16] Some claim comparative law is still not a subject in its own right, while others claim that comparative law, properly pursued, is an essentially philosophical activity. ÖRÜRÜ *supra* note 10 at 4 & W. Ewald, *Comparative Jurisprudence (1): What Was it Like to Try a Rat?,* 143 U. PA. L. REV. 1889, 2111-2112 (June 1995).

[17] P. John Kozyris, *Comparative Law in the 21st Century: New Horizons and New Technologies*, 69 TUL. L. REV. 165-169 (1994) [hereinafter KOZYRIS] & ÖRÜRÜ *supra* note 10 at 17.

[18] All Civil Law systems are conglomerates of medieval European customs and the learning about Roman law that, after having been lost with the fall of the Roman Empire, was rediscovered in the 12th century. But the customs were different in different parts of Europe. RHEINSTEIN *supra* note 5 at 417.

[19] ZWEIGERT *supra* note 7 at 15. Modern comparative law started in Paris in 1900 when Édouard Lambert and Raymond Saleilles suggested a common law of mankind (droit commun de l'humanité) to which comparative law was necessary. They held comparative law must resolve the accidental and divisive differences in the law of peoples at similar stages of cultural and economic development, and reduce the number of divergences in law, attributable not to the political, moral, or social qualities of the different nations, but to historical accident or to temporary or contingent circumstances. ZWEIGERT *supra* note 7 at 3.

[20] TVARNØ *supra* note 7 at 25

[21] ZWEIGERT *supra* note 7 at 2. Much of what is called legal history (or history of law) in the Civil Law tradition is baffling and inexplicable to the Common Law lawyer who first approaches it. He/she is used to thinking of legal history as an account of legal

be compared. One can only compare that with which one is acquainted. Knowledge of these phenomena develops by comparison.[22]

Thus, comparative law is partly comparison but mainly the analysis of the different legal systems of the world. Comparative methods have proven to be the best means available for highlighting structural regularities that would otherwise pass unobserved. It would be wrong, however, to expect comparative methods to explain the reasons for these regularities. Comparisons do not serve this purpose.[23] Thus, further analysis of where and why the differences exist may be appropriate.

Comparative law is a school of verity or truth, which extends and enriches the solutions. However, it is perhaps too often the story of similarities and dissimilarities[24] between legal cultures, traditions, systems, families, styles, origins, solutions and ideas.[25] Some hold that an aim for comparative law is to find the "better solution" for the time and place.[26] However, others find the "better solution" of comparative law is not worthy of being described as an academic discipline in its own right.[27] But all seem to agree that comparative law is a science with its own distinct province. Comparative law can help to illuminate the nature of legal phenomena and the relationship between law and political, moral, and other values. It can also help demonstrate the extent to which the form and substance of any legal system are not "natural," but

rules and institutions in their historical, economic, and social context. However, picking up a book on legal history in the Civil Law tradition, he/she is likely to find the bulk of it devoted to a discussion of schools of legal thought and of disputes between legal scholars and their followers. The protagonist or leader of this form of legal history is the legal scholar, and its subject matter is currents of thoughts about the structure and operation of the legal order, John Henry Merryman, THE CIVIL LAW TRADITION: AN INTRODUCTION TO THE LEGAL SYSTEMS OF WESTERN EUROPE AND LATIN AMERICA 60 (2nd ed.) (Stanford, California: Stanford University Press, 1985).

22 SACCO I *supra* note 13 at 5.

23 SACCO I *supra* note 13 at 5.

24 Thus, the definition of comparative law in Black's Law Dictionary is somewhat wrong, as it claims: comparative law is the scholarly study of the similarities and differences between different legal systems. Actually, this is sometimes divided into three subsets: comparative legislation, comparative history of law and descriptive comparative law.

25 FRANKENBERG *supra* note 6 at 425.

26 ZWEIGERT *supra* note 7 at 8, 15 & TVARNØ *supra* note 7 at 25.

27 Jonathan Hill, *Comparative Law, Law Reform and Legal Theory*, 9 OXFORD JOURNAL OF LEGAL STUDIES 101, 113 (1989) [hereinafter HILL] & Alan Watson, LEGAL TRANSPLANTS: AN APPROACH TO COMPARATIVE LAW 1-9 (University Press of Virginia, 1974) [hereinafter WATSON].

result from the implementation of moral and political values.[28]

Research Tip #4.2

The task of the comparatist should be to cherish "difference," which involves some form of appreciation of "the other" and an a priori readiness to accept another system as valid in its own right.[29]

4.2. About the Method

Research Tip #4.3

Comparatists all over the world are perfectly unembarrassed about their adaptable methodology,[30] and see themselves as still being in an experimental stage.

Comparative law can scarcely be called systematic and comparatists remain appropriately eclectic.[31] Yet, modern comparative law is a critical method of legal science. Comparison has no fear of differences, however large they may be, and it measures the extent of those differences – again, be they large or small.[32]

The comparative method is the opposite of the dogmatic. The comparative method is founded upon the actual observation of the elements at work in a given legal system; whereas the dogmatic method is founded upon analytical reasoning. The comparative method examines the way in which, in various legal systems, jurists work with specific rules and general categories. The dogmatic method offers abstract definitions.[33]

Research Tip #4.4

A comparative lawyer may, and probably should, limit his field of research both in the geographical sense and as regards to subject matter.

[28] HILL *supra* note 27 at 115.

[29] Werner F. Menski, COMPARATIVE LAW IN A GLOBAL CONTEXT: THE LEGAL SYSTEMS OF ASIA AND AFRICA 18 (Platinium, London 2000) [hereinafter MENSKI].

[30] Sciences that have to busy themselves with their own methodology are sick sciences. Gustav Radbruch, EINFÜHRUNG IN DIE RECHTSWISSENSCHAFT 253 (12th Ed. 1969).

[31] Hiram E. Chodosh, *Comparing Comparisons: In Search Of Methodology*, 84 IOWA L. REV. 1025, 1044 & 1061(Aug 1999) [hereinafter CHODOSH], HILL *supra* note 27 at 111 & WATSON *supra* note 27 at 11.

[32] SACCO I *supra* note 13 at 7.

[33] SACCO I *supra* note 13 at 24.

But he must remain flexible and must often rely on common-sense to avoid rigorous discussion of theory and method.[34] A comparatist must set out on a voyage of discovery to find the field and yet on another voyage to find the tools.

When comparing closely related systems, it is usually more rewarding to explain the differences; while in two entirely unrelated systems, it is more rewarding to explain the similarities.[35]

Research Tip #4.5

It is necessary to get to know what is behind the formal legal texts and also, even more important, how these function. This requires understanding of the legal culture that produced the texts, and more broadly, the social and economic structures as well as the ethical and political values that support them.[36]

Research Tip #4.6

Laws cannot be grasped in an idealized form outside the context of the society that created them.[37]

A comparatist should not be limited to the staid and dry juxtaposition of the regulations of one legal system with those of another, with little or no critical analysis, for, as such, comparatists do not compare, they contrast. In Europe and North America there has been an almost irresistible tendency of comparative lawyers to translate roughly equivalent (or so it appears) concepts from two or more legal systems and then to contrast them, rather than to analyze their respective socio-legal environments and to study law and legal concepts "in context."[38]

A globally-focused study of legal systems, including the legal systems of Asia and Africa, cannot avoid taking many culture-specific, so-called "extra-legal" factors into account and therefore needs to be holistic, interdisciplinary and plurifocal in analyzing the concept of "law", for which there is no con-

[34] KAHN-FREUND I *supra* note 6 at 42 & FRANKENBERG *supra* note 6 at 417.

[35] ÖRÜRÜ *supra* note 10 at 9 & Michael Bogdan, COMPARATIVE LAW 18 (1994 Kluwer).

[36] KAHN-FREUND I *supra* note 6 at 41 & 47.

[37] KOZYRIS *supra* note 17 at 168.

[38] MENSKI, *supra* note 29 at 14, Pierre Legrand, *How to Compare Now*, 16 LEGAL STUDIES 232, 234 (July 1996) [hereinafter LEGRAND]. Comparative law loses some of its utility, and most of its charm, if it reduces itself to a level of dry, formalistic, historical introductions to foreign legal systems and comparison of legal rules and institutions. KOZYRIS *supra* note 17 at 175.

sensus definition.[39] A deep understanding of law is not found in legislative texts and judicial decisions alone.[40] The range of non-legal, cultural knowledge[41] required is vastly increased when trying to make sense of Hindu law, Islamic law, African law, Chinese law or Japanese law.

Comparative law has far greater utility in substantive law than in the law of procedure, and the attempt to use foreign models of judicial organization and procedure may lead to frustration and thus be a misuse of the comparative method. One cannot take for granted that rules or institutions are transplantable. The use of the comparative method requires a knowledge not only of the foreign law, but also of its social, and above all its political, context.[42]

Research Tip #4.7

To be able to solve his/her issue, a comparatist must often investigate the history of rules and their problems.

He must take into account not only legislative rules, judicial decisions, the "law in the books" - and general conditions of business, customs and practices - but also in fact everything that helps to mold human conduct in the situation under consideration.[43]

Research Tip #4.8

It is wrong to believe that the first step toward comparison is to identify "the legal rule" of the countries to be compared.[44]

Instead of speaking of "the legal rule" of a country, one must speak of the rules of constitutions,[45] legislatures, courts,[46] and, indeed, of the scholars[47]

[39] MENSKI, *supra* note 29 at 51.

[40] MENSKI, *supra* note 29 at 53, LEGRAND *supra* note 38 at 235. Norwegian professor Torsten Echoff has stated: "it has never been proven that a tribe's drum-dance to solve disputes was a poorer solutions-method than what we are used to" (author's translations into English), quoted by Carl August Fleisher, RETTSKILDER OG JURIDISK METODE 256 [Source of Law and the Legal Method] (Oslo, Ad notam Gyldendal, 1998).

[41] FRANKENBERG *supra* note 6 at 411 & 414 & MENSKI, *supra* note 29 at 15.

[42] KAHN-FREUND II *supra* note 6 at 20 & 27 & SACCO I *supra* note 13 at 7-9.

[43] ZWEIGERT *supra* note 7 at 8 & 11 and SACCO I *supra* note 13 at 26.

[44] SACCO I *supra* note 13 at 21.

[45] No one who wishes to describe the law realistically can ignore the existence of sources other than those formerly recognized in the Constitution. Rodolfo Sacco, *Legal Formants* (Installment II of II), *A Dynamic Approach to Comparative Law*, 39 AM. J. COMP. L. 343, 344 (1991) [hereinafter SACCO II].

who formulate legal doctrine – so-called "legal formants" of which a given legal system has many.[48] The jurist concerned with the law within a single country examines all of these "legal formants" and then eliminates the complications that arise from their multiplicity to arrive at one rule. He does so by a process of interpretation. Yet this process does not guarantee that there is, in his system, only a single rule. Several interpretations will be possible and logic alone will not show that one is correct and another false.

Research Tip #4.9
Within each legal system there co-exist different "legal formants," which may or may not be in harmony with each other.[49]

As for court decisions, one must know not only how courts have acted but consider the influences to which judges are subject. Such influences may have a variety of origins. It is a mistake to reduce the comparative method to the study of cases. Judicial decisions have a different significance in countries where the law is based on precedent from those where it is based on statute. It is important to distinguish between the rule announced by the court and the rule it actually applied, or, as a Common Law lawyer would say, between the court's statement of the rule and the holding of the case, that is, the facts on which the court arrived at a certain result.[50]

A jurist who deals with a system that is not his own often has problems of perception with legal formants that do not exist in his own system. Any account of the sources of law is incomplete unless it describes all legal formants of the system. To have a complete account, one must recognize the rules promulgated by organs of the state and enforced by its coercive power are not the only sources of law.[51]

[46] A Common Law lawyer – accustomed to considering judicial precedent as a main source – will find it curious that in Civil Law countries judicial decisions are not supposed to be a source of law at all. A Civil Law jurist will consult works of scholars if these faithfully describe the rule in a statute, and decisions of judges, because these are instances in which this rule has been enforced. SACCO I *supra* note 13 at 21-22.

[47] Scholarly writings, both essayistic and didactic, are a source of law, that is, they form "legal formants" of the system. SACCO II *supra* note 45 at 346. Scholarly writings were far more important in Germany between 1880 and 1900 than in France. In turn, case law has been more important in France than in Italy. SACCO I *supra* note 13 at 33.

[48] SACCO I *supra* note 13 at 22-23.

[49] SACCO I *supra* note 13 at 30 & SACCO II *supra* note 45 at 343.

[50] SACCO I *supra* note 13 at 23, 26 & 27.

[51] SACCO I *supra* note 13 at 33 & SACCO II *supra* note 45 at 344.

Research Tip #4.10
Law cannot be applied unless it is interpreted.[52]

When law is applied, there must be an interaction between a primary source, such as statute or case precedent,[53] and an interpretation. Interpretation[54] is determined and disciplined by all those factors that affect the convictions of the interpreter.[55]

Comparative law can move beyond the field of evaluating differences and similarities between and among systems to become part of an interdisciplinary research, serving the scholar concerned with problems of sociology and politics. Comparative law would be a purely doctrinal study if it were to concern itself only with legal forms.[56]

Comparative legal studies serves three major purposes:[57]

- Understanding - including explanation, knowledge, legal history, jurisprudence and legal science. Disagreements over what should be compared are in part a function of divergent theoretical and practical objectives.[58]
- Reform - including comparative judicial-decision making, and comparative legislation. A fruitful comparative law method has to do much more than set sections of codes or general legislation side-by-side.[59]
- International unification - including cross-border conflict resolution through private and public international law and international organizations.

Comparative law can be divided into:[60]

- Macrocomparison – comparing the spirit and style of different legal

[52] Interpretation is guided by what the interpreter thought and felt even before he started to read and analyze the source. Josef Esser, VORVERSTÄNDNIS UND METHODENWAHL IN DER RECHTSFINDUNG: RATIONALITÄTSGRUNDLAGEN RICHTERLICHER ENTSCHEIDUNGSPRAXIS (Durchges 1972) & SACCO II *supra* note 45 at 344.

[53] See further on this subject below Chapter 5, subsections 5.1.3., 5.2.6.2.1., 5.2.6.2.4., 5.5. & 5.6 (U.S.) & Chapter 7, subsection 7.3.3.2. (Civil Law).

[54] See further on this subject above Chapter 1, subsection 1.4.2.

[55] SACCO II *supra* note 45 at 344-345.

[56] SACCO II *supra* note 45 at 388.

[57] CHODOSH *supra* note 31 at 1069-1070, .

[58] CHODOSH *supra* note 31 at 1074, 1090.

[59] CHODOSH *supra* note 31 at 1075 & Roscoe Pound, *Comparative Law in Space and Time*, 4 AM. J. COMP. L. 70, 75 (1955).

[60] ZWEIGERT *supra* note 7 at 4-5.

systems, the methods of thought and procedures they use. Research is done into methods of handling legal materials, procedures for resolving and deciding disputes, or the roles of those engaged in the law. For example, compare different techniques of legislation, study the different ways of resolving conflicts adopted by different legal systems (by taking into account all actual methods of settling) disputes, and ask how effective they actually are. Thus, there is no concentration on individual concrete problems and their solutions.

- Microcomparison – a comparison that deals with specific legal institutions or problems, that is, with the rules used to solve actual problems or particular conflicts of interest. However, microcomparison may not work at all unless one takes into account the general institutional contexts in which the rules under comparison have evolved and are actually applied.

4.3. A Plan

A basic working-plan for a comparative (law) method is: [61]

1. As in all intellectual activity, begin with the posing of a question or the setting of a working hypothesis. Remember, that the methodology of a science is its rationale for accepting or rejecting its theories or hypotheses.[62] Prematurely crystallized methodological rationales may do more harm than good.[63] The biggest hazard is the formulation of the problem and the choice of the criteria of relevance on the basis of which data are selected and classified for study.[64] For practical reasons, it is necessary to make a somewhat painful selection; therefore, the comparatist must make up criteria of selection.[65]
2. Next, decide the manner in which the survey-investigation will be conducted, that is, in detail describe what one intends to do (not what one hopes for, as it is premature to do that). One may have to reevaluate and re-write this as work proceeds. List which criteria are

[61] Partly from ZWEIGERT *supra* note 7 at 6.

[62] Mark Blaug, THE METHODOLOGY OF ECONOMICS 47 (Cambridge University Press, 1980).

[63] CHODOSH *supra* note 31 at 1032.

[64] CHODOSH *supra* note 31 at 1053 & Sally Falk Moore, LAW AS PROCESS: AN ANTHROPOLIGCAL APPROACH 137 (ROUTLEDGE & K. PAUL, 1978).

[65] ZWEIGERT *supra* note 7 at 42.

used for the selection of the material.[66]

3. Lay out the essentials of the relevant foreign law, country by country, or component by component.[67] Remember that without clarity of purpose, it is difficult to determine the content of what to report. Without specific attention to the choice of content, comparisons are vulnerable to bias and inaccuracy. One of the dangers of comparative law is the temptation to mold the data with a view to substantiating a preconceived thesis.[68] Without developed techniques of contrast and differentiation, the goal of objectivity becomes elusive.[69] Analyze each component that is to be compared in its own environment, that is, in the way a that a person educated in that environment would do it. This includes using words and terms in the way a person in such environment does. The solutions found in the different jurisdictions must be cut loose from their conceptual context and stripped of their national doctrinal overtones so that they may be seen purely in the light of their function, as an attempt to satisfy a particular legal need.
4. Then use this material as a basis for critical comparison, that is, analyze by using, among other things, the methods from chapter 2 and/or 3 of this book. The comparison should be based on the idea of a logical and neutral referent. Thus, the comparatist's own legal system, culture or experience should not become the basis of and provide the conceptual framework for comparison.[70] This includes defining words and terms that are used differently in the environments to be compared.
5. End up with a real result, that is, a critical evaluation,[71] not just a comparison-result. This could be a conclusion or conclusions about the proper policy for the law to adopt, which may involve a reinterpretation of one's own system; it could also be any other kind of result from the comparative analysis. The comparatist must be able to demonstrate and persuade the audience members of the lessons they

[66] FRANKENBERG *supra* note 6 at 430.
[67] ZWEIGERT *supra* note 7 at 43.
[68] HILL *supra* note 27 at 107 & WATSON *supra* note 27 at 12-13.
[69] CHODOSH *supra* note 31 at 1051.
[70] FRANKENBERG *supra* note 6 at 432.
[71] CHODOSH *supra* note 31 at 1052 & ZWEIGERT *supra* note 7 at 43.

should take away from the analysis.[72] The comparatist is in the best position to follow his/her own comparative researches with a critical evaluation – and if he/she does not, no one will.[73]

4.4. Advice & Comments

The basic methodological principle of all comparative law is that the problem must be stated without any reference to the concepts of one's own legal system.[74] In comparative law, always focus on the concrete problem. To ask why a foreign system has not felt the need to produce a legal solution for a particular problem may lead to interesting conclusions about it, or about one's own law.

> **Research Tip #4.11**
> A comparatist must avoid all limitations and restraints, especially in relation to the question of "sources of law."

He/she must encompass the law of the whole world - past and present, and everything that affects the law. The comparatist must make every effort to learn and remember as much as he/she can about foreign civilizations, especially those whose law has engendered the great families of legal systems.[75] Every comparatist learns that the legal system of every society faces essentially the same problems, but often solves these problems by quite different means.

The right method must largely be discovered by gradual trial and error. It is extremely doubtful whether one could draw up a logical and self-contained methodology of comparative law, which could claim to work effectively. Thus, a detailed method cannot be laid down in advance. Most probably, the science of comparative law will always remain an area where only sound judgment, common sense, and even intuition, can be of any help.

Modern comparative law is a more realistic method of legal science, which not only shows up the emptiness of legal dogmatism, but develops a new and particular system related to demands for suitable rules in life; there-

[72] CHODOSH *supra* note 31 at 1086. The scholar has no other power than the one that comes from his capacity to persuade. SACCO II *supra* note 45 at 349.
[73] ZWEIGERT *supra* note 7 at 46.
[74] ZWEIGERT *supra* note 7 at 10.
[75] ZWEIGERT *supra* note 7 at 36.

fore, it is functional and appropriate. Legal science in general is sick, but comparative law can cure it.[76]

When making a choice among variables, the comparatist should remember the following:

- classification
- prototypes and
- micro/macro distinctions.

Classification, or the differentiation of phenomena into categorical schemes or taxonomies, is a common tool of comparative legal studies.[77] Nevertheless, there are four fundamental flaws in the use of classification in comparative legal studies. First, many classifications are a starting point for comparison rather than a conclusion based on any preceding comparative study. Second, many scholars seek to justify classifications by reference to a limited number of comparative variables. Third, differentiating criteria are often poorly or inconsistently applied. Fourth, even those who object to specific classifications or to classification in general suffer from the same weaknesses they identify in the work of others.[78] A starting point should - instead of working with pre-existing categories of classification - be developing a set of classifications from independent study.[79]

The work of thoughtful comparatists illustrates the difficulties encountered in conventional classificatory systems. Without questioning the categories as starting points, many exhibit the strong tendency to search for explanations of the categories instead of selecting key differentiating features prior to making the categorization. In other words, the comparison tends to take place after the categorization rather than before. Classifications are then justified by reference to a limited number of essential variables. Differentiating

[76] ZWEIGERT *supra* note 7 at 34.

[77] Even political scientists pay deference to categories that are based on facially inconsistent differentiating criteria. Some scholars have classified legal culture families into Roman-Germanic, Common Law, socialist law, and non-Western law. Others have been critical of this form of scholarship. CHODOSH *supra* note 31 at 1091 & endnote 302.

[78] That is, classifications tend to rely on primarily polar contrasts, e.g., black and white, without gray, or the existence or non-existence of differentiating variables. CHODOSH *supra* note 31 at 1090 & 1091 & endnote 303.

[79] "[C]lassification is a beginning rather than an end, a preliminary step 'designed to facilitate study of otherwise unwieldy bodies of information.'" "It is a prerequisite to thinking and speaking about the underlying differences and similarities among various objects." CHODOSH *supra* note 31 at 1091 & endnote 304 & Schlesinger, COMPARATIVE LAW: CASES, TEXT, MATERIALS 284-85 (6th ed.) (Foundation Press, 1998).

criteria are often poorly or inconsistently applied.[80]

Comparative treatments of prototypes of a law, process, or institution (that are then investigated cross-nationally) may be based on a false and implicit equivalence of parochial prototypes with universals. Second, the prototypes are frequently defined too ideally and consequently may lack any real-world plausibility. Third, prototypes may also carry embedded value judgments. Fourth, similar to classification, the use of prototypes appears to be inescapable.[81]

Both the choice of micro or macro levels of analysis and the identification of the appropriate unit of comparison pose a set of methodological concerns.[82]

By focusing on differentiation - a method of distinguishing comparative similarities and difference - one can identify six commonly-applied cross-referential[83] principles that structure the relationship between two or more concepts or the phenomena they attempt to grasp: dichotomy, overlap, relativity, interdependence, equivalence and indeterminacy.

By realizing that comparison involves three distinct, yet related, types of choice (the why, what and how), even an uneventful search for methodological rationales may open a wide array of unforeseen channels of fruitful comparative inquiry.[84]

Comparisons may be compared and differentiated[85] in part by identifying the potentially contrasting purposes that motivate them.[86] Understanding the

[80] CHODOSH *supra* note 31 at 1106-1107.

[81] CHODOSH *supra* note 31 at 1107-1109.

[82] CHODOSH *supra* note 31 at 1109.

[83] By "cross-referential" is meant the understanding of two expressions in terms of one another. This term is used instead of many alternatives, such as "opposite," "opposed," "polar," or "antithetical." Each of these alternatives assumes a significant contrast, indeed a mutual exclusivity. Cross-reference may include an equivalent relationship between two terms and is intended to be neutral as to whether the existence of two terms denotes contrast or similarity. CHODOSH *supra* note 31 at 1115-1126 and endnote 429.

[84] CHODOSH *supra* note 31 at 1130.

[85] Another set of purpose-related justification requires additional explanation, however. Purposes may be accepted or rejected in terms of their practicability. That is, one might agree with the purpose of understanding, reform, or unification, yet disagree that comparison itself can advance the objective. Therefore, to agree or disagree with an articulated purpose may depend on one's view of how well the comparison proceeds from beginning to end. CHODOSH *supra* note 31 at endnote 295.

[86] On the level of methodology, a comparison of purposes would carry an obvious risk that many comparisons could be rejected on the basis of the underlying motivations of the comparatist. Illuminating this as a point of disagreement is to be encouraged; however,

role of purpose in comparison necessitates a differentiation and evaluative comparison of such purposes.[87] Many disagreements can emerge from the choice of comparative variables.[88] Comparisons tend to focus on a particular subset of variables, while ignoring others. However, these comparative variable choices are infrequently explained or justified.[89]

In many comparisons, purpose, content and mode of differentiation each play a significant roles. Insufficient consideration of the complex interaction of these three features of comparison is likely to render poor results.

> **Research Tip #4.12**
> It is a good idea to check the legal dictionary of each jurisdiction to be compared.[90]

For example, is "code" used in the American sense (all legislation combined into one updated and compiled "act"), and if not (does "code" relate to the copying or influence of the French Code Civile?[91]), how so?

> **Research Tip #4.13**
> What in other contexts would be regarded as a good knowledge of a foreign language may not be adequate for the comparatist.[92]

It is not rare for a language to be combined with more than one legal language. Words do not have absolute permanent meanings. Comparatists are continually confronted with problems of translation. The question is often whether one has to use the terminology of the era of a statute's making (and, in the U.S., also of a court's decision), or replace it with modern terminology. Word and concept may be related in different ways and any theory of legal

transforming this into a universally applicable rationale for rejecting comparisons would be very undesirable. Developing rules that would proscribe comparisons motivated by some purposes and not others would severely limit the scope of permissible comparative inquiry. CHODOSH *supra* note 31 at endnote 296.

[87] CHODOSH *supra* note 31 at 1089-1090.

[88] CHODOSH *supra* note 31 at 1090.

[89] This insufficiently explored problem is a critical issue in the explanation of social systems. CHODOSH *supra* note 31 at 1090 & endnote 301.

[90] For U.S. law, see Black's Law Dictionary (8th ed.)(St. Paul: West Publishing, 2004).

[91] ZWEIGERT *supra* note 7 at 85-118.

[92] WATSON *supra* note 27 at 11.

translation must consider them.[93]

To reach any sound conclusions, one must be able to establish connections between class interest and legal superstructure, legal rules and institutions.[94]

An example of a questionnaire for use in a specific comparative project is printed as Appendix 1 in Mauro Bussani & Ugu Mattei, The Common Core Approach to European Private Law Project, 3 COLUMBIA JOURNAL OF EUROPEAN JOURNAL 339, 343 (1997/98).

4.5. When to stop

A comparatist should go as deep as possible into his/her chosen systems. A presumptive rule for the comparatist is that if he finds that there are great differences or indeed diametrically opposite results, he should be warned and go back to check again whether the terms in which he posed his original question were indeed purely functional, and whether he has spread the net of his researches quite wide enough.[95]

Research Tip #4.14

If there are great differences or diametrically opposite results, go back to check whether the terms in which the original question was posed were indeed purely functional, and whether the scope of the research is broad enough.

4.6. Further Reading (updates at corresponding website)

The URL for the corresponding website is <www.hssph.net/legalrm> with a full alphabetic bibliography.

Chodosh, Hiram E., *Comparing Comparisons: In Search of Methodology*, 84 IOWA LAW REVIEW 1025 (Aug 1999)

COMPARATIVE LAW - A HANDBOOK (Edited by Esin Örücü & David Nelken)(Oxford; Portland, Or.: Hart, 2007)

Comparative Law Research at GlobaLex at

<www.nyulawglobal.org/globalex/index.html#>.

[93] SACCO I *supra* note 13 at 11, 12 & 14.
[94] SACCO II *supra* note 45 at 389.
[95] Zweigert *supra* note 7 at 40.

CRUZ, PETER DE, COMPARATIVE LAW IN A CHANGING WORLD (3rd Ed)(London/New York: Cavendish 2007)

ELGAR ENCYCLOPEDIA OF COMPARATIVE LAW (Edited By Jan M. Smits)(Edward Elgar Publishing Limited, 2008)

Ewald, W., *Comparative Jurisprudence (1): What Was it Like to Try a Rat?*, 143 UNIVERSITY OF PENNSYLVANIA LAW REVIEW 1889 (June 1995).

Frankenberg, Günter, *Critical Comparisons: Re-Thinking Comparative Law*, 26 HARVARD INTERNATIONAL LAW JOURNAL 411 (1985)

Hill, Jonathan, *Comparative Law, Law Reform and Legal Theory*, 9 OXFORD JOURNAL OF LEGAL STUDIES 101, 113 (1989)

INTERNATIONAL ENCYCLOPEDIA OF COMPARATIVE LAW, Enclyclopedic Work Series (Edited By K. Zweigert And K. Drobnig)(The Hague: Martinus Nijhoff)

Kahn-Freund, Otto, *Comparative Law as an Academic Subject*, 82 THE LAW QUARTERLY REVIEW 40 (1966)

Kahn-Freund, Otto, *On Uses and Misuses of Comparative Law*, 37 MODERN LAW REVIEW 1 (1974)

Kozyris, P. John, *Comparative Law in the 21st Century: New Horizons and New Technologies*, 69 TULANE LAW REVIEW 165 (1994)

Legrand, Pierre, *How to Compare Now*, 16 LEGAL STUDIES 232 (July 1996)

MENSKI, WERNER F., COMPARATIVE LAW IN A GLOBAL CONTEXT: THE LEGAL SYSTEMS OF ASIA AND AFRICA (Platinium, London 2000)

MERRYMAN, JOHN HENRY, DAVID S. CLARK & JOHN OWEN HALEY, COMPARATIVE LAW: HISTORICAL DEVELOPMENT OF THE CIVIL LAW TRADITION IN EUROPE, LATIN AMERICA, AND EAST ASIA (Matthew Bender & Co, 2009)

MERRYMAN, JOHN HENRY, THE CIVIL LAW TRADITION: AN INTRODUCTION TO THE LEGAL SYSTEMS OF WESTERN EUROPE AND LATIN AMERICA (2nd ed.) (Stanford, California: Stanford University Press, 1985).

Örürü, Esin, & Unde Venit, *Quo Tendit Comparative Law?*, in COMPARATIVE LAW IN THE 21ST CENTURY (Andrew Harding and Esin Örürü (Ed.), Kluwer, 2002)

Pound, Roscoe, *Comparative Law in Space and Time*, 4 AMERICAN JOURNAL OF COMPARATIVE LAW 70 (1955)

Rheinstein, Max, *Comparative Law – Its Functions, Methods and Usages*, 22 ARKANSAS LAW REVIEW 415 (1946)

Sacco, Rodolfo, *Legal Formants, A Dynamic Approach to Comparative Law (Installment I of II)*, 39 AMERICAN JOURNAL OF COMPARATIVE LAW 1 (1991)

Sacco, Rodolfo, *Legal Formants, A Dynamic Approach to Comparative Law (Installment*

II of II), 39 AMERICAN JOURNAL OF COMPARATIVE LAW 343 (1991)

SCHLESINGER, COMPARATIVE LAW: CASES, TEXT, MATERIALS (6th ed.) (Foundation Press, 1998)

Stein, Eric, *Uses, Misuses – and Nonuses of Comparative Law*, 72 NORTHWESTERN UNIVERSITY LAW REVIEW 198 (1977-78).

THE OXFORD HANDBOOK OF COMPARATIVE LAW (Editor: Reiman & Zimmerman)(England: Oxford University Press 2007)

WATSON, ALAN, LEGAL TRANSPLANTS: AN APPROACH TO COMPARATIVE LAW (University Press of Virginia, 1974)

ZWEIGERT, K., & H.KÖTZ, INTRODUCTION TO COMPARATIVE LAW (3rd ed.) (Tony Weir trans., Clarendon Press, Oxford, 1998)

CHAPTER 5

Methods in the U.S. – A Common Law Method

2010 was a year when legal research tools in the United States witnessed significant changes, advances and developments.

In 2007, we saw the beginnings of a revolution in legal education in the United States. Early in 2007, Harvard Law School announced "the most sweeping changes to its first-year curriculum in 100 years, requiring first-year law students to take ... a class on legislation and regulation, another covering global legal systems, and a third focusing on problems and theories."[1] Other leading law schools were likewise revising their curriculums to reflect the new world legal order. Stanford Law School was "in the process of rolling out joint-degree programs and 12 cross-disciplinary courses ..." with a special emphasis on international law.[2] The Columbia Law School dean remarked that "the global economy is becoming more interconnected, so thinking how to teach comparative and international law becomes more and more important every year."[3]

Since 2007, law schools' interests in globalization and international studies have only intensified.

As a front-page story from the National Law Journal[4] reports:

> Nearly 130 of the 200 American Bar Association-approved law schools already offer ABA-sanctioned programs in foreign countries . . . and now the

[1] Tresa Baldas, *Several Schools Adjust Their Curriculums*, THE NATIONAL LAW JOURNAL, Monday, September 10, 2007, p. S1.

[2] *Idem.*

[3] *Idem.*

[4] Karen Sloan, *Globalization: Law schools get serious*, THE NATIONAL LAW JOURNAL, November 29, 2010, p. 1.

organization is weighing whether to offer accreditation to overseas law schools.[5] At least two relatively new foreign law schools – Jindal Global Law School near Delhi, India, and Peking University of Transnational Law – have announced plans to seek accreditation should the ABA move forward with that initiative.

The lawyer of today cannot only rely upon his or her own national legislation or rules but has to take into consideration foreign law, and this is especially true between Europe and the United States. What happens on one side of the Atlantic Ocean is quickly felt upon the other.

An article in Harpers Magazine makes an interesting observation about how law making on one side of the Atlantic effects (not just affects) law making on the other:

> [I]n 1976, the U.S. Congress passed the Toxic Substances Control Act . . . which granted the government the authority to track industrial chemicals and to place restrictions on any that proved harmful to humans or the environment. Because the United States was the world's preeminent economic power, other major chemical producers Germany, France, and Britain soon brought their national regulations into line with United States law.[6]

As Professor Michele DeStefano Beardslee of the University of Miami School of Law has said, "The lawyers of tomorrow, if they want to be successful, are going to have to interact with businesspeople from around the world."[7]

The purpose of this book is to introduce American legal research to Europeans and European legal research to Americans so that they can speak the

[5] See Don J. DeBenedictis, *Foreign Law School Accreditation Proposal Draws Controversy*, SAN FRANCISCO DAILY JOURNAL, Thursday, December 2, 2010, p. 1 quoting Stanford Law professor Michael Klausner as saying "I see no reason why a U.S.-style legal education cannot be provided outside the U.S."

[6] Mark Schapiro, *Toxic Inaction*, HARPER'S MAGAZINE, October 2007, p. 78, 79. However, the European Union has taken over the leading role by signing the following international agreements: Air Pollution, Air Pollution-Nitrogen Oxides, Air Pollution-Persistent Organic Pollutants, Air Pollution-Sulphur 94, Antarctic-Marine Living Resources, Biodiversity, Climate Change, Climate Change-Kyoto Protocol, Desertification, Hazardous Wastes, Law of the Sea, Ozone Layer Protection, Tropical Timber 82, Tropical Timber 94, CIA's The World Factbook-European Union, <www.cia.gov/library/publications/the-world-factbook/print/ee.html>.

[7] Karen Sloan, *Globalization: Law schools get serious*, THE NATIONAL LAW JOURNAL, November 29, 2010, p. 1.

same legal research language, a necessary first step for cross-Atlantic collaborations. The book is also the first legal research text to address the internationalization of the American law school curriculum.

5.1. U.S. Common Law Basics for Non-Americans

5.1.1. Introduction

The United States is a startling vast country, 3,000 miles (4.828 km) coast to coast, and that does not include its two detached states, Alaska and Hawaii.[8] Everything in the United States is "super sized." Americans drive enormous automobiles[9] and the American Dream is to live in a large single-family house.[10] Everything in America, it seems, is done on a grand scale, including law-making. It has been said that the United States is a litigious society and this is reflected in court statistics.[11] Most of this litigation occurs in the states, and not at the federal level,[12] and it is the state courts that apply and create the

[8] For comparison: The European Union's area is 4,324,782 square kilometer (one-half the size of the U.S.) and has a population of 490,426,060 (190,000,000 more than the U.S.), <www.cia.gov/library/publications/the-world-factbook/print/ee.html>. The E.U. is the largest single market in the world with a $15.4 trillion economy and the largest trading partner of the U.S. Trade flows across the Atlantic are running at around €1.7 billion a day.

[9] The gasoline prices in the U.S. are only 1/3 of the prices in most of the rest of the world.

[10] According to HARPER'S MAGAZINE, the "percentage change since 1990 in the average size of an American master bathroom" is 50%. *Harper's Index*, HARPER'S (October 2007), p. 15 (citing National Association of Home Builders (Washington)). Nevertheless the Great Recession perhaps has had an effect here. The average size of new single-family homes completed in 2009 dropped to a nationwide average of 2,438, about 100 square feet smaller than 2007, according to the National Association of Home Builders (NAHB). Kim Palmer, *In American homes, living (not so) large is the next big thing*, THE WASHINGTON POST, Sunday, November 21, 2010, p. A2.

[11] During the 12-month fiscal year 2005-2006, more than 9.2 million cases were filed in the California court system. Judicial Council of California, 2007 COURT STATISTICS REPORT. California is an important state, with a large population, but, still, that is just the number of court filings for one of fifty states and the District of Columbia.

[12] By comparison, in 2006 there were a little over 300,000 cases filed in the United States District courts (the federal trial level court of general jurisdiction). Of these, 259,541 were civil filings and 56,532 were criminal filings. See: Administrative Office of the United States Courts, FEDERAL COURT MANAGEMENT STATISTICS 2006, <www.uscourts.gov/fcmstat>.

Common Law.

Since 2007, the world has experienced an economic crisis labeled by many in the United States as the "Great Recession." Despite this economic downturn, litigation remains a brisk business (and despite the fact that attorneys have not been immune from the crisis and many have lost their jobs). And according to the very popular Above the Law legal news and gossip blog, "[o]n New Years Eve [2010], John Carney - our former colleague, from his days at Dealbreaker - noted on CNBCs NetNet that the ABA issued a paper entitled The Value Proposition of Going to Law School NetNet called the report an official warning from the ABA about the perils of going to law school." In spite of the economy and the ABA's sounding of the alarm the nation's federal trial courts experienced increases in the numbers of new civil and criminal cases filed in the 12-month period ending March 31, 2010..

The number of new civil cases filed in U.S. District Courts rose to 282,307 – a 9.2 percent increase over the previous 12-month period. The number of new criminal cases filed rose to 77,287 – a 3.7 percent increase.[13]

To the lawyer from the continent of Europe, Common Law has always been something rich and strange. At every step, the European lawyer comes across legal institutions, procedures, and traditions, which have no exact counterpart in the Continental legal world. The European lawyer scans the common legal scene in vain for much that seems to him or her to be an absolute necessity in any functioning legal system, such as a civil code, a commercial code, a code of civil procedure, and an integrated structure of legal concepts rationally ordered. The European finds that legal technique, instead of being directed primarily to interpreting statutory texts or analyzing concrete problems so as to "fit them into the system" conceptually, is principally interested in precedents and types of court cases.

It is nearly impossible for any scholar to do proper research on United States law without the use of computer-assisted legal research (CALR) databases, such as the ubiquitous LexisNexis and Westlaw research systems (although, as noted below, more and more competitors are appearing on the scene). Being able to sift, search, cull, and skim from millions and millions of reported and, with greater frequency, unreported court decisions is what American lawyers and law students do, and they do it all of the time.

Since 2007 and especially in 2010 there have been many and dramatic developments in computer-assisted legal research. 2010 saw remarkable changes and advanced in American legal research, particularly case research.

[13] U.S. District Court Filings Continue to Climb, at <http://www.uscourts.gov/NEWS>.

2010 is when Westlaw released its truly revolutionary and addictive new product interface, "WestlawNext" (as of this writing LexisNexis is preparing to roll out its competitive product called Lexis Advance). 2010 is when "Bloomberg Law" made a renewed pitch to provide serious competition to the LexisNexis Westlaw duopoly (called "Wexis" by some).[14] 2010 is also when "Law.gov" started its series of workshop, the results of which have the potential to be far more revolutionary than WestlawNext or anything else we have seen in legal publication, because Law.gov provides the promise of free and open access to legal information from all branches (legislative, executive, and judicial) and from all levels (federal, tribal, state, and local) of American government.

The concept of free legal information – i.e., "open access" – may not seem like a radical notion to the European lawyer, but in America, for far too long, far too much legal information has been locked away behind very expensive pay walls.[15] Google, Inc. took a big step forward in 2009 towards breaking down these paywalls with its inclusion of legal opinions in its Google Scholar database.[16]

These are exciting times for legal start-ups too. Companies such as Occam, Inc. (described in further detail in section 5.5.4.) are just getting ready to launch. When Law.gov takes root, these start-ups offer fascinating possibilities to change the way lawyers do effective legal research.

The federal government and several states have made significant recent inroads with the publication and dissemination of legal information. As of December 20, 2010 the Federal Digital System (FDsys) has become the United States Government Printing Office's official system of record for online Government information. The date December 20, 2010 also marked the start of the countdown for the sunset of the previous online system, GPO Access. In 2011, GPO Access will continue to be updated in parallel with FDsys, and in mid-2011, GPO Access will be officially retired.[17]

[14] Russell Adams, *Bloomberg Hangs New Shingle*, THE WALL STREET JOURNAL, Thursday, July 8, 2010, p. B8; Andrew Edgecliffe-Johnson, *Bloomberg Law's discounts challenge information suppliers*, FINANCIAL TIMES, Monday, November 29, 2010, p. 19.

[15] See *Law.gov: Legal Documents for the People*, STANFORD LAWYER, Fall 2010, p. 2.

[16] Anurag Acharya, *Finding the laws that govern us*, THE OFFICIAL GOOGLE BLOG, <http://googleblog.blogspot.com/2009/11/finding-laws-that-govern-us.html>. Writing on the Spindle Law Blog, a third year law student writes about her "infatuation with Google Scholar." See Laura Bergus, "*One Year of Legal Research Innovations, A Law Student Perspective*," SPINDLE LAW BLOG.

[17] "Not only is FDsys a powerful tool for the public to access online, authoritative Federal information, but it also serves as a preservation repository for the content and a content

According to a letter from Richard G. Davis, Interim Superintendent of Documents at the U.S. Government Printing Office, FDsys provides enhancements to GPO Access that will allow users to:

1. Easily search across multiple publications or collections of Government publications from a single search box.
2. Perform an advanced search against robust metadata about each publication from a single search page.
3. Construct complex search queries using advanced Boolean and field operators.
4. Refine and narrow searches by applying filters, sorting search results, and searching within search results.
5. Retrieve individual Government documents and publications in seconds directly from each search result.
6. View more information about a publication and access multiple file formats from a "More Information" Web page that is available from each search result.
7. Access metadata or information about Government publications in standard formats such as MODS and PREMIS.
8. Download content and metadata packages together as a single ZIP file
9. Browse for a specific Government publication and browse within the publication using its table of contents.
10. Utilize enhanced help options including context specific field level help and a searchable online help system.

5.1.2. State sovereignty

When one performs American legal research, one should regard the United States as a federal union of fifty fairly independent states, each with its own constitution. Thus, one can think of the U.S. as not so much one nation but actually more like the European Union of twenty-seven member states.

The United States Congress in Washington D.C. has limitations upon what issues it may legislate upon, and the federal courts in the United States similarly have limitations upon what cases they may hear.

management system for Federal agencies. " 'The Fdsys': the new GPO Access," LLRX.com, <http://www.llrx.com/fdsys.htm>. See also subsections 5.2.4. & 5.2.5. <http://www.fdlp.gov/component/content/article/19-general/866-fdsyssysofrecord>.

While there is by and large no federal general Common Law,[18] all American lawyers and law students search for federal law precedents.

The United States can be regarded as a gigantic laboratory for legal policy and the critical method of comparative law is important for any lawyer and student in the U.S.[19]

Even though the U.S is regarded as a Common Law country and traces its origins to England, its Common Law varies from the Common Law found in England and the Commonwealth nations. English Common Law is inapplicable if conditions in America make it inappropriate. Nor is there such a thing as "a common American law" (even though it is to a certain degree taught in law schools).

England does not have a constitution, whereas the United States has a constitution creating civil rights[20] and giving the U.S. Supreme Court and lower federal courts the power to declare whether a federal statute is unconstitutional. The Constitution of the United States bestows the U.S. Congress with legislative competence only in limited and special areas, whereas England has a Parliament that can legislate for the entire nation without any limitation and has courts that cannot declare a statute unlawful.

5.1.3. Life for the American law student

Cases, cases, cases. That is what American law students read morning, noon and night.[21] Their textbooks are even called "casebooks."[22] By one estima-

[18] See *Erie Railroad Company v. Tompkins*, 304 U.S. 64 (1938) and 28 U.S.C. § 725 (2000).

[19] Modern comparative law is a critical method of legal science…a discipline where a detailed method cannot be laid down in advance, K. Zweigert & H.Kötz, INTRODUCTION TO COMPARATIVE LAW 33, 251 (3rd ed.)(Tony Weir trans., Clarendon Press, Oxford, 1998).

[20] However, England has the so-called "Magna Carta Libertatum" ("Great Charter of Freedoms") of 1215, which led to the rule of constitutional law today. It influenced many common law and other documents, such as the United States Constitution and Bill of Rights, and is considered one of the most important legal documents in the history of democracy.

[21] However, this is changing in regards to upper level courses with the new curriculum of the leading law schools in the U.S.

[22] "In the first year of law school, much of the focus of law is on courses arising from common law rules … Rather than using traditional textbooks that talk about the law, these courses expose students directly to the law itself through reading assigned in casebooks. A traditional casebook focuses on only one area of law (for example, Torts or Criminal Law) … the casebook contains clusters of edited cases – actual opinions written and published by judges in various jurisdictions. These cases have been care-

tion, a typical United States law student will read between forty and fifty cases a week,[23] every week of his or her first year of law school (and in the United States full time law students take three years to earn their Juris Doctor (J.D.)[24] degree, which is the degree most lawyers in the United States have). Indeed, one of the very first assignments for Stanford Law School students in their first-year Legal Research and Writing (LRW) course is to read Owen Kerr's truly excellent "How to Read a Judicial Opinion: A Guide for New Law Students".[25]

Students devour, discuss, and dissect a stream of these cases, seemingly without end. Federal cases, state cases, English cases, really old cases, bad cases, elegant cases, cases written in verse, unpublished cases, cases decided just today, etc. Case analysis – that is the life of an American law student.

So what is a case? In the United States, judges make decisions and then write opinions. Understanding legal research requires an understanding of its unique vocabulary. So let us take a moment to explain what an opinion precisely is. According to the very helpful legal reference book The Legal Research Dictionary: from Advance Sheets to Pocket Parts, Second Edition:[26]

fully selected and carefully edited by the casebook based on what the author wants you to learn … Some of these cases may contradict one another (they are collected from different jurisdictions that may apply different common law rules), some show evolution in the law, … some show exceptions to a dominant rule … and some are just poorly decided (included to make you think about what does and doesn't make sense)." Ruth Ann McKinney, READING LIKE A LAWYER: TIME-SAVING STRATEGIES FOR READING LAW LIKE AN EXPERT (Durham, North Carolina: Carolina Academic Press 2005).

[23] Professor Ruth Ann McKinney, Clinical Professor of Law and Director of the Legal Writing & Learning Resources Center at the University of North Carolina School of Law has researched the law school experience and estimates that "the average American law student is assigned about three to four cases a night in three classes a night. So, on average, the average law student is reading between eight and twelve cases a night, five nights a week. I estimate they are reading between forty and fifty cases a week." E-mail correspondence from Ruth McKinney, dated September 18, 2007, on file with the authors.

[24] This is a much lower degree than the European "Doctor Juris" degree, which is the highest law degree and requires writing a dissertation, getting it accepted by a law scholar committee and finally passing a "defense" of the thesis asserted in the dissertation.

[25] Available at: <http://volokh.com/files/howtoreadv2.pdf>.

[26] Elyse H. Fox, THE LEGAL RESEARCH DICTIONARY: FROM ADVANCE SHEETS TO POCKET PARTS (2nd ed.)(Chapel Hill, N.C.: Legal Information Services, 2006).

> *Opinion*. Technically, the written statement of the court explaining its decision, i.e., a written explanation by the court of why it took the action it did. Opinions may be very long or very short. They state the facts of the case, the procedural history of the case, and the holding that resulted in the court's decision. Opinions may be signed by an individual judge, or unsigned and designated as issuing from the court as a whole ("*per curiam*": by the court). Sometimes the opinion is designated as not for publication . . . Different types of opinions may be written, and one case may have several opinions (majority opinion, minority opinion, concurring opinion, plurality opinion, *per curiam* opinion, memorandum opinion, rescript opinion). Judges do not always write an opinion to accompany their decisions; sometimes the court issues its decision with no opinion at all but only with an order (order by the court, summary order, summary disposition). Informally, opinion is sometimes used interchangeably with decision, but technically, decision is the action the court takes and opinion is the written explanation.'

Judges from all levels – trial and appellate – and even administrative law judges (ALJs), quasi-judicial officials from the Executive Branch, write opinions.

In their opinions, judges apply law to fact situations and, on appeal, only the questions of law are reviewed. Unlike in Europe, where all is de novo, appellate courts in the United States will not overturn facts that were decided by the trier-of-fact (which could be a jury or a judge if the defendant waived a jury trial). Appellate courts only consider questions of law. It is this exposition of law – written opinions of *appellate* judges -- that American law students study. More on this later when we discuss case law research.

This case-centric approach to legal studies carries over to all three years of the American law students' education. Indeed, it is not unusual to see a second or third year student hunched over at the computer, searching, for hours – in vain – for the "white horse" case,[27] a case that perfectly matches the issue being researched, so named because of a fact pattern identical to the one being researched, right down to the color of the horse that the defendant rode off upon.

Why are students so focused on case law? It traces to the first Latin phrase

[27] Bryan A. Garner, A DICTIONARY OF MODERN LEGAL USAGE (2nd ed.) (New York: Oxford University Press, 1995), (a law library must-have) offers this definition: "White-horse case; horse case; gray mule case; goose case; spotted pony case; pony case. These are terms meaning 'a reported case with virtually identical facts, the disposition of which should determine the outcome of the existing case.' The terms are now less commonly used in the law school than formerly; but they are useful terms." [hereinafter GARNER].

they learn in law school, *stare decisis*, succinctly defined by Black's Law Dictionary as:

> [Latin "to stand by things decided"] The doctrine of precedent, under which it is necessary for a court to follow earlier judicial decisions when the same points arise again in litigation.

Third Circuit Court of Appeals Judge Ruggero Aldisert, who literally wrote the book on judicial opinion writing[28] defines precedent[29] thusly:[30]

> A judicial precedent attaches a specific legal consequence to a detailed set of facts in an adjudged case or judicial decision, which is then considered as furnishing the rule for the determination of a subsequent case involving identical or similar facts and arising in the same court or a lower court in the judicial hierarchy.

Since the United States is a Common Law country (with the exception of some laws from the State of Louisiana and the U.S. territory of Puerto Rico), court cases establish legal principles. A judicial decision "determines the outcome of a particular case, and also may regulate future conduct of all persons within the jurisdiction of the court."[31] It establishes a precedent.[32]

> "The doctrine of *stare decisis*, or adherence to precedent, requires courts to decide cases consistently with their past decisions involving the same or similar facts and legal principles. Lower courts in a particular jurisdiction are bound not only by their own past decisions, but also by the precedents of higher courts in that jurisdiction. Although a court in State A will not regard the judicial precedents from other states as mandatory authority, the court may nevertheless consider them to be persuasive authority, particularly when there is no precedent in State A on the issue raised is the current case."[33]

Because of this doctrine of *stare decisis*, American lawyers and law students must be able to locate all the mandatory (the "law") and, in order to argue well, the most persuasive additional precedents that relate to their re-

[28] Ruggero J. Aldisert, OPINION WRITING (Bloomington, IN: AuthorHouse, 2009).

[29] Compare as for Civil Law in Chapter 7, subsection 7.3.3.2. and Research Tips 7.18 & 7.19.

[30] *Frederico v. Home Depot*, 507 F.3d 188 (3rd Cir. 2007).

[31] West's ENCYCLOPEDIA OF AMERICAN LAW.

[32] The term "precedent" is used differently in Civil Law, where "precedents" are only those court decisions that have been acknowledged to be important by the society and by scholars.

[33] LESSONS IN LEGAL RESEARCH: A MANUAL FOR INSTRUCTORS (LexisNexis, 2004).

search assignments and their clients' cases. And for this reason, many lawyers and law students turn to case law databases first to tackle their research.

A major goal of this chapter is to prove that starting legal research by plowing though case law databases, however, is not the road to effective legal research.

5.1.4. Law Making Bodies in the United States

In this chapter the term "government" is given an American meaning.[34] Government actors are defined as those individuals - elected or appointed - who have some official role in the legal regulation of American life or commerce. These government actors belong to one of three branches of government:

- The Legislative
- The Executive
- The Judiciary

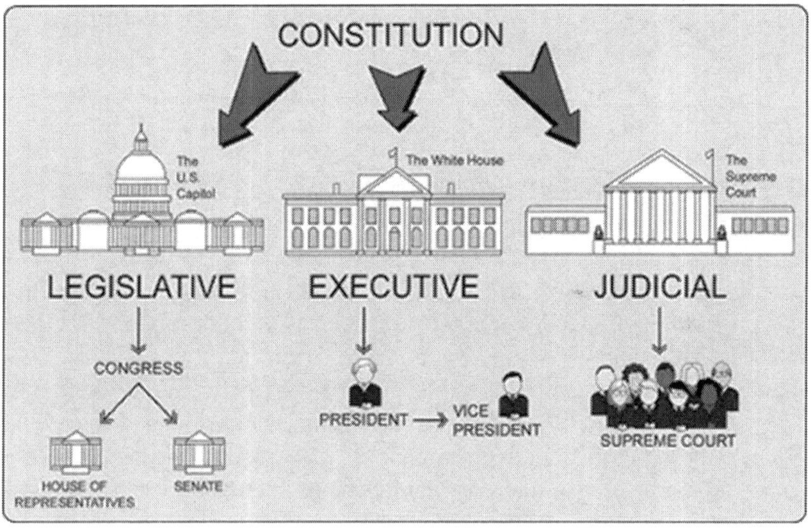

Table 6: United States Three Branches of Government

As discussed above, judges in the United States make "law" by issuing decisions. However, courts are not the only law-making arm in the United States.

[34] On the subject in Civil Law, see Chapter 7, subsection 7.1.1.1. and table 33.

But what, exactly, is "law?" According to West's Encyclopedia of American Law, "… the word law refers to any rule that if broken subjects a party to criminal punishment or civil liability." In other words, failure to obey the law could result in either going to jail or paying someone else money, often a lot of money.

The United States has three branches of government, as illustrated above in Table 6, and each branch produces its own body of law, as guided by the United States Constitution.

- The Legislative Branch produces statutes.
- The Executive Branch issues orders, regulations and administrative opinions.
- The Judicial Branch writes those millions of judicial decisions (also called opinions or just "cases" – the terms are used interchangeably) which are the focus of law school education and comprise the bulk of the content in the gigantic computer-assisted legal research databases LexisNexis and Westlaw (together "Wexis").

All of these types of law, and how to research them, are discussed in detail below. But before we get there, it is important to recognize that these three branches are not operating independently of each other. The White House policy office assists with the drafting of legislation; legislation is enacted with an understanding that courts will flesh out further meaning. In 2010, the U.S. Congress passed major health care reform legislation, dubbed "Obamacare" in some circles. Since enactment and as of this writing "so far in three lawsuits against the plan, two federal judges appointed by Democrats have upheld the law; one Republican-appointed judge has declared an important part of it unconstitutional."[35] This does not mean that the law is doomed. As Stanford law professor and former United States Court of Appeals federal judge Michael McConnell has remarked, "It's not impossible that some kind of interplay between the administration, a more skeptical Congress and a somewhat more skeptical judiciary could lead to improvement in the legislation."[36]

Indeed, inter-branch interplays happen all of the time in the United States.

[35] John Schwartz, *The Supreme Court: Judicial Math, Beyond 5-4*, THE NEW YORK TIMES, Sunday, December 19, 2010, p. WK3.

[36] *Idem.*

5.1.5. Tools for Legal Research in the U.S.

Bibliographic resources in the law are broadly divided into two categories:[37]

- *Primary sources* are those publications – in print or online – that contain the actual text of law, such as statutes, code sections, agency regulations, court decisions, or decisions of administrative law judges (ALJs). These may be government produced sources or commercial sources, but the contents are the work-product of government actors.
- *Secondary sources* are those publications – again, either in print or online – that explain the law. The publications are almost always commercially produced and are authored mainly by attorneys or law professors.

Primary:

<u>Judicial</u>	<u>Legislative</u>	<u>Administrative</u>
Cases	Constitutions	Regulations
Rules of Court	Statutes	Decisions
	Ordinances	
	(Legislative History)	

Secondary:

-Treatises

-Restatements

-Practitioner Aids

-Law Reviews

Table 7: Primary and Secondary Sources of Legal Research

[37] See also table 2 in Chapter 1, subsection 1.2.2.

5.2. Effective Legal Research

> **Research Tip #5.1**
>
> Secondary First. Before undertaking research in legal primary authorities it is always wise to locate good secondary sources that explain the area and then do some background reading first.

The most effective way to begin almost any legal research project is by first consulting a secondary source. This is true for both the novice and highly experienced legal researcher. And this remains true even when using new tools such as WestlawNext (described below). Getting a grounding in secondary sources and learning what are the best search words and phrases will always result in better legal research results. Not only will a secondary source get research off to its best start but also, for an experienced researcher, some legal questions can be answered solely with a good secondary source, although we will see there is always the caveat that all relied upon statutes or cases must be checked for their currency – that is, to determine if the are "still good law." Thus, "citators," such as Shepard's, described later in this chapter (see below section 5.6), are needed to determine all-important currency.

5.2.1. Secondary Sources First

Effective United States legal research involves starting with a secondary source. There are different types of secondary authorities, and any can serve as a launch point. All of these secondary authority research tools are footnote-rich and have numerous reference and connections to other research tools, both primary and secondary. Therefore, it matters little which secondary source one starts with, with just a few scope and coverage caveats as described below.

The important thing to remember is that a secondary source – treatise, legal encyclopedia, legal dictionary, looseleaf set, law review article, etc. – will provide the spark which starts the research engine, in a process that looks like the table below on next page.

> **Research Tip #5.2**
>
> As mentioned above, and it bears repeating, this "secondary first" approach remains valid even when using next-generation research tools such as WestlawNext or Lexis Advance. The researcher will get far better results if he or she understands the legal terms of art before conducting online search.

For example, if researching an issue involving real estate law, better results will be obtained using the search term "broker," rather than realtor, since this is how the case law has been indexed (that is, how certain, controlled vocabulary terms have been applied to cases to organize their legal content for subsequent research retrieval).

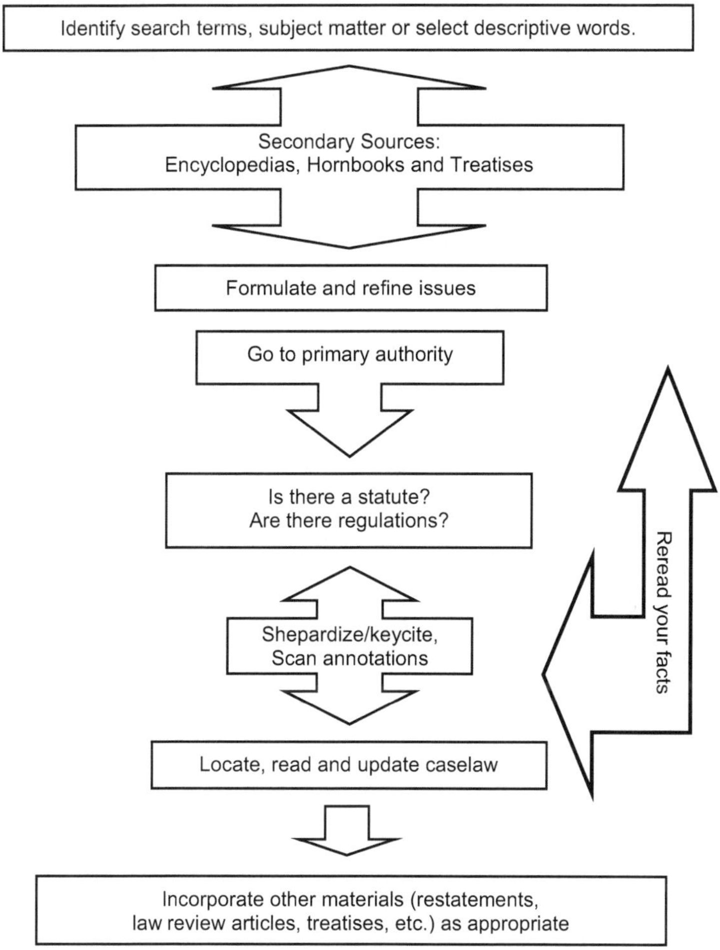

Table 8: Research Flowchart for U.S.

5.2.1.1. Treatises

The most successful legal research is often started by identifying a good legal treatise and getting background and context there. What is a legal "treatise?" Treatises are monographs that are comprehensive guides to discrete areas of law, written by experts in the field. The American Bar Association (ABA) has produced a very useful book[38] called "Association's List of Recommended Law Books for Libraries."[39] This list of a few hundred major treatises is divided by topic.

If, for example, an American law student or lawyer wanted to research an issue of copyright law, the list provides citations to three classic works on copyright:

- Nimmer on Copyright
- Copyright principles, law, and practice by Paul Goldstein,
- Latman's The copyright law by William F. Patry.

And any of these would be excellent starting points.

Treatises give an overview to the researcher new to the subject and then an in-depth analysis not found in other secondary sources, such as legal encyclopedias. One small caveat with treatises: the authors may have a certain point of view, which needs to be considered.

However, as a starting point, treatises are nonpareil. They will always lead the researcher to the most important cases and statutes in the subject area (at least as of time of publication). These cases and statutes will then give the researcher "hooks" to pull in more law for analysis and synthesis. So, in addition to offering background and explanation of the law, treatises are also case-finding and statute-finding tools, with an expert in the field identifying the relevant cases and statutes.

A treatise will cite many cases and discuss some of these cases in far greater detail than others. A case which gets, say, three pages of discussion in a treatise is going to be a much more useful research "hook" than a case which merely gets cited in a "string citation" (a group of cases standing for a similar proposition) or in a footnote. When a treatise gives greater depth of treatment to a particular case, then the researcher should consider that case as

[38] The last published edition is the second as of 1986 RECOMMENDED LAW BOOKS (2nd ed.) (Ed. James A. McDermott) (Illinois, Chicago: Committee on Business Law Libraries, Section of Corporation, Banking and Business Law, American Bar Association, 1986).

[39] A form of this title – modified/ updated by Stanford Library - is available on the book's corresponding website to this book, <www.hssph.net/legalrm>.

one of the most important ones and use that case for subsequent research.

Research Tip #5.3

Pay attention to the depth of treatment cases receive in secondary sources. Cases with greater treatment can be the most useful research "hooks." A case discussed in detail with numerous pages of commentary will be a better "hook case" than one given merely two sentences or less coverage.

5.2.1.2. Looseleaf services

The three copyright treatises listed above are all "*looseleaf services.*" Looseleaf services are very common and very popular in United States law libraries.

A looseleaf service is a book that, traditionally, is published in big spiral binders, so that pages can be easily added or removed.

There are two categories of loose-leaf services:

- Newsletter type and
- Interfiled type.

The above-listed three treatises are all of the interfiled variety. This means that any pages can be removed as the law changes and new pages interfiled throughout the volumes.

The newsletter type of looseleaf service is frequently a weekly publication, and each week a new issue is added to the binder, but no pages are ever removed. An example of this type is the very popular BNA[40] United States Law Week.

Major looseleaf sets, such as CCH's[41] Federal Standard Tax Reporter are complete libraries in themselves, and attorneys practicing tax law, for example, can often find an answer to a client's question by consulting this set alone.

Looseleaf sets can be complicated and some of them use unusual numbering sequences. Almost all looseleaf sets have a section explaining how to use the set. The researcher should carefully read these pages first.

Looseleaf sets are traditionally published in print, but more and more of these sets are offered as online databases as well - with the advantage that they are kept current online and no one has to remove or add pages.

Looseleaf sets on various topics can be found by consulting Legal Loose-

[40] Bureau of National Affairs.

[41] Commerce Clearing House.

leafs in Print, by Arlene L. Eis and published by InfoSources Publishing Company. One can also search the websites or print catalogs from some of the major looseleaf publishers, such as Thomson West (or Thomson Reuters), BNA, and LexisNexis, among others.

Looseleaf services will occasionally reproduce cases that the editors deem to be especially significant. These cases then bear citations to the looseleaf publications. For example, the U.S. federal appellate case *Ringgold v. Black Entertainment Televi-sion, Inc.*, has been reprinted in three different looseleaf sets, as well as in *American Law Reports*. Its citation, with all of these parallel citations added, looks like this:

> *Ringgold v. Black Entertainment Television, Inc.*, 126 F.3d 70, 44 U.S.P.Q.2d (BNA) 1001, Copy. L. Rep. (CCH) P27,693, 150 A.L.R. Fed. 813, 25 Media L. Rep. 2387 (2d Cir. 1997).

Research Tip #5.4

Pay attention to the number of parallel cites a case has. A case that has been selected by various secondary source editors for inclusion may indicate an especially noteworthy case and one that will serve as a very strong research "hook."

5.2.1.3. Hornbooks

"*Hornbook*"[42] is a term used to describe one-volume treatises on specific subjects of law. They may or may not be published by the West Publishing Company (now a part of Thomson West) as part of their Hornbook Series®.[43] Readings from popular hornbooks, such as Prosser on Torts, are of-

[42] Dr. Johnson described the hornbook as "the first book of children, covered with horn to keep it unsoiled." Pardon's New General English Dictionary (1758) defined it as "A leaf of written paper pasted on a board, and covered with horn, for children to learn their letters by, and to prevent their being torn and daubed." It was used throughout Europe and America between the late 1400s and the middle 1700s. Shaped like an old-fashioned butter paddle, the first hornbooks were made of wood. The paper lesson the child was to learn was fastened to the wooden paddle and covered with a piece of horn. ...As the art of printing advanced, the hornbook was supplanted by the primer in the book form we know today. Subsequently, West Publishing Company developed its 'Hornbook Series,' a series of scholarly and well-respected one volume treatises on particular areas of law. Today they are widely used by law students, lawyers and judges." Prefatory page to Dan D. Dobbs, LAW OF REMEDIES: DAMAGES, EQUITY, RESTITUTION (2nd ed.) (West Group Hornbook Series®, 1993).

[43] A complete list of the West Hornbook series at <www.thomson.com/content/legal/brand_overviews/wg_hornbook>.

ten made assigned reading by American law school professors. Hornbooks are useful to read when researching a new area of law or when time is limited. Even if time is not limited, a hornbook remains an excellent research starting point.

5.2.1.4. Legal Encyclopedias

A legal encyclopedia looks like any other big multi-volume encyclopedia. It covers many topics – some in more depth than others – and it is well indexed. The difference between a legal encyclopedia and, say, Encyclopedia Britannica (other than the legal focus to the subject matter) is that legal encyclopedias are footnote-abundant. And this is a very common characteristic with all legal secondary sources - the text explains the law and the footnotes are rich with citations to statutes, cases and, sometimes, regulations. It is not unusual to see a page of a legal encyclopedia with just a few lines of text, those few lines of text citing dozens and dozens of primary authorities. And the footnotes contain a wealth of legal research leads and pointers to primary sources.

In the United States the two most common legal encyclopedias with national coverage are *American Jurisprudence*, 2d edition (AmJur) and *Corpus Juris Secundum* (CJS). One or both of these will be found in every American law library in print. In addition, both now being published by the West Publishing Company are available in Westlaw. AmJur is also available in West's competitor, LexisNexis, although that could very well change in the near future.

AmJur and CJS provide an analysis of both state and federal law. However, if a researcher is dealing with an issue purely of state law, then a state-specific encyclopedia – if there is one – could be a better tool to use. California is an especially important law-producing state and there are two legal encyclopedias for the state. First is California Jurisprudence, published by Thomson West, and then there is the unique treatise known as Witkin's Summary of California Law, which is also now published by Thomson West. Witkin's Summary of California Law is highly regarded by judges in California and anyone researching issues of California law would be well advised to begin his or her research with Witkin's.

5.2.1.5. Law Review Articles

When American law students think about secondary sources, they are often first drawn to law review articles. Perhaps the reason for this is that law review articles are usually written by law school professors.

Every law school in the United States produces law reviews.[44] At Stanford Law School there are several being published, including: Stanford Environmental Law Journal, Stanford Journal of Civil Rights and Civil Liberties, Stanford Journal of International Law, Stanford Journal of Law, Business & Finance, Stanford Law & Policy Review, Stanford Technology Law Review, and the major one, the Stanford Law Review. Tomorrow a new one could easily be born.

Within a typical law review, content is divided into:

- articles
- comments
- notes

Comments and notes are usually written by law students and are shorter in length. The articles are usually written by law professors – although practitioners, judges and others also author law review articles – and are well-researched, rigorously cite-checked and can be excellent places to begin research. Some attorneys always begin their research with law review articles.

Unlike legal encyclopedias, which seek to cover all of Anglo-American jurisprudence, law review content is selective and there are not many duplicate efforts (indeed, editors of law reviews seek unique content). So if there is an article related to your legal research topic, you are off to a good start; if there is nothing, then you will have to turn your attention to a different secondary source.

When reading law review articles, keep in mind that the authors have a definite point of view as to what the law should be and make strong policy arguments to advance such points of view. Nonetheless, the authors' footnotes can contain truly a wealth of valuable resources and reference librarians and other skilled researches "mine" these footnotes heavily.

Law professors have a habit of sometimes giving their law review articles very clever titles, which do not obviously lead the researcher to the subject.[45] Therefore, using an index is especially important when trying to track down law review articles on a particular topic. The careful researcher will consult an index to law reviews (and other periodicals) rather than searching the full text content of these journals in the LexisNexis and Westlaw databases.

The principal law review index, which has been around the longest, and

[44] It is different in Europe - see Chapter 3, section 3.1.5.

[45] For example, a law review article entitled "A Toxic Nightmare on Elm Street," is about a real estate broker's liability for misrepresentation.

has the most historical coverage, is Wilson's Index to Legal Periodicals and Books (available in print and online in WilsonWeb[46]). It is a fine index, but not completely comprehensive; lesser works – articles less than 5 pages in length, for example – are not indexed.

For current research, we usually steer researchers to a more comprehensive index, one now produced by the Gale division of Thomson Publishing (although it started with the Information Access Corporation with a hard push from law librarians and the American Association of Law Libraries (AALL), notably by Stanford Law School Professor J. Myron Jacobstein[47]). This index, unfortunately, goes by different names. In print it is called the Current Law Index. Online it can be called either LegalTrac or the Legal Resource Index (LRI). Whatever it is called, it is arguably the best tool for finding contemporary law review articles.

There is also the Index to Foreign Legal Periodicals, which is arranged much like the Index to Legal Periodicals, but surveys foreign (that is, non US, Canadian, English, Irish, Australian and New Zealand journals – all of which are included in both the Legal Resource Index (a/k/a LegalTrac, a/k/a Current Law Index) and Index to Legal Periodicals and Books.

5.2.1.6. Legal Scholarship Network

The Legal Scholarship Network of the Social Science Resource Center (<www.ssrn.com>)[48] is a resource for seeing the future.[49] SSRN is where many law professors post copies of their working paper drafts of articles that have been accepted for publication in forthcoming law journals. The website is an excellent place to see what is coming down the legal scholarship pike

[46] <www.wilsonweb.com>.

[47] "As Association of American Law Libraries president in 1978-79, Mike [Jacobstein] was the right man at the right place at the right time. He personally pushed through AALL's support of a new index of legal periodicals, a move that eventually led to an agreement with Information Access Corporation and the creation of Current Law Index and its Read Only Memory-Computer Original Microform (COM) counterpart, Legal Resources Index, the forerunner of today's LegalTrac. Although this was a controversial move at the time, it was an important first step away from the binding hold of tradition. The days of ossified indexes and limited coverage of materials are hard to remember, but there is a reason for that." Robert C. Berring, Mike Jacobstein, *Truly a Giant*, 97 LAW LIBRARY JOURNAL 633 (2005). This product was a milestone in American legal research.

[48] SSRN - Social Science Research Network – at <www.ssrn.com>.

[49] Similar, HeinOnline (in detail described in section 5.5.5. below) beautifully presents the past.

and to read the very latest legal thinking.

The Social Science Research Network's "16th year was 'sweet'. The eLibrary <http://ssrn.com/search> has delivered over 41.3 million downloads to date and grown to over 314,000 documents from 149,000 authors."[50] The vast majority of the documents uploaded to SSRN are available to the world for free. Law schools, such as Stanford, pay SSRN in two ways. A larger fee goes to SSRN for it to be able to publish law school working paper journals, such as the Stanford Law School Public Law & Legal Theory Research Paper Series.[51]

The law school also pays a smaller fee to SSRN to subscribe to its journal of abstracts. SSRN's Legal Scholarship Network (LSN) publishes well over 100 of these journal, called "subject matter eJournals." One eJournal that may be of particular interest to readers of this book is the Legal Information & Technology eJournal, edited by two law school law library directors.

> A recent issue [LSN Legal Information & Technology eJournal, Vol 2, No. 35, 12/15/2010], for example, contains abstracts to the following items:
>
> - Laws, Sausages and Bailouts: Testing the Populist View of the Causes of the Economic Crisis
> - Languages, Legal Origins, and Culture before the Courts: Cross Citations between Supreme Courts in Europe
> - Legal Encyclopedias: Research as "Well Begun"
> - On the Respective Roles of National Libraries, National Archives and Research Data Centers in the Preservation of and Access to Research Data
> - Database Ownership: Myth or Reality?

The third item, "Legal Encyclopedias: Research as 'Well Begun,'" certainly reinforces our message of "secondary first."

Readers with a law school affiliation should check with the library and see if it provides a subscription service to the LSN eJournals; if so, the reader is encouraged to receive as many as he or she would like. It is an excellent way to keep up with legal scholarship. A complete list of the eJournals can be found at <http://www.ssrn.com/lsn/index.html>.

[50] 2010 Year-End President's Letter.

[51] <http://www.ssrn.com/lsn/index.html>.

5.2.1.7. Blogs and blawgs

While on the subject of law professor publishing, a new avenue for keeping up with current legal thinking is with blogs or, as law blogs are often called, *blawgs*. This area is growing so quickly that any list of blogs would be out of date as soon as it is published. But a good starting point is the Law Professors Blog at:

<www.lawprofessorblogs.com>.

One of the blogs there that American law librarians read upon a daily basis is the Law Library Blog at:

<http://lawprofessors.typepad.com/law_librarian_blog>.

The Law Library Resource Xchange is a very valuable source for keeping current with developments in legal research at <LLRX.com>.

New on the Blawg frontier is also the Legal Scholarship Blog:

<http://legalscholarshipblog.com>

This blog is a collaborative service from faculty and staff at the University of Pittsburgh School of Law and the Gallagher Law Library at the University of Washington School of Law. The blog features law-related calls for papers, conferences, and workshops - with links to relevant websites and papers as well as an event calendar - along with scholarly resources for Research Deans and current and prospective law professors.

The reference librarians at Stanford Law School maintain a useful blog called Legal Research Plus, which follows legal research developments both in the United States and worldwide. It can be read at:

<http://legalresearchplus.com>.

Throughout this book we will call your attention to other particularly useful blogs as well.

5.2.1.8. American Law Reports (ALR)

American Law Reports (ALR) is a series, published by Thomson West, which can also be a highly useful starting point for research. American Law Reports does two things: It republishes selected decisions and it publishes "annotations" about those decisions or other legal developments. It is the annotations for which this set has value.

Cases published by ALR will carry an ALR citation as one of the parallel citations to the case (more on this below). Researchers looking for good cases to build their arguments upon are wise to pay attention to the number of citations a case carries. Cases that are published in commercial publications, such as ALR, indicate that the editors of these publications deemed the cases to be noteworthy.

The American Law Reports annotations do not cover the gamut of legal subjects. Like law reviews, the coverage is selective. If, however, a topic you are researching is covered, then you are in tremendous luck. American Law Reports seeks to collect and analyze all of the relevant cases on that particular topic. Although called an "annotation," an ALR piece is really much more like a detailed, comprehensive-in-scope law review article, but far more objective and without a scholar's particular, subjective point of view. ALR annotations offer "blackletter"[52] law principles and a collection of the cases – all of the cases – on a particular topic. ALR annotations are kept current with "pocket parts" (paper inserts in the back of each volume) supplementation, and there is even a toll-free phone number that researchers can call to get these very latest cases on the topic.

American Law Reports are published in print and are available electronically in LexisNexis and Westlaw and the annotations are automatically kept current there.

American Law Reports also have a detailed index and a "*digest*"[53] for finding annotations. This "digest" now uses the West Key Number system taxonomy, which is discussed in detail below.

While most of the American Law Reports annotations deal with important cases, the set also addresses important statutory developments. For example, in 2007 President George W. Bush signed into law changes that Congress passed (at the president's urging) to the Foreign Intelligence Surveillance Act of 1978 (FISA). Since this is so timely and so important, the editors at the American Law Reports wrote an annotation: "Validity, Construction and Application of Foreign Intelligence Surveillance Act of 1978 (50 U.S.C.A. sec. 1801 et seq.) Authorizing Electronic Surveillance of Foreign Powers and Their Agents."[54]

[52] "Blackletter" is a term "applied to legal principles that are fundamental and well settled." See GARNER *supra* note 27.

[53] A digest is an essential case-finding tool. It is a multivolume index to the law consisting of major topic headings, thousands of subheadings, and headnotes (short summaries of legal propositions stated in published court cases).

[54] 190 A.L.R. Fed. 385 (2007).

Research Tip #5.5

The careful researcher should always pay close attention to an opinion's citation(s). If the case is reproduced in American Law Reports, this is a signal that the researcher may have found a particularly noteworthy case. Such cases, when Shepardized, can lead to a treasure trove of additional material. The corresponding ALR annotation seeks to provide totally comprehensive coverage of cases on the topic as well.

For example, the cite, alone, to

> *Ringgold v. Black Entertainment Television, Inc.*, 126 F.3d 70, 44 U.S.P.Q.2d (BNA) 1001, Copy. L. Rep. (CCH) P27,693, 150 A.L.R. Fed. 813, 25 Media L. Rep. 2387 (2d Cir. 1997).

tells the researcher a lot about it, without even having read the opinion.

These citations inform the researcher that the case has been selected for inclusion in the secondary source American Law Reports, Federal and is therefore the subject of a research annotation there. Remember that ALR "annotations" are not brief notes but expansive articles collecting all of the cases on a certain point. In addition to being the subject of an ALR annotation, this case has also been selected for publication in various looseleaf services published by Commerce Clearinghouse (CCH) and the Bureau of National Affairs (BNA). BNA publishes both United States Patent Quarterly (USPQ) and the Media Law Reporter. The message here is clear: This may be an especially important case; pay attention to it, its holding, and the subsequent cases and secondary sources that cite to it.

5.2.1.9. Restatements of the Law

Restatements of the Law, published by the American Law Institute, are officially "secondary sources" yet they are so highly-regarded and so frequently-cited that they come close to being "primary sources." They are not technically primary sources because they are not produced by law-makers, at least not writing in their official capacities. The authors of the restatements are panels of highly distinguished law professors, judges, and practitioners.

Restatements of the Law are "blackletter" principles of law. The authors have made an effort to "restate" what they law is for the different areas studied. Restatements of the Law have been prepared for the following subjects:

- Agency
- Conflict of Laws

- Contracts
- Employment Law
- Foreign Relations Law of the United States
- Judgments
- The Law Governing Lawyers
- Property
- Restitution and Unjust Enrichment
- Security
- Suretyship and Guaranty
- Torts
- Trusts
- Unfair Competition

A complete catalog of American Law Institute publications can be found at:

<www.ali.org>

All topics with the exception of Restitution and Security have been published in a second or third edition. The restatements contain detailed Reporter's Notes citing statutory and case authority.

Restatements are not ideal as a research starting point, but once applicable restatement sections are determined from other sources they can make the law easier to understand and provide numerous citations for continuing the research.

The restatements, even if a little difficult to begin research with, are extremely important and judges rely upon them heavily. According to a column in the National Law Journal,[55]

> "We are told that lawyers and judges have no time to read because of their heavy workload. But they have time to read and digest the Restatements of the Law and the lengthy comments that are appended to them as well as the voluminous Reporters' Notes. ... this past year alone there were more than 3,000 citations to Restatements."

Restatements tell you what the law is perhaps better than any other secondary source.

[55] Aaron D. Twerski, *Legal Scholarship: It should be relevant again*, THE NATIONAL LAW JOURNAL, September 3, 2007, p. 22.

5.2.1.10. Legal Dictionaries

Last, but not least, are legal dictionaries. There are many different legal dictionaries, but the two main ones are Black's Law Dictionary (available in Westlaw) and Ballentine's Law Dictionary (available in LexisNexis). Earlier above we gave the Black's definition for *stare decisis*. To show how dictionaries can be helpful in research, here is Ballentine's definition of negligence.[56]

> TERM: negligence.
>
> TEXT: 1. A word of broad significance which may not readily be defined with accuracy. *Jamison v Encarnacion*, 281 US 635, 74 L Ed 1082, 50 S Ct 440. The lack of due diligence or care. A wrong characterized by the absence of a positive intent to inflict injury but from which injury nevertheless results. *Haser v Maryland Casualty Co.* 78 ND 893, 53 NW2d 508, 33 ALR 1018. In the legal sense, a violation of the duty to use care. *Fort Smith Gas Co. v Cloud* (CA8 Ark) 75 F2d 413, 97 ALR 833. The failure to perform an established duty which proximately causes injury to the plaintiff. *Northern Indiana Transit v Burk*, 228 Ind 162, 89 NE2d 905, 17 ALR2d 572. The failure to exercise the degree of care demanded by the circumstances; the want of that care which the law prescribes under the particular circumstances existing at the time of the act or omission which is involved. The omission to do something which a reasonable man, guided by those considerations which ordinarily regulate human affairs, would do, or doing something which a prudent and reasonable man would not do. 38 Am J1st Negl § 2. More particularly, the failure of one owing a duty to another to do what a reasonable and prudent person would ordinarily have done under the circumstances, or doing what such person would not have done, which omission or commission is the proximate cause of injury to the other.
>
> 2. A negligent act is one from which an ordinarily prudent person would foresee such an appreciable risk of harm to others as to cause him not to do the act, or to do it in a more careful manner.
>
> 3. What constitutes "operation" or "negligence in operation" within statute making owner of motor vehicle liable for negligence in its operation.
>
> AUTHORITY:
>
> 1. 38 Am J1st Negl § 2.

[56] Copyright (c) 1969 Ballentine's Law Dictionary (LexisNexis Law Publishing, a division of Reed Elsevier, plc.).

2. *Haralson v Jones Truck Lines*, 223 Ark 813, 270 SW2d 892, 48 ALR2d 248.

3. Anno: 13 ALR2d 378.

Note that this one dictionary definition provides references to a legal encyclopedia (American Jurisprudence), numerous "hook" cases, and an American Law Reports annotation. With these key references, the researcher can easily expand research about the tort of negligence.

Any of the above secondary sources will provide the researcher with citations to primary sources, including the United States Constitution, federal and or state statutes, administrative rules and decisions, and cases, often numerous cases.

Many treatises and looseleaf services are available online in LexisNexis, Westlaw or other computer-assisted legal research (CALR)databases. Westlaw has a box at the upper-right hand side of the search welcome screen entitled "Secondary Sources" with links to Black's Law Dictionary, American Jurisprudence, American Law Reports, and much more. In LexisNexis, the "Research System" screen includes a section "Secondary Legal" which includes links to Matthew Bender publications, restatements, BNA publications, and much more. An advantage to using a secondary source online in LexisNexis or Westlaw is that most of the cited sources will have links to the full text of those sources.

5.2.2. The Constitution of the United States of America – the "supreme law of the land"

Before we move along to the next step in the legal research process – seeking statutes, we must say a word about the United States Constitution. Article VI of the United States Constitution presents its legal importance:

> "Article VI
>
> Section 1, Clause 2, Supreme law.
>
> This Constitution, and the Laws of the United States which shall be made in Pursuance thereof; and all Treaties made, or which shall be made, under the Authority of the United States, shall be the supreme Law of the Land; and the Judges in every State shall be bound thereby . . . "

The annotated text of the Constitution is found in the different compilations of the United States Code, discussed below. Also, the United States Library of Congress has prepared a very useful massive volume The Constitution of the United States of America which includes text, commentary, historical analysis and summaries of important case law.

In addition to the many thousands of cases that have interpreted the United States Constitution, researchers also look to what the framers of the Constitution intended, "since its words so seldom resolve a legal issue. … The Philadelphia Constitutional Convention in 1787 did not create an official record of its proceedings, but James Madison and other delegates kept extensive notes. Debates of state conventions, which ratified the Constitution, are also available. Finally, The Federalist, with essays by James Madison, John Jay, and Alexander Hamilton supporting the Constitution's adoption, is considered an essential source of contemporaneous opinion."[57]

Each state in the United States has its own constitution, and these are most easily found published in that state's annotated code.

5.2.3. Legal Citations

And now a word about legal citation. American lawyers and judges are obsessed with correct legal citation. It begins in law school where many American law students struggle with (and learn to despise) different citation manuals.

Used at Stanford Law School, and widely used elsewhere, is *The Bluebook: A Uniform System of Citation*, 19th edition (2010).[58] This is commonly called just "the bluebook" and checking citations for style is called "*bluebooking*." There are few more tasks dreaded by American law students than "bluebooking."

There are other citation manuals, such as *ALWD Citation Manual: A Professional System of Citation*, 4th Edition (2010), written by the Association of Legal Writing Directors (ALWD) and published by Aspen Publishers.

For a United States Code section, the citation is fairly straightforward and the Bluebook gives these examples:

[57] See David S. Clark and Tugrul Ansay, INTRODUCTION TO THE LAW OF THE UNITED STATES 39 (2nd ed.) (The Hague/New York: Kluwer, 2002) (Chapter 3: The Sources of Law) [hereinafter CLARK]. THE FEDERALISTS PAPERS (ed. By Isaac Kramnick) (Harmondsworth, Middlesex, England: Penguin, 1987).

[58] The Bluebook is compiled by the editors of the Columbia Law Review, the Harvard Law Review, the University of Pennsylvania Law Review, and the Yale Law Journal.

> Citation of an entire statute, the Comprehensive Environmental Response, Compensation, and Liability Act, as codified in the United States Code:
>
> Comprehensive Environmental Response, Compensation, and Liability Act, 42 U.S.C. §§ 9601-9675 (2000).

First is given the official name of the act. 42 is the United States Code title number. §[59] is a symbol meaning "section sign" and when paired, §§, it becomes plural, for sections. 9601-9675 is the span of code sections that contain the full statute. And 2000 is the date of the code.

The citation for an individual provision of the United States Code is set forth thusly:

> 28 U.S.C. § 1291 (2000).

It should be noted that the Bluebook requires citation to the official United States Code. This is a bit of a fiction in the United States. Lawyers and law students do not really use the official United States Code – it is published far too slowly for current legal research. Instead, lawyers and law students use one of the two commercial code publications, United States Code Annotated (West) or United States Code Service (LexisNexis). These sets, in addition to presenting their voluminous case citations, keep the code current. There are "pocket parts" (paper inserts in the back of each volume) and these "pocket parts" are supplemented by monthly updates. So lawyers use the unofficial but cite to the official. Everybody does it, at least when they are adhering to Bluebook rules.

But as the Bluebook itself notes, "[m]any state and federal courts promulgate local citation rules, which take precedence over Bluebook rules in documents submitted to those courts. … When preparing court documents, always check the most recent version of the court's local citation rules."[60]

5.2.4. Statutes

Effective legal research begins with a reading of secondary sources. When reading these secondary sources, the researcher should always be on the lookout for statutory references. Aside from the fact that statutes are controlling, they are also perfect research "hooks" for pulling in more information,

[59] This symbol is used differently in Europe, see chapter 3.

[60] THE BLUEBOOK: A UNIFORM SYSTEM OF CITATION Preface, p. V (19th ed.) (Cambridge,, Massachusetts: Harvard Law Review Assn., 2010).

including the always sought-after cases. The researcher in the United States can often pick and choose from caselaw. But if there is a statute on point, it is controlling and must be read and cited. It is also the "hook" on which all the relevant cases and additional secondary authority can easily be located. Legal research systems in the United States will annotate statutes with case citations, helping the researcher to find case law.

The researcher's threshold question when looking for primary sources is:

- Is there a statute?
- So what is a statute?
- How does it differ from a code?

It is critically important to understand the distinction between statutes and codes and the process of codification in the United States. It should be emphasized that the question "is there a statute" can often be answered by a secondary source, such as a treatise, complete with a full citation. Secondary sources really can save the careful researcher a lot of precious research time. But finding the key statutes is essential, as legislation, when it applies, is controlling. An applicable statute cannot be overlooked.

Before considering the statutes versus code question, a quick review of how a bill becomes law is in order – that is, how the legislative branch of government works.

The United States Congress is bicameral, consisting of two houses:

- The Senate, and
- The House of Representatives.

Without question, the best book for understanding United States federal law making at the legislative level is Walter J. Oleszek's CONGRESSIONAL PROCEDURES AND THE POLICY PROCESS. The table above points out the fundamental differences between the House and the Senate of the United States Congress.

Proposed legislation is introduced as a 'bill." A bill can be introduced in either house of Congress. The bill is first assigned to a committee and hearings can be held. The committee votes on the bill and then the floor of the House or Senate, depending upon where the bill was introduced, also votes. If the bill passes the committee vote and then the floor vote, its name is changed to "act" (but it still is not yet law) and it is sent over to the other house where the process is repeated. If the act passes votes in committee and on the floor there, then it goes to the president for his (or, perhaps soon, her) signature. It is now a law. Only a small percentage of bills become law; in the 111th Congress it was just 3%, according to Harper's Index, January 2011, p. 11.

Once the bill becomes law, it is assigned a law number, called the Public

Law number. This number consists of the number of the Congress, e.g., 110, followed by a number assigned to laws as they are created sequentially, one after another.

House	Senate
Shorter term of office (two years)	Longer term of office (six years)
Adheres closely to procedural rules on floor activity	Operates mostly by unanimous consent
Narrower constituency	Broader, more varied constituency
Originates all revenue bills	Sole power to ratify treaties and to advise and consent to presidential nominations
Policy specialists	Policy generalists
Less press and media coverage	More press and media coverage
Power less evenly distributed	Power more evenly distributed
Less prestigious	More prestigious
More expeditious in floor debate	Less expeditious in floor debate
Strict germaneness requirement for floor amendments	No general germaneness rule for floor amendments
Less reliance on staff	More reliance on staff
More partisan	Somewhat less partisan
Strict limits on debate	Unlimited debate on nearly every measure
Methods of operation stresses majority rule	Traditions and practices emphasize minority rights

Table 9: Several Major Differences between the House and Senate[61]

For example, Public Law 109-1, abbreviated P.L. 109-1, "To accelerate the income tax benefits for charitable cash contributions for the relief of victims of the Indian Ocean tsunami," was the first law passed by the 109th Congress. These public laws are also known as session laws, since a bill must be passed within one session of Congress. If a bill fails to become law in a particular session of Congress, it cannot be carried over to the next session. The whole process must begin anew.

Federal laws are first published as "slip laws" – literally on slips of paper (although one law can be hundreds of pages long) and then they are published, one after another, in a set of books called the Statutes at Large.

The two tables on the following pages illustrate the process.[62]

[61] Source: Walter J. Oleszek, CONGRESSIONAL PROCEDURES AND THE POLICY PROCESS (8th edition)(CQ Press, 2011). Reprinted with permission.

[62] *Idem.* & from HowlawsmadeWIRTH_BW copy.jpg at <www.writingonlife.com/howlawsmadewirth2-jpg-jpeg-image-2450x1207-pixels/>. < http://www.indecisionforever.com/files/2010/06/howlawsmade.jpg>.

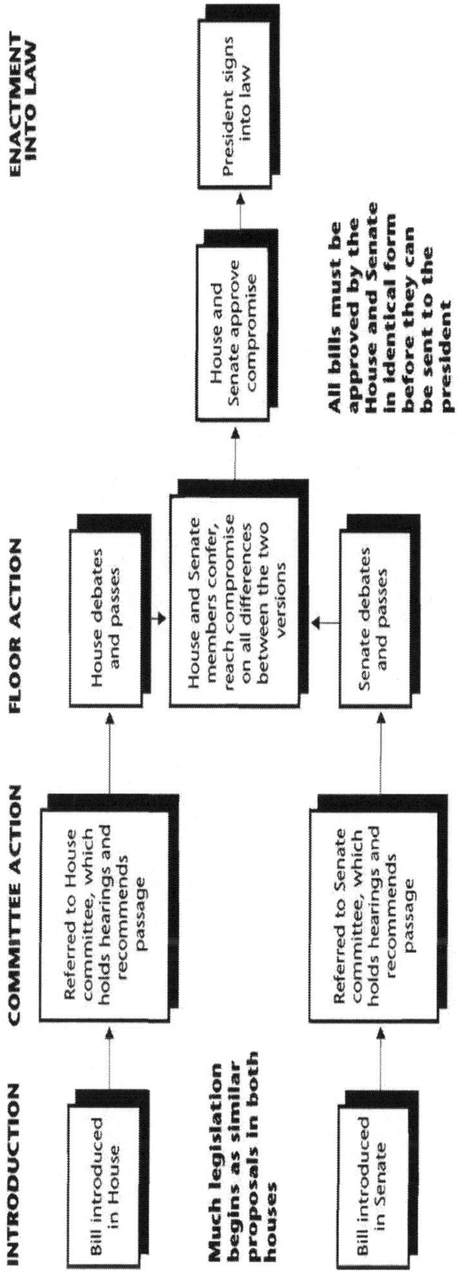

Table 10: How a Bill Becomes Law

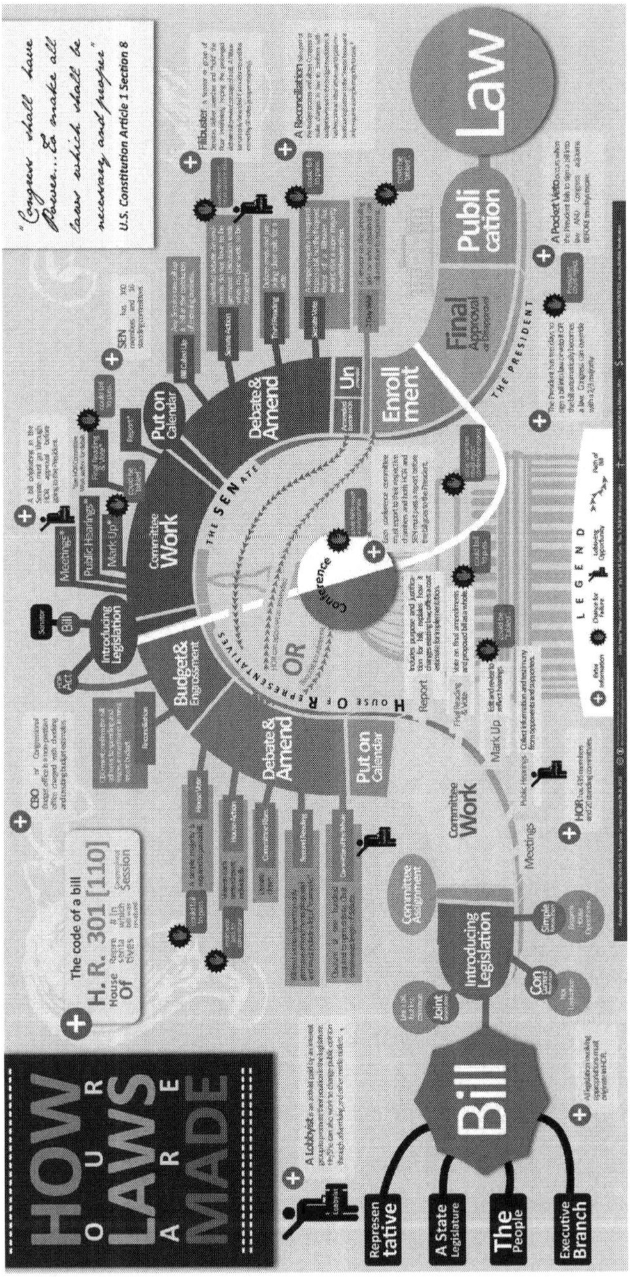

Table 11: How our laws are made

All of this activity, going as far back as the 93rd Congress as of this writing, is also documented online at a wonderfully rich and free U.S. Government website called *Thomas* (named after Thomas Jefferson), available at <Thomas.loc.gov>. Anyone interested in lawmaking at the national level in the United States should explore this site very carefully.

Legislative law-making in the United States is an active, organic process. Laws are constantly being amended, or repealed. Therefore, for current research purposes, a book that contains a static representation of the law, such as the Statutes at Large, is of little value.

Statutory research is most effectively conducted in published codes. A code is best defined as a subject arrangement of public laws. But it is more than that too: in addition to arranging the laws by subject, the Law Revision Counsel's office in Congress organizes, edits slightly and adds numerous enhancements to facilitate research. From its website: "The Office of the Law Revision Counsel prepares and publishes the United States Code, which is a consolidation and codification by subject matter of the general and permanent laws of the United States." (<http://uscode.house.gov>).

The United States Code, as officially published by the government, can be accessed from the Government Printing Office (GPO) Access website. In 2010 this website migrated to the new Federal Digital System, FDsys.[63] This is a perfect starting point for locating laws from any branch of government in the United States. GPO is the office charged with publishing law from Congress and regulations from the Executive Branch administrative agencies. The website can be accessed at <www.gpoaccess.gov>.

The government published official version of the United States Code has severe limitations, however. Its chief limitation is the slowness that it is published and revised. As mentioned above, laws are constantly being amended and attorneys in the United States need to know what the law looks like today. A question United States attorneys constantly ask about statutes (and cases) is: "Is it still good law? "

To answer that question best, research needs to be accomplished in one of the annotated codes that are commercially published. There are two main ones:

- *United States Code Annotated*, published by Thomson West, and
- *United States Code Service*, published by LexisNexis.

[63] See further subsection 5.2.5.

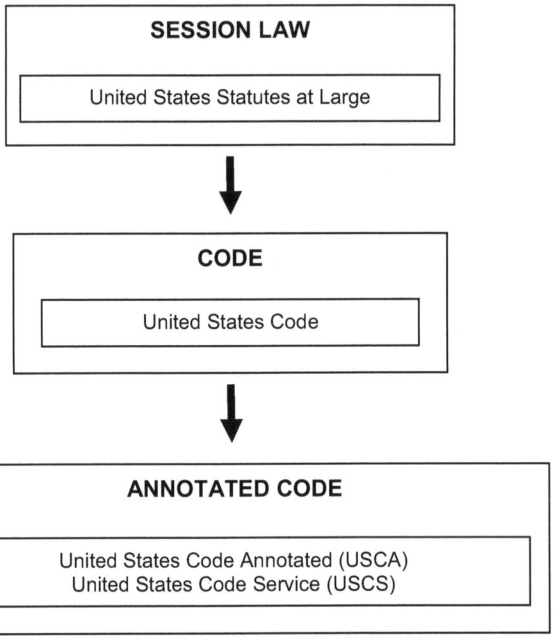

Table 12: From Session Law to Code to Annotated Code

Both of these annotated codes do the same thing: They publish the United States Code and keep it current, with monthly updates and cumulative "*pocket parts*" (paper inserts in the back of each volume). This is very important as an American attorney's primary concern is always with currency. This is such an significant consideration, that, in addition to consulting a current annotated code, attorneys will always "*Shepardize*" important code sections. Shepardizing is explained in detail below, but what it involves is using specialized legal research citator tools – such as Shepard's Citations or *KeyCite*® – for citation verification.

These commercial annotated editions of the United States Code are expensive. Yet they are also essential research tools not just for their currency, but for the "annotations" that they contain. For any code section, if there are cases that have interpreted, construed, ruled on the Constitutionality, or even just cited in any way the code section, then the case is briefly described and given a full citation within an annotation, which follows the code section. For some code sections there are hundreds, even thousands, of case annotations. The annotations present the cases in an organized arrangement by topic and each case is given a short summary of its legal holding.

The annotated codes are extremely useful for these annotations, as attorneys and law students can quickly scan these case annotations to locate cases for further research. Each annotation will include a case citation with which the case can be retrieved, either from a book or from an online database such as LexisNexis or Westlaw.

So how does a researcher find a code section in one of these codes? An excellent starting point – for this and most research – is with the index volumes. Carefully produced indexes are found in both USCS and USCA.

It also helps if you know which title of the United States Code is applicable to your research. The United States Code is divided into 50 titles, with the following subject classifications:[64]

Title Number	Title name
TITLE 1	General provisions
TITLE 2	The congress
TITLE 3	The president
TITLE 4	Flag and seal, seat of government, and the states
TITLE 5	Government organization and employees
TITLE 5A	Government organization and employees (appendix)
TITLE 6	Surety bonds [repealed]
TITLE 7	Agriculture
TITLE 8	Aliens and nationality
TITLE 9	Arbitration
TITLE 10	Armed forces
TITLE 10A	Armed forces (appendix)
TITLE 11	Bankruptcy
TITLE 11A	Bankruptcy (appendix)
TITLE 12	Banks and banking
TITLE 13	Census
TITLE 14	Coast guard
TITLE 15	Commerce and trade
TITLE 16	Conservation
TITLE 17	Copyrights
TITLE 18	Crimes and criminal procedure
TITLE 18A	Crimes and criminal procedure (appendix)
TITLE 19	Customs duties
TITLE 20	Education
TITLE 21	Food and drugs
TITLE 22	Foreign relations and intercourse
TITLE 23	Highways
TITLE 24	Hospitals and asylums
TITLE 25	Indians
TITLE 26	Internal revenue code

[64] Source: GPO Access, <www.gpoaccess.gov>.

TITLE 26A	Internal revenue code (appendix)
TITLE 27	Intoxicating liquors
TITLE 28	Judiciary and judicial procedure
TITLE 28A	Judiciary and judicial procedure (appendix)
TITLE 29	Labor
TITLE 30	Mineral lands and mining
TITLE 31	Money and finance
TITLE 32	National guard
TITLE 33	Navigation and navigable waters
TITLE 34	Navy [repealed]
TITLE 35	Patents
TITLE 36	Patriotic and national observances, ceremonies, and organizations
TITLE 37	Pay and allowances of the uniformed services
TITLE 38	Veterans' benefits
TITLE 38A	Veterans' benefits (appendix)
TITLE 39	Postal service
TITLE 40	Public buildings, property, and works
TITLE 40A	Public buildings, property, and works (appendix)
TITLE 41	Public contracts
TITLE 42	The public health and welfare
TITLE 43	Public lands
TITLE 44	Public printing and documents
TITLE 45	Railroads
TITLE 46	Shipping
TITLE 46A	Shipping (appendix)
TITLE 47	Telegraphs, telephones, and radiotelegraphs
TITLE 48	Territories and insular possessions
TITLE 49	Transportation
TITLE 50	War and national defense
TITLE 50A	War and national defense (appendix)

Table 13: United States Code, 2006 Edition

The fifty titles of the United States Code have been in place since it was first created. But the Code is on the cusp of major change. As noted law librarian Mary Whisner reports,[65]

> ". . . after being encompassed within 50 titles for its entire life, the United States Code is poised to move beyond - to 51, National and Commercial Space Programs; 52, Voting and Elections; 53, Small Business; 54, National Park System; and 55, Environment. The prospect of title 55 is particularly exciting. Over the decades, a wide range of topics have been shoehorned into title 42, the Public Health and Welfare; it is a huge title, with over 7000 pages. Title 55 will pull out the environmental laws and organize them in a more coherent way."

[65] Mary Whisner, *The United States Code, Prima Facie Evidence, and Positive Law*, 101 LAW LIBRARY JOURNAL 545 (2009).

If a lawyer or law student was researching, say, railroads, he or she would find all of the laws on railroads codified in title 45 of the United States Code. This information can be helpful for, in addition to the excellent multi-volume main index to the set, each title of the United States Code also has its own separate index. Armed with the knowledge that title 45 contains all of the federal railroad statutes, the researcher could then use the index to title 45 for more efficient and precise index searching.

Research Tip #5.6

If you know the United States Code title for your research area, use the index that accompanies that title, rather than the general index.

All of the code editions include useful tables for research, with the two most useful tables being these:

Acts Cited by Popular Name (e.g., "Patriot Act")

The researcher will frequently be asked to retrieve a statute by its so-called popular name, such as The Patriot Act. But the actual name of this legislation is the Uniting and Strengthening America by Providing Appropriate Tools Required to Intercept and Obstruct Terrorism Act of 2001. The Acts Cited by Popular Name table will steer the researcher to the correct name of the statute and also give its citation, where the researcher can find it in the United States Code.

In addition to the Popular Name Table found in any addition of the United States Code there is another very useful publication called Shepard's Acts and Cases by Popular Names. This set, published by LexisNexis, provides citations to both federal and state legislation, indexed under popular names. It also lists many cases that have come to be known by a popular name, such as "Miranda" (that is, *Miranda v. Arizona*, 384 U.S. 436 (1966)).

Statutes at Large table, showing where the Acts of Congress are found in the Code.

Secondary sources will often cite to a Public Law as published in the Statutes at Large, particularly when citing to new legislation, and the researcher will need to convert that citation to a United States Code cite in order to perform effective and current research and find the text of the statute as codified. The Statutes at Large Table will enable the researcher to pinpoint exactly where the statutory provides became codified. One statute could have its sections codified in a number of different titles of the United States Code, so this is a very useful locating tool. The United States Congress has made a copy of this table available online at:

<http://uscode.house.gov/classification/table3.pdf>

In addition to titles and code sections, the United States Code organizes its content into "chapters." It is always very important for the careful researcher to review all of the code sections found with a particular chapter of the title he or she is researchers.

Readers may be familiar with the phrase "Chapter 11 bankruptcy." This is a particular type of bankruptcy proceeding available to debtors in the United States. It is called a "Chapter 11" bankruptcy because all of the legal requirements for a particular type of financial reorganization are grouped together in Chapter 11 of the title of the Untied States Code dealing with bankruptcy, (which also happens to be Title 11). When researchers cite to United States Code sections, however, they do not cite to the chapter numbers, only title and section. But researchers should not limit their statute analysis to code sections in isolation – the entire chapter in which the cited code section is found could also be applicable to the research.

5.2.4.1. State legislation

The state law legislative process is very similar to the federal law-making process. In California, for example, the process is as illustrated in the next table.

The two houses of the bicameral state legislature are:

- the California Senate and
- the California Assembly.

The states publish the passed laws chronologically as "session laws" in a volume called Statutes and Amendments to the Codes and these session laws are later codified and published in annotated codes (also called compiled codes or revised codes).

State law is not written solely by legislators. In California, and in many other states, the people themselves can write laws, by writing initiatives and referendums, often referred to as ballot propositions. See Tom McNichol, *The Propositioners – How a small number of legal specialists make their clients' cases to voters*, CALIFORNIA LAWYER, November 2010, p. 26.

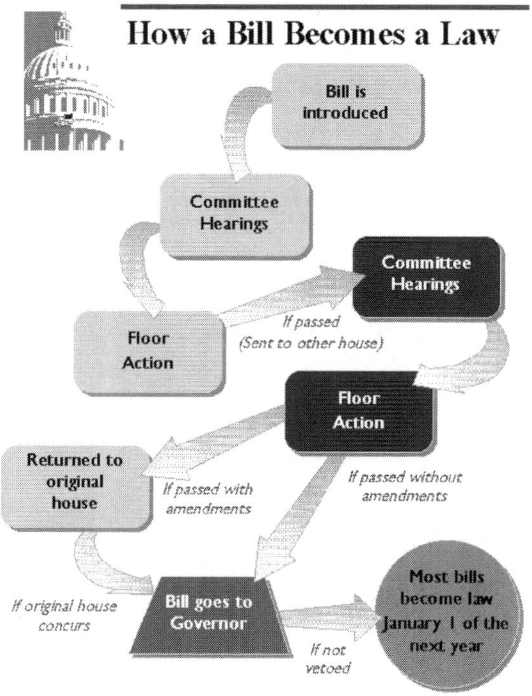

Table 14: How a Bill Becomes Law in California

Another law making body is the National Conference of Commissioners on Uniform States Laws (NCCUSL).[66] NCCUSL consists of selected lawyers who draft models law in an effort "to promote uniformity in state law, on all subjects where uniformity is desirable and practicable, by voluntary action of each state government." The most famous examples here are, perhaps, the Uniform Commercial Code and the Uniform Penal Code. All of NCCUSL's legislative efforts can be found in a set of books titled Uniform Laws Annotated.

For more on NCCUSL see Travis McDate, *Uniform laws aren't always uniform or law*, STUDENT LAWYER, February 2009, p. 12.

Of great interest to the authors of this book is a uniform law being proposed that will address the publication of state legal materials, "Authentica-

[66] <www.nccusl.org> (Uniform Law Commission).

tion and Preservation of State Electronic Legal Materials Act."[67]

Again, successful research is done with the codes, not with the earlier session laws, and the best entry point is usually the code index. Each state code will also include tables that refer researchers from the session law citation to the code citation.

Unlike the United States Code, which is one single code divided into fifty titles, in California there are 29 separate and distinct codes that all have their own names and these names are an important part of the citation. For example, California Business and Professions Code, § 6060 sets forth the requirements for being a lawyer in California.

> West's Ann.Cal.Bus. & Prof.Code § 6060
>
> West's Annotated California Codes
> Business and Professions Code
> Division 3. Professions and Vocations Generally
> Chapter 4. Attorneys
> Article 4. Admission to the Practice of Law
> § 6060. Qualifications; examination
>
> To be certified to the Supreme Court for admission and a license to practice law, a person who has not been admitted to practice law in a sister state, United States jurisdiction, possession, territory, or dependency or in a foreign country shall:
>
> (a) Be of the age of at least 18 years.
>
> (b) Be of good moral character.
>
> (c) Before beginning the study of law, have done either of the following:
>
> (1) Completed at least two years of college work, which college work shall be not less than one-half of the collegiate work acceptable for a bachelor's degree granted upon the basis of a four-year period of study by a college or university approved by the examining committee.
>
> (2) Have attained in apparent intellectual ability the equivalent of at least two years of college work by taking any examinations in subject matters and achieving the scores thereon as are prescribed by the examining committee.

[67] May 2010 Interim Draft available from the authors. and on the book's website under Chapter 5.

(d) Have registered with the examining committee as a law student within 90 days after beginning the study of law. The examining committee, upon good cause being shown, may permit a later registration.

(e) Have done any of the following:

(1) Had conferred upon him or her a juris doctor (J.D.) degree or a bachelor of laws (LL.B.) degree by a law school accredited by the examining committee or approved by the American Bar Association.

(2) Studied law diligently and in good faith for at least four years in any of the following manners:

(A) In a law school that is authorized or approved to confer professional degrees and requires classroom attendance of its students for a minimum of 270 hours a year.

A person who has received his or her legal education in a foreign state or country wherein the Common Law of England does not constitute the basis of jurisprudence shall demonstrate to the satisfaction of the examining committee that his or her education, experience, and qualifications qualify him or her to take the examination.

(B) In a law office in this state and under the personal supervision of a member of the State Bar of California who is, and for at least the last five years continuously has been, engaged in the active practice of law. It is the duty of the supervising attorney to render any periodic reports to the examining committee as the committee may require.

(C) In the chambers and under the personal supervision of a judge of a court of record of this state. It is the duty of the supervising judge to render any periodic reports to the examining committee as the committee may require.

(D) By instruction in law from a correspondence law school authorized or approved to confer professional degrees by this state, which requires 864 hours of preparation and study per year for four years.

(E) By any combination of the methods referred to in this paragraph (2) .

(f) Have passed any examination in professional responsibility or legal ethics as the examining committee may prescribe.

(g) Have passed the general bar examination given by the examining committee.

(h)(1) Have passed a law students' examination administered by the examining committee after completion of his or her first year of law study. Those

> who pass the examination within its first three administrations upon becoming eligible to take the examination shall receive credit for all law studies completed to the time the examination is passed. Those who do not pass the examination within its first three administrations upon becoming eligible to take the examination, but who subsequently pass the examination, shall receive credit for one year of legal study only.
>
> (2) This requirement does not apply to a student who has satisfactorily completed his or her first year of law study at a law school accredited by the examining committee and who has completed at least two years of college work prior to matriculating in the accredited law school, nor shall this requirement apply to an applicant who has passed the bar examination of a sister state or of a country in which the Common Law of England constitutes the basis of jurisprudence.
>
> The law students' examination shall be administered twice a year at reasonable intervals.
>
> CREDIT(S)
>
> (Added by Stats.1939, c. 34, p. 353, § 1. Amended by Stats.1953, c. 1090, p. 2578, § 1; Stats.1959, c. 1084, p. 3148, § 1; Stats.1970, c. 251, p. 513, § 1; Stats.1971, c. 1748, p. 3740, § 14; Stats.1972, c. 1285, p. 2559, § 4.3; Stats.1973, c. 1052, § 1; Stats.1974, c. 316, p. 631, § 1, eff. May 31, 1974; Stats.1987, c. 239, § 1.) ; Stats.1990, c. 707 (A.B.3946), § 1; Stats.1996, c. 168 (S.B.1950), § 1; Stats.1996, c. 866 (S.B.1321), § 3; Stats.2001, c. 46 (S.B.817), § 1; Stats.2002, c. 664 (A.B.3034), § 12.)

Note how following the code section is a section called "Credit(s)." All codes – state and federal – follow this practice of presenting the legislative history in citation form immediately following each code section. With this information the researcher can determine when the legislation was first created and obtain citations to all subsequent amendments.

The codes of California are found in two publications: West's Annotated California Codes and Deering's California Codes Annotated.

The codes are also found in all of the various computer-assisted legal research databases, including the two giants in the market, LexisNexis and Westlaw.

And, of course, more and more legislative information is being made available on the Web by the states. In California, bills, bill status information, codes and more are available at <www.leginfo.ca.gov/>.

LexisNexis and Westlaw are heavily used by United States attorneys and these services offer many "bells and whistles" for researching statutory law not available on official (and free) websites. LexisNexis and Westlaw have current and past editions of state and federal codes.

Searching LexisNexis and Westlaw databases can be done in a number of ways. Documents, especially code sections, can easily be called up by citation, using a very powerful FIND feature.

Documents can also be located using one of two search strategies for searching full text material:

- Combining Terms and Connectors or using
- Natural Language.

Due to the brevity of many code sections and also the non-intuitive language used by legislators, full text searching for code sections can be frustrating and non productive.

Most American law students start their LexisNexis and Westlaw searching using Natural Language. They drill down to a search window, select "Natural Language" and then type in whatever comes to mind. With Natural Language, there is always a search result, as the computer will run its sophisticated algorithms and provide the best matched documents. Natural Language searching is least effective with statutory searches (and most effective with case searches).

More precise searching can be done using Terms & Connectors (more on this with case law, below).

Each document is divided into parts – LexisNexis calls these parts "segments" and Westlaw calls them "fields." Search precision can be gained by applying Terms & Connectors searching to just segments or fields.

Both LexisNexis and Westlaw offer many special features for doing statutory research online. For example, LexisNexis offers this succinct summary of its various statutory searching capabilities:

> Researching statutes can be challenging. LexisNexis provides several tools to make the process quick and easy. Below are some of the more common statutory research tasks and how to perform them on LexisNexis.
>
> Get a Statute by Citation
>
> - Sign-on with your ID & Password at <www.LexisNexis.com/lawschool>.
> - Click the Research System tab at the top of the page.
> - Click the Get a Document tab at the top of the page.
> - Type 18 U.S.C. 3109 in the Get by Citation form and click the red Get button.
>
> Use the blue Citation Formats link when you are unsure of the proper format to retrieve a citation.
>
> Get a Statute by Popular Name

- Click the Search tab at the top of the page.
- Click Federal Legal – U.S. > United States Code Service (USCS) Materials > USCS Popular Names Table.
- Type Cyber Security Enhancement Act of 2002 as a terms & connectors search.
- Bullet Table of Contents and click the red Search button.

Retrieve the Public Law, P.L. 107-296, to see the Act as enacted and where it is codified within the United States Code.

Search Statutes through Table of Contents Headings

- Click the Search tab at the top of the page.
- Click States Legal – U.S. > Ohio > Statutes & Regulations > OH – Page's Ohio Revised Code Annotated.
- Type Burglary as a terms & connectors search.
- Bullet Table of Contents and click the red Search button

If you want to search a specific title of a code then scroll down and check the box next to the desired title before clicking the search button.

Use the Practitioner's Toolbox

- Retrieve 18 U.S.C. 3109 through the Get a Document tab.
- The Practitioner's Toolbox is located to the right of the statute's heading.

1. History – provides a link to the statute's direct history.
2. Interpretive Notes & Decisions – provides a link to a topical Table of Contents for the cases citing the statute (also called annotations).
3. History; Ancillary Laws and Directives – provides a link to the statute's indirect history.
4. Related Statutes & Rules – provides links to related statutes & rules.
5. Research Guide – provides links to related secondary sources.

Use the Practitioner's Toolbox to quickly and easy locate related cases, statutes & secondary sources.

Find Statutory Interpretation through Annotations

- Retrieve 18 U.S.C. 3109 through the Get a Document tab.
- Click Interpretive Notes & Decisions in the Practitioner's Toolbox.
- Click the green down arrow for Warrantless Searches.

You can also use the FOCUS Terms bar at the top to search through the Annotations for a specific issue.

Browse through Statutes

- Retrieve Cal Bus & Prof Code 23007 through the Get a Document tab.
- Click the Bluebook Browse link at the top middle of the page.
- Click the Next Arrow to view the next section of the California code.
- Click the Previous Arrow to view the preceding section of the California code.

Through Book Browse you can browse through an entire code if necessary.

Shepardizing Statutes

- Click the Shepard's tab at the top of the page.
- Type 18 U.S.C. 2234 in the Enter Citation to be Checked form and click the red Check button.
- Select the link for Exact Match from the report list.

If you need the Citing References for a specific subsection select the appropriate report from the report list. If no report exists for your subsection then there are no references.

Printing Statutes Only

- Retrieve 42 U.S.C. 2000e through the Get a Document tab.
- Click the blue Print link at the top right of the statute.
- Click Custom in the drop-down menu under Document View.
- Click the Clear All button and select the Text segment.
- Click the OK button then the red Print button.

Using the Text segment reduces the number of pages printed from over 200 to 3 by printing only the text of the statute without editorial enhancements.

Table 15: Researching Statutes on LexisNexis[68]

Despite all of the electronic features offered by LexisNexis (described above) and Westlaw (which offers similar functions), using a code in print still offers the researcher, particularly a researcher new to United States law, some distinct advantages. The major advantage is the ease in seeing the statutory language in context – the reader can simply flip pages back and forth to read the other, nearby code sections within the same chapter and quickly grasp the organization of the laws. While this process can also be done online in LexisNexis or Westlaw, it requires some skill, and since these databases are very expensive, it can also be cost-effective for the lawyer in the United States to simply pick up a hard-copy volume of the code.

5.2.4.2. Legislative Histories

In addition to a careful reading of the statute (as found in its code section(s)), and perusing the various subsequent cases that have construed or interpreted the statute, researchers in the United States also on occasion try to glean "legislative intent" by looking backward and reading the legislative history of a

[68] Source: LexisNexis Total Practice Solutions.

statute. As noted below, legislation can be ambiguous, even intentionally so; the documents in the legislative history are often used to try and understand a more precise meaning of the statute.

There is a long-running debate on the use of legislative histories in the United States. Some judges use them; others will not.[69]

As a bill winds its way through Congress, a paper trail is created. And this paper trail can help shed light on the meaning and interpretation of the statutory language. As part of the legislative compromise, statutory language often ends up being vague, and cases and legislative history documents are used to try and make the precise meaning of the statute more clear.

To compile a legislative history means to gather all of the following documents:

- The bills (as introduced and as amended)
- Committee reports
- House or Senate Documents
- Debates text
- Hearings transcripts (sometimes)

Of all of these documents, the committee reports are considered the most important part of the legislative history.

Each bill is assigned to a committee, where it either "dies" or advances. If the committee recommends passage, a committee report is usually issued.

From committee, the bill goes to the full body (House or Senate) where the bill may be debated. Debates are published in the Congressional Record. If the bill passes the first body it is then introduced in the other; at this point it becomes an "act." The act is assigned to committee and the process is repeated. At this point there are generally two reports: A House Report and a Senate Report.

In the House and Senate versions of the legislation are at variance, the legislation will be considered by a conference committee, composed of both senators and representatives. Here the committee will try and hammer out a

[69] See Charles Rothfeld, *Read Congress's Words, Not its Mind, Judges Say*, THE NEW YORK TIMES, April 14, 1989, p. B5 and James J. Brudney, *Liberal Justices' Reliance on Legislative History: Principle, Strategy, and the Scalia Effect*, OHIO STATE PUBLIC LAW WORKING PAPER NO. 95, Center for Interdisciplinary Law and Policy Studies Working Paper Series No. 64. Professor Brudney's article "conducts an in-depth examination of Supreme Court Justices' reliance on legislative history during the Burger, Rehnquist, and early Roberts eras."

single, agreed-upon final version of the legislation. This conference committee will issue a report, usually called a House Report (even though the committee consists of both House and Senate members). A very useful print source for the text of these reports can be United States Code Congressional and Administrative News (USCCAN[70]), published by Thomson West, which normally will publish important excerpts from at least one committee report for each public law. USCCAN can be an excellent starting point and, with a limited research budget, it may be all that is needed to answer a statutory question.

The president may publish a message when signing the bill into law. These signing statements are also published. If the law started as a House bill, the message is published as a House document; if originally a Senate bill, the message is published as a Senate Document.

The issuance of signing statements has created recent controversy in the United States.[71] The United States General Accountability Office, the government's oversight agency, did a study of presidential signing statements and drew this conclusion:[72]

> "Federal courts infrequently cite or refer to presidential signing statements in their published opinions, and these signing statements appear to have little impact on judicial decision-making. When they do cite signing statements, it is for a variety of reasons. The most common use of a signing statement is to supplement discussion of legislative history such as committee reports. … The federal courts have only in rare instances treated presidential signing statements as an authoritative source of statutory or constitutional interpretation."

[70] USCCAN - United States Code Congressional and Administrative News - is a West Group publication that collects selected Congressional and administrative materials for publication in a single resource. USCCAN is published in monthly pamphlets that contain a cumulative subject index and cumulative Table of Laws Enacted in addition to the selected documents. Among other documents, USCCAN publishes the full text of new federal laws, selected committee reports from the House and Senate, signing statements, presidential proclamations, executive orders, reorganization plans, President's messages, Federal regulations, proposed constitutional amendments, Federal court rules, and sentencing guidelines - all arranged in chronological order. When published in bound volumes, the legislative history documents are placed in separate volumes apart from the rest of the materials published by USCCAN.

[71] See Dahlia Lithwick, *Sign Here – Presidential Signing Statements Are More Than Just Executive Branch lunacy*, SLATE, posted Jan. 30, 2006.

[72] United States Government Accountability Office, Presidential Signing Statements Accompanying the Fiscal Year 2006 Appropriations Acts, June 18, 2007.

All of the above documents, for more recent legislation at least, are available online in *Thomas* (<Thomas.loc.gov>). Earlier documents are found in a variety of locations depending upon the date of the legislation. Where to look for certain documents depends upon the date of the legislation. And since compiling a legislative history can be a very time-consuming process, it is always a good first step to see if someone has already done the work. Various publications, such as Sources of Compiled Legislative Histories, will identify where compilations may already exist.

The best single-source online database for legislative history material is LexisNexis's Congressional Publications database. This database indexes all documents that have been produced by Congress and includes the full text of many of them, with more being added all of the time. As this 3rd edition of our book went to press, the information firm ProQuest acquired Congressional Publications from LexisNexis. In the near future the name of the database will most likely change, but the content will no doubt remain extremely rich for anyone doing legislative history research.

Compiled legislative histories usually omit hearing transcripts. This is because hearing transcripts are not considered part of the legislative history. The reason for this is that the hearings are the publication of the comments made by people who have been invited to Washington to provide testimony to Congress, in an effort to educate the law-makers. In other words, these are not the words of the law-makers themselves, but the words of various experts; as such this testimony cannot be used to determine legislative intent. Nonetheless, hearings can contain extremely useful information and should not be overlooked when doing exhaustive research on a topic.

Research Tip #5.7

Want a quick understanding of what a statute is all about?

Use USCCAN!

Find the statute in USCCAN and locate the report(s) printed or excerpted there. Often this "thumbnail" sketch helps a lot and it is quick and easy.

5.2.5. Regulations and administrative law decisions.

If the researcher's first question is: Is there a statute? His or her very next question should be: Are there regulations?

Regulations are laws issued by administrative agencies, which are part of the United States Executive Branch of government. Agencies issue regulations pursuant to Congressional authority. For every agency regulation there is a source statute. It is important to remember that administrative rulemaking is delegated authority, delegated to the Executive Branch.

Administrative agencies can write highly detailed regulations on subjects that far exceed the competence of Congress. For example, in 1973 Congress passed the Endangered Species Act, with the laudable intent of preserving endangered species in the United States.

On September 11, 2007, the Fish and Wildlife Service, an administrative agency, charged with authority pursuant to the Endangered Species Act, issued a ruling on the copepod Acanthocyclops columbiensis's status as an endangered species.[73] Congress just does not possess the expertise to make such fine rulings on different amphipods.

The reach and effect of administrative rules should not be underestimated and, indeed, regulations may adversely affect clients more than any other source of law.

We were putting the finishing touches on the first edition of this book during the waning months of the administration of President George W. Bush, and as a New York Times[74] article pointed out, "With Congress in Democratic hands and his political capital all but spent by the Iraq war, Mr. Bush has scant hope of pushing significant domestic legislation through Congress. But he still controls the executive branch and can accomplish much through regulation and executive edict."

Indeed, as the authors of this book were making our final edits of the first edition, "President Bush and his cabinet and staff [were] busily writing far-reaching rules to keep his priorities on the environment, public lands, homeland security, [and] health in safety in place ..."

Of course, any new president might very well undo all of this last-minute law making, as "[o]ne of Mr. Bush's first official acts as president was to withdraw the Clinton regulations that had not yet been published in the Federal Register and delay the effective date of those that had."

Ostensibly, the reason why agencies issue regulations is that these deal

[73] 72 Fed. Reg. 51766.

[74] John M. Broder, *A Legacy Bush Can Control*, THE NEW YORK TIMES, Week in Review, Sunday, September 9, 2007, p. 1. The history of regulation in the United States is truly fascinating and one of the best expositions on this history is found in the CONGRESSIONAL QUARTERLY'S FEDERAL REGULATORY DIRECTORY (Washington D.C.: Congressional Quarterly Inc., 1979/80). The first chapter, "Federal Regulation: An Introduction," gives a highly readable and interesting history of regulation in the United States.

with areas of law that are far too detailed and technical for Congress to address. Agencies have the subject expertise to flesh out the legal requirements for the broad areas that Congress wants regulated – such as, for example, the minutiae of particulate matter concentrations in air pollution.

Agency activities are well-documented in a very important publication called the Federal Register. The Federal Register serves two chief functions:

- It provides announcements of proposed regulations, including contact information where public comments can be made
- It publishes the final regulation. This is the first place of publication.

The Federal Register is a very important tool and many lawyers in the United States routinely read it looking for proposed regulations in areas that could affect their clients.

When a proposed regulation is first published in the Federal Register a government official's name and contact information are always provided. This contact person, for a period of time anyway, knows more about the proposed regulation than probably any other individual on the planet. Researchers needing more information would be wise to try and contact this official.

The United States Government Printing Office (GPO) does an excellent job of publishing the Federal Register online and it even enables anyone to sign up for automated delivery and updates. It is listed on the GPO Access page under Executive Resources at:

<http://<www.gpoaccess.gov/index.html>.

Anyone interested in researching United States law should peruse this website with great care.

The Federal Register, much like the Statutes at Large, publishes laws one after another, with no subject arrangement. This makes it a good tool for current awareness, but not a good tool for subject matter research.

Like the statutes from Congress, the regulations from Executive Branch agencies are also codified – that is, placed in a subject arrangements. The code for federal regulations is called the Code of Federal Regulations, abbreviated as CFR.

Just like the United States Code, the Code of Federal Regulations is divided into 50 titles. Some, but not all, of the subjects of these titles overlap with the subjects of the United States Code titles.[75] Here is a chart that compares the two codes:

[75] See subsection 5.2.3. above (at footnote 65) and indented text above Research Tip 5.6.

	USC	CFR
Title 1	General provisions	General provisions
Title 2	The Congress	[reserved]
Title 3	The President	The President
Title 4	Flag and seal, seat of government, and the states	Accounts
Title 5	Government organization and employees	Administrative personnel
Title 6	Domestic security	Homeland security
Title 7	Agriculture	Agriculture
Title 8	Aliens and nationality	Aliens and nationality
Title 9	Arbitration	Animals and animal production
Title 10	Armed forces	Energy
Title 11	Bankruptcy	Federal elections
Title 12	Banks and banking	Banks and banking
Title 13	Census	Business credit and assistance
Title 14	Coast guard	Aeronautics and space
Title 15	Commence and trade	Commerce and foreign trade
Title 16	Conservation	Commercial practices
Title 17	Copyrights	Commodity and securities exchanges
Title 18	Crimes and criminal procedure	Conservation of power and water resources
Title 19	Customs duties	Customs duties
Title 20	Education	Employees' benefits
Title 21	Food and drugs	Food and drugs
Title 22	Foreign relations and intercourse	Foreign relations
Title 23	Highways	Highways
Title 24	Hospitals and asylums	Housing and urban development
Title 25	Indians	Indians
Title 26	Internal revenue code	Internal revenue
Title 27	Intoxicating liquors	Alcohol, tobacco products and firearms
Title 28	Judiciary and judicial procedure	Judicial administration
Title 29	Labor	Labor
Title 30	Mineral lands and mining	Mineral resources
Title 31	Money and finance	Money and finance: Treasury
Title 32	National guard	National defense
Title 33	Navigation and navigable waters	Navigation and navigable waters
Title 34	Navy [repealed]	Education
Title 35	Patents	Panama canal
Title 36	Patriotic and national observances, ceremonies, and organizations	Parks, forests, and public property
Title 37	Pay and allowances of the uniform services	Patents, trademarks, and copyright
Title 38	Veterans' benefits	Pensions, bonuses and veterans' relief
Title 39	Postal service	Postal service
Title 40	Public buildings, property, and works	Protection of environment

Title 41	Public contracts	Public contracts and property management
Title 42	The public health and welfare	Public health
Title 43	Public lands	Public lands: Interior
Title 44	Public printing and documents	Emergency management and assistance
Title 45	Railroads	Public welfare
Title 46	Shipping	Shipping
Title 47	Telegraphs, telephones, and radiotelegraphs	Telecommunication
Title 48	Territories and insular possessions	Federal acquisition regulations system
Title 49	Transportation	Transportation
Title 50	War and national defense	Wildlife and fisheries

Table 16: Titles of USC and CFR Compared

Each title of the CFR is divided into chapters – just like the United States Code. The chapters combine regulations on the same subjects. The chapter numbers are designated with Roman numerals. The use of chapters is a useful organizational tool, which should not be overlooked.

The chapters are further divided into parts. The parts are finally divided into sections. When you cite to a CFR regulation you do not cite to the part number, although it is "part" of the citation!

> For example, the regulation found here:
>
> Title 6--homeland security
> Chapter I--department of homeland security, office of the secretary
> Part 25_regulations to support anti-terrorism by fostering effective
> Sec. 25.4 Designation of qualified anti-terrorism technologies.
>
> Is cited thusly: 6 CFR § 25.4

The regulations in the Code of Federal Regulations are organized by part and subpart and together these are cited as a section.

5.2.5.1. How to find regulations

Since regulations are issued pursuant to Congressional authority, for every regulation there is an authorizing statute. All of the indexes to the CFR include a Parallel Table of Authorities where the researcher with a United States Code section citation can see if there are regulations listed for that code section. The Parallel Table of Authorities is also online at

<www.access.gpo.gov/nara/cfr/cfr-table-search.html>

in both text and PDF versions.

The official CFR also includes an index volume. The government-produced index, however, is weak and not nearly detailed enough for complete legal research. Several commercial enterprises have produced much more detailed indexes to the Federal Register and Code of Federal Regulations, such as the highly-detailed and excellent indexes published by Congressional Information Service, Inc. (CIS).

The Federal Register and the CFR are published by the United State Government Printing Office (GPO). In addition to the print volumes, available at most law school libraries in the United States as part of their Government Depository status, electronic versions going back to 1996 are available on the GPO Access website (<www.access.gpo.gov>). In 2010, GPOAccess migrated to the Federal Digital System (FDsys) page, a vastly improved interface and with many added features.[76] Here the researcher will find browse, text search, and citation search features for all issues of the CFR that are online.

The full text of the CFR is online at the GPO Access website and in all of the various computer-assisted legal research databases, including LexisNexis and Westlaw.

However, the most efficient way to search the CFR online is to NOT search the CFR online, but instead to conduct a search in the Federal Register. The Federal Register contains every word found in the CFR, plus many more words. When a proposed or final rule is discussed in the Federal Register there is considerable discussion of the rule and its impact. The Notice of Proposed Rulemaking or Final Rule can contain very helpful text discussing the historical background and perceived need for the regulation, summary and discussion of comments received, the anticipated financial impact, and more – all this information providing a large body to additional text for online searching.

For example, the Federal Aviation Agency has enacted a rule commonly referred to as the "sterile cockpit rule" which prohibits non-essential communication in the cockpits of commercial airplanes when the plane is flying under 10,000 feet (i.e., during takeoff and landing).

The phrase "sterile cockpit" does not appear in the regulation. So if a researcher looked for that phrase in the CFR he or she would not find it. However, that phrase is used in the discussion of the rule as published in the Federal Register.

[76] FDsys at <http://www.gpo.gov/fdsys/>.

A search of the Federal Register for "sterile cockpit" results in one document found, "Final Rule, Elimination of Duties and Activities of Flight Crewmembers Not Required for the Safe Operation of Aircraft," 46 Federal Register 5500 (1981). Reading through the "Background" section of this document leads the researcher to other research phrases used, such as "cockpit sterilization." A new online search in LexisNexis of the Federal Register (**not** the Code of Federal Regulations) of cockpit w/2 steril! (the word cockpit within two words of any word beginning with the root "steril") produces two documents, the Final Rule and the Notice of Proposed Rulemaking.

> **Research Tip #5.8**
>
> The best way to search the CFR online is to not search the CFR. Search the Federal Register instead! The Federal Register contains all of the words found in the CFR – including the exact text of regulations -- plus many, many more words, including much less technical language.

> **Research Tip #5.9**
>
> Never look at a code section in isolation. Always read the sections immediately preceding and following, and it is best to look at all of the sections in the same chapter.

Lawyers and law students will also "*Shepardize*" CFR cites for history and citing references.

5.2.5.2. How to Update Regulations

Just like researching the United States Code, or the state codes, the research does not stop once the relevant sections are identified. The researcher always has to ask: Is this still good law? - Are there cases?

Updating the CFR in print is a cumbersome process. A research tool called List of Sections Affected, or LSA, needs to be consulted.

The CFR volumes are printed upon an annual basis, with the following schedule:

CFR Tables	Dates of Annual Revision
Titles 1-16	January 1
Titles 17-27	April 1
Titles 28-41	July 1
Titles 42-50	October 1

Table 17: Dates of Annual Revision of CFR Titles

The List of CFR Sections Affected (LSA) contains a lists of proposed, new, and amended Federal regulations that have been published in the Federal Register since the most recent revision date of a Code of Federal Regulations (CFR) title. It is published by the Office of the Federal Register, National Archives and Records Administration.

Each LSA issue is cumulative and contains the CFR part and section numbers, a description of its status (e.g., amended, confirmed, revised), and the Federal Register page number where the change(s) may be found. The LSA is issued monthly; however, on FDsys, the LSA also contains three supplemental services:

- List of CFR Parts Affected Today: Lists the parts affected by change(s) appearing in most current issue Federal Register. The Federal Register is published Monday through Friday, except Federal holidays.
- Current List of CFR Parts Affected: Lists the CFR parts affected by change(s) since the last monthly issue of the LSA.
- Last Month's List of CFR Parts Affected: Lists only the CFR parts affected by change(s) during the last month.

Whether done in paper or online , to bring CFR sections up-to-date, the researcher must consult the most recent LSA pamphlet, and also the most recent issue of the Federal Register. The Federal Register volumes will pick up where the LSA pamphlets leave off. Each issue of the Federal Register has a cumulative parts affected table so, at most, the re-searcher will only need to consult at most two issues of the Federal Register – the one which covers the month after the most recently monthly pamphlet and the most recent one available if it is from a later month. When the re-searcher moves from the LSA pamphlets to the Federal Register, he or she loses the granularity of updating by specific *section* and has to look at the broader *part* for updates.

This can be a confusing process. One way to for the researcher to ensure that he or she is not missing relevant material is to "mind the gap." All issues of the CFR are dated with an "as of" date. So the researcher should look very closely at all dates to ensure there are no gaps in coverage – from the month and year of the CFR to the current month and year.

All of the updating tables – in the pamphlets or in the Federal Register – make reference to Federal Register pages on which the regulation under investigation has been affected. So the researcher will have to find those pages of the Federal Register – either in print or online – to determine the current status of the regulation. It is time-consuming and annoying that current official codes are not available outside the expensive databases of LexisNexis and Westlaw. But happily this is rapidly changing.

Fortunately, all this manual updating is no longer needed due to a great new government database called the Electronic Code of Federal Regulations (eCFR). The eCFR provides the full text of the entire CFR and it is completely up to date, within one day! No further updating is needed. It is available at: <http://ecfr.gpoaccess.gov> and it is one of the best things the United States government has done for law librarians and legal researchers.

Further, and rolled out just in 2010, FDSys takes updating the CFR to a new level of customization and simplicity. At FDsys the user can use drop down boxes to update the regulation in one very easy step by choosing a date range for the CFR Parts Affected from the Federal Register. It is as current, if not more current, than anything LexisNexis or Westlaw can offer and, best of all, it is free.

Table 18: Enhanced Regulatory Searching on Westlaw[77]

Both LexisNexis and Westlaw keep their versions of the Code of Federal

[77] Source: Dan Henry, Esq., Thomson West Account Representative.

Regulations current. These databases cost money,[78] but attorneys' time costs money too – often lots of it – and it is more cost-effective to use a CALR database to retrieve a current CFR section than it is to update the material manually.

Regulatory research can be confusing, with all of the extremely technical language being used. The government-produced print index is weak and the parallel table of authorities has omissions. If a first check of the index and table reveal no regulations, it is not a safe assumption that there are none. It is better to check the annotated United States Code for CFR references, but even here the system is not perfect. Westlaw has devoted substantial resources to improving this situation and they now offer what is arguably the best index to the CFR with their Regulations Plus (RegsPlus) index. On top of that, Westlaw has now annotated the CFR, so that case law citations can also easily be found. With eCFR and RegsPlus, what was once difficult research has been made easy and complete.

5.2.5.3. Executive Orders

The President of the United States, as head of the Executive Branch, issues Executive Orders. These have the force of law – often a very powerful source of law. It was an Executive Order, for example, which interned Japanese-Americans to relocation camps during World War II.[79] Presidential Executive Orders are published in Title 3 of the Code of Federal Regulations, as well as being available in a variety of other locations including the Weekly Compilation of Presidential Documents, Public Papers of the Presidents, and our favorite source, HeinOnline.

5.2.5.4. Regulations.gov

Participatory government took a gigantic electronic step forward when the United States created this relatively new website. Regulations.gov is a site where the public can find, view, and post comments on proposed regulations and other administrative agency actions. The technology easily enables thou-

[78] As of March 2006, for example, under per-minute charges, it costs $ 7.16 per minute to search the CFR database in Westlaw. Westlaw® Plan 1 Pricing Guide, on file with the authors.

[79] Executive Order 9066 was a presidential executive order issued during World War II by U.S. President Franklin D. Roosevelt on February 19, 1942, using his authority as Commander-in-Chief to exercise war powers to send ethnic groups to internment camps. 7 Fed. Reg. 1407 (Feb. 25, 1942).

sands, if not millions, of people to comment upon proposed rules; a question remains if the technology enables a thoughtful electronic processing of those comments. Regulations.gov allows anyone to participate in the rule-making process and to view all of the comments made by others.

5.2.5.5. Agency decisions

Agencies do more than write regulations. Agencies also possess a quasi-judicial function. Administrative Law Judges (ALJs) hold hearings and settle disputes. As part of this judicial function, ALJs will issue decisions. As Armstrong and Knott point out: "Publication of administrative decisions is irregular at best."[80]

Unlike the decisions from the courts of the Judicial Branch, agency decisions do not follow the same rules of stare decisis. So, while certainly of great importance to the parties of the dispute, the decisions are not binding on others and do not create precedent.

But since it is more likely than not that an agency will follow its own rulings, these decisions are nonetheless important to lawyers representing clients in similar matters.

Some agencies, like the Federal Communications Commission, issue carefully bound published complications of their decisions; others do not.

The best sources for the text of administrative law decisions are the agency websites themselves and also the pricey LexisNexis and Westlaw databases.

Looseleaf services, discussed above, sometimes will include selected administrative agency decisions. A very useful table which indicates what looseleaf services have this information is: "Sources of Federal Regulatory Agency Rules, Regulations and Adjudications," found in Appendix D to Morris L. Cohen, Robert C. Berring and Kent C. Olson, How to Find the

[80] J.D.S. Armstrong and Christopher A. Knott, WHERE THE LAW IS: AN INTRODUCTION TO ADVANCED LEGAL RESEARCH 174 (2nd ed.) (St. Paul: Thomson West, 2006). "Generally speaking, there are three different ways that agency decisions are made available to researchers; on the agency's website, in official publications of the agency, or in commercial publications. It is increasingly common for agencies to make hearing decisions available on their websites. You should know, however, that often these decisions are reproduced with no indexes or finding aids, and are usually arranged by date or party name. There is rarely any kind of subject access to the decisions. A few agencies publish their decisions in official reporters ..."

Law.[81]

5.2.5.6. State administrative law resources

Each state in the United States also has three branches of government: Legislative, Judicial and Executive. The Executive branch for the states all issue regulations, much the same way as the federal Executive branch does.

Most states have some version of a notice publication similar to the Federal Register, although it will be called by different names. In California, it is called the Notice Register. Since states generate far few regulations than the many federal agencies, no state issues its register upon a daily basis. A few states do not publish a register at all.

But all states codify their regulations and some sort of code is available. In California it is the California Code of Regulations.

For more on state regulations, a good resource is William H. Manz, Guide to State Legislative and Administrative Materials.[82]

5.2.5.7. Online sources of administrative law

Since law students use online sources of administrative law in the United States to 90% or more of their research online,[83] the charts (Table 19-21) below is offered as guidance to locating the following administrative materials online:

- Federal Register
- Code of Federal Regulations (CFR)
- Administrative Agencies
- Administrative Decisions
- California Administrative Law

[81] Morris L. Cohen, Robert C. Berring and Kent C. Olson, HOW TO FIND THE LAW (9th ed.) (St. Paul, Minnesota: Thomson West publishing as part of its Hornbook Series, 1989).

[82] William H. Manz, GUIDE TO STATE LEGISLATIVE AND ADMINISTRATIVE MATERIALS (2002 ed.) (Buffalo, New York: William S. Hein, 2002).

[83] Erika V. Wayne & J. Paul Lomio, BOOK LOVERS BEWARE: A SURVEY OF ONLINE RESEARCH HABITS OF STANFORD LAW STUDENTS 6-7 (Robert Crown Law Library Legal Research Paper Series, Research Paper No. 2) (2005) <www.law.stanford.edu/publications/projects/papers/OnlineResearchSurveys.v211.pdf>.

Federal Register	Code of Federal Regulations
Federal Register (print) There is also an index to the Federal Register, published by CIS. Also, historical indexes to the Federal Register are available on HeinOnline from 1936-1995.	Code of Federal Regulations (print) There is also an index to the CFR in USCS.
LexisNexis Congressional 1989- Search by keyword, FR citation.	LexisNexis Congressional Search by keyword, CFR citation, statutory authority.
GPO Access 1995-	GPO Access 1997- (some titles 1996-) eCFR (National Archives and Records Administration) A beta version of the CFR that incorporates changes in rules and regulations to present a currently updated CFR.
LexisNexis 1980- Westlaw 1980- HeinOnline 1936-1998	LexisNexis Historical version back to 1981. Westlaw Historical version back to 1984.

Table 19: Sources for the Federal Register and the Code of Federal Regulations

5.2.6. Case Law Research

Last, but certainly not least, we come to the law produced by the Judicial Branch of government.

Some might argue that judges do not make law. In fact, on the home page of the Administrative Office of the United States Court's Understanding the Federal Courts, it states:

> "Through fair and impartial judgments, the federal courts interpret and apply the law to resolve disputes. The courts do not make the laws. That is the responsibility of Congress. Nor do the courts have the power to enforce the laws. That is the role of the President and the many executive branch departments and agencies."[84]

[84] <www.uscourts.gov/understand03/content_1_0.html>.

Administrative Agencies	Administrative Decisions
The United States Government manual The United States Government manual at the GPO	Finding the Law[85] Appendix C - Sources of Federal Regulatory Agency Rules, Regulations and Adjudications
Federal regulatory directory	Federal Administrative Decisions and Other Actions (University of Virginia) Extensive list of agencies and links to administrative decisions if available on the Internet.
United States Federal Government Agencies Directory (Louisiana State University) Federal Web Locator (Center for Information Law and Policy) Both web sites have complete listings for executive agencies.	
LexisNexis Federal Legal - U.S. : Administrative Agency Materials : Individual Agencies Westlaw Other Administrative & Executive Materials	LexisNexis Federal Agency Decision File and Federal Legal - U.S. : Administrative Agency Materials : Individual Agencies Westlaw Other Administrative & Executive Materials

Table 20: Sources for Administrative rules and decisions

California Code of Regulations and Notice Register
California Code of Regulations This California Code of Regulations (CCR) Website contains the text of the regulations that have been formally adopted by state agencies, reviewed and approved by the Office of Administrative Law, and filed with the Secretary of State. California Regulatory Notice Register Full text of the Notice Register starting July 2000 and table of contents only from January 1998. California State Agencies

Table 21 California Code of Regulation and Notice Register

In this regard, it can be suggested that courts "explain" the law, as they apply it to facts under their review. Explaining the law is how we defined secondary sources, above. However, no one in the legal research world would suggest that compilations of judicial opinions are secondary sources.

Legal research properly begins with an examination of true secondary sources, and then a careful review of all controlling statutes and regulations.

[85] Robert C. Berring, FINDING THE LAW (11th ed.) (St. Paul, MN: West Publishing, 1999).

This is the best way to begin legal research. But legal research always includes case analysis, and generally this is where the research process slows and then stops.

One reason why legal research bogs down in the case law realm is the sheer vastness of the body of law involved. Whereas one could, conceivably, read from cover to cover the entire United States Code (although arguably would not be the same person afterwards), there are millions and millions of cases out in the case law universe, and that is counting only the published cases. By the year, 2000 there were an estimated 5.2 million published judicial decisions "with about 100,000 cases added annually."[86]

LexisNexis and Westlaw became the gigantic economic forces (with annual sales in excess of $1 billion) that they are because of their case law resources. They have branched out to include everything a lawyer needs in his or her practice, but the case law core remains their raison d'être

In the United States there are two parallel court systems: federal and state. Table 22 summarizes the differences.

The federal system includes the courts mentioned in Table 23 below.

The United States District Court is the trial level court for federal cases. In addition to settling disputes this court also has a role in interpreting federal statutes. Federal District Court Judge D. Brock Hornby writes about "the business of the U.S. District Courts" and makes this observation about the court's "increased demands for law exposition":[87]

> Congressional lawmaking carries a particular implication for federal courts' work. When Congress drafts a statute, it cannot possibly foresee all the disputes it will encompass or engender. As a result, statutory language often turns out ambiguous for particular circumstances. Sometimes, to submerge disagreement so as to get the law enacted, Congress intentionally chooses ambiguous language. Either way, users ask federal courts to expound upon what the new law means and the circumstances to which it applies. America's laws continue to multiple (about 1,900 pages of new statutes per session in the 1950s, 6,750 pages per session in the 1990s; about 14,477 new Federal Register pages in 1960, 80,322 in 2002) and, with them, insatiable demand for authoritative interpretation. The demand comes from individual users. It

[86] CLARK *supra* note 57, at 38.

[87] D. Brock Hornby, *The Business of the U.S. District Courts*, 10 GREEN BAG 2d 453, 457 (Summer 2007) citing statistics from Barnes, *Adversarial Legalism, the Rise of Judicial Policymaking, and the Separation of Powers Doctrine, in* MAKING POLICY, MAKING LAW: AN INTERBRANCH PERSPECTIVE 35 (Miller & Barnes, eds.)(Washington, D.C.: Georgetown University Press, 2004) and Marc Galanter, *The Vanishing Trial*, 10 DISP. RESOL. MAG. 3 (Summer 2004).

comes also from user segments, such as American business (e.g., trade association lawsuits), consumers, and the public (e.g., environmental groups). Alternative dispute resolution (mediation and arbitration) does not provide the authoritative interpretation; only courts do.

The 94 U.S. judicial districts are organized into 12 regional circuits, each of which has a United States court of appeals (see further Appendix 3). A court of appeals hears appeals from the district courts located within its circuit, as well as appeals from decisions of federal administrative agencies.

In addition, the Court of Appeals for the Federal Circuit has nationwide jurisdiction to hear appeals in specialized cases, such as those involving patent laws and cases decided by the Court of International Trade and the Court of Federal Claims.

Comparing Federal and State Court Systems	
The U.S. Constitution is the supreme law of the land in the United States. It creates a federal system of government in which power is shared between the federal government and the state governments. Due to federalism, both the federal government and each of the state governments have their own court systems.	
The Federal Court System	**The State Court System**
STRUCTURE	
Article III of the Constitution invests the judicial power of the United States in the federal court system. Article III, Section 1 specifically creates the U.S. Supreme Court and gives Congress the authority to create the lower federal courts.	The Constitution and laws of each state establish the state courts. A court of last resort, often known as a Supreme Court, is usually the highest court. Some states also have an intermediate Court of Appeals. Below these appeals courts are the state trial courts. Some are referred to as Circuit or District Courts.
Congress has used this power to establish the 13 U.S. Courts of Appeals, the 94 U.S. District Courts, the U.S. Court of Claims, and the U.S. Court of International Trade. U.S. Bankruptcy Courts handle bankruptcy cases. Magistrate Judges handle some District Court matters.	States also usually have courts that handle specific legal matters, e.g., probate court (wills and estates); juvenile court; family court; etc.
Parties dissatisfied with a decision of a U.S. District Court, the U.S. Court of Claims, and/or the U.S. Court of International Trade may appeal to a U.S. Court of Appeals.	Parties dissatisfied with the decision of the trial court may take their case to the intermediate Court of Appeals.
A party may ask the U.S. Supreme Court to review a decision of the U.S. Court of Appeals, but the Supreme Court usually is	Parties have the option to ask the highest state court to hear the case.

under no obligation to do so. The U.S. Supreme Court is the final arbiter of federal constitutional questions.	
	Only certain cases are eligible for review by the U.S. Supreme Court.
SELECTION OF JUDGES	
Article III, Section 1 of the Constitution states that federal judges are to be nominated by the President and confirmed by the Senate. They hold office during good behavior, typically, for life. Through Congressional impeachment proceedings, federal judges may be removed from office for misbehavior.	State court judges are selected in a variety of ways, including • election, • appointment for a given number of years, • appointment for life, and combinations of these methods, e.g., appointment followed by election.
TYPES OF CASES HEARD	
• Cases that deal with the constitutionality of a law; • Cases involving the laws and treaties of the U.S.; • Ambassadors and public ministers; • Disputes between two or more states; • Admiralty law, and • Bankruptcy.	• Most criminal cases, probate (involving wills and estates), • Most contract cases, tort cases (personal injuries), family law (marriages, divorces, adoptions), etc. State courts are the final arbiters of state laws and constitutions. Their interpretation of federal law or the U.S. Constitution may be appealed to the U.S. Supreme Court. The Supreme Court may choose to hear or not to hear such cases.
ARTICLE I COURTS	
Congress has created several Article I or legislative courts that do not have full judicial power. Judicial power is the authority to be the final decider in all questions of Constitutional law, all questions of federal law and to hear claims at the core of habeas corpus issues. • Article I courts are U.S. Court of Veterans' Appeals, the U.S. Court of Military Appeals, and the U.S. Tax Court	

Table 22: Comparing Federal and State Court Systems[88]

The federal system includes the courts mentioned in Table 23 below.

[88] Source: <www.uscourts.gov/outreach/resources/comparefedstate.html>.

Table 23: The United States Federal Courts[89]

The United States District Court is the trial level court for federal cases. In addition to settling disputes this court also has a role in interpreting federal statutes. Federal District Court Judge D. Brock Hornby writes about "the business of the U.S. District Courts" and makes this observation about the

[89] Source: *Understanding Federal Courts, Administrative Office of the Courts*, <www.uscourts.gov/understand03/media/UFC03.pdf>.

court's "increased demands for law exposition":[90]

> Congressional lawmaking carries a particular implication for federal courts' work. When Congress drafts a statute, it cannot possibly foresee all the disputes it will encompass or engender. As a result, statutory language often turns out ambiguous for particular circumstances. Sometimes, to submerge disagreement so as to get the law enacted, Congress intentionally chooses ambiguous language. Either way, users ask federal courts to expound upon what the new law means and the circumstances to which it applies. America's laws continue to multiple (about 1,900 pages of new statutes per session in the 1950s, 6,750 pages per session in the 1990s; about 14,477 new Federal Register pages in 1960, 80,322 in 2002) and, with them, insatiable demand for authoritative interpretation. The demand comes from individual users. It comes also from user segments, such as American business (e.g., trade association lawsuits), consumers, and the public (e.g., environmental groups). Alternative dispute resolution (mediation and arbitration) does not provide the authoritative interpretation; only courts do.

The 94 U.S. judicial districts are organized into 12 regional circuits, each of which has a United States court of appeals (see further Appendix 3). A court of appeals hears appeals from the district courts located within its circuit, as well as appeals from decisions of federal administrative agencies.

In addition, the Court of Appeals for the Federal Circuit has nationwide jurisdiction to hear appeals in specialized cases, such as those involving patent laws and cases decided by the Court of International Trade and the Court of Federal Claims.

5.2.6.1. State court system

The state court model runs parallel to the federal system, with litigation starting in trial courts and a first appeal following by an appeal to the state's highest court, usually, but not always, called the state Supreme Court.

A state court structure, using California[91] as a model, looks like this:

[90] D. Brock Hornby, *The Business of the U.S. District Courts*, 10 GREEN BAG 2d 453, 457 (Summer 2007) citing statistics from Barnes, *Adversarial Legalism, the Rise of Judicial Policymaking, and the Separation of Powers Doctrine, in* MAKING POLICY, MAKING LAW: AN INTERBRANCH PERSPECTIVE 35 (Miller & Barnes, eds.)(Washington, D.C.: Georgetown University Press, 2004) and Marc Galanter, *The Vanishing Trial*, 10 DISP. RESOL. MAG. 3 (Summer 2004).

[91] The California Judicial System is the largest court system in the United States, with 2,000 judicial officers and 19,000 employees, serving 34 million people. Source: Administrative Office of the Courts, CA Judicial Branch Fact Sheet, Jan. 2004.

COURT OF LAST RESORT
California Supreme Court
▪ Chief Justice and 6 Associate Justices ▪ Justices appointed by Governor and confirmed by voters statewide for 12-year terms ▪ Required by the Constitution to review all death penalty judgments ▪ Has authority to review decisions of CA courts of appeal (reviewed 8,917 filings in 2001-2002 issued 101 opinions) ▪ Appellate court with final authority on matters regarding the California Constitution and state law
INTERMEDIATE APPELLATE COURT
California Courts of Appeal
▪ 105 justices in 6 appellate districts, 9 court sites and 19 divisions ▪ Justices appointed by Governor and confirmed by voters statewide for 12-year terms ▪ 25,465 cases filed in 2001-2002 ▪ Have appellate jurisdiction over cases that superior courts hear and in other areas decided by statute ▪ Establish precedent for superior courts to follow, correct errors
COURTS OF GENERAL JURISDICTION
California Superior Courts
▪ 1,498 authorized judges in 58 counties ▪ Judges are elected by voters in their counties to serve 6- year terms ▪ Over 8 million cases filed in 2001-2002 ▪ Decide cases by applying the law to the facts in individual cases ▪ Trial courts with original jurisdiction in criminal, civil, family, probate, mental health, small claims, juvenile and traffic matters

Table 24: California Court Structure

It should be pointed out that once a case is filed in a court, it can move up and down the court system in almost elevator-like fashion, unlike the flow of litigation in European courts. Sometimes the litigation moves in a one-direction linear fashion: Complaint filed, answer filed, hearing held, decision reached. End of the story. But more often than not, the litigation rides through the court system as if on an elevator. There can be interlocutory appeals (appeals heard by an appellate court before the initial litigation is concluded); motions are constantly filed and there are often mini-hearings on those motions; and even once a judgment is reached it often is not the end of the story. That judgment may get appealed to a higher court, and that higher court may then remand the matter back to the trial court for reconsideration. Up, down, turn around.

An illustrative example is a long row of court decisions concerning the federal Child Online Protection Act (COPA):[92]

American Civil Liberties Union v. Reno, 1998 WL 813423 (U.S. District Court for E.D.Pa. Nov 23, 1998) (NO. CIV. A. 98-5591)
Temporarily Restraining Order issued
American Civil Liberties Union v. Reno, 31 F.Supp.2d 473 (U.S. District Court for E.D.Pa. Feb 1, 1999)
Affirmed by
American Civil Liberties Union v. Reno, 217 F.3d 162 (U.S. Courts of Appeals for 3rd Circuit (Pa.) Jun 22, 2000)
Vacated by
Ashcroft v. American Civil Liberties Union, 535 U.S. 564, 122 S.Ct. 1700 (U.S. Supreme Court, May 13, 2002)
On Remand to
American Civil Liberties Union v. Ashcroft, 322 F.3d 240 (U.S. Court of Appeals for 3rd Circuit (Pa.) Mar 6, 2003)
Affirmed and Remanded by
Ashcroft v. American Civil Liberties Union, 542 U.S. 656, 124 S.Ct. 2783 (U.S. Supreme Court, Jun 29, 2004)
On Remand to
American Civil Liberties Union v. Gonzales, 478 F.Supp.2d 775 (U.S. District Court for E.D.Pa. Mar 22, 2007)

Most appeals are taken as a matter of right. However, most appeals to the United States Supreme Court are at the Supreme Court's discretion, and this application process is commenced in most instances by filing a petition for certiorari, or "cert. petition." If the Court agrees to hear the appeal, then cert. is granted; if they decline, then it is denied. Of course, the U.S. Supreme Court receives many more applications than it can possibly handle, so the justices pick and choose wisely as to which ones need to be decided, and these are generally the most pressing legal issues of the day. And the elevator stops at the Supreme Court. Once it issues its decision, that's the end of the process for those litigants. A common saying is that "the Supreme Court is not final because it is infallible but it is infallible because it is final."[93]

[92] Codified as 47 U.S.C. § 231 (1998).
[93] *Brown v. Allen*, 344 U.S. 443, 540 (1953) (Jackson, J., concurring).

5.2.6.2. Publication of judicial decisions

5.2.6.2.1. Published and unpublished

Judges write opinions. These are also called decisions, or orders or rulings. They are also called cases. All these terms refer to the same thing: a writing of the court. These opinions can be published or unpublished – that is up to the judge – he or she decides whether or not a particular decision should be published. There used to be a huge distinction between published and unpublished decisions, with unpublished opinions having no precedential value. This distinction is rapidly eroding and legal researchers seek out both published and unpublished opinions as various courts lift the injunction against citing unpublished decisions.

> "After years of extensive debate, reams of commentary and vigorous opposition from several circuit judges and many attorneys, the Committee on Rules of Practice and Procedure and the U.S. Supreme Court have answered 'yes' to the question of whether unpublished federal opinions are citable. Rule 32.1 of the Federal Rules of Appellate Procedure, effective Dec. 1 [2006], lifts restrictions on citing unpublished federal opinions . . . "[94]

The increased drive to cite unpublished decisions has become controversial, and a working paper posted to the Legal Scholarship Network offers this analysis in its abstract:[95]

> This Article advances a relatively simple thesis - unpublished opinions should be non-precedential, at least until these opinions can be readily researched by all attorneys. Unfortunately, based upon the questionable assumption that technological advances have made unpublished opinions readily available, some jurisdictions have recently given unpublished opinions full precedential value and this trend appears to be the next frontier in the crusade over unpublished opinions. In truth, although unpublished opinions are increasingly available, many unpublished opinions are not as readily available as published opinions. By affording precedential value to these difficult to research unpublished opinions, jurisdictions will possibly create ethical and legal malpractice problems for attorneys.

[94] Paul D. Fogel and David J. de Jesus, *Unpublished Opinions*, Forum Column, DAILY JOURNAL, December 20, 2006.

[95] Andrew T. Solomon, *Making Unpublished Opinions Precedential: A Recipe for Ethical Problems & Legal Malpractice?,* 26 MISS. C. L. REV. 185 (2007).

> This Article does not attempt to comprehensively report on which unpublished opinions, on both the state and federal levels, are readily available. Instead, it focuses upon the availability of Fifth Circuit unpublished opinions and shows an example of a jurisdiction which has made some of its unpublished opinions precedential, even though those opinions are difficult, and sometimes virtually impossible, to research. The Article ultimately makes two recommendations: (1) the Fifth Circuit should change its rule regarding the precedential value afforded to unpublished opinions, and (2) other jurisdictions should avoid the Fifth Circuit's mistake and only consider making unpublished opinions precedential when those opinions are readily available and can be comprehensively researched. By adopting these recommendations, courts will minimize the risk that attorneys will face ethical and legal malpractice problems for failing to use binding unpublished opinions in their client representation.[96]

5.2.6.2.2. Official and unofficial

An "official" report is one that is published by the government itself or pub-

[96] *Rules for Unpublished Opinions Violate Due Process, Suit Says*, by Linda Rapattoni, Daily Journal Staff Writer, October 5, 2007: An Orange County law firm sued the California Supreme Court and an appellate division Thursday, contending rules barring lawyers from citing unpublished opinions violate due process and equal protection rights. The suit appears to be the first to challenge the rules in federal court. Bisnar Chase of Newport Beach filed the complaint in U.S. District Court in San Francisco in *Hild v. California* (Supreme Court, C075107JCS). The Hild suit alleges the appellate court violated the new guidelines the state Supreme Court adopted when it filed its June 25, 2007, opinion. In Joshua Hild, vs. Southern California Edison Co., a three-justice panel of the 2nd District Court of Appeal rejected the verdict in an unpublished opinion. A petition for review is pending before the California Supreme Court. Courts don't do it regularly, but the California Supreme Court has reviewed unpublished opinions on a number of occasions. California Constitution, Article VI, Section 14 states it's up to the courts to decide which opinions they publish. "The Legislature shall provide for the prompt publication of such opinions of the Supreme Court and the courts of appeal as the Supreme Court deems appropriate," it says. The U.S. Supreme Court last year adopted Rule 32.1 allowing citation of unpublished opinions, which the 9th U.S. Circuit Court of Appeal, whose jurisdiction includes California, had opposed. California's system is much larger than the federal system and has a constitutional requirement to give a longer reason for each opinion than the one to two paragraphs typical in federal opinions. - - From a Civil Law point of view, it would held that any decision (written or unwritten - as long there exist proof of the courts decision) of any court in a democratic and civilized country can be used in a later case. Only in non-democratic countries can you be forbidden to refer to a previous court decision. Another aspect is of cause (from a Civil Law point of view) is whether the case can be said to be "precedence", thus requiring a (Civil Law) court to build its decision on the previous case.

lished by a commercial publisher under contract with the government. All other reports are "unofficial." When a court releases its decision, the text of opinion itself will be exactly the same whether published officially or unofficially. What might differ between unofficial and official versions are editorial enhancements. This official/unofficial distinction is a minor one, important only for some citation rules. Generally speaking, an official citation must be given before an unofficial citation. But these citation conventions are rapidly changing, especially with the very heavy reliance upon online versions of court decisions.

5.2.6.2.3. Trial and appellate courts

Cases start with a trial court. In the federal system, this is the United States District Court. Many of the decisions of the United States District Court are published. In the state system, a case also begins with a trial court. Often this is called a "superior court" but state trial courts go by other names as well. In New York, for example, the trial court is given the very confusing designation of "supreme court." State trial court decisions are seldom published.

5.2.6.2.4. Reporters

Judicial opinions are published in sets called "reporters." Therefore, a published opinion is also called a *reported* opinion.

Usually state court trial opinions are not published. There are several reasons for this. One reason is that decisions are often reached without a written opinion. And even if the trial court judge does write an opinion, it is recognized that it is binding only upon the parties to the litigation – there is not a wider precedent setting value to the trial court ruling. There are exceptions, and some very notable trial court decisions have been published; but this is rare.

Decisions of the federal trial court, the United States District Court, are different. These are considered more important and are often published.

5.2.6.2.5. Publication of Federal Court Decisions – U.S. Supreme Court

Everything the United States Supreme Court does is published – every decision, every order, every ruling. The first reports of the U.S. Supreme Court followed the early English method, called nominative reports. Commercial reporters would write down the decisions spoken from the bench. These early decisions were cited by the name of the reporter. This practice of citing to named reporters ceased is most jurisdictions by the middle of the 19th century.

By tradition, the first ninety volumes of U.S. Supreme Court decisions are cited by including the name of the commercial reporter. For example, 2 U.S. (2 Dallas) 3 (1791).

Decisions of the U.S. Supreme Court are published officially in the United States Reports and unofficially in Supreme Court Reports, Supreme Court Reporter, Lawyers' Edition, BNA[97] U.S. Law Week, and CCH's[98] United States Supreme Court Bulletin and in many online databases, including the Supreme Court's own website, LexisNexis, Westlaw, and the many new alternatives to LexisNexis and Westlaw that are cropping up such as Bloomberg Legal, FastCase, LoisLaw, Justia, Versuslaw and Wikilaw.[99]

Any discussion of the U.S. Supreme Court must include a reference to a resource-rich blog, SCOTUSblog.com (SCOTUS is an acronym for Supreme Court of the United States). This blog is one of the very most important and popular law blogs in the United States.

This blog reports on the activities of the United States Supreme Court and includes detailed analysis and discussion of each term of the Court. Previews and summaries of arguments are posted. In addition, somehow – and we do not know how they do this – there are times when the SCOTUSblog site will include the text of the latest Supreme Court decisions before they are even posted on the official Supreme Court website at

<www.supremecourtus.gov>.

Anyone interested in understanding United States law would be wise to read SCOTUSblog.com upon a daily basis, at least when the Supreme Court is in session (from the first Monday in October to its summer adjournment).

American Law Reports also follows the Supreme Court very closely and a recent annotation is this one: "2006-2007 United States Supreme Court Review," 21 A.L.R. Fed. 2d 559 or 26 A.L.R. 6th 659 (2007).

5.2.6.2.6. Lower Federal Court Reporting

The decisions of the United States Court of Appeals are published in print only by the West Publishing Company in its Federal Reporter. There is no

[97] Bureau of National Affairs.

[98] Commerce Clearing House.

[99] <http://about.bloomberg.com/about/professional/blaw.html>, <www.fastcase.com>, <www.loislaw.com>, <www.versuslaw.com>, <www.justia.com>, and <www.wikilaw.com>.

official reporter. Decisions from the United States District Court are published in print by the West Publishing Company in its Federal Supplement and Federal Rules Decisions. There is no official reporter.

Very early United States federal cases were published in Federal Cases. This is a set organized by West with cases arranged in alphabetical order. The more significant cases during the period 1789 to 1880 were published in Federal Cases. Cases in this set are numbered consecutively and, by tradition, that number is used as part of the case citation.

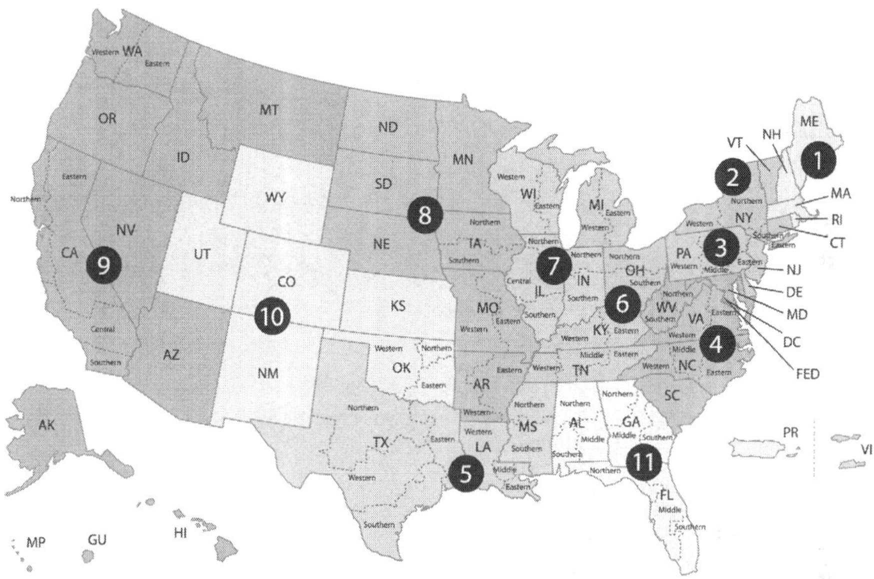

Table 25: Geographic Boundaries of U.S. Courts of Appeals & U.S. District Courts[100]

Between 1880 and 1932 all federal cases were published in the Federal Reporter. In 1932, the trial court decisions were pulled out from the Federal Reporter and published instead in the Federal Supplement.

Federal Rules Decisions contains decisions of the United States District Courts that involve criminal or civil rules. This set only contains District

[100] Source: *Administrative Office of the U.S. Courts*, <www.uscourts.gov>.

Court decisions, even if a Court of Appeals considers a federal rule upon appeal (the appellate decision, if published, is published in the Federal Reporter). There is no overlap between the Federal Rules Decisions and Federal Supplement – a published case is either in one or the other.

In 2001, the West Publishing Company, in our opinion, got a little carried away and began to publish unpublished decisions. This set is called the Federal Appendix and it contains opinions issued by the U.S. Courts of Appeals that are not published in the Federal Reporter. Opinions are included from all circuits except for the 5th and 11th, which do not provide their "unpublished" opinions to any publisher.

The United States Court of Appeals, as indicated, are divided by circuits as shown in Table 25 (see also Appendix 3).

5.2.6.2.7. Publication of State Court Decisions

With fifty states plus the District of Columbia, there is a wide variety in how state judicial opinions are published. The West Publishing Company has tried to make some sense of it all with their National Reporter System.

The West Publishing Company has divided the states into seven regions.

Reported appellate decisions from the states that fall within these regions are then published in:

- Atlantic Reporter,
- North Eastern Reporter,
- North Western Reporter,
- Pacific Reporter,
- Southern Reporter,
- South Eastern Reporter, and
- South Western Reporter.

In states like California, with its separate official reports, the West reporters are unofficial. In some other states, the West Publishing Company is under contract to publish the decision, so they are official. Some states use other publishers or their own printing office. In some states with no official reports and no contract with West, the West reporters remain unofficial but are the only source for a print citation. All of this is rapidly changing in the online world and the next edition of this book will most likely see a radically different landscape of court reporting and citation.

Early state cases, like early federal cases, are sometimes cited by a nominative reporter. The first edition of Price and Bitner[101] has a detailed appendix will all nominative reporters identified.

Of course, no United States law student and increasingly few attorneys use actual books for their case law research. Few in the United States will ever pick up a bound reporter of decisions. Instead, most lawyers and law students reply upon online databases for their case law research. Nonetheless, the citation fiction requires that cases be cited by their print versions.

For example, a student or lawyer wishing to cite the very famous *Miranda decision*[102] – regardless of where he or she finds it – cites it thusly:

> The name or title of the case is *Miranda v. Arizona*. It is reported (published) in volume 384 of United States Reports (the official and therefore preferred citation) beginning at page 436. The case was decided in 1966.
>
> The case citation could also look like this:
>
> 384 U.S. 436, 10 Ohio Misc. 9, 86 S.Ct. 1602, 10 A.L.R.3d 974, 16 L.Ed.2d 694, 36 O.O.2d 237, 39 O.O.2d 63 (1966).

Since the *Miranda* case is extra important it is published in a lot of different places. This multiple publication effect can aid a researcher who is plowing through the LexisNexis or Westlaw database combing through lots and lots of cases. Cases with more citations than others can be bigger, more important cases. A cite to ALR means that the case is published in American Law Reports and therefore the subject of a detailed, lengthy annotation there. This can be research pay dirt.

Research Tip #5.10

Pay attention to the number of places a case is reported.
Cases with lots of different reports are extra important.
Cases with ALR citations can especially lead to fruitful sources.

5.2.6.2.8. Indexing Case Law

John West, the traveling salesman who, with his brother Horatio, founded the West Publishing Company in 1876, was a genius. He had no law training, but he saw the need for lawyers to be able to locate needed court deci-

[101] Miles O. Price and Harry Bitner, EFFECTIVE LEGAL RESEARCH: A PRACTICAL MANUAL OF LAW BOOKS AND THEIR USE (New York: Prentice Hall, 1953).

[102] *Miranda v. Arizona*, 384 U.S. 436 (1966).

sions. His company has taken on, and succeeded, to create a taxonomy for law. A gigantic super index called the West Digest System. It is a marvel. And for the European lawyers reading this, you might be interested to know that the man currently in charge of the West Digest System, Dr. Dan Dabney, has his office in Switzerland.[103]

Dan Dabney spoke at the 2005 American Association of Law Libraries annual convention during a program entitled "Indexes, Taxonomies, and the Google Generation." Law librarian Bill Ketchum reported on the talk for a library journal and made this comment about Dr. Dabney's presentation:[104]

> Taxonomies
> "We call a system of classification, especially a hierarchical one, a 'taxonomy.' … West's Key Number System is a taxonomy of legal concepts. A system thus organized with entries and sub-entries to show the contexts in which a term is used (and that it may occur in more than one context) can be extremely useful to a researcher. Dan Dabney pointed out that in law we often want not only the answer to the question, but also the limits of that answer, such as when and how rule applies or does not apply. In text searching you do not see these 'boundaries.' You don't have a good map of the information space …"

Traditionally – and, again, all of this is changing rapidly in the online world – when a judge wrote an opinion that he or she wanted published, it was sent to the publisher, more often than not, the West Publishing Company. There a team of editors would review the opinion for grammar, punctuation and other minor-league editing tasks, and confer with the judge on any possible needed changes.

After that first editorial task was completed, the opinion went to the big league editors, the editors charged with assigning "key numbers" to the opinion. These editors had to work their way up the chain at West – they all had to serve time as minor league editors and, in addition, they all had to possess law degrees and each had to be a member of a state bar. West would not allow just anyone to index court opinions.[105]

[103] Dan Dabney, Senior Director, Thomson Global Services, Landis-Gyr-Strasse 3, CH-6300 Zug, Switzerland, Phone: +41 (0)41 709 04 49, Email: daniel.dabney@thomson.com.

[104] Bill Ketchum, *Indexes, Taxonomies, and the Google Generation*, SCALL NEWSLETTER, September 2005.

[105] For a glimpse into the famous West Publishing Company, a company that has affected legal research more than any other, see Jill Abramson, John Kennedy and Ellen Joan Pollock, *Inside the West Empire*, THE AMERICAN LAWYER (October 1983), p. 90.

The key numbers are part of the West American Digest System. The key number system is a patented system. West has taken law as a subject and divided it into over 400 subject areas, called topics. These subjects are then further divided into subtopics, which are subdivided into what are called "Key Numbers." "There are over 100,000 individual Key Numbers used in the arrangement."[106] The topic and subtopic together comprise the key number.

Key number editors assign a key number for every point of law found in an opinion. There can be anywhere between one and dozens of key numbers for any one opinion.

The editors then write a little paragraph summarizing the point of law represented by the key number. These paragraphs, along with the key numbers, are superimposed upon each opinion. The key number with its paragraph of text is called a headnote. Headnotes are numbered and the corresponding paragraphs in the judges' opinions are linked by the same number placed in brackets (the brackets indicate that this numbering is done by someone other than the judge who wrote the opinion). If a researcher wanted to read only that part of the opinion that corresponded to a certain headnote, he or she could then look for the headnote's bracketed number in the opinion. For a lawyer, for whom time is literally money, this helps speed the research process.

Digest volumes are then created by rearranging all of the headnotes into a topic and subtopic arrangement. Since cases are published chronologically, it is only by copying and then rearranging the headnotes into a topical scheme that case law research – before the computer anyway – can be accomplished.

Digests are the print index to case law. They are terrific tools for finding cases.

There are three ways to use a Digest:

- First, if you know nothing, just start in the Descriptive Word Index. Look up the words that come to mind until you find a reference to a Digest Topic and then turn to the table of contents for that topic.
- Second, if you know the Topic, but don't have a specific headnote, you can turn to the Outline of Law that is presented at the beginning of the topical area. For example, Negligence as a topic leads to these general subtopics (k stands for key numbers):

  272 NEGLIGENCE
  I. In general, k200-k205

[106] West's ANALYSIS OF AMERICAN LAW: GUIDE TO THE AMERICAN DIGEST SYSTEM (2007 ed.) (St. Paul: Thomson West, 2007).

Ii. Necessity and existence of duty, k210-k222
Iii. Standard of care, k230-k239
Iv. Breach of duty, k250-k259
V. Heightened degrees of negligence, k272-k276
Vi. Vulnerable and endangered persons; rescues, k281-k285
Vii. Sudden emergency doctrine, k291-k295
Viii. Dangerous situations and strict liability, k301-k307
Ix. Trades, special skills and professions, k321-k323
X. Sports, games and recreation, k331-k333
Xi. Fires, k341-k344
Xii. Negligent entrustment, k351-k355
Xiii. Proximate cause, k370-k454
Xiv. Necessity and existence of injury, k460-k463
Xv. Persons liable, k480-k484
Xvi. Defenses and mitigating circumstances, k500-k575
Xvii. Premises liability, k1000-k1320
Xviii. Actions, k1500-k1750
Xix. Criminal negligence, k1800-k1809

- Third, if you have a headnote, you can turn directly to that part of the digest and locate all of the cases – state and federal - that contain the headnote topic and subtopic – that is, all the cases that address the same points of law. This pinpoint approach works whenever you have a relevant case in hand, such as a case found from reading secondary sources.

Publishers other than West also publish court decisions and produce their own digests to the reporters. However, the West system is the granddaddy of them all and the one used the most widely.

Think of the digest as the index to case law. In other words, the digest is used to find cases.

It should be noted that when a case is reported by more than one publisher, the headnotes are the intellectual property of the publisher, and not written by the court. Therefore, there will be differences. Even though both publishers are working with the same published decision, they will index the opinion differently. In the California case of *Northwestern Mutual Insurance v. Farmers' Insurance*,[107] for example, the version in the official reporter contains sixteen headnotes while the version in the unofficial West reporter contains twenty-one headnotes, with some different topics chosen.

The American Digest System is the most comprehensive digest of Ameri-

[107] *Northwestern Mutual Insurance Co. v. Farmers' Insurance Group*, 76 Cal. App.3d 1031, 143 Cal. Rptr. 415 (1978).

can cases. The set is enormous both in coverage and size. It is divided into several units, each covered all of the reported case decisions – state and federal – for a specific time span.

The Century Digest covers the period up to 1896. The "key number" arrangement used in this first digest is slightly different than that in subsequent units. A cross-reference table can be found in volume 21 of the First Decennial digest (and a very common characteristic of law books is that whenever there is a major revision, there is usually a table that will lead the researcher from the old system to the new one).

Digests topics slowly evolve over time and sometimes reflect the mores of the times. For example, the original topic "bastards" become "illegitimate children" and later became "children out-of-wedlock."

The Decennial Digests cover ten-year chunks of time. These are followed by the General Digest, which picks up where the latest decennial leaves off.

There is also the Federal Digest, covering all federal cases; and two digests for the Untied States Supreme Court:

- United States Supreme Court Digest and
- United States Supreme Court Digest: Lawyer's Edition.

For the regional reporter system, there are the following digests:

- Atlantic Digest,
- North Western Digest,
- Pacific Digest,
- South Eastern Digest,
- Southern Digest.

There are no regional digests for the South Western or North Eastern reporters.

There are state digests for nearly every state and for big states, like New York and California, there are more than one digest available. In addition to indexing state court decisions, the state digests will include federal court cases that arose in those states.

Of course, the preferred research tool is the computer, and users can create customized digests in both Westlaw and LexisNexis.

To create a customized digest in Westlaw, first click on "Site Map" at the top of any Westlaw screen. Then click on "Key Number Digest (Custom Digest)."

Westlaw has harnessed the power of the computer to take its digest system one step further with push-button ease for the law student or attorney unfamiliar with the key number system. Westlaw's new KeySearch feature will guide the researcher through the process of finding applicable topic and key numbers. The KeySearch system begins with the researcher clicking on very general legal areas and then guides the researcher to narrower and narrower topics until a precision-based research screen is presented.

While Westlaw got the big head start on LexisNexis in the case indexing arena, and the complete West Digest System is fully integrated in the massive Westlaw database, LexisNexis too provides case indexing tools and in recent years has devoted substantial efforts to increase its case indexing research tools.

LexisNexis also now writes headnotes for its decisions. Unlike Westlaw, however, the LexisNexis headnotes are taken straight from the text of the opinion, verbatim.

In LexisNexis to find cases by topic or headnote click the Search tab at the top of the Research System. Click by topic or Headnote in the red bar under the Search Topic. One can then explore the topic using two approaches.

- Option 1: Find a Headnote Topic through a terms search (e.g., type negligence and click the red Find button to retrieve all the topics related to negligence).
- Option 2: Explore Legal Topics. Find a Headnote Topic by drilling-down through all of the Search Advisor categories. Once one has selected a Headnote Topic one will find related case law and secondary sources through the search form for that topic. One can then search cases and secondary sources covering the Topic with terms or retrieve all the cases with one's Headnote topic.

LexisNexis also enables the researcher to easily find more cases once he or she has found something that looks useful. In reading a case online in LexisNexis, if the researcher locates a headnote that is on point, all he or she has to do is click on the blue "More Like This Headnote" link at the end of the headnote quote. The researcher can then define what jurisdictions he or she is interested in and then hit the red Search button and the database will cull all similar cases from that jurisdiction.

5.3. Boolean Searching and Natural Language Full Text Searching

LexisNexis and Westlaw offer much, much more than "just" topical searching. The databases, as discussed above, can be searched using Terms & Connectors or Natural Language.

Terms & Connectors searching gives the researcher the ability to construct highly detailed, highly specific searches, leading to very focused results.

For example, a Westlaw Terms & Connector search, using field limitations, might look something like this:

Sy ((employ! /s will) or ("wrongful term!) or (unjust pre/2 dismiss!)) and date(after 2000)

This search would limit itself to the synopsis field where the editors have written a paragraph summarizing what the case is about. It would use the Boolean "or" to retrieve cases with certain words and phrases appearing in certain word order as typed in by the researcher.

Another example on narrowing a search:

(AU(Lomio) & ((Cyberspace Internet) /s "Domain name")) & DA(AFT 12/31/1999) % Child-pornography

This search will deselect any document containing the word child pornography (or spelled child pornography or child-pornography) and only search for documents after 31 December 1999, which have Lomio as author and contain a sentence with the phrase domain name and either the word cyberspace or internet.

Searching the synopsis field or the Key Numbers can give the skilled researcher great precision in his or her results. However, it is very important to stress here that the words in the synopsis and the words in the Key Numbers are not the words of the judge. Synopsis fields and Key Numbers, while excellent tools for gaining search precision, should never be cited as legal authority – only the words of the judge count as precedent.

Successful Terms & Connectors searching, using the powerful Boolean search engine, requires practice and it is only by trial and error that law students become accomplished in such searching. Fortunately, American law schools pay flat fees for LexisNexis and Westlaw access, enabling their students to gain proficiency through heavy use. It is really the only way to learn. If you are about to attend a United States law school, there will be abundant opportunities to receive training on both the LexisNexis and Westlaw system. To quote famous law librarian Bob Berring: "Take the training!"[108]

[108] "The most important message we can give you is: TAKE THE TRAINING. … Westlaw and LexisNexis are both designed with very snazzy front ends that make them easy to use intuitively. Let's face it, a chimp could use these systems and get results. Do not limit yourself like that. Take the systems seriously. … Each of these systems has incredible power if you know how to use it. … Westlaw and LexisNexis are full-blown universes of information. There is always more than you think." Robert C. Berring and Elizabeth A. Edinger, LEGAL RESEARCH SURVIVAL MANUAL (St. Paul, Minnesota: West Group, 2000).

LexisNexis and Westlaw are incredibly powerful research tools and a complete explanation of all of their features is far beyond the scope of this book. But listed below is a chart showing just some of the tools available to construct searches for precision. But, again, to echo the words of Professor Berring: ""Take the training!"

Westlaw and LexisNexis use nearly the same Boolean connectors (but be aware that a space in Westlaw means the Boolean OR, and phrases must be carefully placed within quotation marks).

Connector etc.	Type	Retrieves documents	Example
AND	& AND	Both terms	Narcotics & warrant
OR	[a space] OR	Either term or both terms	Car automobile
Grammatical connector	/p	Terms in the same paragraph	Hearsay /p utterance
Grammatical connector	/s	Terms in the same sentence	Design /s defect
Grammatical connector	+s	First term preceding the second in the same sentence	Attorney +s fee
Numerical connector	/n	Terms within n terms of each other (where n is a number from 1 to 255)	Personal /3 jurisdiction
Numerical connector	+n	The first tem preceding the second by n terms (where n is a number from 1 to 255)	42 +7 1942
Phrase	" "	Terms appearing in the same order as in the quotation marks	"attractive nuisance"
Exclude	% but not	Search terms following the percent symbol is deselected	NOT California
Round bracket/ parentheses	( )	Parentheses work in the same way that they do in algebra. Thus, the items in the parenthesis are searched first before the items outside of the parenthesis.	"California law" ("European law")

One joker character in a word	*	To search with one viable character. E.g. to retrieve grew and grow	Gr*w
Two joker characters in a word	**	To search a word with two viable characters. E.g. jury, juror (but not jurisdiction)	Jur**
Compound words	-	A search on a compound word to retrieve all variations (whistleblows, whistle-blow, whistle blow	Whistle-blow
Root Expander/ variant endings	!	To retrieve words with variant endings (contributed, contributor, contributory)	Contribut!
Author	AU( )	Search only a particular author	AU(Lomio)
Court	CO( )	Search only a particular court	CO(Ohio)
Judge	JU( )	Name of the judge writing the lead opinion	
Attorney	AT( )	Names of counsel	
Docket-number	DN( )	Docket number assigned to the case	
Date	DA(mm/dd/year)	To search for documents of a specific date	DA(12/31/2000)
After a date	DA(AFT mm/dd/year)	To search for documents after a given date	DA(AF 12/31/1999)
Before a date	DA(BEF mm/dd/year)	To search for documents before a given date	DA(BEF 12/31/2000)
In-between dates	DA(AFT mm/dd/year and BEF mm/dd/year)	To search for document between to given dates	DA(AFT 12/31/2000 and BEF 12/31/2001)

Table 26: Terms and Connectors Search Capabilities in LexisNexis & Westlaw

LexisNexis and Westlaw each have toll-free numbers (in the United States these are the so-called 800 numbers) and each now offers their customer service via online chat features. Both companies maintain stables of research attorneys standing by 24-hours a day, 7 days a week, waiting to take your research call or respond to your online chat. Use them, as they can try a variety of searches – on their dime – and then walk you through a productive search. Law firm librarians call this research technique "fishing for free."

> **Research Tip #5.11**
> Fish for Free!
> Use the LEXISNEXIS and WESTLAW toll free phone numbers or
> their Instant Message services
> to get the research attorneys to run searches for you and
> to help devise a successful research strategy.

If you do not have access to LexisNexis and Westlaw training sessions but have an account, there are numerous tutorials on each vendor's website,[109] and each company produces tons of literature showing how to use their products. Find out who your LexisNexis and Westlaw representative are and ask for their help.

5.4. WestlawNext

In 2010 Westlaw rolled out its new user interface called "WestlawNext". But it's more than just a different interface; it is a new way of doing legal research. The researcher only needs to know two pieces of information:

- The jurisdiction that the issue arose in, and
- What the issue is.

In framing the issue, as mentioned above, it is helpful, but not necessary, to consult a secondary source first to generate good search words and phrases. However, time spent with a good secondary source is always time well spent and knowing the correct terms of art will improve search results, even with products such as WestlawNext.

With WestlawNext the user can disregard Boolean connectors[110] altogether and simply type in the Google-like query box a string of search terms or phrases. He or she then checks the box for the jurisdiction to be covered and then hits "search." The system decides what databases to consult, not the researcher.[111]

[109] <www.lawschool.Westlaw.com> and <www.LexisNexis.com/lawschool/learning/tutorials>.

[110] However, Boolean still works with WestlawNext and "Power Users" will continue to use Boolean for better results.

[111] The results have been very impressive.

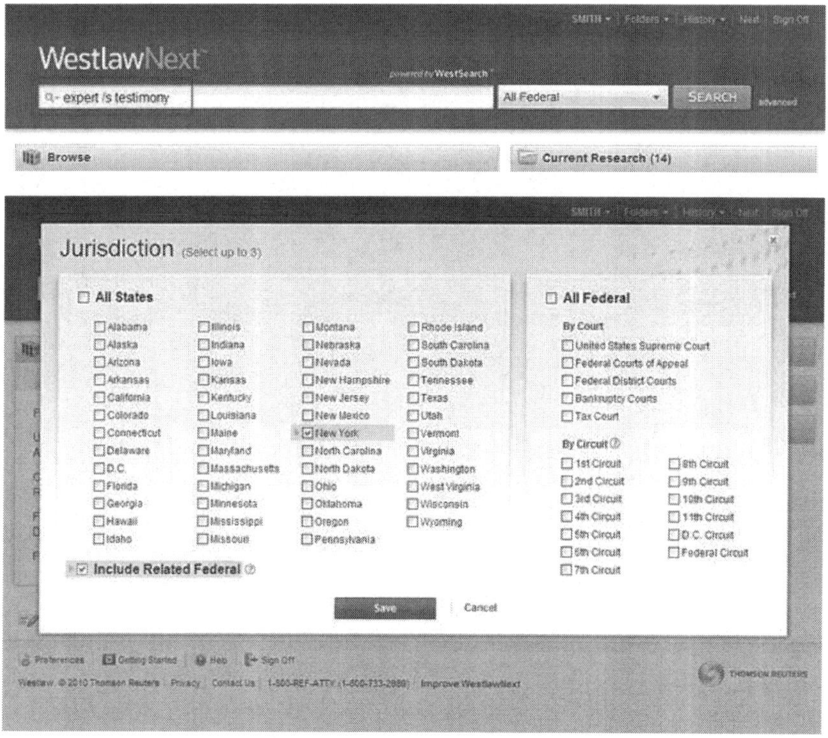

Table 27: WestlawNext screen shot

The result will return cases, statutes and regulations, without the researcher having to consider whether there might be a controlling statute.

This automatic generation of relevant statutes is a major step forward in legal research. Often in the past a researcher, being weaned and raised on case law research, has jumped right into the case law database of LexisNexis or Westlaw and, as a result, has overlooked the critical "is there a statute" step. WestlawNext automatically prevents this from happening. This is a major step towards more effective and complete legal research.[112]

[112] See WestlawNext for Legal Research Game 1: 2 home runs and 1 strike out <http://legalresearchplus.com/2010/10/23/westlawnext-for-legal-research-game-1-2-home-runs-and-1-strike-out/>. See also Jeffrey Isaac Ehrlich, *Westlaw's new upgrade – WestlawNext*, PLAINTIFF, May 2010, p. 30.

As the screen shots below show, WestlawNext is really as easy as one, two. WestlawNext uses "WestSearch, the world's most advanced legal search engine, to emulate the best practices of experienced legal researchers and return the right results, ranked by relevance. Type a Boolean terms and connectors query or terms describing your issue into the search box at the top of the page."

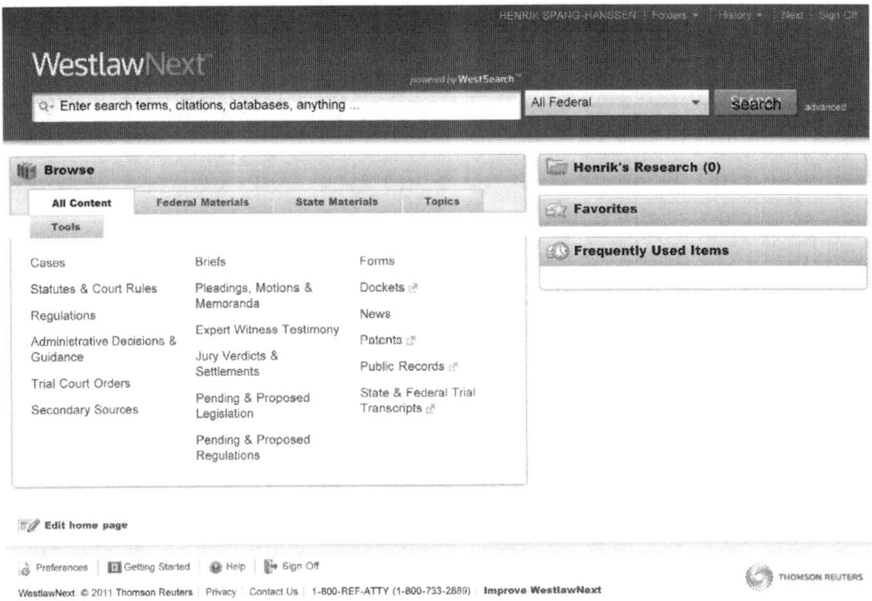

Table 28: WestlawNext's "homepage" after logon

5.5. LexisNexis and Westlaw are not the only online games in town

Courts are increasingly publishing their decisions on their own websites. For links to federal court websites see CourtLink at

<www.uscourts.gov/courtlinks>.

And if you are a European lawyer or law student who would like to get a free taste of American decisional law jurisprudence, a brilliant student from the Stanford Advanced Legal Research class makes this suggestion:[113]

> "... [C]ertain judges' opinions have more precedential value, or clearer statements of the law, than others. The classic example here is Judge Posner [a judge on the Seventh Circuit Court of Appeals in Chicago since 1981] who writes clearly and is well-respected throughout the entire judicial system. A case-on-point from him might be more persuasive than one by another jurist. If you are looking ... for a well-established point of law, consider searching Project Posner, which is a database of all of Judge Posner's opinions. Posner's writing is clear and persuasive and he has been a judge for a long time, so he has considered many different issues. Project Posner is at <www.projectposner.org>.Project Posner is now in "Archive Mode" but it still holds value.

Various aggregator databases are pulling the cases from court websites and creating easily searchable databases of judicial opinions.

5.5.1. Law.gov

The Free Law Movement has begun! Making legal content available on the Web for free is what Law.gov is all about, and as more and more legal content is being made available as public documents other players can enter the market for so long dominated by Lexis and Westlaw.[114]

5.5.1.1. The Promise and Potential of Law.gov

In the United States, the individual states are certainly not united in their approach to the publication of their primary laws. The fifty states plus the District of Columbia all have varied policies and information access philosophies. Some states, such as Oklahoma and New Mexico, have made great gains in making its law freely available and searchable; other states, such as Vermont, can make it exceedingly difficult or even impossible to locate some current law online. Most states deny official status to their online law, directing the researcher to often hard-to-obtain print publications for the official

[113] Thomas Nosewicz, Case Research Pathfinder, available on the Stanford Law School Advanced Legal Research wiki, <sliki.jot.com> (anyone who requests free access may be invited).

[114] See Russell Adams, *Bloomberg Hangs New Shingle*, THE WALL STREET JOURNAL, Thursday July 8, 2010, p. B8. The story includes a graphic credited to Outsell, Inc., which shows LexisNexis with $2.5 billion in revenue having a little more than 20% market share and Westlaw with $4.6 billion in revenue having nearly 40%. "Globally, the top three companies [Thomson Reuters's Westlaw; Wolters Kluwer's CCH and other publications; and LexisNexis] control 75% of the market."

texts. Many states claim copyright over their statutes. And that is just at the state level. When you fold in laws from cities and counties – so-called "local law" – it truly becomes a mish-mash of formats, standards, policies, disclaimers, and copyright assertions. There is no effort to coordinate the online publication of America's legal "operating system." Until Law.gov came along, that is.

Law.gov

Law.gov is a movement, an idea, and a concept that law should be online and available for free to all. A number of information visionaries are behind the Law.gov movement but none more active than Public.Resource.org's Carl Malamud

Law.gov received its official launch at a workshop held at Stanford Law School on January 12, 2010. Since that first workshop, there have been 14 further workshops at leading law schools throughout the country. As a result of these workshops, Public.Resource.org has posted the adopted Law.gov Principles and Declaration:

> LAW.GOV PRINCIPLES AND DECLARATION
>
> The primary legal materials of the United States are the raw materials of our democracy. They should be made more broadly available to enable an informed citizenry.
> Primary legal materials include documents of primary authority issued by governmental bodies, such as court opinions, statutes, and regulations. They also include the supporting documents and other media issued and maintained by those bodies, such as dockets, hearings, forms, oral arguments, and legislative histories. These materials can be found in every branch, at every level, national, tribal, state and local, and should be available to anyone with the will and the heart to obtain them.

The following principles should govern the dissemination of primary legal materials in the United States:

1. Direct fees for dissemination of primary legal materials should be

avoided.

2. Limitations on access through terms of use or the assertion of copyright on primary legal materials is contrary to long-standing public policy and core democratic principles and is misleading to citizens.
3. Primary legal materials should be made available using bulk access mechanisms so they may be downloaded by anyone.
4. The primary legal materials, and the methods used to access them, should be authenticated so people can trust in the integrity of these materials.
5. Historical archives should be made available online and in a static location to the extent possible.
6. Vendor- and media-neutral citation mechanisms should be employed.
7. Technical standards for document structure, identifiers, and metadata should be developed and applied as extensively as possible.
8. Data should be distributed in a computer-processable, non-proprietary form in a manner that meets best current practices for the distribution of open government data. That data should represent the definitive documents, not just aggregate, preliminary, or modified forms.
9. An active program of research and development should be sponsored by governmental bodies that issue primary legal materials to develop new standards and solutions to challenges presented by the electronic distribution of definitive primary legal materials. Examples include the automated detection and redaction of private personal information in documents.
10. An active program of education, training, and documentation should be undertaken to help governmental bodies that issue primary legal materials learn and use best current practices.

Adherence to these principles by governmental bodies is not just good for democracy and justice, it will spur innovation and will encourage:

1. Broader use of legal materials in all parts of our education system, including our law schools.
2. Researchers in law schools, universities, and other research institutions to have broader access to bulk data, spurring important research on the functioning of our government.
3. Innovation in the legal information market by reducing barriers to entry.

4. Savings in the government's own cost of providing these materials through adherence to best current practices.
5. Small businesses to understand rules and regulations they must deal with, reducing their costs and increasing their effectiveness.
6. Increased foreign trade by making it easier for our foreign partners to understand our laws.
7. Better access to justice by making legal information more broadly available to citizens.

How we distribute the raw materials of our democracy is a foundational issue in our system of government. Access to the raw materials of our democracy is a prerequisite for the rule of law and access to justice and makes real the principles of equal protection and due process.

To the European reader these tenets may not seem revolutionary at all. But in the United States, law publication has been a private enterprise function done only with corporate profits as a motivation. Law.gov seeks to make public – genuinely public – law from all three branches of government, and at all levels, for the first time ever. Under the present system much of primary law is owned by corporations and locked behind pay walls, expensive pay walls at that. Even the government itself is paying large sums of money to these corporations to access its own legal information. Law.gov has the goal to make law accessible to anyone. This will force innovation – from the biggest existing players to individuals with visionary ideas who may create new legal research tools.

5.5.1.2. RECOP

At the end of 2010, one of the new visionary companies, Fastcase, announced that it "will collaborate with Public.Resource.org on a weekly feed of national caselaw updates – the nation's first public broadcast of standardized judicial opinions for bulk download." This project, called RECOP for Report of Current Opinions, is Law.gov's first major step to "make the nation's primary legal materials available to everyone.

As the Fastcase press release on RECOP points out "Legal publishers shouldn't be competing on the availability of public law – everyone should have that. They should be competing on who has the smartest tools, the best service, and who creates the most value . . . "[115]

[115] Public.Resource.org and Fastcase Announce Public Caselaw Feed, PRWeb at

5.5.2. Justia.com

A useful, free and popular legal database is Justia.com. This resource is rapidly developing as a leading source for free docket information (federal court filing records), in addition to court decisions, regulations and law blogs.

Justia's mission is to make legal information and resources free and easy to find online, and law librarians applaud such efforts. Legal research has become big business in the United States and we librarians take some blame for ceding so much of the legal landscape to commercial enterprises.

Justia aggregates government cases, codes and regulations, as well as community-generated content such as blogs, and provides them in easy to use databases that are freely accessible to all.

Individual Justia projects include the following:

- US Federal District Court Opinions and Orders - database and the full text of district courts' opinions and orders since 2004. Researchers can do a full-text search of the opinions, or browse decisions by state, court, type of lawsuit and judge. Researchers can also subscribe to RSS feeds of new cases in particular categories, courts or judges. The database is updated daily.
- US Supreme Cases - database of all US Supreme Court Decisions since the 1790s with links to secondary sources including legal blogs and online databases such as Google Book Search. For cases recent cases there is access to mp3 audio of most Supreme Court oral arguments from Oyez.org.
- US Federal Case Filings - database providing US District Courts' civil case filings. Researchers can Search new cases by state, court, lawsuit type (e.g., patent law) or party name. Researchers can also subscribe to RSS feeds of search results to receive updates of new cases. Includes opinions and orders where available.
- US Regulation Tracker - database of the federal register, allowing you to track new regulations of specific federal agencies and subscribe to RSS feeds for daily updates.
- Justia has partnered with the Stanford Law Library to publish and annotate decisions of the California Supreme Court. The site is available at scocal.stanford.edu
- Blawg Search - searchable database of blog posts of over two thousand law blogs published by law professors, lawyers, judges, legal re-

<http://www.prweb.com/releases/Fastcase-LawGov/Public-Law-RECOP/prweb4912854.htm>.

searchers and librarians or search legal podcasts or browse the law blog directory. Updated multiple times a day.

For some federal district court cases Justia is now downloading all of the Electronic Court Filing (ECF) filings by the parties (a pre-alpha version can be viewed at

<http://news.justia.com or http://news.justia.com/cases/>.

Mary Minow, a lawyer and librarian who maintains the LibraryLaw Blog, has been focusing on cases involving libraries

<http://news.justia.com/cases/library>,

and Justia includes all of the Google cases

<http://news.justia.com/cases/google>.

5.5.3. Bloomberg Law (BLAW)

Bloomberg is a name well known in the United States.

Bloomberg, the successful, well-financed, and widely-known provider of business and financial data and news, began working in 2005-2006 to create and disseminate its Bloomberg Law (BLAW) suite of services to law firms as well as to a number of law schools. It is now in direct competition with the duopoly of Westlaw (owned by Thomson Reuters) and LexisNexis (a unit of Reed Elsevier) – "Wexis" – in the online legal research market in the United States. A key emphasis of BLAW is to integrate Bloomberg's established, extensive business and financial data and news coverage seamlessly with its new legal research and analysis tools. (See generally Russell Adams, *Bloomberg Hangs New Shingle: Financial-Data Firm Enters Legal Research, Challenging Westlaw, LexisNexis*, Wall St. J., Jul., 8, 2010, sec. B, col. 1, p. 8.)

Substantial time, money, and effort have clearly been invested in BLAW's design and resources. Law-related materials available in BLAW consist, like in LexisNexis and Westlaw, of:

- primary law sources – both federal and state statutes and federal and state cases, the Bloomberg Law Citator (BCIT) service, and federal and state court dockets; and
- secondary sources, such as the Bloomberg Law Digest (BBLD), organized into core legal topics like civil procedure, corporate law, international trade law, and securities law, and subject-specific, customized Bloomberg Law Reports (BBLR) – generally published

weekly or monthly – in areas like bankruptcy, class actions, executive compensation, insurance law, and sustainable energy.

In its BCIT product, for instance, Bloomberg provides helpful citation analysis summaries for federal and state cases by visual symbols, which show "positive," "negative," and various other treatment categories. BCIT also valuably covers the direct history of the case being checked so that a user can, with only a single "click," display a case's progress through the courts. Citing references can be sorted conveniently by date, court, and analysis. All such references are hyperlinked so that users can jump directly to them. Although Bloomberg is still developing BCIT, it appears to be growing into a serious competitor to LexisNexis' Shepard's Citations and Westlaw's KeyCite (see section 5.6 below).

As indicated, BLAW also incorporates federal and state docket searching, which can be set up flexibly and conveniently depending on a particular user's needs. U.S. federal court dockets are provided by records mined from the national system known as PACER (Public Access to Court Electronic Records). Bloomberg is working to ramp up its state court docket materials on BLAW. However, significant expansion of state court information will be required before the state case docket component of BLAW becomes truly effective and reliable.

The Bloomberg Law Digest continues to grow with the development of unique BLAW headnotes and numbering. Nevertheless, given the only 90 or so headnote categories it has so far, BBLD also needs a great deal of fleshing out before it can claim to be as comprehensive as something like West's 400+ "Key Number" digest system.

Bloomberg Law Reports, meanwhile, have garnered praise in academic circles for their high quality in covering over 30 specific subject areas. Yet they too will have to increase in scope and number to truly catch up to Wexis.

Although it arguably does not yet provide the breadth and depth of legal resources present on Westlaw and LexisNexis, BLAW represents an obvious milestone in U.S. online legal research. And BLAW already offers, as discussed above, some other, definitely significant features in, for example, the traditional Bloomberg strengths of business and financial data and news provision, as well as in federal and state court docket access – which are areas increasingly important to all practitioners, teachers, and students of the law.

But LexisNexis and Westlaw are firmly entrenched at the law schools (see section 5.8 below) and law students have not shown interest in learning Bloomberg Law. Recent monthly usage reports regarding Bloomberg Law at Stanford Law School show no student use whatsoever – the only users are a handful of staff and librarian researchers.

Bloomberg Law, perhaps following the lead of WestlawNext, rolled out a new Web interface in January 2011 to a group of beta-testers.

Can Bloomberg break into the market tightly controlled by LexisNexis, Thomson Reuters and Wolters Kluwer? Only time will tell. But as Outsell analyst David Curle points out ". . . Bloomberg looked unlikely to make big inroads in the short term, but its 'deep pockets' made it a long-term challenger."[116]

5.5.4. Occam, Inc.

Occam, Inc. is an example of a competitor that is creating value with its very smart tool.

Attorneys in the United States are notorious for their extreme paper consumption. It has been estimated that "each attorney in the U.S. consumes the paper equivalent of one ton of wood per year, making the legal profession the single biggest user of paper."[117]

Any attorney deep in the thicket of litigating a case can easily fill a conference room table with piles and piles of paper. There is the complaint, the document that initiates the litigation, followed by a seemingly endless stream of litigation documents – briefs, motions, responses and other pleadings. Together this material consists of the record.

Occam is a company with a novel and creative approach to legal research: mining this record. The beauty of the Occam approach is that no search skills are needed; it is effortless and automatic search, guiding the attorney to important precedents based upon the Occam sifting of the record. The attorney can devote his or her time to applying relevant caselaw rather than trying to figure out how to find it.

Unlike traditional legal search engines, which require an attorney to manually establish context either by foraging through databases, constructing lengthy search queries, or both, Occam utilizes data-mining techniques to automatically pull the context from the various documents contained in the litigation record. The result is a legal search engine that can provide relevant results even without a query and/or return search results ranked according to the specific litigation at hand.

For example, an attorney representing a plaintiff in a biotechnology pat-

[116] Andrew Edgecliffe-Johnson, *Bloomberg Law's discounts challenge information suppliers*, FINANCIAL TIMES, Monday, November 29, 2010, p. 19.

[117] Susan L. Ward, *Green Law Firms Are Where It's At*, NEW JERSEY LAW JOURNAL, April 1, 2008.

ent litigation before Judge Ronald M. Whyte of the Northern District of California would – without entering any search queries – be shown earlier patent decisions issued by Judge Whyte, patent decisions concerning biotechnology patents, and patent decisions favorable to plaintiffs.

Alternatively, Occam's approach could be deployed via a very simple 'Google-like' interface. An attorney working on a patent who enters a query "damages" would retrieve opinions concerning damages in the patent context. An attorney working on a tort case who entered the same query would retrieve opinions concerning damages in the tort context. As more information is mined from the litigation record, increasingly nuanced and intuitive search results are achievable. In other words, as the record grows so does Occam's search sophistication.

Occam is the type of new legal research tool that can be built upon making United States law freely available to all takers.

5.5.5. HeinOnline

An extremely popular database in the United States is HeinOnline. This database contains, among other things, the full text of many, many law re-views – going all the way back to their beginnings, although some recent journal content has a "rolling wall" and is unavailable for a short period of time (one or two years, for instance) Hein is changing its approach, here. In the past, the coverage was chiefly historical; now a significant portion of the law review content is current. If the Stanford Law Library could only afford two databases, they would be Westlaw and HeinOnline.

While HeinOnline's value at the Stanford Law Library is mainly for its law review content, HeinOnline has much, much more to offer. In addition to its vast collection of law journals, HeinOnline contains the Congressional Record Bound volumes in their entirety; complete coverage of the U.S. (Supreme Court) Reports back to 1754; famous world trials dating back to the early 1700's, legal classics from the 16th to the 20th centuries; the United Nations and League of Nations Treaty Series; all United States Treaties; the Federal Register from its inception in 1936 onward; and the CFR from its inception in 1938 onward. And, unlike LexisNexis or Westlaw, access to HeinOnline is not metered, but covered by a flat-rate annual fee. Attorneys can search all the great HeinOnline content without worrying about running up large search charges.

To see just how much material is available on HeinOnline please see the Overview of Collections at

<www.heinonline.org/home/about/Overview.html>.

and follow the HeinOnline blog available there too, in order to keep up with added features and content enhancements.

5.6. Shepardizing

"*Shepardizing*" is such an important step in the American law research process that it deserves its own section in the book.

> "Shepardizing" traces back to a set of books started by Frank Shepard in 1873. Mr. Shepard's books became known as Shepard's citators. Not many people live to see their last name turned into a verb but because of Frank Shepard, untold numbers of law students and young lawyers have been to told to "Shepardize their cases."

Shepard's Citations is a citator, one of two such tools preminent in American law. The other one is called *KeyCite.*

What a citator does – whether Shepard's (in LexisNexis) or and KeyCite (in Westlaw) – is basically two things:

- One, it tells you the particular history of the case being checked. It answers that critically important question of currency, "is this case still good law."
- Two, it gives you a list, with treatment analysis, of all the subsequent cases which have cited your case.

Citators serve another, lesser, function in listing other research resources, such as secondary sources that cited your case, but usually researchers have found those sources before they turn to their Shepardizing (here we are using Shepardizing in a generic sense, to mean citation analysis accomplished with either Shepard's or KeyCite) task.

LexisNexis and Westlaw both use colorful icons to help the researcher see what treatment their cases have received.

Some opinions are stronger precedents than others. It is not just that judges cite earlier opinions. The way that they cite these earlier opinions can say a lot about what the later judges think about the earlier opinions.

Sometimes the later judge will like the earlier opinion a lot and wants to add to its importance, to strengthen it. The way he or she does this is by following the case, and Shepard's will make a note – using the letter "f" for followed – in its print volumes.

Sometimes the later judge will not like the earlier opinion at all but does not want to overrule the earlier decision. So the later judge might distinguish his or her case from the earlier one, as a "polite" way of eroding or weakening the earlier court's holding; this is noted by Shepard's with the letter "d" in the print volumes. Or the later judge might not be so polite and expressly criticize the earlier opinion, again without actually striking it down. Or the later judge might like the holding from the earlier court but see a need to explain it better. All of these subsequent actions and others – criticized, distinguished, explained, followed, harmonized, limited, overruled, reversed, questioned – are duly noted by Shepard's.

There is a table of abbreviations in the front of every Shepard's volume that spells out all of the abbreviations used in the set. And this is a very common characteristic with law books: They will often rely heavily upon abbreviations and present the user with a table of abbreviations, usually in the front of the book.

Detailed instructions are found in the front of the print volumes of any Shepard's set. Listed below as Table 29 are the instructions found in the front of Shepard's California Reports.

> The following example shows how citations appear in Shepard's California Citations, Case Edition, as well as how various notations are used to reflect Shepard's legal analysis. These examples should be studied in conjunction with the Preface (pages viii through xi) and the Citing Sources information (pages vi and vii).
>
> To Shepardize® a decision in Shepard's California Citations, Case Edition, use the Table of Contents (page v) to find the division that corresponds to the reporter in which the decision or ruling was published; then, refer to the volume and page (or paragraph) number of the decision or ruling to find citations to that authority. To create all such citations, be sure to consult all bound volumes and the current soft-covered supplements to Shepard's California Citations, Case Edition.
>
> The citations in the examples are provided solely for illustrative purposes and should not be relied upon for research.
>
> The illustration on previous page shows that the *Alvarez* case was reported in Volume 14 of the California Reports, Fourths Series at page 968. The case name, together with its date and parallel citations, gives you the information necessary to cite Alvarez correctly in ones brief or memorandum of points and authorities. By looking at all citing references to *Alvarez* one can:
>
> - find out how *Alvarez* has been treated over time
> - find cases which have discussed the same points of law as Alvarez
> - Discover the strength and weaknesses of ones position and that of ones opposing counsel.

Following the history of the case, one will find citations preceded by editorial, or treatment letters. These letters indicate how subsequent cases have treated or interpreted *Alvarez*. In this example you can see that *Alvarez* was followed by the court in 56CA4th1249, with references to headnote 3. *Alvarez* was cited in the dissenting opinion of 18C4th690. It was also cited in the opinion found at 56CA4th1103. However, the "#" preceding this citation indicates that one should further research this citation before citing it as legal authority.

ILLUSTRATION

CITED CASE

California Reports Fourth Series

Vol. 14	Volume number in easy-to-find box
-968-	Page number in large bold print
California v Superior Court of Los Angeles County (Alvarez) 1997	Case name and date
(60CaR2d93) (928P2d1171)	Cross references
De 03-12-1997	Review Denied
#s 43CA4th616	History showing Questionable precedent
#s 47CA4th1819	

CITING CASES

17C4th162	
j 18C4th690	Citation from dissenting opinion
56CA4th402	
# 56CA4th1103	Questionable precedent
f 56CA4th^{3}1249	Citation showing significant treatment and headnote analysis
57CA4th73	
57CA4th^{1}76	Citing case showing headnote analysis
f 57CA4th626	Citation showing significant treatment
58CA4th^{1}251	
59CA4th^{6}838	
# 60CA4th1411	
7CalL(7)30	Citation from law review

Table 29: How to Use Shepard's California Citations

Few American lawyers or law students use Shepard's in print anymore, however. The Shepardizing process is so important and the lawyer's time so expensive, that it is usually cost-effective to Shepardize online. Using Shepard's in print requires consulting multiple volumes and there is always a time delay. Online offers ease and currency, and researchers do not have to know what the treatment abbreviations stand for – it is all explained in full online.

In their online systems, both LexisNexis and Westlaw use color-coded icons to alert the researcher to the nature of the subsequent treatment.

The final step in doing legal research is updating the law. However, in practice one will often find it best to update as one proceeds through the phases of finding the law and reading the law. The legal research must include careful attention to updating the legal authorities that govern the problem. This include the use of:

- Citators (Shepard's and/or KeyCite)
- Pocket parts and supplements
- Looseleaf reporter services
- - Computerized searches

Shepardizing/KeyCiting (cases, statutes and regulations)

Makes it possible for legal researchers to ascertain a known authority's history and current status.
To "Shepardize" means to determine the subsequent history of a case, that is, has a case been overruled, modified, followed, criticized, distinguished, etc. In the early 1870's Frank Shepard, devised a method for extracting this information and indexing it. Today, the system is owned by LexisNexis. KeyCite© is Westlaw's equivalent to determine whether a case, statute or regulation is good law and to retrieve citing references.

The two companies' citator-systems are described below.

Citators do not inform whether a court decision has been appealed or a statute made the subject of a proposed amendment, as the deciding factor for the sytems is whether a court has changed a previous opinion or a legislature has passed a bill changing a previous statute. Thus, the systems do not indicate whether a change might be in process.

If a scholar has access to Westcheck or LexisNexis' CheckCite,[118] these features should be used to check citations in a dissertation before delivering the final version of the paper.

[118] These are features offered by Westlaw and LexisNexis to check citations in a Word document, and the check will generate a report send from Westlaw/LexisNexis on incorrect or incomplete citations. CheckCite (1) collects the citation from a document, (2) verifies citations through the Shepard's Citations Service, (3) generates a summary report that tags problem cites for immediate attention, (4) checks quotations that occurred in the document – character for character – and reporting even punctuation differences.

Signals in LexisNexis (Flag and Citation)

In Shepard's pay special attention to the following indications:

For CASE LAW:

Red hexagon (traffic "stop" sign) – warns that the case has been negatively affected by later action. Check its citations carefully for strong negative history or treatment.

- O – overruled – the citing case expressly overrules or disapproves all or part of the case being Shepardized.
- Q – Questioned – the citing opinion questions the continuing validity or precedential value of the case being Shepardized because of intervening circumstances, including judicial or legislative overruling.

Yellow triangle – warns that the case may have lost some of its value as precedent. Check its citations for potentially cautionary history or treatment.

- C – criticized – the citing opinion disagrees with the reasoning/result of the case being Shepardized, although the citing court may not have authority to materially affect its precedential value.
- D – distinguished – the citing case differs from the case being Shepardized, either involving dissimilar facts or requiring a different application of law
- L – limited – the citing opinion restricts the application of the case being Shepardized, finding that its reasoning applies only in specific, limited circumstances.

Blue circle - indicates that either citing references with analysis or citation information is available.

- E – explained – the citing opinion interprets or clarifies the case being Shepardized in a significant way.
- F – followed – the citing opinion relies on the case being Shepardized as controlling or persuasive authority.

History

- R – Same case reversed on appeal.

Treatment of case

- C –Soundness of decision or reasoning in cited case criticized for reason given.
- D- Case at bar different either in law or fact from case cited for reason given.
- E – Statement of import of decision in cited Case. Not merely a restatement of the facts.
- H – Apparent inconsistency explained and shown not to exist.
- O – Ruling in cited case expressly overruled.
- Q – Soundness of decision or reasoning in cited case questioned.

For STATUTES:

- C – constitutional – the citing case upholds the constitutionality of the statute, rule or regulation being Shepardized.
- F – followed – the citing opinion expressly relies on the statute, rule or regulation being Shepardizing as controlling authority.
- Rt – retrospective – the citing opinion discuses retrospective or prospective applica-

tion of the statute, rule or regulation being Shepardized.

- U - unconstitutional – the citing case declares unconstitutional the statute, rule or regulation being Shepardized.
- V - void/invalid – the citing case declares void or invalid the statute, rule or regulation being Shepardized because it conflicts with an authority that takes priority.
- Va – valid – the citing case upholds the validity of the statute, rule or regulation being Shepardized.

Signals in Westlaw (Flag and Citation)

KeyCite uses the following signals for CASES:

Red flag – warns that a case is no longer good law for at least one of the points it contains.

Yellow flag – warns that the case has some negative history, but has not been reversed or overruled.

Blue H - indicates that the case has some history.

- Direct History – traces the same case through the appellate process and includes both prior and subsequent history. Note, it does not contain information on whether a previous decision is under re-consideration/has been appealed.
- Negative Indirect History – lists cases outside the direct appellate line that may have a negative impact on the precedential value of the case in question.
- Related References – lists cases that involve the same parties and facts as the case in question, whether or not the legal issues are the same.

Green C – indicates that the case has citing references but no direct or negative indirect history. The number of stars tells the depth the case has been examined by other cases).

- **** Examined - extended discussion of the cited case, usually more than a printed page of text.
- *** Discussed - substantial discussion of the cited case, usually more than a paragraph but less than a printed page.
- ** Cited - some discussion of the cited case, usually less than a paragraph.
- * Mentioned - brief reference to the sited case, usually in a string citation.
- " Citing case directly quotes the cited case

KeyCite uses the following signals for STATUTES:

Red flag –indicates that a section of a statute has been amended or repealed by a recent session law.

Yellow flag –indicates that pending legislation is available for a section (sections merely "referenced," that is, mentioned, in pending legislation are not marked with a yellow flag) or that the section was limited on constitutional or preemption grounds or its validity was otherwise placed in the following categories:

- Updating Documents – lists citation to recent session laws that have amended or repealed the section.
- Pending Legislation – lists citations to pending bills that reference a federal statute.
- Credits – lists in chronological order citations to session laws that have enacted, amended ore renumbered the section.

- Historical and Statutory Notes – describe the legislative changes affecting the section.

Green C – gives a list of documents that cite the statute. The documents are listed in the following order:

- Pending legislation
- Cases from United States Code Annotated and state statute notes of decisions
- Additional cases on Westlaw that do not appear in notes of decisions
- Administrative materials
- Secondary sources

Table 30: Updating the Law

LexisNexis and Westlaw have added impressive additional features to basic Shepardizing, and both Shepard's in LexisNexis and KeyCite in Westlaw can be used to find additional authority. Lawyers in the Untied States are always looking for legal authority to buttress their arguments. Both Shepard's online and KeyCite offer "depth of treatment" and analysis features that enable the researcher to cull through thousands of citing decisions and find the ones that best fit the arguments being made.

In LexisNexis the "FOCUS – Restrict By" link enables the researcher to add custom restrictions, such as jurisdiction or depth of treatment, add headnotes or additional terms, and limit the research in a variety of manners.

In Westlaw, the researcher can similarly manipulate the KeyCite results by clicking on the "Limit KeyCite History Display" arrow at the bottom of the screen.

But neither Shepard's nor KeyCite is self-starting. One must bring a citation to the citator to begin the Shepardizing process and find subsequent materials.

We have discussed using Shepard's and/or KeyCite to check whether or not found cases are "still good law." But citators are used for all of the laws discussed in this chapter. The careful researcher will always run their statute and regulation citations through citators. Statutes and regulations, in addition to cases, can – and should – be "Shepardized."

Shepardizing a statute can produce a longer case list than the cases found in the annotated code. The code editors will be selective in deciding what cases to include within the case annotations, whereas the citators pull them all in – if a case cites a code section, regardless of how or why, Shepard's and KeyCite will list the case citation. If the research aim is to leave no stone unturned – and often in United States legal research it is – then the diligent researcher will check all of his or her important statutes and regulations for case citations using Shepard's and/or KeyCite. It is the practice in some American law firms that important primary sources be checked for current validity in both Shepard's and KeyCite.

Research Tip #5.12
As important as Shepardizing is, there are limitations to citators that the thorough researcher needs to be aware of.

But Shepard's and KeyCite have limitations. A major limitation is explained in this article from the San Francisco Daily Journal:[119]

> Legions of lawyers and law students have been told: "Shepardize your cases to make sure they are still good law."
>
> This is a cautionary tale of one statute, three cases, and the limits of Shepardizing. (By "Shepardizing," I mean the use either of the two legal citators: Shepard's Citators on LexisNexis or KeyCite on Westlaw.) The tale was told to me by a Stanford law student doing real-world research for a clinical case he was assigned.
>
> The statute in question is 28 U.S.C. § 1291, which grants the federal courts of appeal jurisdiction over "final decisions of district courts." One of the cases that the student found was the Ninth Circuit's 1982 opinion in *Gough v. Perkowski*, which held that "an order disqualifying counsel in a civil case **is** immediately appealable" (emphasis added). Shepardizing or KeyCiting this case shows every indication that this holding is still good law. No red flag; no red stop sign.
>
> The other case the student found was *Koller v. Richardson Merrell, Inc.*, from the D.C. Circuit. It also held, in 1984, that an "order disqualifying counsel was immediately reviewable." If you check this case's citation in Shepard's or KeyCite, red flags abound and you are pointed to its vacation on appeal by the United States Supreme Court in *Richardson-Merrell, Inc. v. Koller* (1985).
>
> The Supreme Court vacated the DC Circuit's opinion in *Koller*, holding that an order disqualifying counsel in civil case is **not** subject to immediate appeal. The Court also therefore remanded with instructions that the court of appeals dismiss the appeal for want of jurisdiction.
>
> The Supreme Court writes the supreme law of the land; its precedents bind even the Ninth Circuit. Yet there is no citator link from *Gough* to *Koller*. Why? Simply because the Supreme Court did not cite *Gough* in its opinion. The Court cites to cases from the Eleventh, Second, and Federal Circuits as

[119] J. Paul Lomio, *Caveat Citator (Or Why Shepardizing Your Cases Isn't Always Enough)*, SAN FRANCISCO DAILY JOURNAL, January 31, 2008. Reprinted in full with permission.

allowing immediate appeal when it notes that "the Courts of Appeals [are] divided on the appeal-ability of orders disqualifying counsel in a civil case." These three cases are all redflagged because they are cited in the Court's decision.

Both Shepard's and KeyCite do, to their credit, tell you that the briefs in the Supreme Court appeal of *Koller* cited *Gough*, but the careful researcher would then have to be extra alert to the possibilities and then to have connected all of the dots.

So what should a reasonable researcher do? Read the statute. First. Foremost. Always. And Shepardize it. If you run the federal statute through Shepard's or KeyCite, the Supreme Court decision, of course, appears.

A hurried researcher searching full-text only in the Ninth Circuit database and then Shepardizing the results could be seriously midled. One option would be to use databases that include all precedential law – i.e., the circuit PLUS the Supreme Court, but this search strategy did not occur to our student.

In my opinion, the quickest, easiest and best approach is to read the statute in an annotated code and to peruse the annotations. A reading of the annotations is especially helpful in this instance, as both the United States Code Annotated and the United States Code Service have easy-to-find case notes under the subject of "disqualification" enabling the researcher to quickly hone in on the relevant cases among the tens of thousands that have cited this statute. The annotations review is a task easily accomplished in just a few minutes either online in LexisNexis or Westlaw, or with actual search charge-free books, a medium which may be unfamiliar for today's law students..

Research Tip #5.13

So what should a reasonable researcher do? Read the statute in an annotated code. First. Foremost. Always.

And Shepardize it. Always.

Another limitation to Shepard's and KeyCite is that they do not tell the complete story. These citator services s list cites to later cases, but not to docket entries. If a case has been appealed further, existing citators do not include that very pertinent piece of information. So if a lawyer was relying, even in part, on a recent opinion from the United States District Court, in addition to "Shepardizing" the case the attorney would be wise to check PACER or CourtLink or Bloomberg Dockets to ensure that a Notice of Appeal has not been filed and that an appeal is not pending.

Research Tip #5.14

Check the docket! If a replied-upon recent opinion has been appealed, a citator will not reveal that critical piece of information. The appeal information is obtained from the docket sheet, and the citators do not link to docket sheets.

Shepardizing is critically important, and a lawyer can face sanctions for failure to use a citator. See, for example, *Gosnell v. Rentokil*, 175 F.R.D. 508, 510 n. 1 (N.D. Ill. 1997) **But** the Shepard's and KeyCite history feature do not tell the complete history. The diligent research will dig deeper.

5.7. When to Stop Researching

Regardless of whether the researcher is using traditional tools of print digests and reporters or the latest electronic tools such as WestlawNext or Occam, the question of knowing when to stop the research process remains the same.

In all of the legal research classes at Stanford, students frequently ask the question: How do I know when to stop researching? There is no easy answer to this question as research, in theory, could be never-ending – one case always leads to another.

Sometimes it becomes a practical matter. The client or supervising attorney may allot a research budget, and the researcher simply stops when this budget is used up – usually measured in time increments. For example, a supervising attorney may say to the researcher, "do not spend more than 5 hours on this assignment." So the researcher stops when the five hours have elapsed. It can be as simple as that. When given a small research budget – such as five hours – it is important to check for valuable resources, such as American Law Reports annotations, since these are comprehensive for the subjects addressed. The researcher should not waste his or her time – and his/her client's money – by beginning the research trolling through expensive case law databases.[120] He or she should turn to a secondary source first.

If the researcher is not constrained by a research budget, then the process of "looping" will begin to give the researcher some confidence to stop re-

[120] LexisNexis and Westlaw can be frightfully expensive. For example, as of March 2006, using Westlaw's Per Minute Charges plan one minute in the ALLCASES database cost $ 16.63. If the Westlaw contract was for Transactional Charges instead, each pressing of "Enter" would have racked up a charge of $ 159.00. Careless searching can results in thousands of dollars of charges.

searching. He or she will keep coming upon the same leading cases, the same statutory language, and the same cited regulations. Once the researcher sees the same key references over and over again, and gets the sense that these are the controlling laws, the time will have come to stop.

Of course, tomorrow a new case could come along and completely change an earlier and replied-upon holding. For this reason both LexisNexis and Westlaw allow the diligent researcher to set up automated Shepard's and KeyCite searches with the latest developments sent directly to the researcher's e-mail address or hand-held device, such as an iPhone or Blackberry. The attorney could be walking up the courthouse steps to try a case when the hand-held will light up with an important new precedent to consider.

5.8. Hybrid Legal Research is Most Effective

This chapter discussed both books (for example, treatises and print codes) and online databases (for example, LexisNexis and Westlaw). The most effective research adopts a strategy of using both books and the computer. Knowing when to use books, rather than an immediate online search, is a bit of an art, rather than a science. But generally speaking, treatises are easier to use in print, especially when using a particular title for the first time, than they are online (if they are online), and this is largely due to the fact that they have detailed indexes.

Codes are also more useful when used in print, since it is so much easier to see the code sections in their organizational context.

However, earlier in this chapter it was pointed out that it is nearly impossible for any scholar to do proper research on United States legal material without the use of computer-assisted legal research (CALR) databases, such as the ubiquitous LexisNexis and Westlaw research systems. This remains very much the case as law students, lawyers, and judges all turn to these databases for the bulk of their research needs. As one law firm librarian points out: "These are tools that lawyers need every day to get their job done."[121]

According to a survey of the 200 largest law firms in the United States, conducted by Law Firm Inc., law firm libraries spent an average of US$ 1,234,631 for LexisNexis searching in 2006, up from US$ 999,825 and an

[121] Comment by Trish Webster, library manager for the Detroit, Michigan law firm of Honigman Miller Schwartz and Cohn, reported in Alan Cohen, *Sleuth in the Stacks*, CALIFORNIA LEGAL PRO (Fall 2007), p. 4, 5.

average of US$ 1,681,399 for Westlaw searching, up from US$ 1,494,588.[122]

No legal research text – not this one or any other – can adequately teach how to use LexisNexis or Westlaw. These databases contain vast amounts of legal materials and offer search engines more sophisticated than anything out there. No amount of Google searching can yield legal materials with the depth and precision offered by LexisNexis or Westlaw. Both LexisNexis and Westlaw enable conceptual searching. Both LexisNexis and Westlaw developed powerful search engines over twenty-five years ago, well before the World Wide Web, and each company has devoted millions of dollars since to continually improve the searching capabilities.

LexisNexis and Westlaw maintain heavy marketing presences at American law schools. Law school representatives, all with law degrees, teach a variety of free classes on online legal research, both in group settings and individual sessions. The best way – the only way, really – to learn how to use LexisNexis and Westlaw successfully is to take advantage of this hands-on training. European (and other) law students or lawyers who visit law schools in the United States should seek out the librarian and make enquiries about LexisNexis and Westlaw training opportunities. It is an opportunity not to be missed.

Research Tip #5.15
Seek Out Opportunities to
get hands-on training
with Bloomberg Law, LexisNexis & Westlaw.

5.9. Conclusion

The government of the United States can be thought of as a three-ring circus: the Executive, Legislative, and Judicial branches are the three rings of government. And like at the circus, there is a show going on all of the time in all three rings.

These three rings extend to both the state level as well. So, in a sense, there are at least fifty-one circus shows going on all of the time in the United States.

But unlike fifty-one separate circuses, there is constant interaction between the different branches of government in the law-making and review Big Tent.

[122] *Idem* at 5.

For example, on September 12, 2007, a federal judge (Federal Judicial Branch) in the state of Vermont ruled that the states (via their Executive Branch agencies) had the legal right to regulate greenhouse gas emissions from automobiles.[123] The decision was a review of regulations written by California and then adopted verbatim by eleven other states (state laws are often models for other states). The 244 page written opinion is called *Green Mountain Chrysler-Plymouth-Dodge et al v. Crombie et al.* There are actually multiple plaintiffs and defendants involved with this litigation and one of the plaintiffs, who lost the case, The Alliance of Automobile Manufacturers, reported that it was "considering the options, including an appeal."[124] The deadline for such an action was November 13, 2007, which – at the time - was after this book had gone to press. Researchers who want to know what has happened will need to call up the case in LexisNexis or Westlaw and click on the "Shepardize" or KeyCite button.[125]

5.10. Further Reading (updates at corresponding website)

> The URL for the corresponding website is <www.hssph.net/legalrm> with a full alphabetic bibliography.

5.10.1. Books

ALDISERT, RUGGERO J., OPINION WRITING (Bloomington, In: Authorhouse, 2009).

AMERICAN JURISPRUDENCE (2d Ed.)(West Publishing)

AMERICAN LAW REPORTS (Thomson West)

ANALYSIS OF AMERICAN LAW: GUIDE TO THE AMERICAN DIGEST SYSTEM (2007 Ed.) (St. Paul: Thomson West, 2007).

ARMSTRONG, J. D. S., WHERE THE LAW IS: AN INTRODUCTION TO ADVANCED LEGAL RESEARCH (St. Paul, MN : West, 2009) - This book covers all of the basics. It deals more with sources of law than with research strategies.

BALLENTINE'S LAW DICTIONARY (Available In Lexisnexis).

BARKAN, STEVEN M., FUNDAMENTALS OF LEGAL RESEARCH (New York, NY: Foundation Press : Thomson Reuters, 2009) - Without question this is the most complete, most

[123] *Green Mountain Chrysler Plymouth Dodge Jeep v. Crombie*, --- F. Supp. ---, 2007 WL 2669444 (D.Vt, September 12, 2007)(No. 2:05-CV-302, 2:05-CV-304).

[124] Healey, James R., *Judge Says States Can Regulate Emissions*, USA TODAY (September 13, 2007), p. 1B.

[125] But have in mind Research Tip 5.13 & 5.14.

comprehensive text on legal research – if you cannot find an answer elsewhere, look here. It is the *magnum opus* of legal research.

BERRING, ROBERT C., FINDING THE LAW (11th Ed.) (St. Paul, Mn: West Publishing, 1999).

BERRING, ROBERT C., LEGAL RESEARCH SURVIVAL MANUAL (St. Paul, MN: West Group, 2002) - We urge you to read this slim volume, just a pamphlet really. It is written with humor and clarity and the hour or so it takes to read cover-to-cover is well worth the time for anyone interested in American legal research.

BLACK'S LAW DICTIONARY (Available In Westlaw)

BRYAN A. GARNER, A DICTIONARY OF MODERN LEGAL USAGE (2nd Ed.) (New York: Oxford University Press, 1995) - A Law Library Must-Have

BURNHAM, WILLIAM, INTRODUCTION TO THE LAW AND LEGAL SYSTEM OF THE UNITED STATES (West Group, 2006) – A good introduction book for foreigners

Clark, David S., and Tugrul Ansay, INTRODUCTION TO THE LAW OF THE UNITED STATES (2nd ed.) (The Hague/New York: Kluwer, 2002)

COHEN, MORRIS L. & KENT C. OLSON, LEGAL RESEARCH IN A NUTSHELL (10 ed.)(St. Paul: West, 2010) – Contains a List over State Research Guides in Appendix B.

CORPUS JURIS SECUNDUM (West Publishing).

Eis, Arlene L., LEGAL LOOSE-LEAFS IN PRINT (Infosources Publishing Company).

FEDERAL REGULATORY DIRECTORY (Washington, D.C.: Congressional Quarterly Inc., 1979) - In addition to being a directory of Executive Branch agencies, this book, now in its 14th edition, provides fascinating reading about the history and development of regulation in the United States. Sections include Reasons for Regulation, Early History and Growth of Regulation, The Development of Social Regulation, Regulatory Tools, Implementation Techniques, Dispute Resolution, Analysis in the Regulatory Process, Regulatory Personnel, Accountability and Oversight, and Reform and the Future.

FOX, ELYSE H., THE LEGAL RESEARCH DICTIONARY : FROM ADVANCE SHEETS TO POCKET PARTS (2nd ed.) (Chapel Hill, N.C.: Legal Information Services, 2006) - Any discipline has its own language and jargon. This very useful book will help learn the language of legal research.

LESSONS IN LEGAL RESEARCH: A MANUAL FOR INSTRUCTORS (Lexisnexis, 2004).

Manz, William H., GUIDE TO STATE LEGISLATIVE AND ADMINISTRATIVE MATERIALS (2002 Ed.) (Buffalo, New York: William S. Hein, 2002).

MURRAY, MICHAEL D., 1965- LEGAL RESEARCH METHODS (New York, NY: Foundation Press : Thomson Reuters, 2009) - This slim book does detail research strategies and is especially useful for its Boolean illustrations.

OATES, LAUREL CURRIE, 1951- JUST RESEARCH (Austin [Tex.]: Wolters Kluwer Law &

Business; [New York]: Aspen Publishers, 2009) - This book also goes into research strategies, including useful strategies for successful Google searches. It also includes excellent chapters on researching local law, something most other legal research texts do not include

OLESZEK, WALTER J., CONGRESSIONAL PROCEDURES AND THE POLICY PROCESS (8th Edition)(Cq Press, 2011)

OSBECK, MARK K., IMPECCABLE RESEARCH : A CONCISE GUIDE TO MASTERING LEGAL RESEARCH SKILLS (St. Paul, MN: West, 2010) - Contents include: A five-step strategy for impeccable legal research: Step 1: formulate a research plan and generate search terms. - - Step 2: consult secondary sources. - - Step 3: conduct your search for primary authorities. - - Step 4: expand and update your case research. - - Step 5: analyze and organize your research results. The book also provides "Ten tips for the summer associate and the beginning lawyer," a "Trouble-shooting guide," and an explanation of Secondary sources of law versus Primary sources of law.

PRINCE, MARY MILES, PRINCE'S BIEBER DICTIONARY OF LEGAL ABBREVIATIONS (6 Ed.)(New York: William S. Hein & Co, 2009)

RECOMMENDED LAW BOOKS (2. Ed.) (Ed. James A. Mcdermott) (Illinois, Chicago: Committee On Business Law Libraries, Section Of Corporation, Banking And Business Law, American Bar Association, 1986) -- List of recommended law books for libraries -- This list of a few hundred major treatises is divided by topic -- An (Stanford Library) updated version is available on our book's corresponding website at <www.hssph.net/Legalrm>.

RESTATEMENTS OF THE LAW (American Law Institute)

SOLAN, LAWRENCE M., THE LANGUAGE OF STATUTES: LAWS AND THEIR INTERPRETATIONS (Chicago, IL, University of Chicago Press, 2010)

SURRENCY, ERWIN C., A HISTORY OF AMERICAN LAW PUBLISHING (New York: Oceana Publications, 1990).

THE BLUEBOOK: A UNIFORM SYSTEM OF CITATION (19th ed.) (Cambridge, Massachusetts: Harvard Law Review Assn., 2010)

THE FEDERALISTS PAPERS (Ed. By Isaac Kramnick) (Harmondsworth, Middlesex, England: Penguin, 1987)

West's Encyclopedia Of American Law.

WILSON'S INDEX TO LEGAL PERIODICALS AND BOOKS (Available in Print and Online in Wilsonweb At <Www.Wilsonweb.Com>).

WITKIN'S SUMMARY OF CALIFORNIA LAW (10th ed.)(San Francisco: ThomsonWest, 2005)

5.10.2. Articles

Abramson, Jill, John Kennedy and Ellen Joan Pollock, *Inside the West Empire*, THE AMERICAN LAWYER, October 1983, p. 90 - This article tells the story of West Publishing Company from its founding and explains how the company wooed the judiciary to become the legal research empire that it is today.

Beal, Dave, *Thomson Reuters' Brain*, TWIN CITIES BUSINESS, November 2009, p. 38 - Continues the story of West Publishing and discusses its recent technological advances and the role of the company's information scientists.

Dorsey, Tobias A., *Some Reflections on Not Reading the Statutes*, 10 GREEN BAG 2D 283 (2007)

Ehrlich, Jeffrey Isaac, *Westlaw's new upgrade* – WESTLAW NEXT: REPORT OF AN EARLY ADOPTER, PLAINTIFF, May 2010, p. 30.

How Laws Are Made (Ben's Guide to U.S. Government) - The graphic illustration at <http://bensguide.gpo.gov/9-12/lawmaking/index.html> might from a non-US perspective: be of value.

iCivics - a web-based education project initiated by Former Justice Sandra Day O'Connor so students can get the information and tools they need for civic participation, and give teachers better materials at <www.icivics.org/teachers/subjects (This page can be useful for non-American to learn about the basics on the US 3 branches).

Johnson, Charles W., How Our Laws are Made (Revised and Updated)(U.S. House of Representatives) at

<http://frwebgate.access.gpo.gov/cgi-bin/getdoc.cgi?dbname=105_cong_documents&docid=f:sd014.pdf>.

Kerr, Owen, *How to Read a Judicial Opinion: A Guide for New Law Students*, Available at: <http://volokh.com/files/howtoreadv2.pdf>.

Law.gov: Legal Documents for the People, STANFORD LAWYER, Fall 2010, p. 2.

Lee, Jootaek, *Introducing and Integrating Free Internet Legal Research into the Classroom*, UNIVERSITY OF MIAMI LEGAL STUDIES RESEARCH PAPER NO. 2010-05, available at <http://papers.ssrn.com/sol3/papers.cfm?abstract_id=1509673>. - This useful article on the pros and cons of free Internet legal research also explains and cites to cases where lawyers have been subjected to court sanctions for failure to Shepardize.

McDade, *Legislative history is easy to find with various databases*, STUDENT LAWYER, December 2006, p. 10.

Patrick, Jeremy J., *Beyond Case Reporters: Using Newspapers to Supplement the Legal-Historical Record* (June 16, 2010). Available at SSRN:

<http://ssrn.com/abstract=1625978>.

Segal, David, *Is Law School a Losing Game*, NEW YORK TIMES, Sunday, January 9, 2011, p. WK1 - This lengthy report on the state of the legal profession documents the large debts and difficult job market today's law students are facing and the growing supply demand imbalance. According to the article, "Since 2008, some 15,000 attorney and legal-staff jobs at large firms have vanished, according to a Northwestern Law study. Associates have been laid off, partners nudged out the door and recruitment programs have been scaled back or eliminated." Meanwhile, "About 43,000 J.D.'s were handed out in 2009, 11 percent more than a decade earlier, and the number of law schools keeps rising -- nine new ones in the last 10 years, and five more seeking approval to open in the future."

Sloan, Karen, *Judges Are Paying More Attention to Law Review Articles, Study Finds*, NEW YORK LAW JOURNAL, Tuesday, August 3, 2010, p. 6

Tress, Will, *Lost Laws: What We Can't Find in the United States Code*, 40 GOLDEN GATE UNIVERSITY LAW REVIEW 130 (2010) - This article traces the development of the United States Code, explains the positive law titles, the use of "riders," the function of the Office of Law Revision Counsel, problems with the U.S. Code and proposed solutions.

Whisner, Mary, *The United States Code, Prima Facie Evidence, and Positive Law*, 101 LAW LIBRARY JOURNAL 545 (2009) - The author examines the history of the U.S. Code, explains why it is only "prima facie evidence of the law," and discusses the efforts of the Office of the Law Revision Counsel to enact Code titles into positive laws. The author also writes about the addition of additional titles to the United States Code.

Whisner, Mary, *Enact Locally*, 102 LAW LIBRARY JOURNAL 497 (2010) - In this article the author discusses the wide range of topics that can be covered by local law. The Green Bag recently included Mary Whisner's "Enact Locally" in its list of "Our "Exemplary Legal Writing 2010" honorees.' See: <http://www.greenbag.org/> and <http://www.aallnet.org/products/pub_llj_v102n03/2010-27.pdf>.

5.11. Various Exercises (updates at corresponding website)

Listed below are legal research exercises that cover all of the major topics covered in Chapter 5. Students should approach these exercises with the legal research flowchart as guide (Table 8). Legal research instructors may request an answer key and lecture notes for each exercise by contacting the authors in writing.

5.11.1. Exercise 1

You are an attorney representing a magazine publisher. In order for your client to receive special mailing rates, she must provide information to the federal government, including the circulation numbers for her magazine. She believes that this is a violation of her constitutional rights. Please research this issue and compose an e-mail to your client advising her on her rights and responsibilities here.

5.11.2. Exercise 2

Marian the Librarian just bought a house in Palo Alto, California. Marian first saw the house at an open house and the real estate agent who was showing the house, David Kuokoo, told Marian that the house was in "move-in condition." After buying the house and moving in, Marian found that there was damage to the house's foundation from last year's heavy rains. Marian wants advice on what claims, if any, she might be able to make against Kuokoo. Research this issue and write an e-mail advising Marian on her possible claims and remedies.

5.11.3. Exercise 3

Your client, Paolo Pasticiotti, is a law librarian at a major law school in Northern California. Over the past few years there has been continuous construction outside Paolo's window with the law school's construction of new residence halls and a faculty office building. Students have complained to Paolo that the almost constant beep-beep-beep of the construction trucks when they are in reverse gear is adversely affecting their studying in the library. Paolo wants to take this up with the university project managers but before he does he needs to know what the law, if any, that requires all this beeping. Paolo asks you to research this and wants to know is it federal law, state law, both, neither? Please research this issue and compose an e-mail to Paolo with your findings.

5.11.4. Exercise 4

In addition to these three research exercises, it is sometimes useful to begin the class with an ungraded legal research assessment exercise. Below is a True/False exercise that has been used with the advanced legal research class at Stanford. These questions reflect a complexity that may not be apparent. Legal research instructors may obtain the answer key and notes by contacting the authors in writing.

1. It is possible to Shepardize law review articles.
2. LexisNexis has an index feature in its United States Code Anno-

tated database.

3. Westlaw has an index in its United States Code Service database.
4. The legal abbreviation ALR stands for Alabama Law Review.
5. The highest court of every United States state is called the state Supreme Court.
6. Law.gov is a website where you can find all primary United States law.
7. All opinions of the United States Supreme Court are available online for free.
8. All opinions of the California Supreme Court are available online for free.
9. Regulations from Vermont state agencies are available online for free.
10. The United States Code Annotated is an official publication.
11. All federal agency rules are found in the Code of Federal Regulations.
12. "Secondary first" is a good legal research mantra.

CHAPTER 6

England Resources – Common Law

The United Kingdom (formally the "United Kingdom of Great Britain and Northern Ireland") is divided into the following three legal jurisdictions:

- England and Wales
- Scotland
- North Ireland

A detailed description of the courts in the United Kingdom can be found at Justis.com.[1]

A Guide to the United Kingdom Legal System can be found at GlobaLex.[2]

In the United Kingdom, statutory law increasingly overrides Common Law traditions of judicial law-making, while on the continent, legal theory increasingly acknowledges the fact and necessity of judicial precedent and law-making. Important areas of the law are unified under international treaties. British judges faithfully implement European Union law that is based primarily on Civil Law notions.[3]

The U.K.does not have a constitution, however England has the so-called "Magna Carta Libertatum" ("Great Charter of Freedoms") of 1215, which led to the rule of constitutional law today. It influenced many common law and other documents, such as the United States Constitution and Bill of Rights, and is considered one of the most important legal documents in the history of democracy.

[1] <www.justis.com/support/faq-courts.aspx#ca> .

[2] Sarah Carter & Hester Swift, *A Guide to the UK Legal System, GlobaLex* at <www.nyulawglobal.org/globalex/United_Kingdom1.htm>.

[3] Herbert Hausmaninger, THE AUSTRIAN LEGAL SYSTEM 320 (Vienna: Manzsche Verlags- und Universitätsbuchhandlung, 2003).

The following will deal with England and Wales.

6.1. The Executive & the Cabinet

In the United Kingdom, the executive authority lies with the monarch. This authority is exercised only by, or on the advice of, the Prime Minister and the Cabinet, which is the supreme decision-making committee of the Government and consists of the Prime Minister and most senior Minister. The Cabinet members advise the monarch as members of the Privy Council.[4]

According to the unwritten constitution of the United Kingdom, the monarch has the following powers:

- The power to appoint and dismiss the Prime Minister
- The power to appoint and dismiss other Ministers.
- The power to summon, prorogue and dissolve Parliament
- The power to make war and peace
- The power to command the armed forces of the United Kingdom
- The power to regulate the Civil Service
- The power to ratify treaties
- The power to issue passports
- The power to appoint bishops and archbishops of the Church of England
- The power to create peers (both life peers and hereditary peers).

6.2. The Government

The Government of the United Kingdom, officially known as Her Majesty's Government in the United Kingdom, is the central government of the United Kingdom of Great Britain and Northern Ireland. It consists of those Ministers responsible for the conduct of national affairs, also known as the front-bench. Since 1998, certain areas of central government have been devolved to democratically-accountable governments in Scotland, Wales and Northern

[4] A body of advisors to the British Sovereign. Its members are largely senior politicians, who were or are members of either the House of Commons or House of Lords of the United Kingdom of Great Britain and Northern Ireland. The Privy Council was formerly a powerful institution, but its policy decisions are now controlled by one of its committees, the Cabinet of the United Kingdom.

Ireland.[5]

The Government is led by the Prime Minister, who selects the other members of the Government. The Prime Minister and the other most senior Ministers belong to the supreme decision-making committee, known as the Cabinet. A list of the Ministers and their responsibilities is given at

<www.cabinetoffice.gov.uk/media/416777/lmr100701.pdf>.

The Government is dependent on Parliament to make primary legislation, which means that in practice a U.K. government must seek re-election at least every five years. The monarch selects the Prime Minister as the leader of the party most likely to command a majority in Parliament.

Throughout all parts of the United Kingdom there also are up to three layers of elected local authorities (such as County, District and Parish Councils), in some places merged into Unitary Authorities. However, the Government has substantial influence over local and other authorities by financial powers and grants.

6.3. Acts / Laws & Parliament

As there are no legal restraints imposed by a written constitution, Parliament may legislate as it pleases as long as the UK meets its obligations as a Member State of the European Union. It can make or change law, overturn established conventions or turn them into law. It can even legislate to prolong its own life beyond the normal period without consulting the electorate.

Parliament consists of three parts:[6]

- the House of Commons – First Legislative Chamber or Lower House
- the House of Lords – Second Legislative Chamber or Upper House – It includes two different types of members:
    - the Lords Spiritual (the senior bishops of the Church of England) and

[5] The Government, Prime Minister and Cabinet at <www.direct.gov.uk/en/Governmentcitizensandrights/UKgovernment/Centralgovernmentandthemonarchy/DG_073444[11/>.

[6] Source: Parliament: House of Commons and Lords at <www.direct.gov.uk/en/Governmentcitizensandrights/UKgovernment/Parliament/DG_073604>.

  - o the Lords Temporal (members of the Peerage) whose members are not elected by the population at large, but are appointed by the Sovereign on advice of the Prime Minister
- the Sovereign (the head of the Parliament).

Legislation in England comes from:
- Acts of the United Kingdom Parliament
- Statutory instruments (for example, orders or regulations) made by a Minister or by the Queen-in-Council, generally subject either to parliamentary approval (affirmative procedure) or parliamentary disallowance; these are made either under Acts or by royal prerogative.
- European Union - Decisions, directives and regulations of the European Communities.

The stages as for how laws are made in both chambers are as shown in the Table 31 below.[7]

6.4. Courts

By statute, judges are guaranteed judicial independence.[8]

Since 3 April 2006 the Lord Chief Justice has been the overall head of the judiciary. Previously he was second to the Lord Chancellor, but that office lost its judicial functions under the Constitutional Reform Act 2005. The Lord Chief Justice is also the head of the Criminal Division of the Court of Appeal.

Although the Lord Chancellor is no longer a judge, he still exercises disciplinary authority over the judges, jointly with the Lord Chief Justice. He also has a role in appointing judges.

The judges of the Supreme Court of the United Kingdom are known as Justices of the Supreme Court, and they are also Privy Counselors.

> Before the creation of the Supreme Court, the highest court in England, Wales and Northern Ireland (and the highest court in civil matters in Scotland) was the Judicial Committee of the House of Lords, in which sat the Law Lords (more properly, the Lords of Appeal in Ordinary).

[7] How laws are made in Parliament at <www.direct.gov.uk/en/Governmentcitizensandrights/UKgovernment/Parliament/DG_073671>.

[8] The Constitutional Reform Act 2005.

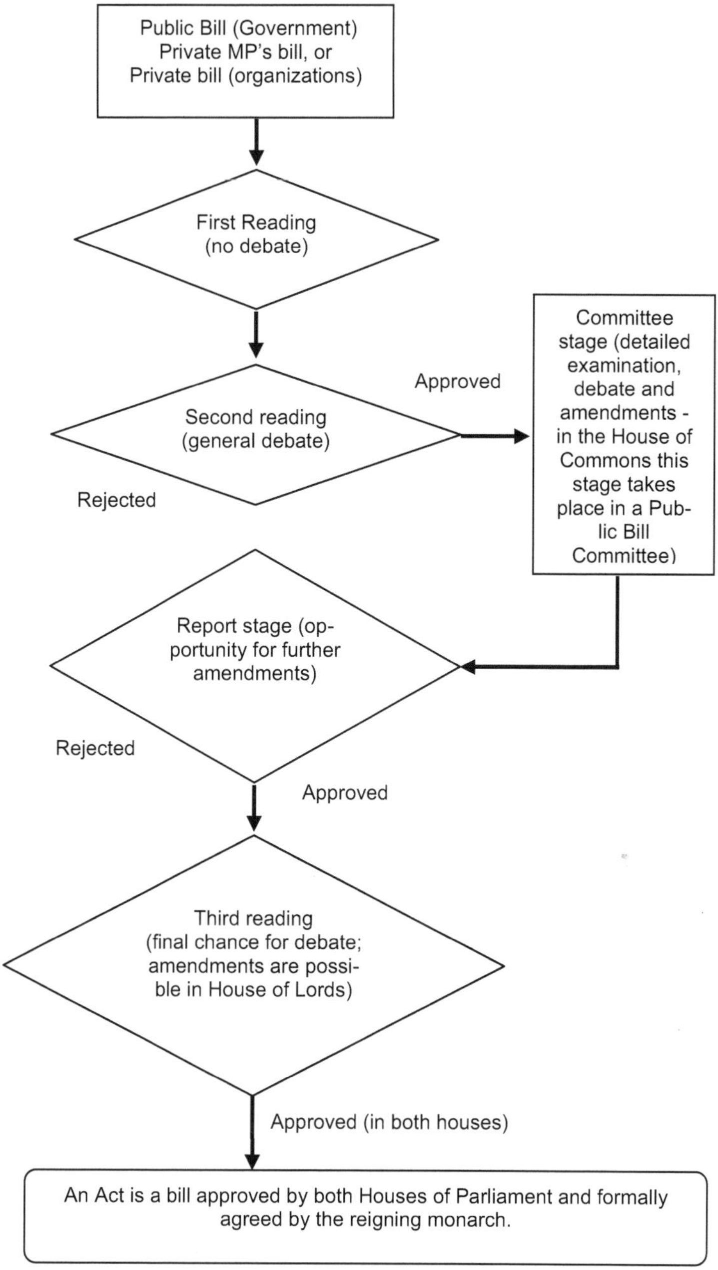

Table 31: How laws are made in both Houses

> As of November 2010, a potential Circuit Judge must satisfy the judicial-appointment eligibility condition (of having been a barrister) for 7 years. A potential District Judge must satisfy the judicial-appointment eligibility condition on a 5-year basis or another type of lawyer, such as a member of the Legal Executives (ILEX Fellows).

The court system in England and Wales consists of the following five levels, with the Supreme Court (until 1 October 2009: the House of Lords) and the Judicial Committee of the Privy Council at the top (see Table 32):[9]

6.5. Citation for case law

The Oxford Bodleian Law Library recommends for neutral citation in England and Wales the following:[10]

- First element: the calendar year, put in square brackets [ ]
- Second element: the abbreviation for the court which heard the case
  - If the citation is to a High Court decision as a whole, the Practice Direction states that the appropriate divisional abbreviation should be placed in ( ) after the case number
  - If the paragraph is from a High Court (EWHC) judgment, the Practice Direction says to drop the (divisional abbreviation) after the case number
- Third element: the unique (case) number - without brackets
- Fourth & last element: any reference to a paragraph is put at the end, with the paragraph number in [ ]

> As of 2009, the following are in use:
>
> UKSC United Kingdom Supreme Court
> UKHL House of Lords (from 2001)
> UKPC Privy Council (from 2001)
> EWCA Civ Court of Appeal Civil Division (from 2001)
> EWCA Crim Court of Appeal Criminal Division (from 2001)
> EWHC High Court (over 2001/2002 see more detail below)

[9] Source Her Majesty's Courts Service: at <www.hmcourts-service.gov.uk/aboutus/structure/index.htm>.

[10] See also: Practice Direction on the form of Judgments, Paragraph Marking and Neutral Citation at <www.hmcourts-service.gov.uk/cms/928.htm> & Practice Direction (Judgments: Neutral Citations) at <www.bodleian.ox.ac.uk/law/guides/citation>.

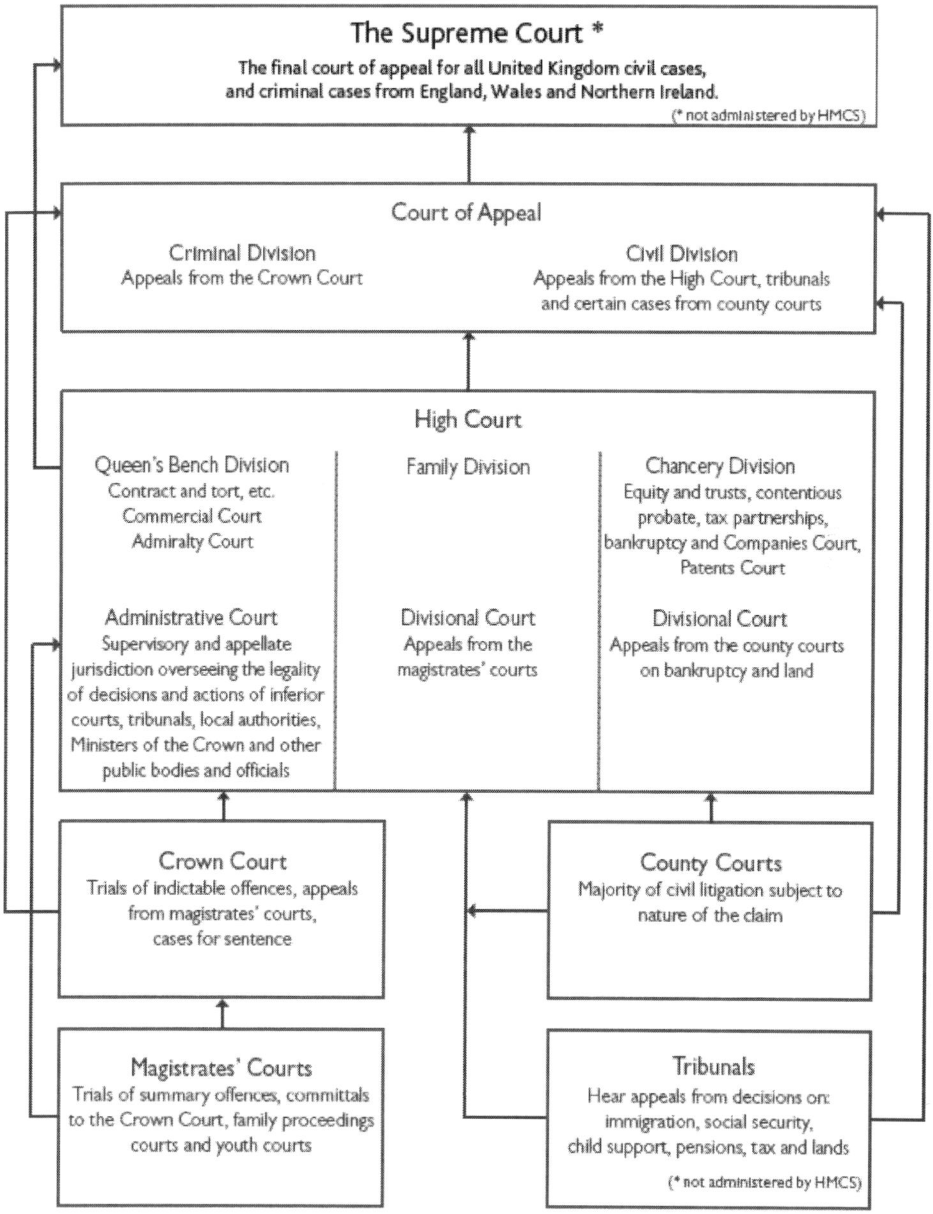

Table 32: Court system in England Wales

The HC divisions are as follows:

Administrative Court (Admin) (from 2001)
Admiralty Court (Admlty) (from 2002)
Chancery Division (Ch) (from 2002)
Commercial Court (Comm) (from 2002)
Family Division (Fam) (from 2002)
Mercantile (Mercantile) (from 2002)
Patents Court (Pat) (from 2002)
Queen's Bench Division (QB) (from 2002)
Supreme Court Costs Office (Costs) (from 2002)
Technology and Construction Court (TCC) (from 2002)

For example:
Radmacher (formerly Granatino) v Granatino [2010] UKSC 42
Ebanks v R [2006] UKPC 11, [2006] 1 WLR 1660
R v H [2003] EWCA Crim 13 at [19]

See also, Oxford Standard for Citation of Legal Authorities at

<www.law.ox.ac.uk/publications/oscola.php> or
<www.oxfordjournals.org/our_journals/oxjlsj/for_authors/oscola_2006.pdf>.

6.6. Sources

6.6.1. Primary Sources

Primary sources in the U.K. are:

- Parliament:
  - Bills - Public Bills are published in two series; House of Commons and House of Lords.
  - Parliamentary Debates - popularly known as Hansard – this gives the official report of what is said in both the House of Commons and the House of Lords.
  - Standing Committee Debates on Bills and Other Standing Committee Debates are in a separate series.
- Statutory Legislation:
  - Public General Acts - The majority of Acts (or Statutes) passed by Parliament are Public General Acts.
  - Local and Personal Acts - These only apply to particular localities or persons.
- Delegated Legislation - This is the term used for the large body of rules, orders, regulations and byelaws created by subordinate bodies

under specific powers delegated to those bodies by Parliament. They are currently known as Statutory Instruments:

  - Statutory Rules and Orders and Statutory Instruments revised to December 31, 1948. (1949-52) London: HMSO
  - Statutory Instruments. (1948-) London: HMSO
  - Halsbury's Statutory Instruments. (1987-) London: Butterworths

- Case Law - A case is only selected for reporting if it raises a point of legal significance. Only a very small proportion of all cases heard and decided by the courts are eventually reported. There is no official series of law reports and there are many different series. Some, such as the All England Law Reports, cover all subjects, whereas others, such as the Criminal Appeal Reports, are restricted to one special area. One major series, The Law Reports, is regarded as having greater authority than others because its reports are checked by the judges before publication.
  A case which is reported in the Law Reports should be cited by its Law Reports reference in preference to any other, e.g.:
  - All England Law Reports. (1936-) London: Butterworths
  - The Times Law Reports. (1884-1952, 1963-) London: The Times
  - Weekly Law Reports. (1953-) London: Incorporated Council
- Laws from the European Union (and in the future, perhaps, the European Convention on Human Rights) are also authoritative sources.

6.6.2. Secondary Sources

Among existing secondary sources can be mentioned:

- Textbooks
- Journals
- Legal Dictionaries
- Major Legal Reference Works e.g. Halsbury's Laws of England 4th ed. (1973-1987) London -- Halsbury's Laws of England is an updated/annotated, encyclopedic treatise on the laws of England published by LexisNexis Butterworths. It includes restatements of the common law with remarks to the relevant judicial authority and the statutory law, which has in many cases codified, modified or supple-

mented common law.[11]

- Butterworths & The Digest: Annotated British, Commonwealth and European Cases. (1971-) London: Butterworths

6.7. Where to find resources

- UKSC decides cases are available from <www.supremecourt.gov.uk/decided-cases/index.html> & <www.lawreports.co.uk/HouseofLords/decisions.htm>.
- Many UK Cases can be found from the British and Irish Legal Information Institute's website. (BAILII) <www.bailii.org/databases.html>.[12] Cases are included in the Law Reports published by the Incorporated Council of Law Reporting at <www.lawreports.co.uk/Publications/newlr.htm>.[13]
- UK Statutes can be found at the UK Statute Law Database (SLD) is the official revised edition of the primary legislation of the United Kingdom made available online.at <www.statutelaw.gov.uk/> (search: Title, Year, Number, Legislation Type).
- The Oxford Bodleian Law Library has a list with links to free online resources at <www.bodleian.ox.ac.uk/law/guides/uk>.
- Oxford Standard for Citation of Legal Authorities at <www.law.ox.ac.uk/publications/oscola.php> or <www.oxfordjournals.org/our_journals/oxjlsj/for_authors/oscola_2006.pdf>.
- UK Office of the European Parliament at <www.europarl.org.uk/>.
- European Commission Representation in the United Kingdom at <http://ec.europa.eu/unitedkingdom/>.
- United Kingdom E.U. publications at <http://ec.europa.eu/unitedkingdom/information/publications/index_en.htm>.

[11] <www1.lexisnexis.co.uk/HSSI/index.htm> & <www1.lexisnexis.co.uk/HSSI/faq.htm> The treatise is named for its original editor and compiler, the Earl of Halsbury. It contains a total of fifty-six volumes.

[12] UK Cases at British and Irish Legal Information Institute (BAILII) <www.bailii.org/databases.html>.

[13] How courts work, see <www.direct.gov.uk/en/CrimeJusticeAndTheLaw/Goingtocourt/DG_181615>.

6.8. Further Reading (updates at corresponding website)

The URL for the corresponding website is <www.hssph.net/legalrm> with a full alphabetic bibliography.

Baker, Lord Justice Scott, *Middle Temple, The Inns of Court and the Present Structure of the English Legal System*, 31 OKLAHOMA CITY UNIVERSITY LAW REVIEW 81 (2006)

Carter, Sarah & Hester Swift, *A Guide to the UK Legal System*, GlobaLex at <www.nyulawglobal.org/globalex/United_Kingdom1.htm>.

Directgov, which is the U.K. government's digital service for in the population of England and Wales, allows one to browse as to various subject matters. It delivers information and practical advice about public services, bringing them all together in one place <www.direct.gov.uk/en/SiteInformation/DG_4004497>.

Justis FAQs – Courts in the United Kingdom (Justis Publishing Ltd.) at

<http://www.justis.com/support/faq-courts.aspx>

MORRIS L. COHEN, ROBERT C. BERRING & KENT C. OLSON, HOW TO FIND THE LAW (Chapter 16 - English and Commonwealth Materials)(9. ed.)(St. Paul, Minn.: West, 1989)

CHAPTER 7

Methods in Europe - A Civil Law Method

7.1. Civil Law Basics for Americans

This chapter and the following can from the perspective of an American reader be taken as an example of how a lecturebook/textbook is written per currently prevailing European culture.

Furthermore, this chapter has - because of page limitations (printing costs) - to be somewhat general in style and content, as the only other alterative would be to provide a chapter for each of the 47 countries in Continental Europe.

The chapter provides necessary basic skills to enable the study of the law of a Civil Law country – that is, in its own environment.

Keep in mind the information on differences given in Chapter One.

Also, see Chapter 3 on the necessary requirements for being able to study a foreign country's law.

For a person who is brought up with and taught Common Law, studying the law of a Civil Law country is somewhat like coming to a whole new world.

Research Tip #7.1

An American lawyer studying the law of a country on the European continent has to disregard nearly everything he or she has been taught on Common Law and focus on trying to feel at home on a completely different planet.

It is not wholly fallacious to explain law in Civil Law countries by saying that the legislator enacts a statute, scholars discover its meaning, and judges, assisted by their conclusions, give the statute a precise application through their decisions. A Civil Law lawyer ("jurist") will consult works of scholars if these faithfully describe the rule in a statute, and decisions of judges, because these are instances in which this rule has been enforced.[1] However, it is very important to notice that courts in continental Europe do not (really – see on exceptions, further in section 3.3.3.2 and 3.3.4.2.) "make" law.[2]

Civil Law is today the dominant legal tradition in most of Europe,[3] all of Central and South America, many parts of Asia and Africa, and even a few enclaves in the Common Law world (that is, the American State of Louisiana and Territory of Puerto Rico, the Canadian Province of Quebec, and Scotland[4]).

Research Tip #7.2
English words and terms are often used with different meanings in continental Europe as opposed to in the U.S.[5]

The following subsections (7.1.1. – 7.1.9.) will try to give the American lawyer an idea of the mindset of a European continental lawyer and a little about the basic legal learning of such an individual.

The rest of the chapter seeks to explain how a Civil Law[6] lawyer does le-

[1] Rodolfo Sacco, *Legal Formants, A Dynamic Approach to Comparative Law* (Installment I of II), 39 AM. J. COMP. L. 1, 21-22, 24 (1991) [hereinafter SACCO I].

[2] However, even in America, at least one famous U.S. Supreme Court Justice, Felix Frankfurter has claimed that in reality the U.S. Supreme Court no longer makes Common Law, as virtually all cases since 1947 have rested on statutory grounds. Felix Frankfurter, *Some Reflections on Reading of Statutes*, 47 COLUM. L. REV. 527 (May 1947).

[3] Except England, Wales & Northern Ireland (which have a form of Common Law distinctive from U.S. Common Law), but including Ireland and Scotland

[4] Scottish law is a hybrid of Civil (Romanistic Legal Family) Law and Common Law elements.

[5] A project for a Dictionary with Civil Law Glossary and Common Law Glossary can be found at <http://civillawdictionary.pbwiki.com>. Also, the Internet Public Library has posted translation-dictionaries that, given a word in one language, will show the identical or related word in another language. See <www.ipl.org/div/subject/browse/ref28.80.00>.

[6] The term "civil law" refers to the Roman law based tradition of continental Europe, from where it has spread to all parts of the globe. Herbert Hausmaninger, THE AUSTRIAN LEGAL SYSTEM 299 (Vienna: Manzsche Verlags- und Universitätsbuchhandlung) [hereinafter HAUSMANINGER].

gal research and to go over the methods he or she uses.[7]

Research Tip #7.3
Beware that legal research approaches in Civil Law vary by country and by topic, and no single procedure will work for all purposes.

7.1.1. Introduction

An American doing research on the law of a Civil Law country must be aware of the major differences between the Civil and Common Law systems, and the effect of these differences on how legal problems are viewed and how research is conducted. See Table 1: Comparison between Common Law and Civil Law thinking, above in Chapter 1.

Any sophisticated comparative[8] lawyer in both the Civil Law and Common Law systems has long ago abandoned discussions of relative superiority or inferiority of the two.[9]

A rule of law may be worked out either by developing the consequences that it involves (American scholars' preference), or by developing the wider principles that it presupposes (the Civil Law scholars' preference).[10]

The American scholar will be astonished by the lack of footnotes/endnotes and citations (and lack of exact page or "pinpoint cite" references)[11] in European scholars' work on the scholarship of others and on court decisions. In Europe, many regard large amounts of footnotes as a plague. As a result, there will often only be a bibliography in the back of the continental European book or article, without page references – and there will hardly ever be a case list. As for court decisions, references will only be made in footnotes,

[7] "Legal method" is the line of action the courts and any other, who have to decide a legal question must use. Jens Evald, RETSKILDERNE OG DEN JURIDISKE METODE 129 [Source of Law and the Legal Method] (2nd. ed.) (Copenhagen: DJØF Publishing, 2000).

[8] Modern comparative law is a critical method of legal science … a discipline where a detailed method cannot be laid down in advance, K. Zweigert & H.Kötz, INTRODUCTION TO COMPARATIVE LAW 33, 251 (3rd ed.)(Tony Weir trans., Clarendon Press, Oxford 1998) [hereinafter ZWEIGERT]. See further below Chapter 7.

[9] John Henry Merryman, THE CIVIL LAW TRADITION: AN INTRODUCTION TO THE LEGAL SYSTEMS OF WESTERN EUROPE AND LATIN AMERICA 3 (2nd ed.) (Stanford, California: Stanford University Press, 1985) [hereinafter MERRYMAN].

[10] MERRYMAN *supra* note 9 at 67 quoting German legal scientist Rudolph Sohm.

[11] In the U.S., "the scholarly backbone of any law review article are the footnotes." Dana Neacşu, *Google, Legal Citations, and Electronic Fickleness: Legal Scholarship in the Digital Environment* at 1 (Social Science Research Network, June 2007). Available at SSRN: <http://ssrn.com/abstract=991190>.

without specific-page citations (and frequently lacking mention of the names of the parties – with only the case reporter, year and first page given).

To the lawyer from a Common Law country, Civil Law is quite strange. It has different legal institutions, procedures, and traditions, and has little interest in precedents and types of cases. The continental lawyer thinks systematically, or in the abstract, and finds – as an absolute necessity, in any functioning legal system – need for a civil act or code, a commercial act or code, a act or code of civil procedure, and an integrated structure of legal concepts rationally ordered.

Thorough research on a foreign[12] law issue can only be undertaken in the language of the jurisdiction. In researching the law of Civil Law countries, lawyers limited to English-language[13] material will be seriously handicapped.[14] However, the increasing availability of "secondary" sources in English, as well as sometimes unofficial translations of parts from information from the country or countries in question, allows quite effective preliminary study of many foreign legal issues. Such study may help the American lawyer to determine the general nature of a problem, and can facilitate communication with any foreign law specialist who may be called upon to assist. Nevertheless, any serious legal problem involving another jurisdiction will require consultation with a lawyer trained (and licensed) in that jurisdiction. This in turn implies that in training future lawyers, each law school (whether in the United States or Europe) should strive to include in its faculty diverse scholars brought up in different legal systems from that of the country of the law school.[15]

During the 17th and 18th centuries, so-called "enlightened periods" in

[12] "Foreign law" here means the domestic law of another national jurisdiction.

[13] It is extremely costly to make authorized translations. The European Commission's Directorate-General for Translation (DGT) is the largest translation service in the world. Located in Brussels and Luxembourg, it has a permanent staff of some 1 750 linguists and 600 support staff. The DGT works only for the Directorates-General and Services of the Commission as each EU institution has its own translation service. See Translation tools and workflow <http://ec.europa.eu/dgs/translation/bookshelf/tools_and_workflow_en.pdf>. See also E.U. Directorate General for Interpretation (DG Interpretation (formerly known as SCIC) <http://scic.cec.eu.int/europa/jcms/j_8/home>.

[14] American law students are frequently, surprised by the lack of foreign primary sources published in English. They need to learn that English is for most of the world not the first language – and thus not the official language used for publication. Thus, American students have – as students of the rest of the world – to learn foreign languages.

[15] It is not just the law courses that are changing. It is also the faculty, *ABA Journal*, July 2007, page 64.

Europe, many continental countries undertook comprehensive and systematic reorganizations of their laws. The resulting legal codifications were "drafted primarily not by legal elites, such as academic scholars or judges, but by philosophically and politically educated representatives of the administration."[16]

Today in Europe – and in the E.U. – nearly all suggestions for amendments of existing legislation or creation of new acts are drafted by government administrators, not by commissions of scholars and other legal experts. However, the latter often will provide white papers[17] with recommendations, but even here usually only after having been appointed by a minister of the particular portfolio and having been given a task-list. Overall, most legislative bills in Europe nowadays come from government proposals, although they can still also come from members of parliament and parliamentary committees.

In continental Europe, law and its enforcement are strictly separated. Accordingly, European lawyers can focus on the law regardless of its enforcement. In contrast, in the Common Law tradition, the conflation of the law of rights and the law of remedies adds enforcement as a necessary element.[18]

Americans talk about government (separate from society), whereas Europeans talk about "the state." In Europe, the debate does not deal with a distinction between public and private spheres and its impact on law, but with the distinction between private and public law.[19]

[16] Ralf Michaels & Nils Jansen, *Private Law and the State: Comparative Perceptions and Historical Observations*, in Rabels Zeitschrift Für Ausländisches Und Internationales Privatrecht, vol. 71, no. 2, 2007 p. 32. [hereinafter MICHAELS-I] However, only to the extent that the particular country belongs to the Germanic Legal Family (see discussion in Chapter 6 below) will Roman law have played an important role, otherwise *idem* at 33. In contrast to European codifications, the American Restatements were initiated as a non-state, professional enterprise and have remained as such.

[17] A white paper is used in many countries and is an official report setting out government policy on an issue to be voted on by the country's parliament. Compare this with "green paper," which is also an "official," heavily researched report on a topic, or a government document that proposes and invites discussion on approaches to a problem (and may lead to issuance of a white paper).

[18] Ralf Michaels & Nils Jansen, *Private Law Beyond the State? Europeanization, Globalization, Privatization*, 54 AM. J. COMP. L. 843, 853 (Fall 2006) [hereinafter MICHAELS-II].

[19] In the United States, the public/private distinction is an illusion, *idem* 853, 857, 858. In Europe, private law is that part of a legal system that deals with the relationships between natural and artificial persons (that is, individuals, business entities, non-profit organizations). It is to be distinguished from public law, which deals with relationships between natural and artificial persons and the state as the other party.

Research Tip #7.4

A characteristic of Civil Law is that (a) public law and (b) private law are treated as inherently different and clearly distinguishable.[20] Furthermore, the term "private law" has a different meaning in European and in American law[21] in general, and the place of private law within each differs.

Thus, The Anglo-American lawyer should be aware of the continental European division between private law in the narrow sense and commercial law, which the Romanistic and Germanic legal families (except Switzerland and Italy) still recognize by having different codes.[22] The areas in European private law are:

- Civil law[23]
- The law of obligations, including Contract law
- Tort law
- Property law
- Family law family-related issues and domestic relations including, but not limited to marriage, civil unions, divorce, spousal abuse, child custody and visitation, property, alimony, and child support awards, as well as child abuse issues, and adoption.
- Succession law
- Labor law
- Commercial law
- Corporations law
- Competition law[24] (including U.S. antitrust law)

Public law in Civil Law has two components: constitutional law (the law by which the governmental structure is made up) and administrative law (the law governing the public administration and its relations with private indi-

[20] MERRYMAN *supra* note 9 at 63.

[21] In the U.S.: The body of law that concerns individual people and their property and relationships. See BLACK'S LAW DICTIONARY (8th ed.) (St. Paul: West. 2004).

[22] Grossly simplified, in Germany, the core of the law is private and the rest is contingent politics; in the U.S., the core of the law is public (regulatory) law and the rest is contingent private ordering, MICHAELS-II *supra* note 18, at 843, 852, 847-851 and footnote 9.

[23] The area of law in Civil Law countries governing relations between private individuals.

[24] In Europe, competition law covers both what in the U.S. is called antitrust law and also the law on pricing and profits (from a pure social and public economic perspective). Competition law covers issues of monopoly and trade practices generally as well.

viduals).

In private relations, public and private parties are equal. In public legal relations, the state is a party and superior to the private individual.

The Civil Law legal technique is directed primarily to interpreting statutory texts or analyzing concrete problems so as to "fit them into the system" conceptually.[25] Instead of searching for precedents in factually similar judicial decisions, a Civil Law lawyer looks first to the abstract provisions of the code for a logical and appropriate legal principle. Among the very helpful sources are extensive article-by-article commentaries on each phrase, paragraph or article of an act or code. These are mostly written by the civil servants of the government ministry that introduced the bill, a judge with specialty in the code in question, or another highly regarded specialists.

Secondary sources – in the Civil Law sense - are the government minister's or secretary's commentaries to the bill when introduced in parliament and officially issued expert white papers upon which the bill was drafted.[26]

The next group in the hierarchy of "law-source" are court decisions, which determine whether the given facts allow the use of an article of a code or act and what result the use of the statute implies – thus determining the decision of the court. However, court decisions in Civil Law countries usually do not have any impact or lawmaking validity (no stare decisis effect).

In those countries having a Parliamentary Ombudsman,[27] statements from that independent official are of particular relevance in the area of administrative law.

In addition to the formal sources of the Civil Law, there is an overlay of concepts and principles - primarily derived from legal scholarship.

Although scholarly articles can provide the researcher some valuable input, they have far from the degree of impact on legislation and court decisions that articles in American law reviews from experts can have in the U.S.

[25] ZWEIGERT *supra* note 8 at 181.

[26] One commentator has asserted that the European teacher-scholar is the real protagonist of the Civil Law tradition, and that the Civil Law is a law of professors. MERRYMAN *supra* note 9 at 68 and footnote 46 below. However, drafts to bills are made by civil servants working in the ministry departments and the European Unions' Commission.

[27] An ombudsman (sometimes named "Parliamentary Commissioner, see ") is an official (usually appointed by the government or by parliament), who is charged with representing the interests of the public by investigating and addressing complaints reported by individual citizens. Ombudsman exist in: Australia, Bulgaria, Croatia, Czech Republic, Cyprus, Denmark, Estonia, European Union, France, Finland, Greece, Iceland, India, Ireland, Israel, Italy, Macedonia, Netherlands, New Zealand, Norway, Philippines, Poland, Portugal, Sweden..

(as references in court decisions or as incentives for a legislative bills, etc.). This is so even though in Europe professors, judges and practitioners – not students – are the editors of law reviews/journals, of which there usually exist only one or two for the whole country.

It is a fundamental mistake to claim, as some American hornbooks on legal research do, that once one has identified the primary and secondary sources of European law that might be relevant the research proceeds much as it would for a problem of U.S. law.[28] This is because the distinction in the U.S. of "primary" and "secondary" sources is differently from the use in Civil Law (where a distinction rather follows by the terms "hard" and "soft" law, see further Chapter 3, sections 3.1.1.1. & 3.3. above). Case law has extreme little impact in Europe.

An American legal researcher should be extremely cautious about using what would typically be his or her normal method of relying primarily on what is stated on a statute's face, as Civil Law lawyers are brought up in a system where statutes have been enacted based on abstract thinking and thus require considering whether interpretations should be made.

Using and interpreting Civil Law codes may necessitate understanding their underlying philosophies. For instance, the Code Civile of France is based on revolutionary thinking and a desire for wholesale change from the past, whereas the German Code is based on a historical study of the past and a desire to codify previous "law."

The Civil Law legal scholar is more interested in developing and elaborating a theoretical "scientific" structure than he is in solving concrete problems. The work of "legal science" is carried on according to the methods of traditional formal logic. Intuition and the subconscious, despite their powerful influence on human affairs, are excluded from this process ("logically formal rationalism"[29]). Thus, insight, history,[30] and theories of the social sciences,

[28] J.D.S. Armstrong & Christopher A. Knott, WHERE THE LAW IS: AN INTRODUCTION TO ADVANCED LEGAL RESEARCH 211 (2nd ed.) (St. Paul: West, 2006).

[29] Max Weber, WIRTSCHAFT UND GESELLSCHAFT; GRUNDRISS DER VERSTEHENDEN SOZIOLOGIE. MIT EINEM ANHANG; DIE RATIONALEN UND SOZIOLOGISCHEN GRUNDLAGEN DER MUSIK (4 ed. ew hrsg. Aufl., besorgt von Johannes Winckelmann, Tübingen 1956); Guenther Roth & Claus Wittich, eds. Max Weber, ECONOMY AND SOCIETY: AN OUTLINE OF INTERPRETIVE SOCIOLOGY, (trans. Ephraim Fischoff [and others], New York: Bedminster Press, 1968). MERRYMAN *supra* note 9 at 64.

[30] A wealth of information about the history of Europe and its institutions since 1945 is available from European NAvigator (ENA) - an educational platform that focuses particularly on the development of a united Europe. ENA is available in English, French, German and Spanish, though some documents are available in other languages at

for example, are excluded as non-legal.[31] However, there is a growing trend away from this point of view.

In Europe today, Civil Law and Common Law show some signs of convergence. In the United Kingdom, statutory law increasingly overrides traditions of judicial law-making, while on the continent, legal theory increasingly acknowledges the fact and necessity of judicial precedent and law-making. Important areas of the law have also been unified under international treaties. British judges faithfully implement European Union law that is based primarily on Civil Law notions. The Court of Justice of the E.U. creatively applies principles from both legal worlds. Yet, despite refreshing input from the Common Law, the dominant legal culture of the European Union and the emerging *ius commune Europaeum*[32] remain very much in the Civil Law tradition.[33]

7.1.1.1. Some terms for the American Student/Scholar to keep in mind

This subsection gives only a broad overview of some terms that will be dealt with more in the following sections, but that the American should be "on guard for."

In Civil Law countries, law students do not undertake research "projects." Instead they perform "scientific" studies and research. Only scholars do legal research projects, and only after they have gained funding for specific projects. In Civil Law countries, students study at universities, not at law schools.

Courses on "legal research" in Europe are not about how and where to find "the law" physically or online. Broadly stated, the legal research courses in Europe deal with the theoretical (scientific) question of "what is law (in the European sense)" and how to (correctly) interpret "the law." These are the

<www.ena.lu>. Using the site is free, although the documents are protected by copyright. ENA is developed by the CVCE (Centre Virtuel de la Connaissance sur l'Europe - Virtual Resource Centre for Knowledge about Europe), a Luxembourg-based public undertaking that is actively supported by the Ministry of Culture, Higher Education and Research.

[31] MERRYMAN *supra* note 9 at 65.

[32] See Glossary in Appendix 1.

[33] HAUSMANINGER *supra* note 6 at 320.

courses taught by law professors and the issue of where physically to find the law is not taught. Providers such as Westlaw and LexisNexis do not offer courses for students outside the U.S. At many universities, only librarians and law professors have access to online databases; therefore, students are obliged to ask a librarian to find articles for them. Only, at a few universities outside the U.S. do students have access to Westlaw and/or LexisNexis – often with only single account-access for all students.

Thus, legal research in the American sense are left to the librarian by most Civil Law scholars, that is, the finding of books and articles on a special subject. Once these are collected by the law/reference librarian, the lawyer/scholar in Europe will examine them and use the "scientific legal method" skills he/she was taught by the law professor while studying law at a Civil Law university.

The scientific legal method deals in broad terms with

- what is the law on a special issue,
- how the law-material is to be interprctatcd and
- which few court decisions are classified as precedent (and therefore to be considered important) – in the Civil Law sense — as opposed to all other (normal) court decisions that have no relevance for a Civil Law lawyer and the courts.

The Civil Law lawyer uses the term "sources of law" in two different ways.[34] He/she uses the term "source of law" and in plural: "sources of law" as in the U.S. meaning,[35] that is, something (such as a constitution, treaty, statute, or custom) that provides authority for legislation and for judicial decisions; a point of origin for law or legal analysis.

However, he/she also employs the term in a way that it would be more

[34] It is also termed *fons juris*, see further footnote 6 in Chapter 1.

[35] In the context of legal research, the term "sources of law" can refer to three different concepts which should be distinguished: (1) it can refer to the origins of legal concepts and ideas; (2) it can refer to governmental institutions that formulate legal rules; and (3) it can refer to the published manifestations of the law. The books, computer databases, microforms, optical disks, and other media that contain legal information are all sources of law. Roy M. Mersky, Donald J. Dunn & J. Myron Jacobstein, FUNDAMENTALS OF LEGAL RESEARCH 1-2 (8th ed.)(University casebook series(New York, N.Y.: Foundation Press, 2002).

proper to call "sources of law" (only with the plural "s"). By this is meant that the Civil Law lawyer uses the phrase as a scientific term, where he/she discusses what should be allowed to be a source of law. For example, should "Custom" or "Legal Cultural Tradition" be allowed to be a "source of law"?

This is bound to be confusing for American readers.

Accordingly, it would seem best to reformulate the latter alternative to "law-foundation-sources" (only with a plural "s"),[36] which term will be used for the reminder of this chapter.

Furthermore, it would seem best to reformulate "sources of law" to "law-source(s),"[37] which term will also be used for the reminder of this chapter.

Civil Law is made by parliament, not by the "government," which latter term is used totally differently from its use in the U.S. The Civil Law term "legislation" refers only to acts by parliament and decrees/rules issued through delegation from such acts. See table below (next page).

Only a few presidents in Civil Law countries have power to issue decrees, as under most Constitutions they are actually not part of the "government" (that is, they are not part of what is called the executive branch in the U.S.). The "government" or "cabinet" is not directly elected by the voters but is a group of people that has the support of the Parliament (or at least is not one voted out by a majority of the parliament members) – the "Parliamentarisme" principle.[38]

Civil Law lawyers do not talk about branches of law. Instead, they talk about the hierarchy of law based on the learning from the basic "legal research-course" on "law-foundation-sources."

[36] The Danish term is "retskilde" and the course is termed "Retskildelære".

[37] The Danish term is "retskildetyper" .

[38] On this, see further Appendix A in Addendum in the back of the book.

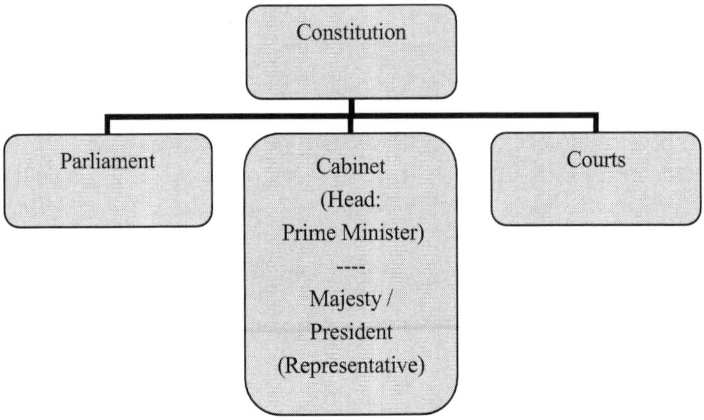

Table 33: Division of power in most European Countries

Moving beyond the "law-foundation-sources" and "law-source(s), another term of special meaning in Europe is the "white paper." It is used in many countries and is an official report setting out government policy on an issue to be voted on by the country's parliament. Compare this with a "green paper," which also is an official report, but one that is usually heavily researched on a specific topic, or else a document that proposes and invites discussion on approaches to a problem (and that may lead in turn to issuance a white paper).

Another point to be emphasized is that Civil Law judges do not fill gaps in "the law" (In the U.S. making law). They are restricted only to filling gaps in a very limited number of areas, that is, to make "close" interpretations of statutory text, or in situations where a statute's text explicitly allows a court to fill in a defined "gap" in the statute or act.

A Civil Law lawyer does not use the term "still good law" (author emphasis). The stare decisis doctrine is not used. Shepardize (citatior) is a word and something a Civil Law lawyer never had heard about during his/her education. In Civil Law one talks about what is "good law", that is, which Acts are the newest and which are the newest cases that is regarded as having precedence. Thus, the Civil Law lawyer do not need to use the word "still" because he/she only is concerned about the "newest," since newest automatically has recalled for ever what was older ("lex posterior principle").

As for the terms as "section," "paragraph," "subsection" and "statute," these are often used as synonyms in Civil Law.

Finally, in Civil Law there is a distinction between "hard" (sometimes termed "binding") and "soft"[39] law. This distinction is sometimes characterized as between "primarily" and "secondary" sources of law; these terms will no doubt be confusing for American readers, as they have a totally different meaning under U.S. Common Law, in which case law is a "primarily source."

7.1.2. State sovereignty

The Member States of the European Union retain full sovereignty. The E.U. is not a true federation like the United States.[40] However, the European Court of Justice has in some decisions expressed another point of view, see below Chapter 3 section 3.3.4.2.

The E.U. does not have any "Constitution" The so-called "E.U. Constitution," which was rejected by some Member States' citizens in referendums, was nothing more than a compilation of previous E.U. treaties with some amendments. Therefore, in terms of public international law, the E.U. Constitution was a treaty between sovereign states.

7.1.3. The European Continental Court System

Overall, the European Civil Law counties' court systems consist of a three-tiered framework, in which the judiciary in overall does not make law, and where appeals only go upwards, that is, the U.S. practice of case remands (sent back to the lower court) is not an option.

Appeals courts in Civil Law countries are often allowed to consider the whole case before them de novo, finding the facts and accepting new evi-

[39] The term "soft law" refers to quasi-legal instruments which do not have any legally binding force, or whose binding force is somewhat "weaker' than the binding force of traditional law. Also, it is associated with international law.

[40] On the so-called "proportionality principle" and "the subsidiary principle," see Chapter 9, section 9.1 and 9.1.3 below.

dence and arguments and pleadings.[41] The reason for allowing this practice during appeals is because a jury system is not used in civil cases in Europe (with extreme exceptions). In other words, in Europe only judges decide civil cases, whether in the first instance or appeal.

Civil Law on the European continent does not entertain the two parallel English court systems of "law" and "equity".[42]

Some states' constitutions in Europe create extra, special court(s), such as an Impeachment Court (to deal with removal of judges or governmental ministers) and/or a Constitutional Court (to deal with interpretation and other significant questions related to the Constitution,[43] including as well as whether or not laws that are challenged are in fact constitutional[44]). Some European countries also have a special highest-level appeal court for administrative justice.[45]

Other states' constitutions allow their supreme courts[46] to decide whether statutes made by their parliaments are unconstitutional.[47] Some European su-

[41] In these instances, new evidence to support the parties' claims and allegations is often submitted by the parties, although entirely new claims and/or allegations require the consent of the other party or the court.

[42] In the United States, this distinction between law and equity remains important in: (a) categorizing and prioritizing rights to property; (b) determining whether the Seventh Amendment's guarantee of a jury trial applies (that is, the determination of a fact that is necessary for the resolution of a "law" claim) or whether the issue can only be decided by a judge (namely, issues of equity); and, (c) the principles that apply to the grant of equitable remedies by the courts. In Common Law legal systems, the law-equity distinction is crucial to understanding almost all important doctrinal areas of law.

[43] Sweden is an interesting case in that it has four Constitutional laws: the Constitution Act, the Act of Succession, the Freedom of the Press Act, and the Freedom of Speech Act, Legal order – Sweden <http://ec.europa.eu/civiljustice/legal_order/legal_order_swe_en.htm>. See unofficial translations into English at <www.servat.unibe.ch/law/icl/sw__indx.html>.

[44] See Albania, Austria, Belgium, Bosnia and Herzegovina, Bulgaria, Croatia, Czech Republic, France, Germany, Greece, Hungary, Italy, Latvia, Lithuania, Republic of Macedonia, Poland, Portugal, Romania, Serbia, Slovakia, Slovenia, and Spain.

[45] France: the Conseil d'État; Finland: Korkein Hallinto-oikeus; Polen: Supreme Administrative Court of the Republic of Poland; Sweden: Högsta Förvaltningsdomstolen.

[46] In various European countries, the court of last resort is called the "Courts of Cassation" rather than the "Supreme Court" (and some of these courts do not deal with constitutional questions): Belgium: Hof van Cassatie (in Flemish) / Cour de cassation (in French); France: the Cour de cassation; Greece: the Areios Pagos; Italy: Corte Suprema di Cassazione; Romania: Înalta Curte de Casație și Justiție.

[47] Since the first Danish Constitution of 1849, the Danish Supreme Court has only once – in the so-called "Tvind Case" – declared a statute unconstitutional. See *Selvejende In-*

preme courts have the privilege to decide which cases should be allowed/ presented before them (thus allowing a second appeal). Other states have a special organ/committee to deal with questions of permission (or "leave").

As for national courts or tribunals of Member States of the E.U., which may be called upon to decide disputes involving E.U. law, they may, and sometimes must, submit questions to the E.U. Court of Justice for a preliminary ruling. The E.U. Court will then provide an interpretation, or review the legality, of a rule of European Community law. Thus, the E.U. Court of Justice works in conjunction with the national courts. But the latter, no matter the high level they may occupy in their own countries, merely apply E.U. law.

In European Civil Law countries, courts typically only employ a jury in the most serious criminal cases, e.g. in cases involving murder. The criminal bench usually consists of a full-time judge together with several lay citizens. Juries are almost never used in civil lawsuits.[48]

Judges in Europe are full-time judge civil servants appointed (not elected) for life (until they reach a mandatory retirement age).[49] Normally, they can only be removed by some kind of an impeachment process.

Some European countries do not allow judges to write dissents. In some countries it is not permitted to indicate with panel decisions which judges were in the majority and which were in the dissent.

During litigation, the parties' attorneys correspond with and meet before a judge or judges in successive court sessions. These sessions normally conclude with a final meeting (sometimes over several days), where counsels present their clients' cases for the court, and where the parties, witnesses, and experts are heard during questioning from counsels and from the judge(s). Counsels finish their presentations by oral pleading and rebuttal.

Due to the dogma of "certainty" in any legal system, it is vital to understand the Civil Law judicial tradition, because the function of the judge within that tradition is to interpret and to apply "the law" as it is technically

stitution Friskolen i Veddinge Bakker v. Undervisningsministeriet [The private independent School in Veddinge Hills v. Danish Ministry of Education], UfR 1999.842 H (Danish Supreme Court, 19 February 1999; docket no. I 295/1998)(holding that §7 of Law no. 506 of 12 June 1996 is illegal as regards the appellant).

[48] In the southern countries of Europe, in criminal cases, a judge will be used to lead the investigation; in northern Europe, in contrast, a special branch of the police will conduct the investigation and present the case before a court.

[49] Only in certain countries do judges come from a self-recruiting professional elite. MICHAEL-I *supra* note 16, at 35.

defined in his or her jurisdiction.[50] A judge under the Civil Law generally does not turn to books and articles by legal scholars or to prior judicial decisions for guidance. Separation of powers between the judicial and legislative branches preserves the latter is lawmaking monopoly. However, some European constitutions allow a judge to declare a statute unconstitutional. Even so, court decisions in Europe are in general not (a source of) law. The doctrine of stare decisis is not followed in Civil Law legal systems, although in practice judges are influenced to some extent by prior decisions. In general, a Civil Law judge is restricted to interpreting the article of a code without filling in any of a code's gaps.

7.1.3.1. Where to find case decisions

In many Civil Law countries, there may be just only one official case reporter, and only a small number of judicial decisions are published. For the legal researcher, even these decisions can be of little value, because numerous European judicial opinions treat solely the legal issue(s) that the courts found necessary to decide the cases upon, and do not deal with all the issues presented. This circumstance is due in no small part to the fact that courts in Civil Law countries do not make law and that the doctrine of stare decisis is not observed.

Reporters will only be published in the official language, which is used in the courts.

Almost always, case law can only be found in hard copies published by the official publisher, which may or may not include, a yearly Table of Contents and/or an Index according to the subject matter of the cases. Some publishers make headnotes for each case. In the last couple of years, in some countries, published case decisions have also been made available online on a subscription basis.

American legal researchers ordinarily cannot find European court decisions in English and, in any event, only the state-authorized translator's documents can be relied upon.

Interestingly, for the American scholar, in Civil Law legal citators such as Shepard's and KeyCite – as well as Bluebook signals – are non-existing.

[50] MERRYMAN *supra* note 9 at 2. Even in American states, which probably have as much legislation in force as exists in Europe, a judge must follow the principle of legislation being superior to judicial decisions (that is, statutes supersede contrary judicial decisions (constitutional questions aside)). *Idem* at 26.

7.1.4. Legislation - Codes

Law - acts, codes,[51] and statutes (the terms in continental Europe are used casually and without any particular distinctions) - is made by national parliaments. As for Member States of the European Union, law may also be made by the European Parliament (see Chapter 4). It must be emphasized that no European country has a "code" like the United States Code[52] that compiles and topically arranges all national statutes. Most of the Civil Law countries that have a code only compile statutes related to what in Civil Law is termed "private law." See above section 7.1.1. and below Table 36.

Statutes are divided into acts, ordinances and regulations. Acts are authored by parliament, ordinances/decrees/rules are authored by the government, and regulations are issued by the authorities/agencies.

It is normally stated in an act when it will come into force. However, it is sometimes the case, that entry into force is governed by a separate, so-called promulgation act, or the government is empowered by the act to determine the date of coming into force and this later takes place by means of a separate published decree in the official gazette/journal. In any case, it is a precondition/ requirement in many Civil Law countries that an act from parliament cannot take effect / go into force before the enforcement date has been published in the national gazette.

Again, the Anglo-American lawyers should remember the continental European division between private law in the narrow sense and commercial law, which the Romanistic and Germanic legal families – except Switzerland and Italy – still recognize by having different codes.

Rules governing a single transaction may be placed in widely separated parts of a Civil Law country's different acts or code, which are abstract in terminology / language, whereas the Anglo-American view is that all aspects of a unitary transaction should be dealt with in the same place in the system

[51] In the United States a code is a complete system of positive law, carefully arranged, edited and officially promulgated; a systematic collection or revision of laws, rules, and regulations (however a Civil Lawyer will soon realize that references to sections or paragraphs might not have been "corrected" as to which section the actual texts is found. For example 8 U.S.C.A. 101 is in fact become 1101).

[52] The Civil Code of the State of Louisiana (the only Civil Law state in the United States), follows the institutions system and is divided into five parts: Preliminary Title; Of Persons; Things and Different Modifications of Ownership; Of Different Modes of Acquiring the Ownership of Things; Conflict of Laws. See WEST'S LOUISIANA STATUTES ANNOTATED, Section 9 (St. Paul: West, 2000).

(usually defined as a "chapter" of the code).[53]

In Civil Law jurisdictions,[54] the codification[55] movement developed out of the philosophy of the Enlightenment and began in earnest in several European countries during the late 18th century. However, it only gained significant momentum with the enactment of the French Napoleonic Code[56] in 1804. The tradition of having a civil code in the European Civil Law countries has been followed in Austria, Germany,[57] Italy, the Netherlands, Portugal, Spain, and Switzerland.[58]

Most Civil Law systems include separate codes or acts of civil procedure and criminal procedure, which should be distinguished from administrative procedure for administrative tribunals or boards of appeal and – where they exist – administrative courts.

In Europe (including the E.U.), it is not common to have an assembled, up-to-date compilation like the U.S. Code. New laws are published in the official journal or gazette in the order they are enacted – similar to the American collection in Statutes at Large.[59] To a certain extent, quasi-official, con-

[53] ZWEIGERT *supra* note 8 at 145.

[54] Even though ancient Rome made compilations like the Corpus Iuris Civilis, much of the ancient Roman era laws were left mostly uncodified. Previously, Denmark had codes such as: The Law of Jutland of 1241 and King Christian V's Danish Code of 1683.

[55] Codification is the process of collecting, arranging, and systematizing and restating the law of a jurisdiction in certain areas, usually by subject.

[56] Code Napoléon (originally called the Code Civile des Français, which entered into force on March 21, 1804), today known as *Code Civile*. .

[57] The Bürgerliches Gesetzbuch (or BGB) is the civil code of Germany. Its development began in 1881 and came into force on January 1, 1900. It is structured as follows: General (covering personal rights and legal personality); Obligations (including sales and contracts); Law of Real Rights (covering things and immovable and movable property); Family Law (domestic relations); Law of Inheritance (succession). The civil codes of Portugal and Switzerland are similar to Germany's.

[58] ZWEIGERT *supra* note 8 at 100-109. .

[59] See <http://thomas.loc.gov/> [press "Public Laws" link]. In the United States, acts of Congress are published (1) chronologically in the order in which they become law on an individual basis in official pamphlets called "slip laws;" and (2) are grouped together in official bound book form, also chronologically, as "session laws", that is, the United States *Statutes at Large* (*Stat.*). (3) Because each Congressional act may contain laws on a variety of topics, many acts, or portions thereof are also split up, rearranged and published in a topical, subject matter codification, that is, the United States Code. Generally, only "Public Laws" are codified. Even in code form, however, many statutes by their nature pertain to more than one topic. Further, portions of some Congressional acts, such as the provisions for the effective dates of amendments to codi-

solidated versions of specific acts will be made available but such versions are not always published in the official journal or gazette; nonetheless, they can often be found in online systems.

Today, European civil servants in ministries ordinarily create the drafts of legislative bills. Expert white papers can influence these bills, but it will most often be a minister who appoints the expert panel that authors a white paper, and so the panel's work is influenced by the government from the very beginning. Thus, European legal scholars do not have real influence on their nations' legislation and, moreover, they are only seldom called upon to appear before a European parliament commission.[60]

As for the structure of an act in Europe, one must beware that in Europe there exists no specific rank-order of the following terms: Title, Chapter, Section, and Paragraph. Furthermore, the terms section, paragraph and (single) statute are sometimes used as synonyms.

> **Research Tip #7.5**
> In Europe, the symbol "§" can be used for a paragraph, section, and even a single statute.[61]

The timeline of legislation in Continental Europe has broadly the pattern shown below in Table 34.

7.1.4.1. Where to find acts/codes

All acts/codes can be found in printed in the official gazette/journal (in the official language). Many European countries also publish new legislation online (in the official language).

As for legislation in Member States of the European Union <http://curia.europa.eu/en/content/outils/liens/index.htm> is often an easy gateway to find links in English language to a country's online database for newer legislation.

Also, see this books corresponding website at <www.hssph.net/legalrm>.

fied laws, are themselves not codified at all, Tobias A. Dorsey, *Some Reflections on not Reading Statutes*, 10 GREEN BAG 2d 283, 288 (Spring 2007).

[60] Unlike in the United States, where law professors are frequently called upon to testify before Congress.

[61] In the United States, the symbol "§" is used for to mean "section." In Europe, the phi-symbol (π) "¶" is never used.

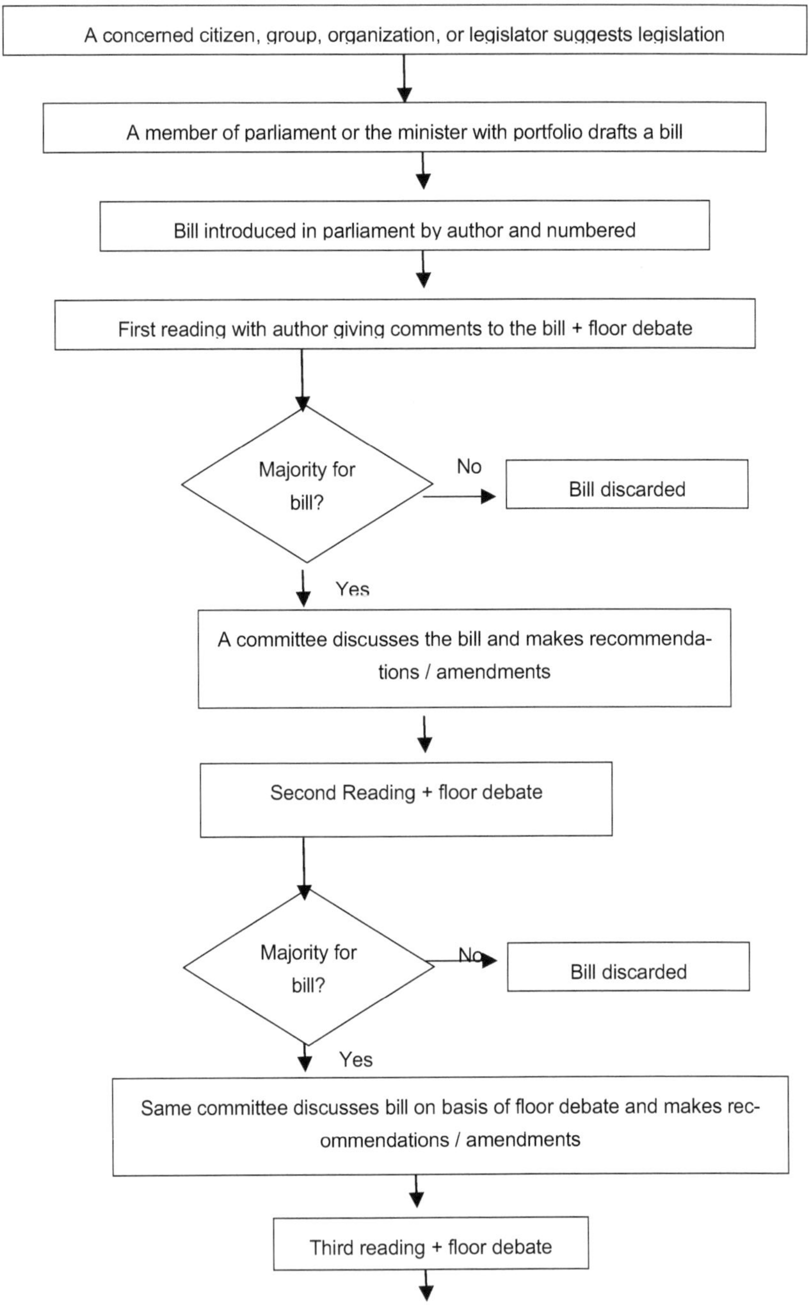
A concerned citizen, group, organization, or legislator suggests legislation
A member of parliament or the minister with portfolio drafts a bill
Bill introduced in parliament by author and numbered
First reading with author giving comments to the bill + floor debate
Majority for bill?
No
Bill discarded
Yes
A committee discusses the bill and makes recommendations / amendments
Second Reading + floor debate
Majority for bill?
No
Bill discarded
Yes
Same committee discusses bill on basis of floor debate and makes recommendations / amendments
Third reading + floor debate

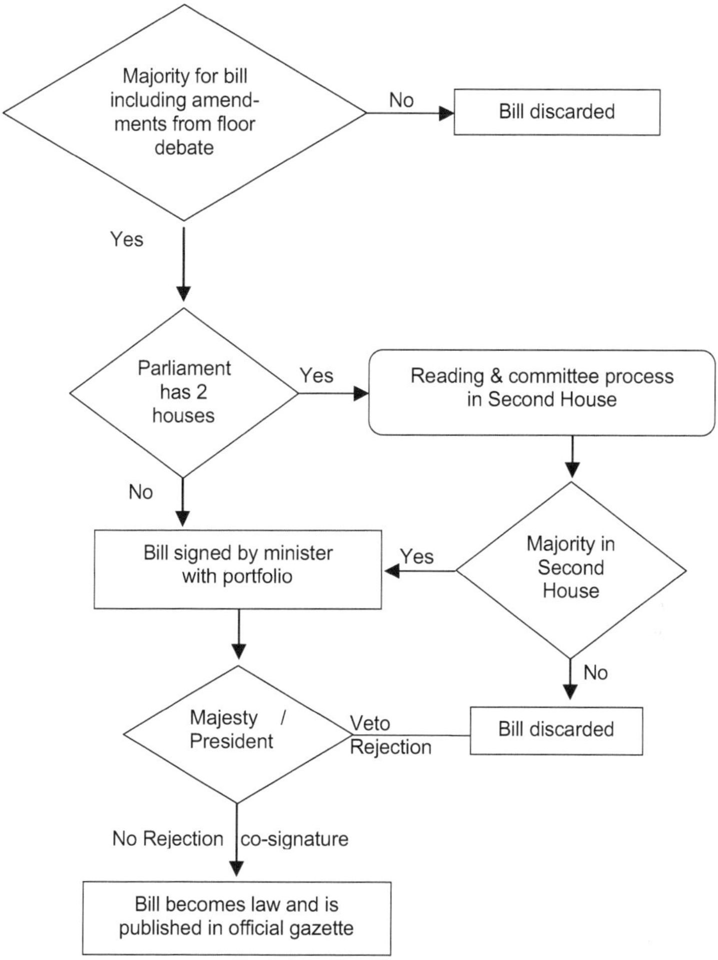

Table 34: Timeline of legislation in Continental Europe

7.1.5. Law Reviews/Journals in Europe

In all European countries, there are academic law journals or reviews,[62] but

[62] Some law journal/review title-words in Europe, if translated directly into English, would be rendered as "Yearbook" or "Weekly Magazine" (e.g., consider "Neue Juristische Wochenschrift" (NJW)).

they are not[63] edited or managed by law students as in the U.S.[64] In addition, they are not related to a single university, but are national or regional publications.[65] A regional or national editorial board consisting of professors, judges, and other highly qualified experts, scrutinizes each submitted article.[66] Consequently, it is much more difficult to get an article printed in a law journal/review in Europe than in the U.S.[67] Normally authors of articles in European law journals/reviews are scholars or persons writing dissertations for a PhD or the higher-ranking European Doctor Juris degree (dr.jur.[68]). It is extremely seldom that articles by law students are published.[69] Thus, some scholars in Europe claim that the quality of articles published in law journals in Europe is much higher than in the U.S. Some even claim American law schools law reviews' student-editorial-boards are nothing but simple paper-printing-producers.[70]

[63] This is also due to the fact that continental European-financed and -run universities do not receive money for law journal/review publication. Also, acting as an editor is not regarded as an educational task for European law students.

[64] In the U.S., membership on law review staff is highly sought after by law students and often has a significant impact on their subsequent careers. Most law reviews select members after their first year of studies, either via a writing competition, or on the basis of grades, or through some combination thereof. Membership is normally divided into staff (second-year students) and editors (third-year students). Submitted articles will frequently be revised by the staff and editors (with/without consent from the authors).

[65] See, e.g., Neue Juristische Wochenschrift (NJW), Österreichische Juristen-Zeitung (ÖJZ), Juristische Blätter (JBl), Ugeskrift for Retsvæsen (UfR), Tidsskrift for Skatteret (TfS).

[66] The author will have the final say about the content of the article before it is printed.

[67] In the U.S., each of the more than 200 law schools has at least one law review.

[68] This is a degree not found in the U.S., where the term "Juris Doctor" (J.D.) only indicates that the person is a "*candidatus*" from a law school. In Europe, a person having been examined by the law faculty of a university is called a "*candidatus juris*" (cand.jur.), which degree is higher than a U.S. J.D. and signifies more a U.S. master degree (J.D. + LLM).

[69] However, some universities have begun publishing law students' work through the law faculties' websites. For example, see "Justicia" (edited by professors and published by DJØF Publishing, Denmark). Some European law school students have been allowed to create American-style law reviews on their universities' website, but the universities' academic staff is not involved and the writings that are published are mostly from the students themselves. See, e.g., Heidelberg Student Law Review (HSLR) at <www.studzr.de/html/menu_oben/uberuns_en.html> and Hanse Law Review (HLR) at <www.hanselawreview.org/cgi-bin/site.pl?user=&site=index>.

[70] U.S. Appeals Court Judge Richard A. Posner has suggested that "law schools 'take back' their law reviews, assigning editorial responsibilities to members of the faculty."

In Europe, because of the high cost of printing (in sometimes "minor" national languages), law review/journal production is most often done by professional firms – and these may be multi-national or international publishers – that also manage distribution. Because of the printing and distribution costs, most European law review articles tend to be much shorter than their American counterparts. In addition, there are several European law journals or reviews that are "cross-border" publications,[71] some on specific topics.[72] European law reviews are also rarely offered in electronic[73] versions (and if so mostly on a subscription basis).[74]

Accordingly, the American legal scholar must be mindful of often only being able to find European law review articles by going to a library and locating a hard copy in the native language.

7.1.6. The Legal Families of Continental Europe.

When studying European continental law – or, rather, Europe excluding England, Wales & Northern Ireland (which have a form of Common Law distinctive from U.S. Common Law[75]), but including Ireland and Scotland[76] – one should be aware of which legal family each country's law being studied be-

Richard A. Posner, *Against the Law Reviews:Welcome to the World Where Inexperienced Editors Make Articles about the Wrong Topics Worse* , 2004 (Dec) Legal Affairs 57. For another view, see Erwin N. Griswold, *The Harvard Law Review – Glimpses of its History as seen by an Aficionado*, Harvard Law Review: Centennial Album 1, 19 (1987) at <www.harvardlawreview.org/Centennial.shtml>.

71 For an example, see Recueil des Cours, the Collected Courses of the Hague Academy of International Law/Académie de Droit International de la Haye (Brill Academic Publishers at <www.ppl.nl/bibliographies/all/?bibliography=recueil>).

72 For an example, see International Journal of Law and Information Technology (published by Oxford University Press, at <http://ijlit.oxfordjournals.org/>).

73 Some of the newer law reviews in the U.S. are only published online.

74 One such exception is Electronic Journal of Information, Law and Technology (JILT), edited by professors from several universities in the United Kingdom. See <www2.warwick.ac.uk/fac/soc/law/elj/jilt/>).

75 The American State of Louisiana is regarded a Civil Law country.

76 Scotland is often said to use the Civil Law system, but in fact it has a unique system that combines elements of an uncodified Civil Law dating back to the Corpus Juris Civilis with an element of Common Law long predating the Treaty of Union with England in 1707. Scottish Common Law differs in that the use of precedents is subject to the courts seeking to discover the principle that justifies a law, rather than to search for an example as a precedent. In addition, the principles of natural justice and fairness have always formed a source of Scottish law. Other comparable pluralistic (or "mixed") legal systems operate in Quebec, the American State of Louisiana, and South Africa.

longs to. This is because the legal family type has a great impact on the way the law of that country is to be interpreted. The "continental" European legal families (see further on this subject in Chapter 6) are:[77]

- The *Romanistic Legal Family* (France,[78] the Benelux countries,[79] Italy,[80] Spain,[81] and Portugal[82]) – The *Code Civile*[83] of 1804 is the heart of private law in France and the great model for the codes of private law of the whole Romanistic legal family. It is a felicitous blend of traditional legal institutions from the droit écrit of the South – influenced by Roman Law – and the droit coutumier of the North – influenced by Germanic-Frankish customary law. The Code Civile bears throughout the marks of its heritage of the pre-revolutionary law (*ancien droit*). There was never any serious discussion of a complete reception of Roman law into France – unlike Germany later on. From two royal ordinances in the 17th century, came the basis for a division between private law, in the narrow sense, and commercial law, which the Romanistic and Germanic legal families – except Switzerland and Italy – still recognize by having different codes, much to the surprise of Anglo-American lawyers. In France and Italy, the highest court in civil and criminal matters differs in characteristic respects from the comparable supreme courts of the Anglo-American and German legal families.[84] The (highest[85]) French Court of Cassation goes in for lapidary "whereas" clauses. Legal studies in France are part of a general education.[86]
- The *Germanic Legal Family* (Germany, Austria, Croatia, Switzerland, Greece) – The effects of Roman law were much greater in

[77] ZWEIGERT *supra* note 8 at 64.

[78] Stéphane Cottin & Jérôme Rabenou, *Researching French Law* (May 2005 with update May 2007) at <www.llrx.com/features/french.htm>.

[79] Belgium, the Netherlands, and, Luxembourg.

[80] Elio Fameli & Fiorenza Socci, *Guide to Italian Legal Research and Resources on the Web* (translated by Deirdre Exell Pirro) (March 2005 with June 2006 update), at <www.nyulawglobal.org/globalex/Italy.htm>.

[81] Olga Cabrero, *Guide to legal research in Spain* (Feb. 2005) at <www.llrx.com/features/spain.htm >.

[82] ZWEIGERT *supra* note 8 at 104.

[83] or Code Napoléon [Napoleonic Code] (originally called the Code civil des Français).

[84] ZWEIGERT *supra* note 8 at 74-80 & 120.

[85] It should be pointed out that besides this Supreme Court for judicial cases (civil justice or criminal justice), France has other Supreme Courts, for example the Conseil d'État (for administrative justice), and Conseil Constitutionnel (constitutional challenges).

[86] ZWEIGERT *supra* note 8 at 130-131.

Germany than in France and enormously greater than in England. Germany consisted of many small principalities until 1871. As there was no common German private law, no common German court system, and no common German fraternity of lawyers, Roman legal ideas and institutions were adopted wholesale in many parts of the country and for many areas of law.[87]The Superior German Court will give reasons that are wide-ranging and loaded with citations like a textbook. Legal studies in Germany, are not part of a general education.[88]

- The *Nordic Legal Family* (Denmark,[89] Finland,[90] Iceland,[91] Norway,[92] and Sweden[93])[94] – Nordic Legal Family law has few, if any, of the "stylistic" hallmarks of the Common Law. Roman law has played a smaller role in the legal development of the Nordic countries than in Germany. The Nordic Legal Family's laws belong to the Civil Law, but form a special legal family, alongside the Romanistic and German legal families. The political and cultural ties between these countries have always been very close – partly based on the fact that the countries for some hundred years was unified. In the 17th century, the countries each promulgated comprehensive codes unifying private law, criminal law, and procedural law. In the 19th century, they began modernization of their codes, and amendments were made in separate reforming laws. In addition, unified laws between the countries were added. Nordic Legal Family members have resisted tendency toward conceptualism and the construction of large-scale integrated theoreti-

[87] ZWEIGERT *supra* note 8 at 133-135.

[88] ZWEIGERT *supra* note 8 at 130-131.

[89] Rasmus H. Wandall, *Researching Danish Law* (July 2006) [hereinafter WANDALL] at <www.nyulawglobal.org/globalex/Denmark.htm>.

[90] *Legal order – Finland* at <http://ec.europa.eu/civiljustice/legal_order/legal_order_fin_en.htm>.

[91] Rán Tryggvadóttir & Thordis Ingadóttir, *Researching Icelandic Law* (2007) at <www.nyulawglobal.org/globalex/iceland.htm>.

[92] Hans Petter Graver, *The Approach to European Law in Norwegian Legal Doctrine,* in Peter Christian Müller-Graff & Erling Selvig, eds., EUROPEAN LAW IN THE GERMAN-NORWEGIAN CONTEXT: ORIGINS AND PERSPECTIVES (Berlin: Berliner Wissenschafts-Verlag GmbH, 2001) & at <www.arena.uio.no/publications/wp03_18.pdf> [hereinafter GRAVER].

[93] *Legal order – Sweden* at <http://ec.europa.eu/civiljustice/legal_order/legal_order_swe_en.htm>.

[94] Usually, Scandinavia is regarded as Denmark, Norway, and Sweden. The Nordic countries are the Scandinavian ones plus Iceland and Finland.

cal systems. All of these countries possess constitutions and neither their royal families/presidents exercise genuine executive power, which power belongs to the government, which constitutes an separate branch pursuant to the constitutions – along with the Parliament and the courts.

7.1.6.1. Some basic books for different European countries written in English by natives

The following is a list of some books written in English by natives giving a basic introduction to the particular country's law and structure:[95]

- Austria - Herbert Hausmaninger, The Austrian Legal System (Manzsche Verlags- Und Universitätsbuchhandlung, 2003 – ISBN 3-214-00289-9)
- Belgium - Hubert Bocken & Walter de Bondt, Introduction to Belgian Law (Kluwer Law International, 2000 - ISBN-13: 978-9041114563)
- Denmark – Anne Gleerup, Ulla Rosenkjær, Leif Rørbæk, An introduction to Danish law (2nd Ed.) (Denmark: Drammelstrupgaard, 2008 - ISBN-13: 978-87-988688-3-5)
- England - Gary Slapper, The English Legal System (9 Ed.) (Publisher: Routledge Cavendish, 2008 - ISBN-13: 978-0415459549)
- France - Introduction To French Law (Editors: E. Picard & G Bermann) (Kluwer Law International, 2008 - ISBN 978-9041124661)
- Germany – Introduction to German Law (Editors: Joachim Zekoll & Mathias Reimann) (2nd Ed.) (Kluwer Law International, 2005 - ISBN-13: 978-9041122612)
- Greece – Introduction to Greek Law (Editors: Konstantinos D. Kerameus & Phaedon J. Kozyris) (3rd Ed.) (Kluwer Law International, 2008 - ISBN 978-9041125408)
- Hungary – Introduction To Hungarian Law (Editors: TuRul Ansay & Atilla Harmathy) (Kluwer Law International, 1998 - ISBN 978-9041110664)
- Israel - Introduction To The Law Of Israel (Editors: Amos Shapira & Keren C. Dewitt-Arar) (Kluwer Law International, 1995 - ISBN 978-9065448354)
- Italy - Introduction to Italian law (Ed. Jeffrey S. Lena & Ugo Mat-

[95] Morris L. Cohen, Robert C. Berring & Kent C. Olson, HOW TO FIND THE LAW (9. ed.)(St. Paul, Minn.: West, 1989).

tei)(Hague/London/New York: Kluwer Law International 2002 - ISBN: 978-9041117076)
- Netherlands - Introduction To Dutch Law (Editors: Jeroen M.J. Chorus, Piet-Hein. M. Gerver & Ewoud H. Hondius) (4th Ed.) (Kluwer Law International, 2007 - ISBN 978-9041122698)
- Poland – Introduction to Polish Law (Editors: Stanislaw Frankowski & Adam Bodnar) (Kluwer Law International, 2005 - ISBN 978-9041123312)
- Sweden - Michael Bogdan (Ed.), Swedish Law in the New Millennium (Stockholm: Norstedts Juridik, 2000 - ISBN 91-39-00628-X)
- Switzerland - Introduction To Swiss Law (Editors: Francois Dessemontet & Tugrul Ansay) (3rd Ed.) (Kluwer Law International, 2004 - ISBN 978-9041122605)
- United States of America - William Burnham, Introduction to the Law and Legal System of The United States (West Group, 2006 – ISBN 0-314-25393-9)

7.1.7. Legal Science and Legal Philosophy

On the European continent, scholars, when studying law, use the following two principal groupings:[96]

- Legal Philosophy – consisting of different legal theories, which explain legal science, including, for example, natural law[97] and legal realism.[98] Each theory analyzes the legal science to explain, what is "law"; what is a legal norm; what is the relation between law and morality; whether "legal science" is an exact science; and what is required for it to be a science, including the role the "legal method" has.
- Legal Science – consisting of "science" in relation to:
    - "Source of law" – the science about the content of norms, prioritization, binding effect, and political legitimation.

[96] Ruth Nielsen & Christina D. Tvarnø, RETSKILDER & RETSTEORIER [Source of Law & Legal Theories] 22-26 (1st ed.) (Copenhagen: Jurist- and Økonomforbundets Forlag [DJØF Publishing], 2005) [hereinafter TVARNØ].

[97] On natural law, see TVARNØ *supra* note 96 at Chapter 7.

[98] U.S. legal realism is similar to the Scandinavian. See TVARNØ *supra* note 96 at 323; Karl Llewellyn, Karl N. Llewellyn, JURISPRUDENCE : REALISM IN THEORY AND PRACTICE (Chicago: University of Chicago Press, 1962); Jerome Frank, LAW AND THE MODERN MIND (New York: Brentano's, 1930).

- Legal politics – (a) de lege ferenda views;[99] and (b) de sententia ferenda views[100]
- Legal history or "history of law" (in the European sense, which is totally different from an American perspective).[101]
- Legal sociology – analyzing the law from a sociological perspective to explain the law's implications on the society and why rules arose.
- Legal dogmatics – systematization, description, interpretation and analysis of existing law (de lege lata) with the aim of solving concrete legal problems.
- Comparative law – comparison of legal systems or legal rules on the basis of a specific - for the concrete question - method of analysis.

7.1.8. Citations

In European countries, formal citation systems do not exist.

American scholars have to accept that their normal exhaustive, pinpoint citation system is so culturally alien in Continental Europe that it should not be employed; they have to learn to use the "European" system.[102]

Examples of some commonly used citations can be found in the Guide to Foreign and International Legal Citation (GFILC), which is edited partly with the help of scholars from each country.[103]

Oxford University has also made available a Standard for Citation of Legal Authorities.[104]

However, the particular country's courts and legal scholars might use dif-

[99] How the law should be (made by legislator).

[100] How a court should use law and rules in relation to specific circumstances.

[101] MERRYMAN *supra* note 9 at 60.

[102] This does not mean the European system is perfect – far from. It often leaves a possibility for a wrong citation because there are no cross-reference in the citation. For example, a case with only citation of the publisher, year and page – without names of the parties – makes it very possible never to be able the case, if its wrongfully citated.

[103] GFILC was published by the New York University Journal of International Law and Politics in 2006. It is available for free download from <www.law.nyu.edu/journals/jilp/gfilc.html >. One would expect that this first edition will be updated and expanded. GFILC is also available in a spiral-bound, paperback form by sending U.S.$20 payable to "Journal of International Law and Politics" to: Circulation Department, Journal of International Law and Politics, 110 West Third Street, New York NY 10012, USA.

[104] Standard for Citation of Legal Authorities (University of Oxford, 2006) at <www.competition-law.ox.ac.uk/published/oscola_2006.pdf>.

ferent ways of make citations.

Especially for court decisions in some European countries there are only made reference to the publisher, year and first page, without any mentioning the parties or the court or date (which lack of sufficient reference sometimes make it hard to find an European case if the year or page is wrongfully cited in a European publication/article).

7.2. Legal Research

7.2.1. Introduction

As mentioned above, research approaches in Civil Law vary by country and by topic, and no single procedure will work for all purposes.[105]

> **Research Tip #7.6**
> The first step when beginning research, as regards any foreign law,[106] is to consult a legal research guide about the country being researched.

In some countries, this information may be available online, but to date it is seldom that the information will be translated into English.[107]

The following sections are based on the approach for Scandinavia[108] (with two Scandinavian countries, Denmark and Sweden, being members of the E.U.)[109] and where the approaches - even being in the same legal family - is not always the same.

[105] In the U.S., legal research methods are frequently taught by law librarians rather than by lawyers/law professors, who do teach such methods in Europe, as librarians there do not engage in teaching legal subjects. A mixture seems to be the right if the aim is to teach international systems and especially on U.S. law., since if a lawyer does not know where to find material in a law library he is lost.

[106] The domestic law of another country.

[107] Some helpful guides in English can be found at "Globalex" <www.nyulawglobal.org>.

[108] Usually, Scandinavia is regarded as Denmark, Norway, and Sweden. The Nordic countries are the Scandinavian ones plus Iceland and Finland.

[109] In Norway's legal culture, legal doctrine is expected to refer to the sources of law as they appear to the judge. In addition, however, legal doctrine is expected to aspire to the status of a science. The Norwegian trend after, World War II, toward internationalization and, at the same time, harmonization with European community law and human rights law, is a factor that must increasingly be taken into account. GRAVER *supra* note 87.

As for member states of the European Union, some guidance in English can be found at <www.ec.europa.eu/civiljustice/legal_order /legal_ order_gen_en.htm>. In addition, in May 2001 the Council of the E.U.[110] decided to establishing the European Judicial Network[111] in civil and commercial matters. This network consists of representatives of the member states' judicial and administrative authorities. It meets several times each year to exchange information and experience and boost cooperation between the member states as regards civil and commercial law. The themes for the network are (similar to menus from its website):

- Legal order
- Organisation of justice
- Legal professions
- Legal aid
- Jurisdiction of the courts
- Bringing a case to court
- Applicable law
- Service of documents
- Taking of evidence and mode of proof
- Interim measures and precautionary measures
- Enforcement of judgements
- Simplified and accelerated procedures
- Divorce
- Parental responsibility
- Maintenance claims
- Bankruptcy
- Alternative dispute resolutions
- Compensation to crime victims

A European Judicial Atlas in Civil Matters provides access to the follow-

[110] 2001/470/EC: Council Decision of 28 May 2001, establishing a European Judicial Network in civil and commercial matters, OJ L 174, 27.6.2001, p. 0025–0031.

[111] REPORT from the Commission to the Council, the European Parliament and the European Economic and Social Committee on the application of Council Decision 2001/470/EC ESTABLISHING A EUROPEAN JUDICIAL NETWORK IN CIVIL AND COMMERCIAL MATTERS, (COM/2006/203 final) and annexes (SEC/2006/579) & Final Report: EVALUATION OF THE FUNCTIONING OF THE EUROPEAN JUDICIAL NETWORK IN CIVIL AND COMMERCIAL MATTERS, submitted by The European Evaluation Consortium (TEEC), all at <http://ec.europa.eu/civiljustice/index_en.htm>.

ing information relevant for judicial cooperation in civil matters (in a chosen language):[112]

- Competent Courts
- Legal Aid
- Serving Documents
- Taking Evidence
- Recognising and Enforcing Judgements
- Compensation to Crime Victims
- Filling in Forms
- Links

> **Research Tip #7.7**
> When starting a survey of a new legal issue, it is helpful to read the first parts of a white paper or comments to a proposed bill, as these often provide a valuable overview of the a specific legal area.

> **Research Tip #7.8**
> When dealing with a rule issued by a governmental body in a Member State of the European Union, one has to look for a legal basis, or "law -source," for the rule not only in national legislation but also in regulations and decisions of the E.U.

Furthermore, one should check whether the rule complies with this legal base or whether it goes beyond the scope of the delegation given to the governmental body.

7.2.2. Legal Methodology

Legal methodology does not give an answer as to which statute or legal rule should be used in relation to a certain legal problem, but instead states on which basis the answer can be found, that is, the method by which a "law-source" is analyzed and used when a legal problem is raised.[113] The aim is to make the lawyer capable of obtaining a correct solution to legal questions by shedding light on which normative factors can be used and when, in order to answer the questions. Legal methodology does not describe the rules of a certain branch of jurisprudence[114] (de lege lata), which latter is answered by le-

[112] See <http://ec.europa.eu/justice_home/judicialatlascivil/html/index_en.htm>.
[113] TVARNØ *supra* note 96 at 27.
[114] In the U.S. "jurisprudence" is defined: 1. Originally (in the 18th century), the study of the first principles of the law of nature, the civil law, and the law of nations. - Also

gal dogmatics.[115]

Research Tip #7.9

The legal method contributes the first bricks to building general understanding of the legal system, its tensions, and also the art and technique of legal research.

The science as to the legal method consists of a theoretical and a practical part. The legal methodology encompasses the normative factors – sources of law – which can be used when deciding legal problems, and provides how these sources of law contribute to legal argumentation. The legal method depends on the situation, that is, it is used when there is a need to analyze and solve concrete problems that require answers as to what is the current law. Its application does not always give an unambiguous answer. Yet the legal method does in some situations imply alternatives. Thus, it is important to consider on what grounding a preference should be made.

Learning legal methodology is the cornerstone for studying law in Europe and doing a European Civil Law lawyer's work.

Research Tip #7.10

Learning legal methodology contributes to and supports an understanding of legal problems, providing the individual with a critical approach to those problems and their solutions (as introduced in courses on legal dogmatics); forucs on the following five questions:[116]

1. What is the definition of a law- source ?
2. Why use a law- source ?
3. How does one use a law-source ?
4. Where are sources of law and who creates them?
5. Where does one find sources of law?

termed jurisprudentia naturalis; 2. More modernly, the study of the general or fundamental elements of a particular legal system, as opposed to its practical and concrete details. 3. The study of legal systems in general. 4. Judicial precedents considered collectively. 5. In German literature, the whole of legal knowledge. BLACK'S LAW DICTIONARY (8th ed.) (St. Paul: Minnesota, 2004).

[115] Peter Blume, JURIDISK METODELÆRE [Legal Methodology] 1-3 & 6 (Fifth Edition, Copenhagen: Jurist- og Økonomforbundets Forlag [DJØF Publishing] 2009) [hereinafter BLUME].

[116] However, as the legal system grows more disordered, the normal legal methodology cannot always stand alone, but works more like a steppingstone for the lawyer's use of the source of law. *Idem* 14-15, 18, 64 & 75.

Research Tip #7.11

When solving a legal research assignment in Continental Europe, the following questions/points should be addressed:

- What is the legal problem?
- Which parts of the given facts are important?
- Which sources of law are relevant?
- Consider and analyze possible arguments pro and con.
- Provide a conclusion.

In general, legal rules are necessary for a society in order to show the individual how to behave and to prevent conflicts. Rules can have one or more of the following three characteristics:

- Substantive-law rules, which describe and lay down what is the standard on a certain issue;
- Procedural rules stating the process to be followed when using a particular substantive-law rule; and
- Rules providing for consequences or sanctions in case of violations.

7.2.3. The Legal Method in Principle

The Legal Method is the lawyer's basic toolbox – to be employed when concrete facts are present and need to be considered and dealt with in legal terms. It is the lawyer's mission to lay down which legal rules must be used and to reach a conclusion. The method consists of many elements, not all of which necessarily have to be used every time or in the same order.

When given a set of facts and a problem, the question is how to effectively identify, consider, and address the legal issue(s) at hand.[117] Initially, one has to examine whether legal material exists.

Research Tip #7.12

In Civil Law countries, the natural starting points for examination are constitutional articles and then acts, either codes or statutes.

After studying the actual text of a paragraph of a code or statute, an interpretation or filling out of its text may be neccssary. At this stage, the aim or in-

117 American law students typically use the so-called IRAC (issue-rule-application-conclusion) system – both for writing memoranda on legal issues and for taking examinations. Some use IWRAC (issue-public int' law- rule-analyse-conclusion).

tent[118] of the statute is significant. Support for ascertaining such intent can be found in the preliminary work to the statutory text. This work can include, for example, the statements given by the person who introduced the bill that became law, the minutes of negotiations in parliament, and white papers.

Then, one should look for administrative judicial precepts that are legally binding. Examples are: rules issued in the government's regulatory process or by government order; rules in the form of government or departmental circular; or, governmental instructions or guidance.

The next step, find decisions where the statute or code has been used. In Civil Law countries, there are two main types : (a) court decisions; and (b) decisions made by an administrative authority. The first will usually have greater weight, because courts often have jurisdiction to review the decisions of administrative authorities.

Furthermore, legal literature can help to encircle the state of the law.

One must determine the legal meaning of the statute, then make an interpretation, with the aim of throwing light on or clarifying what the text of the statute stands for.

An interim conclusion should be reached at this point, concerning whether a reasonable result has been achieved or whether a re-evaluation ought to be undertaken given the circumstances. In the latter case, one should look for legal material addressing the given issue in a broader context – for instance, the aim or intent of a provision in the constitution or in an international treaty (which has been ratified and entered into force). On this basis, one can then decide whether to alter the interim conclusion.[119]

Research Tip #7.13

In order to be able to clarify which rules must be used in a certain legal system – so as to be able to determine what behavior is legal or not – one needs to acquire knowledge to assess whether the rules are appropriate and desirable.

In Europe, such information is designated by a special term of art: "law-foundation-sources."[120]

[118] As opposed to, in the U.S., where some U.S. judges say that legislative intent should not be considered. See JOSEPH L. GERKEN, WHAT GOOD IS LEGISLATIVE HISTORY? JUSTICE SCALIA IN THE FEDERAL COURTS OF APPEALS (Buffalo, New York: William S. Hein & Co., Inc., 2007).

[119] BLUME *supra* note 115 at Chapter 4.

[120] The Danish term is "Retskildelære." See, BLUME *supra* note 115 at 59.

However, as noted above in section 7.1.1.1. this translation into English of "sources of law" is bound to be confusing for American readers. Accordingly, "sources of law" in this chapter is reformulated to "law-foundation-source,"[121] respectively a "law-source"[122] or types of "law-sources."[123]

Note: Americans does not talk about "source of law" but about "sources of law."

7.3. The Method in Detail

Accordingly, up to this juncture in the discussion of legal research in Europe, it is clear that one needs a basic method. Whether that method is proper in turn relies on whether it relates to the law-sources and is recognized by other lawyers. The law-sources function as legal argument, and the legal method is characterized by all the relevant arguments that are brought to light and analyzed in a reasonable and appropriate professional manner to reach an answer in a reasonable and appropriate professional manner to reach an answer to a particular legal question. The application of the method is dependent upon the situation.

Research Tip #7.14

To determine whether the method has been used correctly, it is necessary to have a common understanding of:[124]

1. What a law -source is.
2. How a law -source is used.
3. Which kind of information is considered to be a law -source.

7.3.1. Law-sources

Law-sources in Civil Law countries do not describe an already-existing situation, but instead aim – as of the time they are created – to bring about change and to govern behavior.[125]

[121] The Danish term is "retskilde" and the course is termed "Retskildelære".
[122] The Danish term is "retskilde".
[123] The Danish term is "retskildetyper".
[124] BLUME *supra* note 115 at 59.
[125] BLUME *supra* note 115 at Chapter 5.

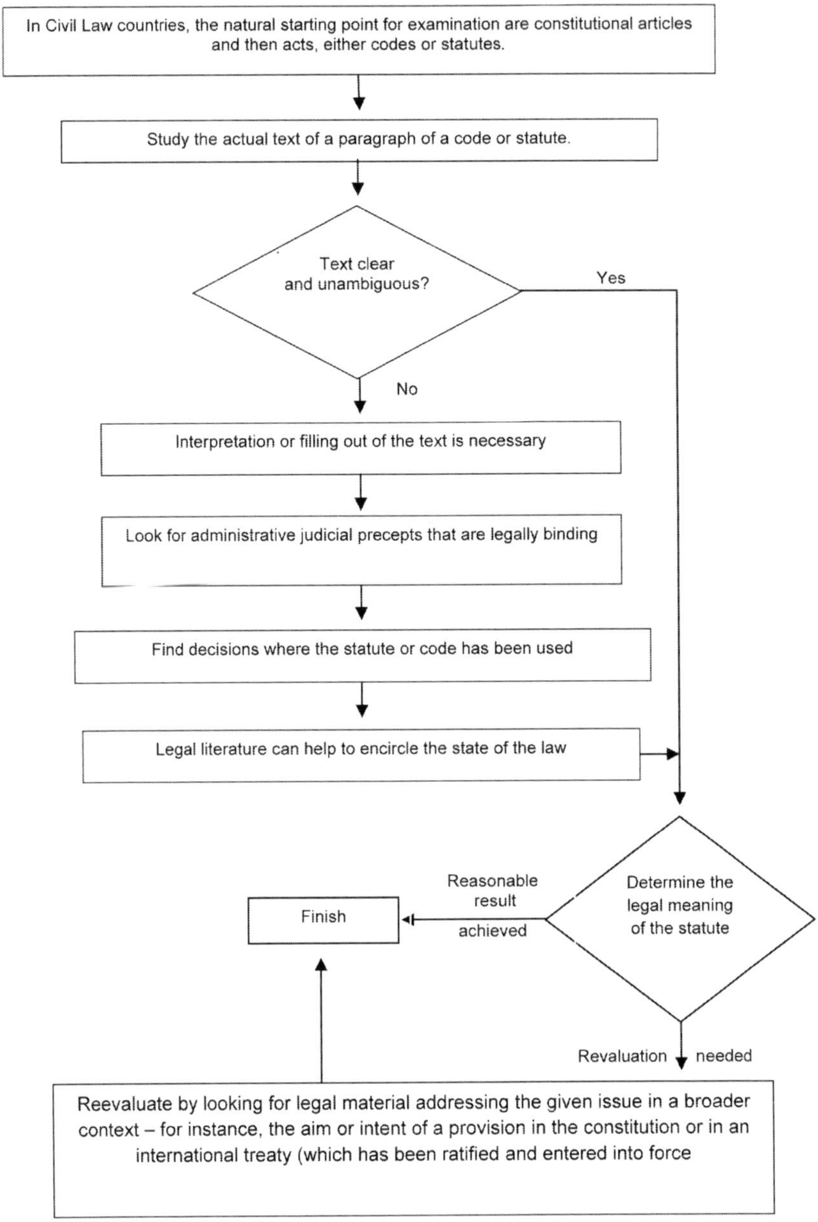

Table 35: Research Flowchart for Civil Law

Only seldom is a single law-source sufficient to lay down what the legal rule is. Often, fragments have to be collected from several sources of law. Thereafter, these legal arguments are harmonized and cumulated into an answer that is persuasive. The precondition is that sources of law be related to something that is subject to legal regulation.

The function of the law-sources is to ensure that a certain legal question always is answered in the same manner. Yet, in practice, lawyers can disagree on what is the necessary or correct legal argumentation. Only seldom do lawyers disagree on whether a certain type of information is a law-source .

In Civil Law countries, there exist several types of law-sources. These types are arranged according to the way they are created, and often divided into a group of binding sources and other(s). In addition, law-sources of national or international nature may be treated differently.

> **Research Tip #7.15**
> Law-sources are divided into two main groups:
>
> "hard law" - juridical precepts, decisions, and customary law,
> &
> "soft law" - preparatory works, statements by the Parliament Ombudsman, legal literature describing already existing rules or law, private source of law, and legal cultural tradition.

But to a certain extent, all sources are equal, as each type may influence the answer to a legal question.[126] See also Chapter 1, Table 3 "Overview of Law-Sources in default Civil Law country".

7.3.1.1. Hard (or binding) law- sources

7.3.1.1.1.. Juridical precepts

A judicial precept is a set of rules, in writing, issued by an authority that has the express power to promulgate it. The value of a certain precept is deter-

[126] BLUME *supra* note 115 at 74. In Finland sources are divided into three groups with the following order: (1) strongly binding sources (constitution, acts, regulations, and custom); (2) weakly binding sources (preparatory legislative work and court decisions); and (3) admissible sources of law, which is not binding (jurisprudence, general legal principles, and factual arguments). See Legal order – Finland at <http://ec.europa.eu/civiljustice/legal_order/legal_order_fin_en.htm>.

mined by the status or rank of its issuing body. Principal examples are: constitutional rules, acts, codes or statutes,[127] regulations or government decrees, government or departmental circulars, (ratified) treaties, and E.U. regulations and directives.

7.3.1.1.2. Decisions

A decision is a legal resolution or judgment of a question raised in a concrete factual context.

One group of decisions is made by the courts. In contrast to strict past practice, nowadays it is recognized that courts in Civil Law countries can "make" law to a certain extent.[128] One exception is a case that is in the Civil Law sense classified to be a "precedence" case – see further in section 7.3.3.2 and 7.3.4.2.[129] The other exception is where an act or statute presumes or expressly permits courts to fill in gaps in legislative schemes. Thus, modern court decisions – as opposed to older ones – can today possess high value as a law-source .[130]

When legislation is old, or when many changes has occurred within a doctrinal area of law, the importance of case law increases.

However, not all case law can be used; it is only cases that constitute precedence that can be used as a law-source - see section 7.3.3.2.

The other group of decisions are made by governmental or departmental bodies. Today, such decisions have great impact on citizens' legal status. Often these decisions can be reviewed by the courts.

In those countries that do not have a special administrative court, an ombudsman's[131] statements – even though not decisions and consequently not binding on the courts – can be regarded as a substitute for an administrative

[127] Acts, codes, and statutes can also be referred to as legislation.

[128] Benjamin Cardozo (US Supreme Court Judge 1932-38) had great respect for precedent and his great respect...and deference to the Legislative Branch. But Cardozo wasn't always an advocate for judicial deference. In his most famous book, THE NATURE OF THE JUDICIAL PROCESS, Cardozo called a chapter *The Judge as a Legislator*. Cardozo: Like legislators, judges must get their experience 'from live itself', and when the law isn't clear, a judge must sometimes 'pronounce judgment...according to the rules which he would establish if he were to assume the part of a legislature." TIME MAGAZINe, July 2009 page 26.

[129] BLUME *supra* note 115 at 67-68.

[130] Also, the E.U. Court of Justice has through the years made new E.U. law – see below Chapter 9, section 9.2.7.

[131] See footnote 27 above.

court decision and thus as a law-source .[132]

In many judicial decisions from Europe, an American reader will not find a structure similar to the one used by most U.S. courts, namely:[133]

- The caption, which is the title of the case – such as Brown v. Board of Education or Miranda v. Arizona. In most cases, the caption reflects the last names of the two parties to the dispute. [134]
- The case citation. This consists of "the name of the court that decided the case, the law book in which the opinion was published (and therefore can be found), and also the year in which the court decided the case."
- The author of the opinion. This will be the name of the judge who authored the opinion.[135]
- The body of the opinion includes:
    - The (self-explanatory) Facts of the Case.
    - The Law of the Case: Here, the court discusses the law, including the law-source it is using to resolve the dispute before it. The basis of the court's authority can help determine the significance of its opinion. The holding of the case – if there is one – and any dicta[136] are included here as well.
    - The Disposition: This usually appears at the end of the main opinion and consists of what action the court is taking with the case. In general, a concurring opinion is an opinion by a judge who would have reached the same result as the majority, but for a different reason. Concurrences and dissents are very important. One needs to read them carefully.[137]

7.3.1.1.3. Customary law

Customary law[138] is ordinarily viewed as denoting customs, which have been followed generally and continuously with a sense of legal obligation. Cus-

[132] BLUME *supra* note 115 at 143.

[133] ORIN S. KERR, *How to Read a Judicial Opinion: A Guide for New Law Students* (Version 2.0 - August 2005), George Washington University Law School, at <http://volokh.com/files/howtoreadv2.pdf>.

[134] Seldom given on the European continent.

[135] Seldom given on the European continent.

[136] Plural form of "*dictum,*" which is an abbreviation of the Latin phrase "obiter dictum," that means "a remark by the way." Dicta are statements in an opinion that are not actually required to resolve the case before the court.

[137] In the evolution of Common Law, a dissenting opinion may become the majority view. This reflects the reality that judicial decisions are often political decisions as well.

[138] In Danish "sædvane."

tomary law is unwritten[139] and accordingly one cannot expect it to be reported. It covers limited areas of contractual practices, land registration, and criminal law; customary law is relevant in relation to some areas of public administration and constitutional matters.[140] Because regulations provided for in written law are nowadays fairly comprehensive, custom is today rarely of any importance as a law-source .

Customary law may be recognized in case law. However, more frequently the source is found in scholarly writing or in the public legal offices that deal with the area of law in question.[141]

7.3.1.2. Soft Law

The term "soft law" [142] covers a broad spectrum of different kinds of sources. This type of law-source is created in a more informal way. It is used in areas where there is a need for a dynamic development or evolution of law in view of continuous changes in the society. Soft law is characterized by giving advice or recommendation and thus not legally binding for the persons it relates to. They can declare / have shape of / content a custom or practice or be the forerunner for a later legal precept. This kind of source can be hard to find, as they are often not promulgated. Doctrines, commercial customs, contractual provisions, and general customs can be supplementary sources of law.

7.3.1.2.1. Preparatory work

The purpose of preparatory or preliminary work is to state the reasons for issuing a precept and to explain the meaning behind specific parts or rules of the precept. In European Civil Law countries, it is an accepted part of the legal method to study preparatory work and include them in legal argumenta-

[139] The term "unwritten" is used differently in the United States. There, the term covers: law that, although never enacted in the form of a statute or ordinance, has the sanction of custom and traditionally included unpublished case law. It is also termed *jus non scriptum, jus ex non scripto, lex non scripta*, and *jus moribus constitutum*. BLACK'S LAW DICTIONARY (8th ed.) (St. Paul: West, 2004).

[140] WANDALL *supra* note 89. For the same in Finland, see <http://ec.europa.eu/civiljustice/legal_order/legal_order_fin_en.htm>.

[141] WANDALL *supra* note 89. BLUME *supra* note 115 at 44, 147, 154-155.

[142] Soft law: 1. Collectively, rules that are neither strictly binding nor completely lacking in legal significance. 2. Int'l law. Guidelines, policy declarations, or codes of conduct that set standards of conduct but are not legally binding. Black's Law Dictionary (8th ed.) (St. Paul: West, 2004).

tion.[143]

The more recent the preparatory work, the more important it is.

The older a statute is, the less reasonable it is for a legal researcher to find support for his or her interpretation in the preparatory work to the statute, as later practice/experience likely has changed the meaning of a statute.

In addition, the more precise the text of a statute is, the less weight should be ascribed to preparatory work.

One should distinguish between preparatory work created before a bill is introduced and preparatory work established during negotiations in parliament. In practice, courts from time to time use white papers, whereas government bodies more often prefer the content of the ministers' comments to the bill.

The fact that a bill never was passed can be used in the negative as regards what the law is.[144]

7.3.1.2.2. Statements by the Parliamentary Ombudsman

An Ombudsman's[145] statements is not decisions and not binding on the courts. However, as a law-source such statements are considered of high authority and are adhered to by the administration. They constitute an indispensable source when researching European administrative law.[146]

7.3.1.2.3. Legal Literature describing already Existing Rules or Law

The part of legal literature that describes the already existing rules or law (de lege lata) – legal dogmatics – can be used for arguments or contributions to a point of view and thereby be regarded as a law-source . However, this "source" should be limited to writings of authors who are widely acknowledged as experts. American researchers should note that legal dogmatics may be far different in use and importance than in American jurisprudence. Works of legal dogmatics in Europe will often imply a sort of production process even though nothing new is created. They contain often review and analysis

[143] In most countries of Europe, it is common practice in the preparation of any major legal reform to engage in extensive study of foreign ideas and experience. Max Rheinstein, *Comparative Law – Its Functions, Methods and Usages*, 22 ARK. L. REV. 415, 424 (1946).

[144] BLUME *supra* note 115 at 96.

[145] See footnote 27 above.

[146] BLUME *supra* note 115 at 143.

of different sources of law in a particular author's paper.[147]

In Civil Law countries, legal dogmatics is divided into the categories show in Table 36.

Private Law (Regulations between private citizens and business, including public firms)	The law of Contracts and Torts
	Property Right
	+ including Law of Persons & Family law
	+ including Consumer Rights
Public Law (Regulations among public bodies and regulations between public bodies and citizens/businesses)	Constitutional law
	Administrative law
	Criminal law
	Law of (legal) Procedure
	+ including Social (welfare) Law
	+ including Environment law
International Law	Public International law
	E.U. law
	International Private law
	+ including Maritime law
	+ including Law of War
General Topics	Jurisprudence
	History of law or Legal History[148]
	Sociology of law
	Legal Informatics
	Legal Economy

Table 36: Disciplines of Legal Dogmatics[149]

To this group of law-source also belong unofficial, published commentaries, which are written commentary on each word/paragraph of the articles of an act contributed by acknowledged scholars, civil servants, or judges.

In some European countries, court decisions may make reference to scholarly writings. However, the citation practice of European courts does not necessarily reveal the influence of academic lawyers on judicial law-making. Italian courts, unlike English and German ones, do not usually make explicit

[147] BLUME *supra* note 115 at 161.

[148] Much of what is called legal history in the Civil Law tradition is baffling and inexplicable to the Common Law lawyer. He or she is used to thinking of legal history as an account of legal rules and institutions in their historical, economic, and social context. However, picking up a book on legal history in the Civil Law tradition, one is likely to find the bulk of it devoted to a discussion of schools of legal thought and of disputes between legal scholars and their followers. The protagonist or leader of this form of legal history is the legal scholar, and its subject matter is currents of thoughts about the structure and operation of the legal order, MERRYMAN *supra* note 9 at 60.

[149] BLUME *supra* note 114 at 163.

reference to academic writings.[150]

In Italy, a statute expressly forbids judges to make reference to scholarly works as authority in the court decisions.[151] Nevertheless, in practice, the courts sometimes do so.[152] Occasionally, Italian courts quote directly from a legal textbook or article without mentioning the author or the work.[153]

In England, in particular, appellate court references to academic literature have increased enormously.[154] These days, judges read academic articles as part of their ordinary judicial activity, and they cite them with authors' names and references.[155]

Unlike English judges, Italian judges hardly ever examine in detail the position of the legal doctrine in their judgments. In Italy, as well as in France, the expression "legal doctrine" refers to legal scholars as a collective entity.[156]

7.3.1.2.4. Private source of law

A private law-source [157] is one that is not issued by an authorized official body, but stems from a practice followed by a group of people – a public kind

[150] Alexandra Braun, *Professors and Judges in Italy: It Takes Two to Tango*, 26 OXFORD JOURNAL OF LEGAL STUDIES 656, 670 (Winter 2006) [hereinafter BRAUN].

[151] "In ogni caso deve essere omessa ogni citazione di autori giuridici" ["In every case every citation of legal authors must be omitted"], Regio decreto 18 dicembre 1941, n. 1368 (Suppl. G.U. 24 dicembre 1941, n. 302), Disposizioni per l'attuazione del Codice di Procedura Civile e disposizioni transitorie [Regal decree No. 1368 of 18 Decembers 1941 (Suppl. G.U. 24 December 1941, no. 302) as Annex to the Code of Civil Procedure, Title Three, Heading Two, Section Three, Article 118, subsection 3], at <www.difensore.it/codici/codiceproceduracivile.htm>. See also Virgilio Andrioli, CODICE DI PROCURA CIVILE E NORME COMPLEMENTARI (Milan: Dott. A. Giuffrè Editore, 1984).

[152] The Italian Supreme Court of Cassation has acknowledged that some academic contributions in the field of leasing have been adopted by the courts. Case 5573 from Suprema Corte di Cassazione, 13 December 1989, Foro ital ano, 1990, I, 46; BRAUN, *supra* note 144 at 671 and footnote 27.

[153] Suprema Corte di Cassazione, 16 May 2000, Case no. 6323, Nuova giurisprudenza civile commentate 2001, I, 357 at 367 (in which the judges quote a passage from C.M. Bianca, Diritto civile, III, Il contratto (1984) at 238 without mentioning the author or the book); BRAUN *supra* note 148 at 671 and footnote 28.

[154] BRAUN *supra* note 148 at 668 and footnote 10.

[155] *In Re OT Computers Ltd (In Administration) Nagra v. OT Computers Ltd*, [2004] Ch 317, 332-333 para 43, [2004] EWCA Civ 653 para 43, [2004] 3 W.L.R. 88 (Court of Appeal, CA (Civ Div), May 2004 - Judge Longmore).

[156] BRAUN *supra* note 148 at 680.

[157] In Danish "kutyme". BLUME *supra* note 115, at 147-158, 202.

of self-regulation. Examples are trade usage or private agreements.

7.3.1.2.5. Legal Cultural Tradition

This "source"[158] cannot be defined accurately and its basis is hard to trace. It can be described generally as using common sense in a legal argument to support the determination of whether a specific or concrete result is in accordance with the legal tradition and the values of a particular legal system. It may refer to considerations of fairness, equality, and feasibility as to societal needs.[159] It influences the decision of whether an intermediate result is reasonable and just; thus, it should be considered only as part of the last and final say on a legal issue.[160]

7.3.2. Use of the source of law

Another issue is to determine whether a specific law-source has to be used. This implies answering the following questions:

Research Tip #7.16

1. Does the source actually exist, and has it has been legally adopted?
2. Is the rule indicated in the source usable for the specific problem?
3. Is the use of the rule influenced by other sources, for example an interpretation of a court decision, is there a more appropriate rule for the issue at hand?

In principle, all sources of law are equal, so there is no hierarchy with some ranked higher than others. However, hard law sources do have priority over soft law ones.[161]

It is not a precondition for the use of a particular source of law that it has been published or made public – for example, a court decision has been published – unless the legal system involved has expressly made it a requirement – for example, a statute has to be publicized in a legal system's legal journal or gazette (before it can come into force). Nevertheless, it is a requirement

[158] In Danish "Forholdets nature".

[159] Former Danish Supreme Court Judge Torben Jensen in *Domstolenes retsskabende, retsudfyldende og responderende virksomhed* [The courts' law-creating, filling out and responding activity], 1990 JOURNAL OF LAW [Ugeskrift of Retsvæsen] (UfR) [subsection] B 441.

[160] BLUME *supra* note 115 at 76. WANDALL *supra* note 89, at 4.5.

[161] BLUME *supra* note 115 at 74.

that the source of law be trustworthy and reliable.[162]

Even if one has knowledge of all sources of law on a specific problem, it is by no means necessary that every one must be used. The requirement is simply that all necessary sources be used for solving the particular legal problem or question.[163]

7.3.3. Interpretation of the law-sources

When one has found those law-sources that might influence the answer to a legal question, the next step is to lay down the legal meaning of each source of law so that one can determine how each one contributes to the legal argument.[164]

> **Research-Tip 7.17**
>
> For written sources of law, this implies an analysis and consideration of the text.
>
> The aim of interpretation165 is to find the legal purpose or meaning, which might be different from the immediate linguistic meaning.166

[162] BLUME *supra* note 115 at 78-80.

[163] BLUME *supra* note 115 at 88-81.

[164] The general contemporary American view of statutory interpretation is that there is not a great deal to say about the subject. The American understanding of statutory interpretation still remains quite limited and a unified theory of statutory interpretation may be unattainable. The phrase "statutory interpretation" might refer to a variety of judicial actions with respect to statutes. Unfortunately, there is no consensus as to which of these judicial actions are covered by the phrase "statutory interpretation," and some commentators contrast that phrase with another – "statutory construction" – to which they assign a different meaning. Other writers treat the phrases as synonymous, each phrase referring to all these judicial actions. Robert Weisberg, *The Calabresian Judicial Artist: Statutes And The New Legal Process*, 35 STAN. L. REV. 213, footnote 1 (January 1983); Daniel A. Farber, *Statutory Interpretation and Legislative Supremacy*, 78 GEO. L. J. 281 (December 1989).

[165] Interpretation, as applied to written law, is the art or process of discovering and expounding the intended signification of the language used, that is, the meaning which the authors of the law designed it to convey to others. HENRY CAMPBELL BLACK, HANDBOOK ON THE CONSTRUCTION AND INTERPRETATION OF THE LAWS 1 (1896).

[166] The American term "comparative interpretation" seems to have a different meaning, as the method of interpretation in the U.S. seeks to ascertain the meaning of a statute or other writing by comparing its several parts and also by comparing it as a whole with other like documents proceeding from the same source and referring to the same general subject. See BLACK'S LAW DICTIONARY (8th ed.) (St. Paul: West Publishing, 2004).

The interpretated sources compile into a "rule" or norm, which is used for legal decision-making. In the compiling process, a determination is made of how to weight each of the sources for the legal question that has to be answered. Ethical and value-based motives can sometimes exercise influence. The interpretation is done ad hoc, in relation to a concrete case (and factual context), so that it is different from case to case. The object of interpretation[167] is to reduce or remove the uncertainty of a legal rule's meaning and to preclude (or at least hinder) unreasonable results.

As explained next below, a number of interpretation methods have been developed.

7.3.3.1. Statutes

Initially, one should note that the different interpretation methods do not influence the determination of the meaning or use of a rule.[168]

- The most important interpretation method is the *Lex Superior Principle* – a rule at a higher level in the hierarchy is to be preferred over a rule on a lower level, that is , a legal rule issued by a lower body has to comply with rules on a higher level.[169]
- A consultative interpretation-rule for choice between rules at the same level is the *Lex Posterior Principle* – a newer statute comes before an older statute. However, there might be some reason why the older statute has not been revoked.[170]
- Another consultative interpretation-rule is the *Lex Specialis Principle* – there is a preference for the rule that deal with specific issue(s) of society; thus, a distinct and specific rule comes before a statute of general content.[171]
- As for rules concerning the relationship between a citizen and the

[167] This involves also the question of whether a law should be given the meaning attributed to it by the legislator at the time of enactment, or whether the statute may be treated as having a kind of independent life of its own and interpreted in the light of changing social conditions.

[168] BLUME *supra* note 115 at 176-178; Legal Order in Sweden at <http://ec.europa.eu/civiljustice/legal_order/legal_order_swe_en.htm>; Legal Order in Finland at <http://ec.europa.eu/civiljustice/legal_order/legal_order_fin_en.htm>.

[169] This principle should be distinguished from the question of hierarchy between the sources of law.

[170] Or *lex posteriori derogat legi priori.*

[171] Or *lex specialis derogat legi generali.*

public ("the state"[172]),where there are several useful rules at the same level, the rule that is in the citizen's interest or favor should be used.[173]

No guideline exists where there is a conflict between an older specific rule and a newer but more general one – or lex posterior contra lex specialis. In such situations, reasonableness, preparatory work to a statute, and legislators' intentions can be considered.

Research Tip #7.18

A U.S. student should take a course on statutory interpretation before doing research on Civil Law as a main issue in Civil Law research is interpretation.

They should at least know the content given above in chapter 1, section 1.4.2.1.

7.3.3.2. Court decisions – Finding Precedential Authority

As courts in Civil Law countries do not (generally) make law,[174] court decisions have only limited value.

Research Tip #7.19

As a law-source , only a decision that can be characterized as having precedential authority[175] is of real interest.[176]

[172] In the European sense, see section 7.1.1 above.

[173] TVARNØ *supra* note 96, at 26.

[174] The French Napoleonic code expressly forbade French judges from pronouncing the law, by prohibiting judges from passing judgments exceeding the matter that was to be judged – because general rules were the domain of the law, a legislative power. In theory, then, there is no case law in France. .

[175] The substantial basis for precedent is a final judgment. Peter Blume, *From Drakon to the Computer and Beyond* in NORDIC STUDIES IN INFORMATION TECHNOLOGY AND LAW 78 (Peter Blume, ed.) (Deventer, Boston: Kluwer Computer Law Series, 1991). As for U.S. common law on the subject of precedent, see Chapter 5, subsections 5.1.3., 5.2.6.2.1., 5.2.6.2.4., 5.5. & 5.6.

[176] DANISH LAW IN A EUROPEAN PERSPECTIVE (2nd ed.) (Dahl, Melchior & Tamm, eds) (Copenhagen: DJOEF Publishing); Joseph Lookofsky, *Precedent and the Law in Denmark* - Danish National Report at the XVIIth Conference of The International Academy of Comparative Law, Utrecht 2006, at <www.cisg.law.pace.edu/cisg/biblio/lookofsky15.html> [hereinafter LOOKOFSKY]. BLUME *supra* note 115 at 134-137.

In rare cases, a decision will provide a more general opinion or point of view on the legal rule(s) involved in the case.

Thus, the primary task in considering decisions from Civil Law countries is to sort out what are the precedential cases, because any other case will not have value as a law-source.

Research Tip #7.20
One has to scrutinize the background and history of a case to figure out whether the decision is regarded as having precedential value.

The crucial element or part of a court decision that is of interest when searching for precedent is the grounds of judgment (ratio decidendi). In a precedential case, a given ground from the court can influence a later, similar case.

Note that to become a precedential case it is not a requirement that is was decided by the highest-ranking court; thus, even a decision of a court of first instance can be a precedential authority – as long as it cannot be appealed. However, of the various court decisions, the most important as sources of law are those of the highest courts

The term "precedent" – as well as the concept of "case law," to which the term precedent is tied – means different things to different jurists in different European Civil Law legal systems. There are differences even between the Scandinavian countries (Denmark, Norway, and Sweden[177]) that belong to the same Nordic Legal Family.[178]

In Denmark, the "bindingness" of any given Danish judgment – which term does not imply that the judgment has to be followed – will depend, in large measure, on the "rank" of the court, which rendered that decision, as well as on that court's relation to courts, which might be expected to "follow" it.[179] Danish courts, including the Supreme Court,[180] consider themselves

[177] Although Finland deserves inclusion in the Nordic Legal Family in certain respects, the Finnish concept of (non-binding) precedent seems distinctly more "Civilian" than Scandinavian. See generally Aulis Arnio Tampere, *Precedent in Finland,* in INTERPRETING PRECEDENT: A COMPARATIVE STUDY (Niel MacCormick, Robert S. Summers & Arthur L. Goodhart, eds.) (Vt.: Ashgate/Dartmouth, 1999) [hereinafter MACCORMICK]. Regarding the concept of precedent in Norway and in Sweden, see generally Svein Eng, *Precedent in Norway*, and Gunnar Bergholtz, *Precedent in Sweden, idem.*

[178] LOOKOFSKY *supra* note 176.

[179] LOOKOFSKY *supra* note 176.

[180] In the Danish Supreme Court decision *Kvistgaard Jern og Metal A/S v. Carsten Tilleman Carstens*, Ugeskrift for Retsvæsen 2005. 2949, 2955 (Decision of 30 June 2005 – No. 178/2004), the Supreme Court expressly based its decision on its own prior prece-

bound by their own prior decisions, at least unless compelling circumstances dictate departure from established precedent. A requirement for becoming precedential is that another (judge) has considered the result and the reasoning of the prior decision to be persuasive. Sometimes, even non-Danish decisions are considered "relevant" by Danish courts, e.g., decisions rendered by the European Court of Justice and the European Court of Human Rights.[181]

In modern times, European legislators to a certain degree, in many of the statutes enacted by parliaments, reflect an intent to leave the development of many fundamental issues and doctrines up to the courts.[182] Thus, a combined law-supplementing and law-function has long been justified and recognized as one of the Danish Supreme Court's most important tasks,[183] and without any formal restraints.[184]

A Danish judgment consists of several segments, including (in civil cases):[185]

- a presentation of the parties' respective claims;
- the parties' allegations;
- a statement of the facts of the case;
- a summary of the testimony of witnesses;
- the court's "reasoning," also referred to as the "premises," that is, the propositions upon which the court's argument is based or from which its conclusion is drawn; and, finally,
- the result.
- If the case is being heard on appeal, the judgment of the appellate

dents. But compare that with the "Maastricht Treaty" case, where the Supreme Court of Denmark took the unusual step of expressly distancing itself from its own prior decision on a similar question in *Helge Tagen v Statsministeren*, UfR 1973.694, (Decision of 28 July 1973), *Hanne Norum Carlsen v. Statsminister Poul Nyrup Rasmussen*, UfR 1996.1300 (Decision of 12 August 1996 – No. 272/1994).

181 LOOKOFSKY *supra* note 176.

182 LOOKOFSKY *supra* note 176.

183 Former Danish Supreme Court Judge, Torben Jensen, *Højesterets arbejdsform in Højesteret* 1661 - 1986 [The Supreme Court's Working Methods (printed in a special edition of the Danish Case Reporter in 1986] (Torben Jensen, W.E. von Eyben & Mogens Koktvedgaard, eds. (Copenhagen: Særudgave af Ugeskrift For Retsvæsen - G.E.C Gads Forlag, 1986).

184 It is otherwise in Norway, where the Norwegian Act of 25 June 1926 (Amending the Law Relating to the Supreme Court) requires that a plenary session of the Supreme Court be convened when two or more members of an ordinary panel (of 5 justices) wish to overrule a previous decision by that Court. Svein Eng, *Precedent in Norway*, in MACCORMICK *supra* note 177, at 201-203.

185 LOOKOFSKY *supra* note 176.

court will also include a full account of the proceedings in the forum below. One reason for this is the fact that a lower court judgment, once appealed, is unlikely to be published on its own.

In all European systems that recognize judge-made law, only "similar" cases have precedential potential, so the facts of a case are obviously important for purposes of "distinguishing" the case at bar from prior decisions.

The key prospective element of a given decision is the court's reasoning (premises), that is , that part which serves to explain and legitimize the precedent-setting court's result (the ratio decidendi – in the U.S. called the "holding").

However, in Europe some court decisions – even by the Supreme courts – are written in such a way that the reader cannot determine the whole scope of a decision, because the premises are so briefly stated or formulated in such an oracle-like fashion that they provide no clear guidance beyond the decision in the given, concrete case.[186]

7.3.4. Relations between National Law and International / E.U. Law

7.3.4.1. Monistic versus Dualistic Idea

Research Tip #7.21

Among scholars and authorities, there exist two different approaches as to whether international law is superior or not to national law: (a) monistic; and (b) dualistic.

Pursuant to a pure monistic concept, the national and international systems constitute a single legal system. Some monists claim international law supersedes national law. Others think the opposite.

Dualists hold that the national and the international legal systems are different, and exist in their own separate spheres. International law has no independent status in national law. It only becomes relevant when and if the national authorities decide to create national law based on international law.

Danish Law recognizes the principle of dualism and requires international legal sources to be incorporated domestically in order to have legal effect for and against its citizens. However, the last two decades have seen the recogni-

[186] Carl Torp, *I anledning af Højesterets 250-aarige Bestaaen*, in UGESKRIFT FOR RETSVÆSEN, 1911, p. 54; LOOKOFSKY *supra* note 176.

tion of international legal sources as a means of safeguarding the rights of individuals in Denmark.[187]

Finland is one of the dualist system countries in which international agreements do not become binding until they have been specifically implemented domestically. Implementing provisions are therefore analogous to national provisions of the same hierarchical rank.[188]

7.3.4.2. National law versus E.U. Law

As discussed in detail in the next chapter, one should note, that so-called Regulations from the E.U. are not to be implemented in national law; opposite so-called Directives.[189]

As for the E.U. Member States, the rules of law have different origins and values, because in each member state different authorities are empowered to adopt rules of law and the different sources of law do not all have the same status.[190]

The European Court of Justice holds that E.U. law[191] supersedes national law. However, not all Member States agree.[192]

The Danish Supreme Court has stated in the so-called "Maastricht Case" that §20 of the Danish Constitution prohibits handing over to an international organization authority to issue legislation or make decisions, if these are in conflict with provisions in the Constitution, including its list of freedoms.[193]

In the so-called "Maastricht Judgment," the German Federal Constitutional Court affirmed that the exercise of sovereign powers by the European

[187] WANDALL *supra* note 89.

[188] Legal Order – Finland at <http://ec.europa.eu/civiljustice/legal_order/legal_order_fin_en.htm>.

[189] On sources of EU and Danish law, see TVARNØ *supra* note 96.

[190] Legal order - General Information at <http://ec.europa.eu/civiljustice/legal_order/legal_order_gen_en.htm>.

[191] Documents with EU legislation often contain large preambles that introduce the legislation and/or express the particular legislative aims. They can be utilized when making legal arguments.

[192] In Finland, in accordance with doctrine on the supremacy of European Union law, E.U. law takes precedence over national law. Legal Order – Finland at <http://ec.europa.eu/civiljustice/legal_order/legal_order_fin_en.htm>. In Sweden, EU legislation applies to a certain extent directly in Sweden without any intermediate legislation. Legal Order – Sweden at <http://ec.europa.eu/civiljustice/legal_order/legal_order_swe_en.htm>.

[193] *Hanne Norup Carlsen et. al. v. Primeminister Poul Nyrup Rasmussen*, UfR 1998.800 H at no. 9.2 (Danish Supreme Court 6 April 1998 – No. I 361/1997).

Union "is based on authorizations from the Member States which remain sovereign and which in international matters generally act through their government ... nowhere does the Union Treaty reflect the common will of the contracting Parties to establish the Union as a distinct legal subject bearing genuine competences."[194]

In contrast, the European Court of Justice has regularly held that E.U. regulations, directives, and agreements are directly, fully, and immediately binding upon E.U. Member States. In the Costa case, the ECJ stated,[195] "By contrast with ordinary international treaties, the EEC Treaty has created its own legal system which, on the entry into force of the Treaty, became an integral part of the legal systems of the Member States and which their courts are bound to apply … By creating a Community of unlimited duration, having … powers stemming from a limitation of sovereignty, or a transfer of powers from the States to the Community, the Member States have limited their sovereign rights, albeit within limited fields, and have thus created a body of law which binds both their nationals and themselves… ." The elements of the E.U. that the ECJ felt were most salient were unlimited duration, a limitation of sovereign rights, and (separately) treaty language that directly binds the Member States to follow European law.

Furthermore, the European Court of Justice has regularly held that international law – especially customary international law regarding the interpretation and effect of treaties – is binding upon the European Union and its organs. In the Racke case, the European Commission questioned whether international law regarding interpretation of treaties – in this case, the doctrine of "fundamental change of circumstances" – had become part of the European legal order. The ECJ emphatically stated that "the European Community must respect international law in the exercise of its powers" and "the rules of customary international law concerning the termination and suspension of treaty relations by reason of a fundamental change of circumstances are binding upon the Community institutions and form part of the Community legal order."[196]

Recently, in the Placanica case, the ECJ held that articles in the EC Treaty

[194] Judgment on the Maastricht Treaty, BVerfGE 89, 155, (Bundesverfassungsgericht, 12 October 1993).

[195] *Costa v. ENEL*, 1964 E.C.R. 585, 593 (European Court of Justice 15 July 1964 - Case 6/64).

[196] *A. Racke GmbH & Co. v. Hauptzollamt Mainz*, 1998 E.C.R. I-3655 para 45-46 (European Court of Justice , 16 June 199 - Case 162/96).

"must be interpreted as precluding national legislation."[197]

7.4. When to Stop

When one is performing research in a Civil Law country, one cannot stop before all sources of law have been located, reviewed, and analyzed. However, if dealing with a foreign law, this requirement is often not achievable.

> **Research Tip #7.22**
> It is a requirement for proper legal research in a Civil Law country always to at least have read all hard sources of law on the issue at hand. In legal research of Civil Law countries, one must be sure all hard law has been studied (including E.U. law for Member States).

7.5. Conclusion / Recap

- Do not use common law / U.S. research methods on Civil Law research
- Find the relevant Civil Law research method for your country & topic
- Do not rely on the meanings & your own country's English words when researching another country
- Only rely on authorized (official) translations
- Learn about the legal family, culture, history, society & language before doing research in a foreign country
- Researching Civil Law requires knowledge about how to interpret text in a statute
- Only research those Civil Law case decisions that are regarded as precedents.

7.5. Further Reading (updates at corresponding website)

The URL for the corresponding website is <www.hssph.net/legalrm> with a full alphabetic bibliography.

[197] *Criminal proceedings against Massimiliano Placanica* (Italy), [2007] 2 C.M.L.R. 25 para 64 & 71-72, [2007] ECR 00, 2007 WL 654380 (ECJ) (European Court of Justice (Grand Chamber), 6 March 2007 - Case C-338/04).

See also above in subsection 7.1.6.1. a list of some basic books for different European countries written in English by natives.

Apple, James G., & Robert P Deyling, *A Primer on the Civil-law System* (Federal Judicial Center, 1995) at

<www.fjc.gov/public/pdf.nsf/lookup/CivilLaw.pdf/$file/CivilLaw.pdf>

Jestaz, Philippe, & Christophe Jamin, *The entity of French doctrine: Some thoughts on the Community of French Legal Writers*, 18 LEGAL STUDIES 415 (1998)

MERRYMAN, JOHN HENRY, THE CIVIL LAW TRADITION: AN INTRODUCTION TO THE LEGAL SYSTEMS OF WESTERN EUROPE AND LATIN AMERICA (2nd ed.) (Stanford, California: Stanford University Press, 1985)

TUORI, KAARLO & SUVI SANKARI, THE MANY CONSTITUTIONS OF EUROPE (Burlington, VT: Ashgate Publishing Company, 2010)

Vogenauer, Stefan, *An Empire of Light: Learning and Lawmaking in Germany Today*, 26 OXFORD JOURNAL OF LEGAL STUDIES 627 (2006)

CHAPTER 8

Russia Resources – Civil Law

8.1. Russia – Short Overview

Russian law belong to the Civil Law tradition. However, as Russia through periods was isolated from Europe, its legal system has different roots than rest of Europe. Both before and after the Bolshevik Revolution of 1917, the Russian legal system has had many characteristics of Civil Law systems and civil codes related to Western Europe. Some have however classified the legal system under the communist period as a separate "socialist" legal tradition based on factors other than the characteristics of legal systems traditionally considered by comparativists.[1] After the fall of communist regime, Russia has essentially rejoined the Civil Law family.[2]

Russia is a federation with capital in Moscow consisting of 83 (previous 89) "Subjects of the Federation" (Regions), which have equal political rights.

Subjects of the Federation have their own legislatures and governments, who act within the competence determined by the Constitution and, in some cases, an agreement between the Federation and the region.

However, in reality most Russian laws are federal and as such have superiority over regional legal acts. Another complication of relations between the Federation and the Regions is the composition of the tax and budget systems. The majority of regions receive financial assistance from the federal budget.

There are over 24,000 municipalities, whose structures are determined by the regional legislation under the legal framework established by the federal laws. They include legislative bodies at the local level.

[1] William Burnham, Peter B. Maggs & Gennady M. Danilenko, LAW AND LEGAL SYSTEM OF THE RUSSIAN FEDERATION 4 (4. Ed)(New York: Juris Publishing, 2009).
[2] *Idem* at 6.

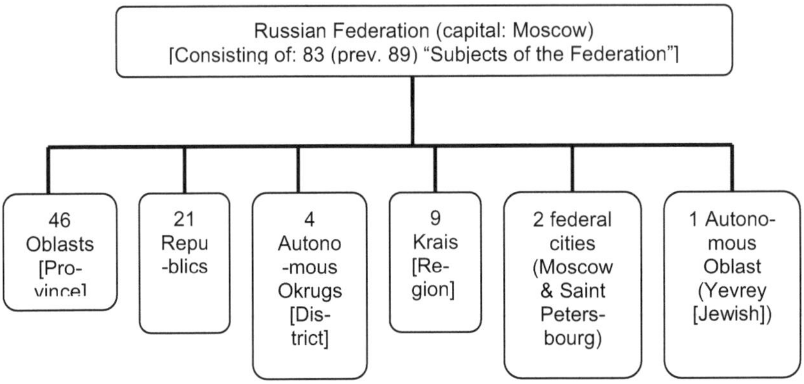

Table 37: State Structure – Subjects of the Federation

The political system established by the Constitution of 1993 gives the president substantial superiority over the other branches of the state. The president is elected for a term of six years directly by the citizens of the Russian Federation (maximum two terms in succession).

The Federal Assembly - or Parliament - is the supreme legislative body of the Russian Federation and consists of two chambers:

- The Federation Council (upper house - 2 representatives from each Subject of the Federation, 1 from the representative and 1 from the executive bodies of the Subject of the Federation (Presently: 166 seats))(Previously: "Congress of People's Deputies of the Russian Federation")
- The State Duma (lower house - 450 deputies for 5-year terms)(Previously: "Supreme Soviet")

The Government consists of the Chairman of the Government, Deputy Chairman of the Government and federal ministers. The chairman is appointed by the president with consent of the State Duma. If the State Duma thrice rejects candidates for Chairman of the Government nominated by the president, the president then appoints a Chairman of the Government, dissolves the State Duma and calls a new election.

The Chairman of the Government of the Russian Federation is the second most powerful official of the Russian Federation. In case of the President's death, resignation or impeachment, the Prime Minister becomes a temporary president until new presidential elections, which must take place within three months. The Prime Minister acting as president may not dissolve the State Duma, announce a referendum or propose amendments to the Constitution.

The President appoints and dismisses the Prime Minister and other members of the Government. The President may chair the meetings of the cabinet and give obligatory orders to the Prime Minister and other members of the Government, the President may also revoke any act of the Government.

The Prosecutor's Office of the Russian Federation is a single centralized system in which lower prosecutors are subordinated to higher prosecutors and the Prosecutor-General. The Prosecutor-General is appointed to the post and relieved from it by the Federation Council on nomination by the President. Prosecutors are appointed by the Prosecutor-General.

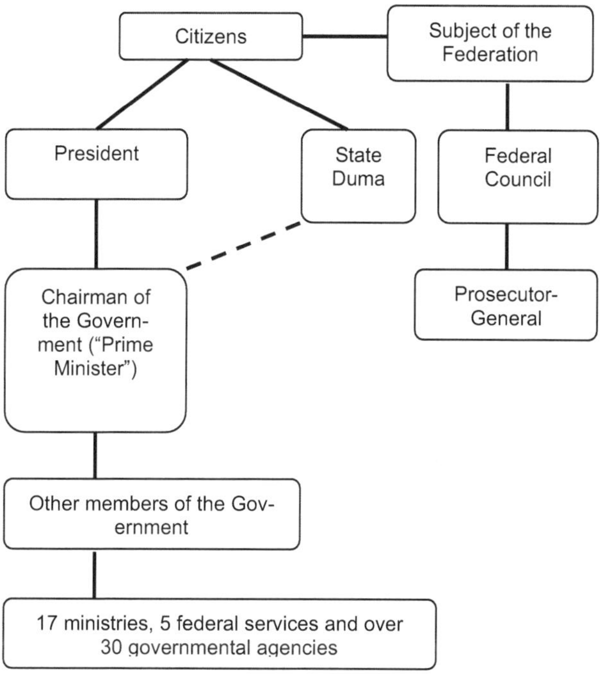

Table 38: Political System of Russia

The legislative process in Russia includes three hearings in the State Duma, then approvals by the Council of the Federation and then transmission to the President. If the President rejects a federal law, the State Duma and the Federation Council again consider the law. If the law is approved in its earlier draft by two-thirds of the total number of deputies of the Council of the Federation and the State Duma, the President must sign it.

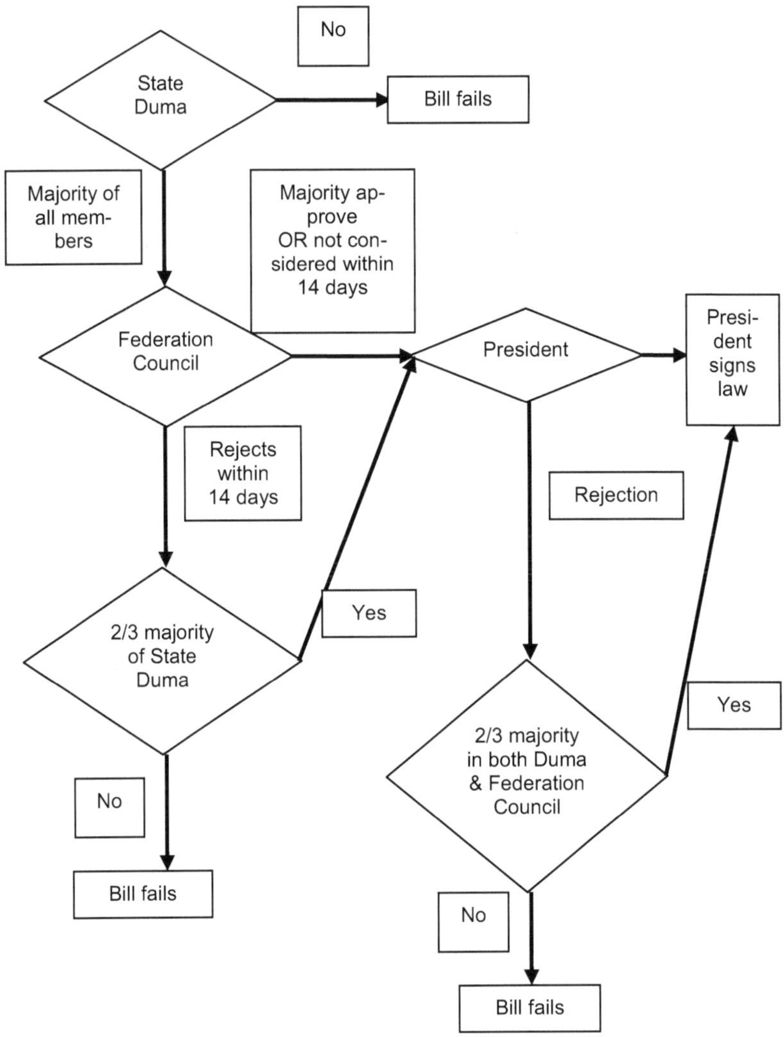

Table 39: Legislative Process in Russia

The framework of the Russian legal system is created by:

- the Constitution, constitutions of the Subjects of the Federation,
- decisions of the Constitutional court,
- decisions and directives of the Supreme Court and the Supreme Ar-

birtazhny Court,

- international treaties (when ratified, they have direct effect and precedence over the domestic legislation),[3]
- federal constitutional laws and federal laws,
- regional laws and ordinances,
- municipal legal acts,
- directives and statements of the Central Bank and governmental ministries and state authorities.

The law of the Russian Federation is divided into several codes.

Conflict between legal acts is resolved according to the juridical power of the legal acts. The Constitution is a supreme power over the whole territory of Russia. Codes and federal constitutional laws, meanwhile, have more power than federal laws.[4]

Decisions rendered by courts are not binding on other courts. However, in practice precedents of the higher courts are becoming an important source of Russian law.

Judges of the three highest courts serve for life and are appointed by the Federation Council after nomination by the President. The President on his/her own appoints judges to the federal district courts. The Minister of Justice appoints judges to regional and city courts.

A comprehensive list (in English) of courts in Russia – arranged by level of court and geographic location, with links to the courts' websites (in Russian) – is provided by World Law Guide by Lexadin at

<www.lexadin.nl/wlg/courts/nofr/oeur/lxctrus.htm>.

The Supreme Court of the Russian Federation has on its website provided an English-language description about the court and its work, at

<www.supcourt.ru/catalog.php?c1=English>.

[3] Tarja Långstöm, TRANSFORMATION IN RUSSIA AND INTERNATIONAL LAW (Leiden: Martinus Nijhoff Publishers, 2003).

[4] <www.russianlawonline.com/content/russia-sources-law>.

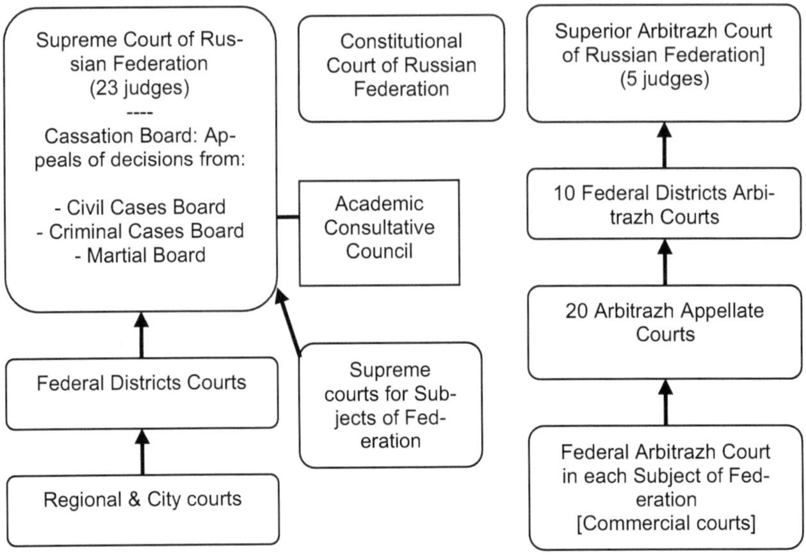

Table 40: Russian Federation Court Systems Superior Arbitrazh Court of Russian Federation [5]

8.2. Miscellaneous Russian material in English

- Garant (subscription required) – A Russian company providing a major database for accessing Russian legislation and court cases in English translation at

  <http://english.garant.ru/>.

  Garant is available through LexisNexis.
- Kodeks (subscription required) - A major Russian database, with translations into English, primarily on business legislation at

  <http://kodeks.mosinfo.ru/>.

[5] The Academic Consultative Council assists the Supreme Court in various legal and academic matters. It comprises members of the Supreme Court itself, academics and practicing lawyers and law enforcement officers. The members of the Academic consultative Council are elected at plenary sessions of the Supreme Court.

Free access to Thematic Glossary of Normative Acts and to New Documents, which are useful in showing what is available on the site in translation.

- Legislation Russia – A World Law Guide by Lexadin that gathers material found on the World Wide Web. Thus, some materials may be outdated at

  <www.lexadin.nl/wlg/legis/nofr/oeur/lxwerus.htm>.

- Courts and Cases Russia – A World Law Guide by Lexadin that provides in English a comprehensive list of courts in Russia (arranged by level of court and geographic location) with links to the courts' websites (in Russian) at

  <www.lexadin.nl/wlg/courts/nofr/oeur/lxctrus.htm>.

8.3. Further Reading (updates at corresponding website)

The URL for the corresponding website is <www.hssph.net/legalrm> with a full alphabetic bibliography.

Burnham, William E., Peter B. Maggs & Gennady M. Danilenko, Law and Legal System of the Russian Federation (4. Ed)(New York: Juris Publishing, 2009)

Butler, William E., Russian Law (1. Ed)(New York, N.Y.: Oxford University Press, 1999)(this has some material that was not incorporated into the later edition).

Butler, William E., Russian Law (2d ed.)(New York, N.Y.: Oxford, University Press, 2002)(comprehensive textbook, including the text of the constitution, a listing of treaties, and a chapter devoted to resource material on Russian Law)

Cox, Lucy, *Material on Russian Federation Law in English: Selection of Sources*, (GlobaLex, August 2008) at <www.nyulawglobal.org/globalex/Russia1.htm>

Guide To International Legal Research (The George Washington International Law Review) (Newark, NJ : LexisNexis Matthew Bender, 2010)

Kavass, Igor I., Law in Russia and the Other Post-Soviet Republics: A Bibliographic Survey of English Language and Literature 1992-1995 (Buffalo, N.Y: William S. Hein & Co., 1997)(provides a thorough bibliographic listing of books, articles, translations of laws and court decisions from law reviews and other journals; access is by author or subject).

Kavass, Igor I., Law in Russia and the Other Post-soviet Republics: A Bibliographic Survey of English Language Literature 1996-2001 (Buffalo, N.Y.: William S. Hein & Co., 2002). (continuation of the earlier work listed directly above).

LÅNGSTÖM, TARJA, TRANSFORMATION IN RUSSIA AND INTERNATIONAL LAW (Leiden: Martinus Nijhoff Publishers, 2003).

Popova, Arina, and Lev S. Soloviev, *A Guide to Legal Research in Russia* (GlobaLex, August 2008) at <www.nyulawglobal.org/globalex/Russia_Legal_Research1.htm>

U.S. Library of Congress, Legal Research Guide: Russia at <www.loc.gov/law/help/russia.php>.

CHAPTER 9

European Union Resources – Civil Law

9.1. Introduction

This chapter on the European Union[1] is updated from first and second editions of the book in light of the so-called Treaty of Lisbon of December 2007, which came into force on 1 December 2009. It consists of the:[2]

- Treaty on European Union (TEU)[3]
- Treaty on the Functioning of the European Union (FTEU)[4]

As this book is primarily aimed for use in teaching courses on legal research methods, note that the brief time normally allotted for such courses cannot begin to cover comprehensive instruction on European Union Law.[5]

Right off the bat, so to speak, a good book on European Union[6] "law" is "Euro-

[1] As of 2007, trade between U.S. & E.U. was running at around €1.7 billion (i.e., $ 2.468 billion) per day. In 2009, the E.U. amounted to over 21% of the world's total economic output in terms of purchasing power parity. World Economic Outlook Database at <www.imf.org/external/pubs/ft/weo/2010/01/weodata/index.aspx>. 161 of the top 500 largest corporations measured by revenue have their headquarters in the E.U. Fortune Global 500 at <www. money.cnn.com/magazines/fortune/global500/2010>.

[2] Consolidated version (sometimes with changed/other text as the Lisbon Treaty) printed in E.U. Official Journal [OJ] C115, 9.5.2008 pp. 0001-0388.

[3] Consolidated version of Treaty on European Union [TEU], OJ C115, 9.5.2008 pp. 0013-0045.

[4] Consolidated version of Treaty on the Functioning of the European Union [TFEU], OJ C115, 9.5.2008 pp. 0047-0199.

[5] Previously called European Community law.

[6] The European Union (EU) is a political and economic union of member states, located in Europe, and established by the Maastricht Treaty of 1993 upon the foundations of the pre-existing European Community. The Vatican, Iceland, Norway, Liechtenstein and Switzerland are not members.

pean Union Law."[7]

Remember that European Union "law" is part of the law of each of the E.U. Member States, who must – to a certain extent – separately implement that "law" from Brussels (Bruxelles).

Research Tip #9.1

European Union "law" should be read and studied through the law of the E.U. Member State on which one is doing research.[8]

Beware that some E.U. "law" may be not even have been "implemented into law" by a Member State (which state be sued by the European Union Commission for such failure to implement).

Soft law[9] on E.U. "law" cannot be found in general but have to be searched through the particular E.U. Member State on which one wants to do research.

The European Union is unique in that it is much more than an international organization.[10] It has legal personality and can conclude treaties with States. The E.U. is not a federation like the United States. Nevertheless, to a certain extent, the E.U. has similarities in function and organization to the United States. Even so, in the E.U., there is no rule similar to the U.S. "Dormant"

[7] Damian Chalmers, Gareth Davies & Giorgio Monti, EUROPEAN UNION LAW (2 ed)(England: Cambridge, 2010). See also, Watt & Dashwood's EUROPEAN UNION LAW (London: Thompson); Woods, Steiner & Twigg-Flesner, EU LAW (England: Oxford University Press).

[8] In the context of the E.U., the term "supranational" usually refers to the institutions that exist to pursue the common E.U. interests, shared by the E.U. Member States. It also refers to the discharge of functions and exercise of powers by those institutions, transcending national boundaries, in the domains where the E.U. Member States, in the treaties, have conferred those functions and powers on them. The supranational approach is often contrasted with the intergovernmental approach that involves keeping supranational institutions, and their role, to a minimum.

[9] Some name it "secondary sources" and others claim there does not exist any secondary sources/soft law in the E.U. See also Table 4 in Chapter 1.

[10] For example, an international organization does not have a "Secretary of State" as the E.U. does. Arguably, it has been incorrectly characterized as an "International Organization" in Chapter 8 of Marcy Hoffman and Mary Rumsey in INTERNATIONAL AND FOREIGN LEGAL RESEARCH: A COURSEBOOK (Martinus Nijhoff Publishers, 2008).

Commerce Clause.[11] Thus, the member states of the E.U. truly have full sovereignty.[12] However, there is also a so-called "proportionality principle" that is, European Union actions must not go beyond what is necessary to achieve the objectives of the Treaty of Rome,[13] except that the E.U. can act in areas where Member States cannot sufficiently achieve an objective but through the Community (the subsidiarity principle).[14]

On December 13, 2007, a major new treaty - a so-called "Reform Treaty" or the Treaty of Lisbon - was signed by leaders of the Member States with its

[11] Even where Congress chooses not to exercise such power, U.S. states cannot regulate, even if Congress "sleeps." See U.S. Supreme Court Chief Justice John Marshall's dicta in *Gibbons v. Cigden*, 22 U.S. 1 (1824).

[12] See Subsection 1 of article 4 of TEU. However, the European Court of Justice holds that E.U. law supersedes national law. The ECJ has regularly held that EU regulations, directives and agreements are directly, fully, and immediately binding upon EU Member States. In the *Costa* case, the court stated that "[b]y contrast with ordinary international treaties, the EEC Treaty has created its own legal system which, on the entry into force of the Treaty, became an integral part of the legal systems of the Member States and which their courts are bound to apply...By creating a Community of unlimited duration, having...powers stemming from the States to the Community, the Member States have limited their sovereign rights, albeit within limited fields, and have thus created a body of law which binds both their nationals and themselves". *Costa v. ENEL* (ECJ 15 July 1964, Case 6/64), 1964 E.C.R. 585, 593. But, not all Member States agree. The Danish Supreme Court has in the so-called "Maastricht Case" stated that under §20 of the Danish Constitution an international organization is prohibited from issuing legislation or making decisions, if these are in conflict with provisions in the Danish Constitution, including its freedom rights. *Hanne Norup Carlsen et. al. v. Primeminister Poul Nyrup Rasmussen*, UfR 1998.800 H at no. 9.2 (Danish Supreme Court 6 April 1998 – No. I 361/1997). See also the so-called "Maastricht judgment" of the German Federal Constitutional Court where it affirmed that the exercise of sovereign powers by the European Union "is based on authorizations from the Member States which remain sovereign and which in international matters generally act through their government...nowhere does the Union Treaty reflect the common will of the contracting Parties to establish the Union as a distinct legal subject bearing genuine competences." Judgment on the Maastricht Treaty, BVerfGE 89, 155, (German Federal Constitutional Court, 12 October 1993).

[13] Or "Treaty establishing the European Economic Community" of 25 March 1957, 298 U.N.T.S. 11.

[14] After Lisbon, Article 5 of Consolidated version of Treaty on European Union [TEU], OJ C115, 9.5.2008 p. 0018 outlines the principles of conferral, subsidiary and proportionality (see also Protocol No. 2, OJ C115, 9.5.2008 p. 0206-0209). Previously, article 5 (ex ante EC art. 3b) of Treaty of Establishing the European Community, OJ C321 E, 29.12.2006 p. 0046.

purpose being to make the E.U. work more efficiently, including merging/eliminating the so-called pillar[15] system.[16] As with the nature of most amending treaties, the Treaty of Lisbon is not intended to be read as an autonomous text. See below section 9.3.2. It came into force on 1 December 2009.

Note that the Council of Europe[17] (an international organization) is not part of the E.U., which latter entity includes the Council of the European Union (one of the legislative institutions of the E.U.) and the European Council. However, most confusingly, all these institutions share certain symbols, such as flag and anthem. The European Union has been a permanent observer at the United Nations since the mid-1970s and a full participant in many major UN conferences. It is also one of the key players in the World Trade Organization (WTO).

Research Tip #9.2

American scholars who want to undertake comparative research on E.U. "law" (and Civil Law) should be careful about using legal terms,[18] even ones well-known in American legal circles, as their meanings may be quite different in Europe (and Civil Law).

Thus, definitions should be carefully checked before any comparison is attempted.

Research Tip #9.3

American scholars cannot use their U.S. legal research methods in researching E.U. "law" and Civil Law (see further above in Chapter 3).

[15] See below section 9.2.9.

[16] The Flexibility Clause within the Treaty of Lisbon allows for adjustments of E.U. competence within the defined parameters of the E.U. The existing clause can only be used in connection with the area of the common market. Art 352 (ex Article 308 TEC) of Consolidated Treaty on the Functioning of the European Union [TFEU], OJ C115, 9.5.2008 p. 0196.

[17] The aim of the Council of Europe is to achieve greater unity among its members, which are all European democracies, including Russia and Turkey, Council of Europe at <www.coe.int/> and Council of the European Union <http://europa.eu/institutions/inst/council/index_en.htm>.

[18] E.U. Glossary at <http://europa.eu/scadplus/glossary/index_en.htm>.

In Europe today, Civil Law and Common Law show several signs of convergence. In the UK, statutory law increasingly overrides Common Law traditions of judicial law-making, while on the continent, legal theory increasingly acknowledges the fact and necessity of judicial precedent and law-making. Important areas of the law are unified under international treaties. British judges faithfully implement European Union law that is based primarily on Civil Law notions. The Court of Justice of the E.U. creatively applies principles from both legal worlds. But despite refreshing input from the Common Law, the dominant legal culture of the European Union and the emerging ius commune Europaeum[19] remain very much in the Civil Law tradition.[20]

To be able to find material on the European Union, it is important for the legal scholar to understand the different E.U. institutions and their function. Thus, the following will broadly describe the main E.U. institutions of importance for the legal scholar.

9.1.1. The Legal Base for the European Union

The E.U. can only take action if it has a "legal base" in the (consolidated version of the) two treaties with amendments from the Treaty of Lisbon - which will later provide new legal bases and allow the E.U. to take action on:

- Public health (such as disease prevention), in response to wider concerns affecting the safety of the general public
- Energy security
- Dealing with natural or man-made disasters
- Sport
- Space policy

No new exclusive competences have been created by the Treaty of Lisbon,[21] e.g., military capabilities remain in national hands.

In the Treaty of Lisbon, the distribution of competences in various policy areas between Member States and the Union is explicitly stated in the following three categories: [22]

[19] See Glossary: Terms & Abbreviations in the Appendix.

[20] Herbert Hausmaninger, The Austrian Legal System 320 (2003 Manzsche Verlags- und Universitätsbuchhandlung).

[21] See Presidency Conclusion's on the Brussels European Council meeting 21-22 June 2007 at <www.consilium.europa.eu/ueDocs/cms_Data/docs/pressData/en/ec/94932.pdf>.

[22] The TFEU also refers to the common foreign and security policy and the coordination of economic and employment policies, which, because of their specific nature, do not

Type of competence	**Exclusive** (full list)[23]	**Shared** (non-exhaustive list)[24]	**Complementary** (full list)
Definition	Only the Union can adopt legally binding acts. The Member States cannot intervene unless authorized to do so by the Union, or to implement measures taken by the latter.	The Union and the Member States can adopt legally binding acts. The Member States being able to do so if the Union has not done so.	The Union can intervene only to support action by Member States (primarily through financial contributions); it may legislate but not harmonize national legislation and regulations.
Subjects	▪ Customs Union ▪ Establishing competition rules required for operation of the internal market ▪ Monetary policy for Member States whose currency is the euro ▪ Conservation of the biological resources of the sea under the fisheries policy ▪ Common commercial (trade) policy	▪ Internal market ▪ Social policy (for the aspects defined in the Treaty of Lisbon) ▪ Economic, social and territorial cohesion ▪ Agriculture and fisheries (excluding conservation of the biological resources of the sea) ▪ Environment ▪ Consumer protection ▪ Transport ▪ TransEuropean networks ▪ Energy ▪ Area of freedom, security and justice	▪ Protection and improvement of human health ▪ Industry ▪ Culture ▪ Tourism ▪ Education ▪ Youth ▪ Sport ▪ Vocational training ▪ Civil protection (disaster prevention) ▪ Administrative co-operation

come under any of the three categories in this table. The areas of competence "underlined" in each of the columns are areas for which there are currently no specific provisions in the Treaties but in which the Union has already taken action, in particular using the provisions relating to the internal market or Article 352 (ex Article 308 TEC) of TFEU.

[23] In addition to these competences, the Union also has as an exclusive competence for the conclusion of international agreements when this is provided for in a legislative act of the Union, when it is necessary to enable the Union to exercise its internal competence or when it is likely to affect common rules or adversely affect their scope.

[24] Although the TFEU deals with the policies indicated by underlining in this column in the article relating to shared competences, they are sectors in which Union action does not have the effect of preventing the exercise of national competences.

		▪ Common safety concerns in the public health sphere (for the aspects defined in the Treaty of Lisbon) ▪ *Research and technological development* ▪ *Space policy* ▪ *Development co-operation*	

Table 41: The Competences of the Union

9.1.2. National Parliaments

With the Treaty of Lisbon, national parliaments have become much more involved in the legislative process.[25] They have the power to have a say at a very early stage, before a proposal is considered in detail by the European Parliament and the Council of Ministers.

Article 1 of Protocol No. 1 on the Role of National Parliaments in the European Union requires that draft legislative acts sent to the European Parliament and to the Council shall be forwarded to national parliaments.

The latter may send reasoned opinions[26] on whether a draft legislative act complies with the principle of subsidiarity,[27] see Protocol No. 2.[28] Thus, national parliaments have now formally been given the task of "watchdog" so that the principle of subsidiarity is respected.[29] National parliaments will have

[25] Art. 3 in Protocol no. 1 on the role of national parliaments in the European Union. OJ C115, 9.5.2008 p. 0204.

[26] Reasoned Opinion (as for the protocol 2 of the Treaty of Lisbon on applying the principles of proportionality) - an opinion with reasons, put forward by a national parliament (or one of its Houses) that a proposal for a law, made by the Commission, is in breach of the principle of subsidiarity. In this case, a reasoned opinion is part of an "early warning system," to be operated by national parliaments.

[27] Protocol No. 1 on the Role of National Parliaments in the European Union, OJ C115, 9.5.2008, p. 0203-0205.

[28] Protocol No. 2 on the Application of the Principles of Subsidiarity and Proportionality, OJ C115, 9.5.2008, p. 206-209.

[29] Art. 12 of consolidated TEU; Protocol no. 1 on the Role of National Parliaments in the European Union; and Protocol no. 2 on the Application of the Principles of Subsidiarity and Proportionality, OJ C115, 9.5.2008 p. 0021, 0203 & 206.

the power to block certain proposals.[30] For example, national parliaments will be able to veto measures furthering judicial cooperation in civil matters.[31]

Consolidated TEU article 12[32] states among other things that national parliaments are to contribute to the good functioning of the Union:

- by taking part in the evaluation mechanisms for the implementation of the Union policies in the area of freedom, security and justice.
- through being involved in the political monitoring of Europol and the evaluation of Eurojust's activities.
- by being notified of applications for E.U. accession.
- by taking part in the inter-parliamentary cooperation between national parliaments and the European Parliament.

The Treaty of Lisbon contains a "Solidarity Clause" committing the Union and its Member States to act jointly in a spirit of solidarity if a Member State is the target of a terrorist attack or the victim of a natural or man-made disaster.[33]

9.1.3. Principles of Conferral, Subsidiarity and Proportionality

Article 5 of Consolidated TEU (see also Protocol No. 2[34]) outlines the principles of conferral, subsidiarity and proportionality as follows:[35]

> "(ex Article 5 TEC):
> 1. The limits of Union competences are governed by the principle of conferral. The use of Union competences is governed by the principles of subsidiarity and proportionality. 2. Under the principle of conferral, the Union shall act only within the limits of the competences conferred upon it by the Member States in the Treaties to attain the objectives set out therein. Competences not conferred upon the Union in the Treaties remain with the Member States. 3. Under the principle of subsidiarity, in areas which do not fall within its exclusive competence, the Union shall act only if and in so far as the objectives of the proposed action cannot be sufficiently achieved by the Member States, either at central level or at regional and local level, but can rather, by reason of the scale or effects of the proposed action, be better achieved at Un-

[30] E.g. art. 69 & 81(3) in fine of consolidated TFEU, OJ C115, 9.5.2008 p. 0074 & 0079.

[31] Art. 85 of consolidated TFEU (art. 69 D in Treaty of Lisbon – ex ante art. 31 TEU), OJ C115, 9.5.2008 p. 0081.

[32] OJ C115, 9.5.2008 p. 0021 (art. 8c in Treaty of Lisbon).

[33] Article 222 (= Title VII of Part V) of the consolidated version of the Treaty on the Functioning of the European Union, OJ C115, 9.5.2008 p. 0148.

[34] Lisbon Protocol No. 2 on the Application of the Principle of Subsidiarity and Proportionality, OJ C115, 9.5.2008 p. 0206-0209.

[35] OJ C115, 9.5.2008 p. 0018 (emphasis added).

> ion level. The institutions of the Union shall apply the principle of subsidiarity as laid down in the Protocol on the application of the principles of subsidiarity and proportionality. National Parliaments ensure compliance with the principle of subsidiarity in accordance with the procedure set out in that Protocol. 4. Under the principle of proportionality, the content and form of Union action shall not exceed what is necessary to achieve the objectives of the Treaties. The institutions of the Union shall apply the principle of proportionality as laid down in the Protocol on the application of the principles of subsidiarity and proportionality."

The pre-Lisbon Consolidated version 2006 of article 5 of Treaty of Establishing the European Community (TEC) stated:[36]

> "The Community shall act within the limits of the powers conferred upon it by this Treaty and of the objectives assigned to it therein. In areas which do not fall within its exclusive competence, the Community shall take action, in accordance with the principle of subsidiarity, only if and in so far as the objectives of the proposed action cannot be sufficiently achieved by the Member States and can therefore, by reason of the scale or effects of the proposed action, be better achieved by the Community. Any action by the Community shall not go beyond what is necessary to achieve the objectives of this Treaty."

The principle of conferral means that the E.U. does not have general competences in its own right, but only those that are specifically conferred upon it by the Member States in the founding treaties and their subsequent modifications. The E.U. can only act on the basis of a provision of the treaties that authorizes it to do so. In treaty terms, competence means the legal capacity or ability to legislate or to take other action. E.U. action must not exceed what is necessary to achieve the objectives of the Treaties.

The principle of subsidiarity is intended to ensure that decisions are taken as closely as possible to the citizenry and that constant checks are made as to whether action at Community level is justified in the light of the possibilities available at the national, regional or local level. The principle implies that the E.U. does not take action (in areas of shared competence) unless it is more effective than action taken at the national, regional or local level.

Protocol 2 provides national parliaments eight weeks to study European Commission legislative proposals and decide whether to send a "reasoned opinion" stating why the national parliament considers it to be incompatible with subsidiarity. National parliaments may vote to have the measure re-

[36] OJ C321 E, 29.12.2006 p. 0046 (emphasis added).

viewed. If one third (or one quarter, where the proposed E.U. measure concerns freedom, justice and security) of votes are in favor of a review, the Commission will have to review the measure and if it decides to maintain it, must give a reasoned opinion to the Union legislator as to why it considers the measure to be compatible with subsidiarity.

9.1.4. Legislative Procedure

The legislative authority is in overall divided between the Council of the European Union and the Parliament.

The E.U. procedures can be listed as follows:

A. Ordinary legislative procedure (Article 294 TFEU)

B. Special legislative procedures:

a. Consultation procedure
b. Consent Procedure (formerly Assent Procedure)
c. Commission and Council acting alone (Article 31 and Article 207(3)).
d. Commission acting alone (Article 106(3) and Article 45(3)(d)).

However, under the "ordinary legislative procedure" ("co-decision" see further table below) only the Commission can initiate legislation and here the Parliament is on an equal footing with the Council. Where "special legislative procedures" (see below), Parliament might have only an advisory opinion (the "consultation procedure," see further table below).

With the Treaty of Lisbon, for the first time in the E.U., one million citizens from different E.U. Member States will be able to directly request that the Commission brings forward an initiative of interest to them in an area of E.U. competence.[37] A direct new source of such public participation will be the fact that legislative procedural meetings, including debates and voting, will be televised.

The Treaty has made significant changes in how E.U. institutions make decisions.

The Treaty of Lisbon increases the use of qualified majority voting in the E.U. Council, and also increases involvement of the European Parliament in the legislative process through extended co-decision-making with the E.U. Council. The below explained co-decision procedure has become the "ordinary legislative procedure" in the work of the Council and the Parliament.

In the few remaining areas - called "special legislative procedures" – the E.U. Parliament either has the right of consent to a Council measure, or vice-

[37] Article 11(4) of Consolidated TEU, OJ C115, 9.5.2008 p. 0021.

versa, except in the few cases where the old consultation procedure applies.[38] Decision-making procedures vary and may allow for a dominant role for either the Council of Ministers or the European Parliament. In some cases, proposals may come from sources other than the Commission. Unanimity is also allowed for in some cases.

The Treaty of Lisbon has introduced a new term: "Delegated Act."[39] Where there are non-essential elements to a legislative measure, power can be delegated to the European Commission to enact detailed measures to supplement or amend these elements. The objective, content, scope and duration of these delegations has to be defined in the original legislative measure. The Council of Ministers and the European Parliament are to supervise the use of this power and may also revoke any such delegation.

Annexes 2-4 of the E.U. Parliament's report on the Treaty of Lisbon list when:[40]

- qualified majority voting[41] (QMV)[42]
- ordinary legislative procedure[43]
- special legislative procedures, including some Council Acts where:
    - Unanimity and consent of European Parliament
    - Unanimity and consultation of European Parliament

[38] Where the Council must consult the European Parliament before voting on the Commission proposal and take its views into account. The Council is not bound by the Parliament's position but only by the obligation to consult it. Parliament must be consulted again if the Council deviates too far from the initial proposal.

[39] Art. 290 of Consolidated TFEU, OJ C115, 9.5.2008 p. 172.

[40] Report on the Treaty of Lisbon (2007/2286(INI)) from the European Parliament's Committee on Constitutional Affairs (Rapporteurs: Richard Corbett & Íñigo Méndez de Vigo), A6-0013/2008, 29 January 2008 at <www.europarl.europa.eu/sides/getDoc.do?pubRef=-//EP//NONSGML+REPORT+A6-2008-0013+0+DOC+PDF+V0//EN&language=EN> [hereinafter E.U. Parl. Report on Lisbon].

[41] A pre-Lisbon weighted voting system (see e.g. Council Decision 2007/4/EC, OJ L1, 4.1.2007 p. 0009) will over time change to a "double-majority" system, see art. 16(3-5) of Consolidated TEU, art. 238 of Consolidated TFEU and art. 3 of Protocol no. 36 on Transitional Provisions, OJ C115 9.5.2008 p. 0024, 0153, 0322.

[42] The present system is so complicated that several websites offers a "Majority Calculator" for Council decisions (in English) at <www.consilium.europa.eu/App/calculette/default.aspx?lang=en&cmsid=1690> & <www.bmwi.de/English/Navigation/European-policy/majority-calculator.html>.

[43] Article 238(1) of Consolidated TFEU states: "Where it is required to act by a simple majority, the Council shall act by a majority of its component members." OJ C115 9.5.2008 p. 0153.

- Qualified majority and consent of EP
- Qualified majority and consultation of EP

are required.[44]

Ireland and the United Kingdom have opted out from the change from unanimous decisions to qualified majority voting in the sector of police and judicial affairs. This decision will be reviewed in Ireland three years after the Treaty of Lisbon enters into force (if approved by public referendum). Both states will be able to opt in to these voting issues on a case-by-case basis.[45]

After the Commission has presented a proposal for a "legislative text," a member of the European Parliament, working in one of the parliamentary committees, draws up a report on the proposal. The parliamentary committee votes on this report and, possibly, amends it. When the text has been revised and adopted in plenary, Parliament has adopted its position. This process is repeated one or more times, depending on the type of procedure and whether or not agreement is reached with the Council.

The co-decision procedure[46] was introduced by the Maastricht Treaty on European Union of 1992 (effective 1993), and was extended and made more effective by the Amsterdam Treaty of 1996 and the Lisbon Treaty. Co-decision gives the same weight to the European Parliament and the Council of the European Union on a wide range of areas (for example, transport, the environment and consumer protection). After the Commission has sent its proposal to Parliament and the Council, they consider it, and discuss it on two successive occasions. After two readings, if they cannot agree, the proposal is brought before a Conciliation Committee made up of an equal number of representatives of the Council and Parliament. Representatives of the Commission also attend the meetings of the Conciliation Committee and contribute to the discussions. When the Committee has reached agreement, the text agreed upon is sent to Parliament and the Council for a third reading, so that they can finally adopt it as a legislative text. The final agreement of the two institutions is essential if the text is to be adopted as a law. However, even if a joint text is agreed to by the Conciliation Committee, Parliament can still reject the proposed law by an absolute majority of its members.

[44] E.U. PARL. REPORT ON LISBON *supra* note 40.

[45] Protocol no. 36 on Transitional Provisions, OJ C115 9.5.2008 p. 0322.

[46] Article 294 of Consolidated TFEU (ex ante TEC Article 251 (ex ante EC art. 189 b)) OJ C115 9.5.2008 p. 0173..

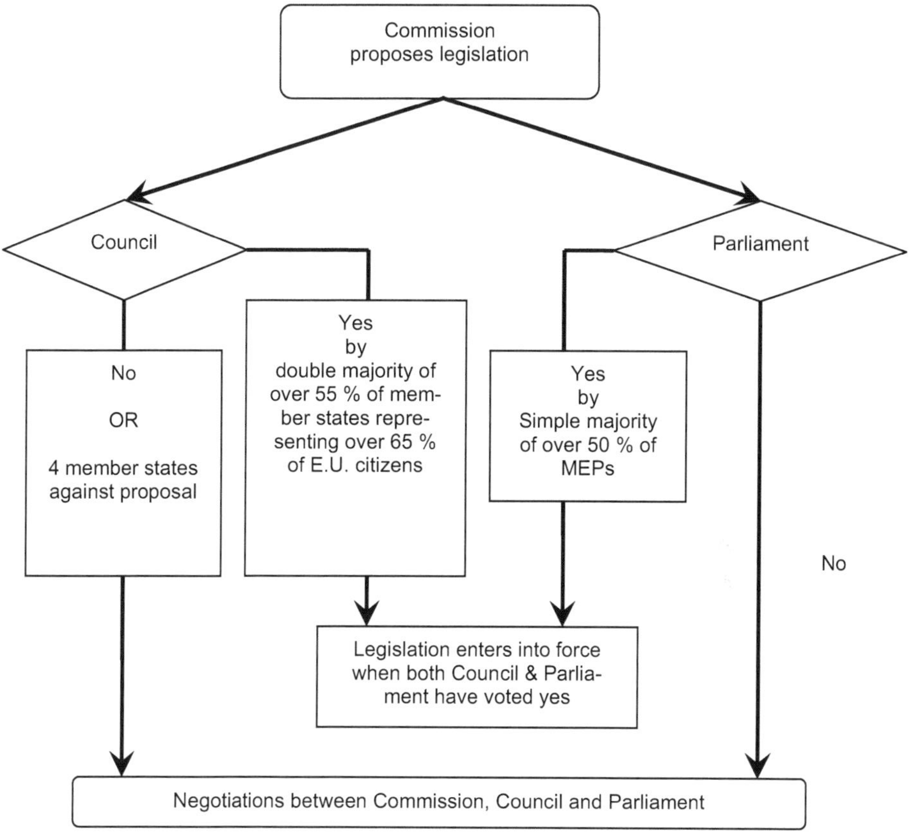

Table 42: Ordinary legislative procedure

The following table explains step-by-step this procedure.[47]

[47] From <http://ec.europa.eu/codecision/stepbystep/diagram_en.htm> and with text-explanation at <http://ec.europa.eu/codecision/stepbystep/text/index_en.htm>.

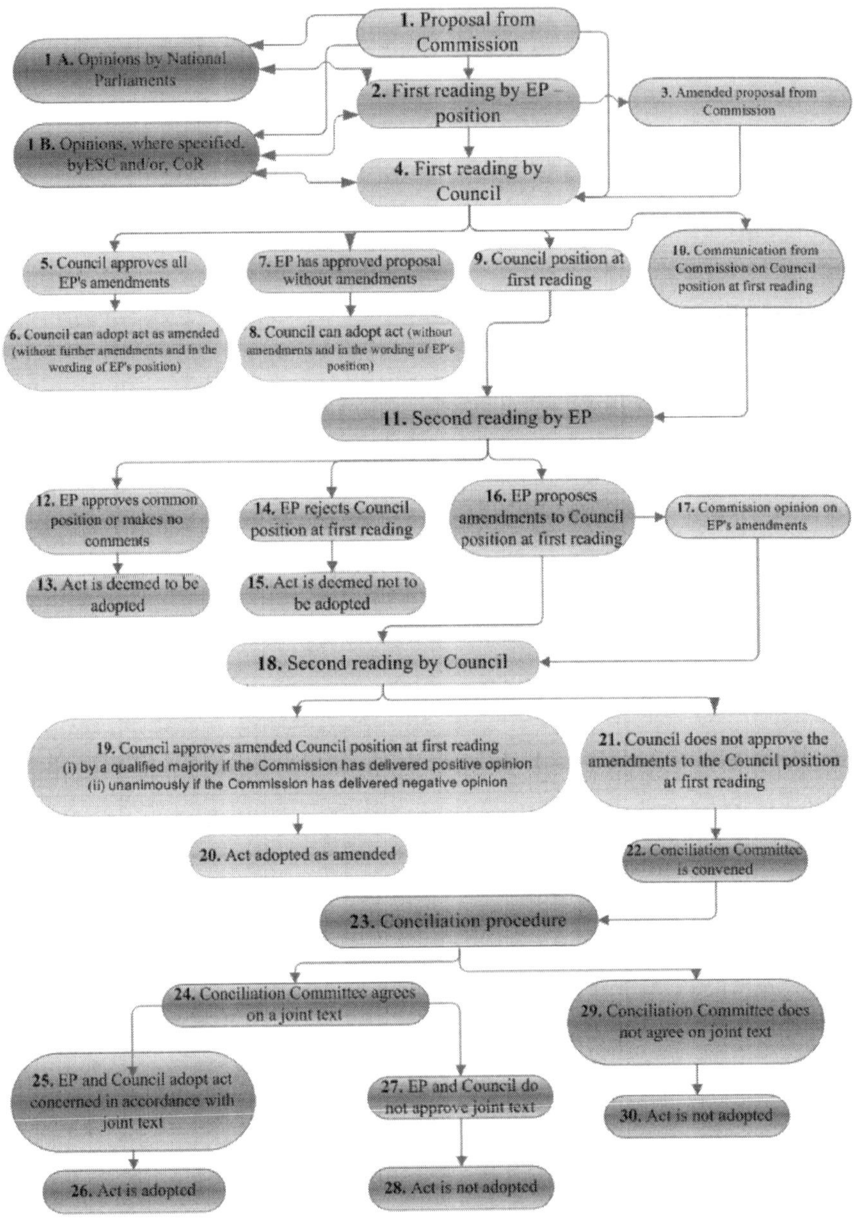

Table 43: Co-decision Procedure

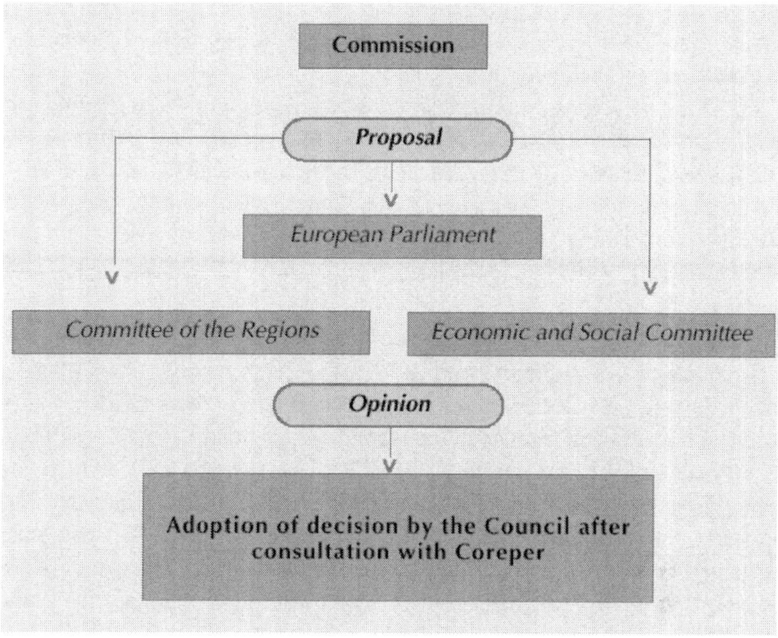

Table 44: Consultation Procedure[48]

9.1.5. Charter of Fundamental Rights

The Charter of Fundamental Rights of the European Union[49] lists political, social and economic rights for E.U. citizens. It is intended to make sure that European Union regulations and directives do not contradict the European Convention on Human Rights, which is ratified by all E.U. Member States.

Unlike the draft of a European Constitution, the Charter of Fundamental Rights is not included in the text of the Treaty of Lisbon, which only provides

[48] On COREPER, see below in 9.2.3. On the Consultation Procedure step-by-step, see <http://www.europeanlawmonitor.org/EU-Information/EU-Legislative-Procedures/EU-Legislation-The-Consultation-procedure.html >.

[49] Charter of Fundamental Rights of The European Union, 2000/C 364/01, OJ C 364 18/12/2000 p. 0001-0022 or at <www.europarl.europa.eu/charter/pdf/text_en.pdf>. See also, EU Charter of Fundamental Rights with commentary at website at <www.eucharter.org>.

a reference to the Charter. Article 6 of Consolidated TEU[50] states that the Charter has the same legal value as the E.U. Treaties, but the Charter shall not extend the competences of the Union.

The United Kingdom, as one of the two countries with a common law legal system in the E.U.[51] and a largely uncodified constitution, as well as Poland, has required a protocol to the Treaty of Lisbon, which clarifies that the Charter does not extend the rights of the courts to overturn domestic law in Britain/Poland.[52]

The Court of Justice will ensure that the Charter of Fundamental Rights is applied correctly.[53]

The Charter is part of national law and, after the Lisbon Treaty, has become directly enforceable in national courts if cases involve the application of E.U. law (article 51(1)). The Charter includes all the civil and political rights contained in the European Convention on Human Rights (ECHR), together with existing E.U. rights, including economic, social and cultural rights. Therefore, it is believed that the E.U. Charter is a more extensive and up-to-date declaration of rights for E.U. citizens. Furthermore, the standard of human rights protection might well be higher than the ECHR's standard of protection. It is clear from article 52(3) of the Charter that the rights conferred by the ECHR only offer minimum protection.[54]

[50] OJ C115, 9.5.2008 p. 0019.

[51] The other is Ireland. See Anglo-American Legal Family below in Chapter 6.

[52] Protocol no. 30 on the application of the Charter of Fundamental Rights of the European Union to Poland and to the United Kingdom, OJ C115, 9.5.2008 p. 0313; Protocol no. 8 relating to Art. 6(2) of the TEU on the accession of the Union to the European Convention on the Protection of Human Rights and Fundamental Freedoms, OJ C115, 9.5.2008 p. 0265; 1st Declaration concerning the Charter of Fundamental Rights of the European Union, OJ C115, 9.5.2008 p. 0337; 53rd Declaration by the Czech Republic on the Charter of Fundamental Rights of the European Union, OJ C115, 9.5.2008 p. 0355; 61st Declaration by the Republic of Poland on the Charter of Fundamental Rights of the European Union, OJ C115, 9.5.2008 p. 0358; 62nd Declaration by the Republic of Poland concerning the Protocol on the application of the Charter of Fundamental Rights of the European Union to Poland and to the United Kingdom, OJ C115, 9.5.2008 p. 0358.

[53] See Discussion document of the Court of Justice of the European Union on certain aspects of the accession of the European Union to the European Convention for the Protection of Human Rights and Fundamental Freedoms, 5 May 2010, at <http://curia.europa.eu/jcms/upload/docs/application/pdf/2010-05/convention_en_2010-05-21_12-10-16_272.pdf>.

[54] <www.eucharter.org/home.php?page_id=66>.

9.1.6. Withdraw or Opt-out

The Treaty of Lisbon introduces an exit clause[55] for members wanting to withdraw from the Union.[56] This formalizes the procedure by stating that a Member State must inform the European Council before it can terminate its membership.

Member States can have opt-outs from some policy areas. For example, regarding the area of justice and home affairs, special arrangements have been made for Denmark, Ireland and the United Kingdom.

Denmark will have to decide whether to renounce its reservations from 1992 (on the Maastricht Treaty). See mainly Lisbon Protocol No. 22 on the Position of Denmark.[57] See also Lisbon Protocol No. 16, 17, 19 and 32.[58]

TEU article 7 provides for the suspension of certain rights of a member state if a member persistently breaches the E.U.'s founding principles (liberty, democracy, human rights etc. outlined in TEU article 2).

9.2. Institutions

Among others, the following institutions working in co-operation serve the E.U.:[59]

- The European Parliament[60] – maximum 750 members + President and no State with more than 96 members or less than a minimum 6 members – on the basis of proportion of population in each State (digressively proportional[61]). Members are elected directly by E.U. citizens for five years.
- The Council (or the "Council of the European Union", "Council of

[55] Article 50 of consolidated TEU, OJ C115, 9.5.2008 p. 0043.
[56] As of 2010, only Greenland – a part of the Kingdom of Denmark – has exited the E.U.
[57] Lisbon Protocol No. 22 on the Position of Denmark, OJ C115, 9.5.2008 p. 0299-0304.
[58] Lisbon Protocols No. 16 on Certain Provisions Relating to Denmark, No. 17 on Denmark, No. 19. on the Schengen Acquis Integrated into the Framework of the European Union, No. 32 on the Acquisition of Property in Denmark, OJ C115, 9.5.2008 p. 0287, 0288, 0290 and 318.
[59] The two main E.U. advisory bodies are the Economic and Social Committee and the Committee of the Regions. Art. 300-307 of consolidated TFEU, OJ C115, 9.5.2008 p. 0177-0179.
[60] Art. 14 of consolidated TEU, OJ C115, 9.5.2008 p. 0022 and art. 223-234 of consolidated TFEU, OJ C115, 9.5.2008 p. 0149-0152.
[61] See glossary in Appendix 1.

Ministers", or "Consilium")[62] – the other key legislation body, along with the E.U. Parliament

- A Presidency of the Council - except for Foreign Affairs[63] - consists of pre-established groups of three Member States (the "Presidency Trios") for a period of 18 months on the basis of equal rotation among the Member States.[64] Each member of the group in turn chair the Council for a six-month period.[65] However, the Foreign Affairs Council (national foreign ministers) is chaired by the E.U.'s "High Representative." (member of the Commission)[66]

- The European Council[67] – gives the E.U. its political direction and sets its priorities (it meets at least 4 times a year)
  - From 1 December 2009 it elects a President[68] for a term of 2 ½ years (but that individual can be removed in the event of an impediment or serious misconduct). The person who is President of the European Council may not hold a national office.[69] The European Council comprises the heads of state or government of E.U. member states, the President of the European Council and the President of the European Commission.
- The Commission[70] – until 1 November 2014[71] consists of one commissioner from each Member State (including its President and Vice-President (= "High Representative of the Union for Foreign Affairs

[62] Art. 16 of consolidated TEU, OJ C115, 9.5.2008 p. 0024 and art. 237-243 of consolidated TFEU, OJ C115, 9.5.2008 p. 0153-0155.

[63] Art. 16(9) of consolidated TEU, OJ C115, 9.5.2008 p. 0024.

[64] Art. 1(1) of 9th Declaration concerning the European Council decision on the exercise of the Presidency of the Council, OJ C115, 9.5.2008 p. 0341.

[65] Art. 1(2) of 9th Declaration concerning the European Council decision on the exercise of the Presidency of the Council, OJ C115, 9.5.2008 p. 0341.

[66] By some nicknamed the "E.U.'s Foreign Minister." The "High Representative is also member of the Commission and its foreign policy head.

[67] Art. 15 of consolidated TEU, OJ C115, 9.5.2008 p. 0023 and art. 235-236 of consolidated TFEU, OJ C115, 9.5.2008 p. 0152-0153.

[68] This new post has incorrectly been referred to as "President of Europe."

[69] Art. 15(5-6) of consolidated TEU, OJ C115, 9.5.2008 p. 0023.

[70] Art. 17 of consolidated TEU, OJ C115, 9.5.2008 p. 0025 and art. 244-250 of consolidated TFEU, OJ C115, 9.5.2008 p. 0155-0157.

[71] Article 17 (Lisbon Treaty Article 1 litra 18 ("Article 9 D, paragraph 5") of consolidated TEU, OJ C115, 9.5.2008 p. 0025.

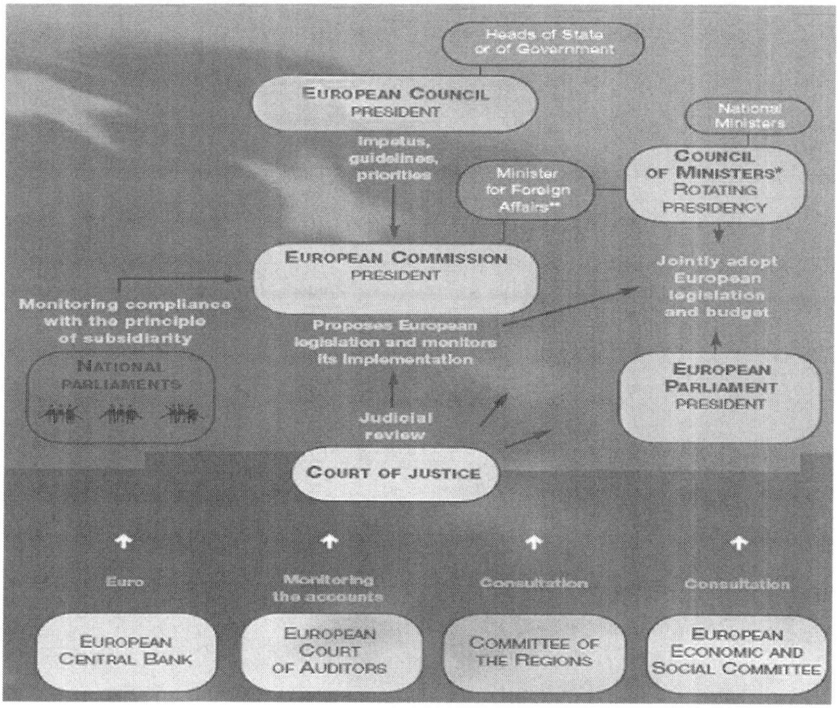

Table 45: European Union Institutions[72]

and Security Policy"[73]))[74] at what time it will be reduced to a number of members corresponding to 2/3 of the Member States and commissioners selected on a basis of equal rotation between the Member States. E.U., High Representative of the Union for Foreign Affairs and Security Policy

[72] Source: E.U. website (2007)..

[73] The vice-President is also "High Representative of the Union for Foreign Affairs and Security Policy. Art. 18, 27 & 34 of consolidated TEU, OJ C115, 9.5.2008 p. 0026, 0032 & 0035 and art. 218(3) & 221 of consolidated TFEU, OJ C115, 9.5.2008 p. 0145 & 0147. This position merges the previous post of High Representative for the Common Foreign and Security Policy and the post of Commissioner for External Relations and European Neighborhood Policy.

[74] Art. 17(4-5) of consolidated TEU, OJ C115, 9.5.2008 p. 0025.

- The only E.U. institution with the power to initiate the law on which the E.U. Parliament and Council have to take a decision.
- Administers the budget and manages Community programs.
- Seeks to ensure that E.U. treaties, law, rules and decisions are complied with.
- Negotiates for the E.U. in international trade aid areas.
- Is independent from and does not seek instructions from any government or other body.

9.2.1. The European Parliament

The European Parliament[75] is the only supranational institution whose members are (since 1979) democratically elected directly by the E.U.'s citizens under a system of population-based proportional representation. It represents the people of the E.U. Member States.[76] Today, the European Parliament is firmly established as a co-legislator, has budgetary powers and exercises democratic controls over all the European institutions. Transnational "Europarties" has been established. MEPs sitting for a 5-year period cannot also be member of national parliaments.

As only the E.U. Commission can initiate legislation in the E.U., the European Parliament is far from having the powers of a national parliament.

Parliament can ask the Commission to present legislative proposals for laws to the Council of the European Union. It plays a genuine role in creating new laws, since it examines the Commission's annual program of work and indicates which laws it would like to see introduced.

Furthermore, the Parliament can raise questions to the Commission and Council; the Parliament can by a two-thirds vote "censure" the Commission; the Parliament can initiate lawsuits against Council or Commission for failure to act; the Parliament can veto a nomination of a Commissioner; and the Parliament has power over the entire E.U. budget.

Parliament has also appointed an Ombudsman,[77] who deals with complaints by individuals or businesses registered in the E.U. against European Community institutions or bodies[78] with a view to reaching an amicable solu-

[75] Article223-234 (ex ante TEC 189-201 (ex ante EC art. 137)) of consolidated TFEU, OJ C115, 9.5.2008 p. 0149-0152. In addition, see relevant articles in TEU.

[76] It serves the second largest democratic electorate in the world (after India).

[77] The Ombudsman's website is <www.ombudsman.europa.eu/home/en/default.htm>.

[78] The Ombudsman investigates complaints against the Commission, Council of European Union, Parliament, Court of Auditors, Court of Justice (except in its judicial role),

tion.

Written or oral questions by members of the European Parliament (MEPs) to the Council and the Commission - as one of Parliament's means of exercising supervision - can be of high value to a researcher.

Parliament wants its work to be known and understood by the public and has provided a register that gives access to documents.[79] The European Parliament Public Register of Documents allows members of the public to carry out research into Parliament's work. It is intended to inform the public of the existence of the various documents produced by Parliament and to give access to them.

9.2.2. The European Commission

The European Commission (formally the Commission of the European Communities)[80] is independent of national governments and represents the European perspective. The European Commission is the only institution empowered to initiate legislation. Furthermore, it is the union's executive branch. Together with the E.U. courts it enforces European law.[81] On the international stage, it represents the European Union, for example in the WTO.

The President of the Commission is appointed by a majority vote in the Council and the Parliament approves or rejects the proposed appointment. Then, in accord with the President appointed, the Member States appoint the 25 Commissioners, except the High Representative of the Union for Foreign Affairs and Security Policy (who is vice-President of the Commission) The College of Commissioners must then be endorsed as a whole by Parliament.

Parliament has the power to censure the Commission. It can force the College of Commissioners as a whole to resign.

9.2.3. The Council of the European Union

The Council of the European Union[82] - or the "Council", "Council of Minis-

European Economic and Social Committee, Committee of the Regions, European Central Bank, European Investment Bank, Europol, and any other European Community body.

[79] <www.europarl.europa.eu/RegWeb/application/registre/simpleSearch.faces>.

[80] Article244-250 (ex ante TEC Article 211-119 (ex ante EC art. 155)) of consolidated TFEU, OJ C115, 9.5.2008 p. 0155-0157. In addition, see relevant articles in TEU.

[81] See "Reasoned Opinion" in glossary, Appendix 1.

[82] To be distinguished from "Council of the European Union", see below section 9.2.4.; and also distinguished from "Council of Europe" (an international organization), see above footnote 17.

ters", or "Consilium[83] consists of a representative of each Member State at ministerial level, authorized to commit the government of that Member State. Membership is fluid, with each government sending the minister appropriate to the subject then under consideration by the Council. The foreign minister is generally regarded as the coordinator and main representative of each government's delegation. The presidency of the European Council is held by each Member State in turn for a six month period, under a rotating system.[84]

To prepare the agenda for its meetings a Committee of Permanent Representatives ("COREPER")[85] exist. It is chaired by the Presidency of the Council of the European Union.

The Council has six main responsibilities:

- Adopting European law – often jointly with the Parliament
- Coordinating the broad economic policies of the Member States
- Concluding international agreements between the E.U. and other countries or international organizations
- Approving the E.U.'s budget together with the Parliament
- Developing the E.U.'s common foreign and security policy
- Coordinating cooperation between the national courts and police forces in criminal matters.

9.2.4. European Council

The European Council[86] – to be distinguished from Council of the European

[83] Article 237-243 (ex ante TEC Article 202-210 (ex ante EC art. 145)) of consolidated TFEU, OJ C115, 9.5.2008 p. 0153-0155. In addition, see relevant articles in TEU.

[84] It is to be distinguished from the Council of Europe, which is a completely separate international organization, not a European Union institution.

[85] See Article 240 of the Treaty on the Functioning of the European Union. Weekly meetings are held in private. It prepares the agenda for the ministerial Council meetings and may take some procedural decisions. It oversees and coordinates the work of some 250 committees and working parties made up of civil servants from the E.U. Member States who work on issues at the technical level. It is chaired by the Presidency of the Council. There are two committees: (I) consists of deputy heads of mission from the E.U. member states in Brussels and deals largely with social and economic issues; (II) consists of heads of mission and deals largely with political, financial and foreign policy issues. Representatives of the Council Secretariat from the relevant Directorates and from the Legal Directorate are also present. There is also a special committee on agriculture.

[86] Article 235-236 (ex ante Article 4 (ex ante art. D)) of consolidated TFEU, OJ C115, 9.5.2008 p. 0152-0153. In addition, see relevant articles in TEU.

Union[87] - meets at least four times a year in what is informally known as the "European Summit" (E.U. summit), and is a closely related but separate body.[88]

From 1 December 2009 it elects a President[89] for a term of 2 ½ years (but that individual can be removed in the event of an impediment or serious misconduct). The person who is President of the European Council may not hold a national office.

The Presidents duties are according to Article 15(6) of TEU:[90]

- Chairs the European Council
- Ensures the preparation and continuity of the work of the European Council in cooperation with the President of the Commission, and on the basis of the General Affairs Council
- Endeavors to facilitate cohesion and consensus within the European Council
- Present a report to the European Parliament after each of the meetings of the European Council
- Ensures external representation of the Union on issues concerning its common foreign and security policy, without prejudice to the powers of the High Representative on the Union for Foreign Affairs and Security Policy.

The European Council comprises the heads of state or government of E.U. Member States, the President of the European Council and the President of the European Commission.

It provides the necessary impetus for the development of the European Union and sets forth its general guidelines and political priorities, taking account of Parliament's recommendations. Each summit begins with a declaration by the President of the European Parliament, setting out the institution's key positions on the subjects to be addressed by the Heads of State and Government. At the end of each summit, the President of the European Council presents a report to Parliament on its outcome and launches a debate with the Members of the European Parliament.

[87] See above section 9.2.3.; and also distinguished from "Council of Europe" (an international organization), see above footnote 17.

[88] Rules of Procedure for European Council, Decision 2009/882/EU of 1 December 2009, O.J. L315, 2.12.2009 p. 0051-0055.

[89] Article 15(5)-(6) & 16(6) of consolidated TEU, OJ C115, 9.5.2008 pp. 0023-0024 (ex ante Lisbon Treaty Article 1, litra 16 ("Article 9 B (5)-(6)"), O.J. C306, 17.12.2007 pp. 0017-0018).

[90] Press-release of November 2009 from General Secretariat of the Council of the E.U.

9.2.5. "Presidents" in the E.U.

The title "President" covers several positions in the European Union. There exists a President for the:

- Commission (appointed by Council of the European Union and Parliament for a 5 year period, renewable once)[91] (the High Representative is also the vice-president for the Commission)[92]
- Parliament ("Parliament's Speaker")(elected by the members of the European Parliament)[93]
- Council of the European Union or Consilium (rotating between member states every 6 month)[94]
- European Council (appointed by the members of the European Council for a 2½-year period, renewable once)[95]
- European Central Bank (non-renewable 8 years period)[96]
- European Court of Justice[97]

[91] Article 17(6)-(7) of consolidated TEU, OJ C115, 9.5.2008 pp. 0025-0026 (ex ante Lisbon Treaty Article 1, litra 18 ("Article 9 D (6)-(7)"), O.J. C306, 17.12.2007 p. 0020). Commission President's website at <http://ec.europa.eu/commission_2010-2014/president/index_en.htm>.

[92] Article 17(7) & 18 of consolidated TEU, OJ C115, 9.5.2008 p. 0026-0027 (ex ante Lisbon Treaty Article 1, litra 18-19 ("Article 9 D (7)" & "9 E", O.J. C306, 17.12.2007 pp. 0020-0021). High Representative of the European Union for Foreign Affairs and Security Policy's websites (Council) <www.consilium.europa.eu/showPage.aspx?id=1847&lang=en> & (Commission) <http://ec.europa.eu/archives/commission_2004-2009/ashton/index_en.htm>.

[93] Article 14(4) of consolidated TEU, OJ C115, 9.5.2008 p. 0023 (ex ante Lisbon Treaty Article 1, litra 15 ("Article 9 A(4)"), O.J. C306, 17.12.2007 p. 0017). Parliament-President's website at <www.europarl.europa.eu/president>.

[94] Article 16(9) of consolidated TEU, OJ C115, 9.5.2008 p. 0024 (ex ante Lisbon Treaty Article 1, litra 17 ("Article 9 C(9)", O.J. C306, 17.12.2007 p. 0019). Consilium-President's website changes every 6 month.

[95] Article 15(5)-(6) & 16(6) of consolidated TEU, OJ C115, 9.5.2008 p. 0023-0024 (ex ante Lisbon Treaty Article 1, litra 16 ("Article 9 B (5)-(6)"), O.J. C306, 17.12.2007 pp. 0017-0018). European Council-President's website at <www.european-council.europa.eu/the-president.aspx>

[96] Article 283 of consolidated TFEU, OJ C115, 9.5.2008 p. 0168 (ex ante TEC Article 112). European Central Bank's website at <www.ecb.int/home/html/index.en.html>.

[97] The term "Court of Justice of the European Union" covers all the existing courts pursuant to the Lisbon Treaty, e.g. the "General Court". Article 253 of consolidated TFEU, OJ C115, 9.5.2008 p. 0158 (ex ante TEC Article 223). Courts' website at <http://curia.europa.eu/jcms/jcms/j_6/>.

9.2.6. European External Action Service & the High Representative

The High Representative of the Union for Foreign Affairs and Security Policy[98] (a five year term) chair the European Council of foreign ministers. The High Representative is assisted by a joint service, the European External Action Service (EEAS),[99] which is composed of officials from the Council, the Commission and the diplomatic services of the Member States.

Besides representing the EU at international fora and co-coordinating the Common Security and Defense Policy, the High Representative is:

- ex-officio Vice President of the European Commission
- responsible of the European Union Special Representatives
- head of the External Action Service and the delegations
- President of the Foreign Affairs Council
- Secretary-General of the Western European Union
- President of the European Defense Agency
- Chairperson of the board of the European Union Institute for Security Studies.

Further duties are according to Article 18 and 27 of TEU:

- Conduct the Union's common foreign and security affairs
- Contributes by his/her proposals to the development of that policy, which he/she will carry out as mandated by the Council, and ensures implementation of the decisions adopted it this field
- Ensures the consistency of the Union's external action and is responsible within the Commission for the responsibilities incumbent on it in external relations and for coordinating other aspects of the Union's external action
- Represent the Union for matters relating to the common foreign and security policy, conduct political dialogue with third parties on the Union's behalf and expresses the Union's position in international organisations and at international conferences
- Exercises autority over the European Action Service and over the Un-

[98] In short, the "High Representative" formerly titled the High Representative of the Common Foreign and Security Policy. Article 17(7) & 18 of consolidated TEU, OJ C115, 9.5.2008 p. 0026-0027 (ex ante Lisbon Treaty Article 1, litra 18-19 ("Article 9 D (7)" & "9 E", O.J. C306, 17.12.2007 pp. 0020-0021). See also, Articles 215, 218, 220-222, 234, 238, 243, 328-329, 331 of consolidated TFEU, OJ C115, 9.5.2008.

[99] See Title V of the consolidated version of the Treaty on European Union, OJ C115, 9.5.2008 p. 0028-0041 and Part V of the consolidated version of the Treaty on the Functioning of the European Union, OJ C115, 9.5.2008 p. 0139-0148.

ion delegations in third countries and at international organizations.[100]

The High Representative is appointed by the European Council acting by qualified majority. However in order to take up their role in the Commission, in particular as a Vice President, the High Representative has to appear before Parliament for questioning and then be subject to Parliament's vote of approval on the proposed Commission.

9.2.7. The E.U. Courts

After the Lisbon Treaty, the Court of Justice of the European Union consists of:[101]

- the (European) Court of Justice (ECJ).[102]
- the General Court (previously the "Court of First Instance").
- specialized courts (including the European Union Civil Service Tribunal).[103]

The ECJ's jurisdiction still excludes matters of foreign policy, all though it now can review foreign policy sanction measures,[104] and can exercise jurisdiction over certain matters concerning the "Area of Freedom, Security and Justice" (AFSJ) not concerning policing and criminal cooperation.[105]

With the Lisbon treaty, a new "emergency" procedure has been introduced into the preliminary reference system, which will require the Court of Justice to act "with the minimum of delay" when a case involves an individual in custody.[106]

The E.U. courts[107] have jurisdiction to give preliminary rulings ("advisory rulings") on the interpretation of E.U. law. National courts cannot determine the validity of a European legal measure. The E.U. courts have the power to settle legal disputes between E.U. Member States, E.U. institutions, businesses, and individuals.

[100] Press-release of November 2009 from General Secretariat of the Council of the E.U.

[101] Article 251-281 (ex ante TEC Article 221-245 (ex ante EC art. 145)) of consolidated TFEU, OJ C115, 9.5.2008 p. 0157-0167. In addition, see Article 19 of consolidated TEU, OJ C115, 9.5.2008 p. 0027 and Protocol no. 3 on the Statute of the Court of Justice of the European Union, OJ C115, 9.5.2008 p. 0210-0229.

[102] Before the Lisbon Treaty: Court of Justice of the European Communities.

[103] Art. 257 of consolidated TFEU, OJ C115, 9.5.2008 p. 0160.

[104] Art. 275 of consolidated TFEU, OJ C115, 9.5.2008 p. 0166.

[105] Art. 276 of consolidated TFEU, OJ C115, 9.5.2008 p. 0166.

[106] Art. 267, in fine, of consolidated TFEU, OJ C115, 9.5.2008 p. 0164.

[107] Article 19 of consolidated TEU, OJ C115, 9.5.2008 p. 0027 (replacing TEC Article 220 (ex ante EC art. 164)).

Only a decision made public in the language of the case is authentic, even though decisions are published in all E.U. working languages. See further Rules of Procedure.[108]

From November 1989, the original E.C. Court, the European Court of Justice (ECJ) was augmented by a lower court, the Court of First Instance (CFI) – renamed by the Lisbon Treaty to General Court. The original purpose of the CFI was to relieve the ECJ of its caseload. The General Court is particularly responsible for actions brought by private individuals, companies, and some other organizations, as well as for cases relating to competition law. It is possible to appeal General Court decisions to the ECJ.

Decisions made by the ECJ are now numbered with a "C" for court, whereas CFI/General Court decisions are numbered with a "T" for tribunal. In the official European Court Reports, ECJ judgments have page numbers preceded by "I-," whereas CFI judgments have page numbers preceded by "II-." Decisions are given without dissent. The General Court can be chaired by only one judge, while the ECJ has 3-5 judges in chambers or 13 judges in a Grand Chamber. There is also a lower court, the European Union Civil Service Tribunal, for "disputes involving the European Union civil service."[109] Its decisions are numbered with a "F":[110]

The judges are appointed by the E.U. Member States from among persons with a legal education.

In E.U. Court proceedings, there is a special lawyer, the "Advocate-General" (AG[111]), who participates and gives his analysis and evaluation on the case and his opinion of a proper result under European law. The AG is an institution that exists in France but not most other Civil Law countries. For an American scholar, the AG can to a certain extent resemble a permanent amicus curiae[112] on behalf of justice. The AG-opinions can definitely be of

[108] Rules of Procedure of the Courts can be found at the courts website under "Texts governing procedure" at <http://curia.europa.eu/jcms/jcms/Jo2_7003/#B>. Consolidated version of 2 July 2010, O.J. C 177 p. 0001-0036 at <http://curia.europa.eu/jcms/upload/docs/application/pdf/2010-04/rp.en.pdf>.

[109] This tribunal has "first instance jurisdiction in disputes between the Communities and their servants referred to in Article 236 of the EC Treaty and Article 152 of the EAEC Treaty, including disputes between all bodies or agencies and their servants in respect of which jurisdiction is conferred on the Court of Justice."

[110] <http://curia.europa.eu/jcms/jcms/Jo2_14954/>.

[111] See further, Chapter 1 on Judges and Advocates General in Rules of Procedure of the Court of Justice Consolidated version of 2 July 2010, O.J. C 177 p. 0001-0036 at <http://curia.europa.eu/jcms/upload/docs/application/pdf/2010-04/rp.en.pdf>.

[112] "Friend of the Court".

value for the legal scholar. With the Lisbon Treaty, the number of Advocates General (appointed by E.U. Member States) has been increased from 8 to 11 and, by a political compromise, a permanent "Polish" Advocate General has been created – as is already the case for Germany, France, Italy, Spain and United Kingdom.[113]

Through its case law, the Court of Justice has identified an obligation of administrations and national courts to apply European Community law in full within their spheres of competence and to protect the rights conferred on citizens by that law (that is, direct application of European Community law), and to display any conflicting national provision, whether prior or subsequent to the Community provision (that is, primacy of Community law over national law).

The Court of Justice has also recognized the principle of the liability of E.U. Member States for breach of Community law.

In addition, the Court of Justice also works in conjunction with the national courts, which are the ordinary courts applying European Community law. Any national court or tribunal that is called upon to decide a dispute involving Community law may, and sometimes must, submit questions to the Court of Justice for a preliminary ruling. The Court will then give an interpretation or review the legality of a rule of Community law.

Of the thousands of judgments rendered by the Court of Justice, the majority, particularly preliminary rulings, clearly have important consequences for the daily life of European citizens. Examples of some of the most important areas of Community law with which Court judgments have dealt include free movement of goods, freedom of movement of persons, freedom to provide services, equal treatment and social rights, and fundamental rights.

The procedure before the Court of Justice is as follows: [114]

[113] Declaration on Article 252 of the Treaty on the Functioning of the European Union regarding the number of Advocates-General in the Court of Justice, OJ C115, 9.5.2008 p. 0350 and Declaration ad Article 222 of the Treaty on the Functioning of the European Union on the number of Advocates-General in the Court of Justice, 18 October 2007, DS 866/07 at <www.consilium.europa.eu/uedocs/cmsUpload/ds00866.en07.pdf>.

[114] The Court of Justice: composition, jurisdiction and procedures page 4 (ECJ, 2007) <http://curia.europa.eu/jcms/upload/docs/application/pdf/2008-11/en_cj_comp.pdf>.

<table>
<tr><th>Direct actions and appeal</th><th></th><th>References for a preliminary ruling</th></tr>
<tr><td colspan="3">Written procedure</td></tr>
<tr><td>Application

Service of the application on the defendant by the Registry

Notice of the action in the Official Journal of the E.U. (Series C)

[Interim measures]

[Intervention]

Defence/Response

[Objection to admissibility]

[Reply and Rejoinder]</td><td>[Application for legal aid]

Assignment of Judge-Rapporteur and Advocate General</td><td>National court's decision to make a reference

Translation into the other official languages of the European Union

Notice of the question referred for a preliminary ruling in the Official Journal of the E.U. (Series C)

Notification to the parties to the proceedings, the Member States, the Community institutions, the EEA States and to the EFTA Surveillance Authority

Written observations of the parties, the States and the institutions</td></tr>
<tr><td colspan="3">The Judge-Rapporteur draws up the preliminary report

General Meeting of the Judges and the Advocate General

Assignment of the case to a formation

[Measures of inquiry]</td></tr>
<tr><td colspan="3">Oral procedure</td></tr>
<tr><td colspan="3">[Hearing; Report of the Hearing]

[Opinion of the Advocate General]

Deliberation by the Judges

Judgment</td></tr>
</table>

Notes:
Optional steps in the procedure are indicated in brackets
Cases disposed of by order do not include all the steps indicated above
Words in bold face indicate a public document

Table 46: Procedure before the Court of Justice

Pursuant to the renumbering (or rather equivalences) of the articles of the Treaty on the European Union (TEU) and of the Treaty establishing the European Community (TEC), brought about by the Treaty of Amsterdam

(1996), the Court of Justice and the (now named) General Court have introduced, with effect from May 1, 1999, a new method of citation of the articles of the TEU, TEC, European Coal and Steel community (ECSC) and Euratom Treaties. That new method is primarily designed to avoid all risk of confusion between the version of an article as it stood prior to May 1, 1999 and the version applying after that date.[115]

The principles on which that method operates are as follows: where reference is made to an article of a treaty as it stands after May 1, 1999, the number of the article is immediately followed by two letters indicating the treaty concerned: E.U. for the Treaty on the European Union; EC for the EC Treaty; CS for the ECSC Treaty; and EA for the Euratom Treaty. Further explanation can be found at <www.curia.europa.eu/en/content/juris/index_infos.htm>.

9.2.8. The European Judicial Cooperation Unit

EUROJUST[116] is a newer European Union body established in 2002[117] to enhance the effectiveness of the competent authorities within E.U. Member States when they are dealing with serious cross-border and organized crime. Eurojust stimulates and improves the coordination of investigations and prosecutions and also supports the Member States in order to render their investigations and prosecutions more effective. Its mission is to enhance the development of Europe-wide cooperation in criminal justice cases. This means that Eurojust is a key interlocutor with the European institutions such as the Parliament, the Council and the Commission. It operates from The Hague in the Netherlands. Eurojust and Europol signed an agreement on close cooperation on June 9, 2004.

The College of Eurojust is composed of one member nominated by each E.U. Member State (as of 1 January 2007 27). The national members are senior, experienced prosecutors or judges; some national members are supported by deputies and assistants.

[115] On the book's corresponding website at <http://hssph.net/legalrm/Research_book_2-Edition_Appendix_4.pdf> tables of equivalences of articles in the different treaties. Note, that these tables indicates more than just a renumbering of articles.

[116] <www.eurojust.europa.eu/>.

[117] Eurojust was created by EU Council Decision 2002/187/JHA of 28 February 2002 setting up Eurojust with a view to reinforcing the fight against serious crime, OJ L 63, 6.3.2002, p. 1–13, amended by EU Council Decision 2003/659/JHA of 18 June 2003, OJ L 245, 29.9.2003, p. 44–46.

9.2.9. The Former Pillars of the European Union

The subject matter dealt with in various of the E.U. treaties before the Lisbon Treaty was sometimes described as the "Three pillars," with the following categorization:

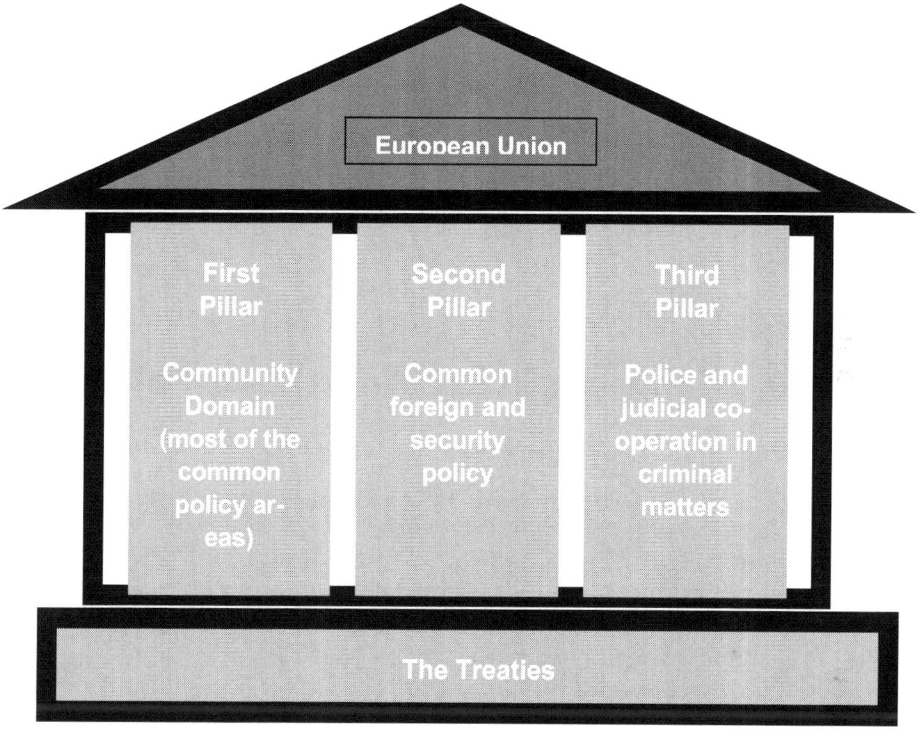

Table 47: The Three E.U. Pillars

The "roof" - general principles TEU Title I (art 1-7)

First pillar (the Community Law) – TEU Title II (art. 8 on the old EC Treaty) & Title IV of the (art 10 on the EURATOM Treaty). The first pillar covers:

- Customs union and a single market
- Agricultural policy
- Structural policy

- E.U. citizenship
- Education and culture
- Trans-European networks
- Consumer protection
- Health
- Research and environment
- Social policy
- Asylum policy
- External borders
- Immigration policy
- Euratom
- European Coal and Steel Community[118]

Second pillar (foreign and security policy co-operation) – TEU Title V (art 11-28). The second pillar covers:

- Cooperation, common positions and measures
- Peacekeeping
- Human rights
- Democracy
- Aid to non-member countries
- Drawing on the WEU (questions concerning the security of the E.U.)
- Disarmament
- Financial aspects of defense
- Long-term: Europe's security framework

Third pillar (police and enforcement co-operation in criminal cases) & Closer co-operation – TEU Title VI (art 29-42) & TEU Title VII (art 43-45) Bottom – Final articles – TEU Title VIII (art 46-53) & Protocols. The pillar includes:

- Cooperation between judicial authorities in civil and criminal law
- Police cooperation
- Combating racism and xenophobia
- Fighting drugs and the arms trade
- Fighting organized crime
- Fighting terrorism
- Criminal acts against children, trafficking in human beings.

When the Treaty of Lisbon came into force, the three pillars was merged into one single pillar. Furthermore, the "roof" now somewhat include the

[118] All assets and liabilities of the ECSC was transferred to the European Community on 24 July 2002. Article 1 of Protocol to the Nice Treaty, OJ C325. 24.12.2002 p. 0182.

Charter on basic rights.[119]

9.2.10. E.U. Member States

Since January 1, 2007 (see map below), the E.U. has consisted of the following Member States: Austria, Belgium, Bulgaria, Cyprus, Czech Republic, Denmark, Estonia, Finland, France, Germany, Greece, Hungary, Ireland, Italy, Latvia, Lithuania, Luxembourg, Malta, Netherlands, Poland, Portugal, Romania, Slovakia, Slovenia, Spain, Sweden and the United Kingdom.[120]

Links to main national websites (in official country language) via ECJ's (CVRIA) website at <http://curia.europa.eu/jcms/jcms/Jo2_7066/>.

The legal order for several Member States of the E.U. is given (English version) at

<http://ec.europa.eu/civiljustice/legal_order/legal_order_ec_en.htm>

and in the CIA World Factbook

<www.cia.gov/library/publications/the-world-factbook/index.html>

and Wikipedia.org both provide helpful initial information on different countries.

Since the last enlargement of 2007, the European Union map is as illustrated on next page. and the European Union is part of the "Supranational European Bodies" (see (interactive) map in Table 49 below.

[119] Charter of Fundamental Rights of The European Union, 2000/C 364/01, OJ C 364 18/12/2000 p. 0001-0022.. See further above section 9.1.5.

[120] Candidate countries are: Croatia, former Yugoslav Republic of Macedonia, Turkey and Iceland. Potential candidate countries: Albania, Montenegro, Bosnia-Herzegovina, Serbia, Republic of Kosovo. On the enlargement process, see <http://europa.eu/about-eu/member-countries/index_en.htm >.

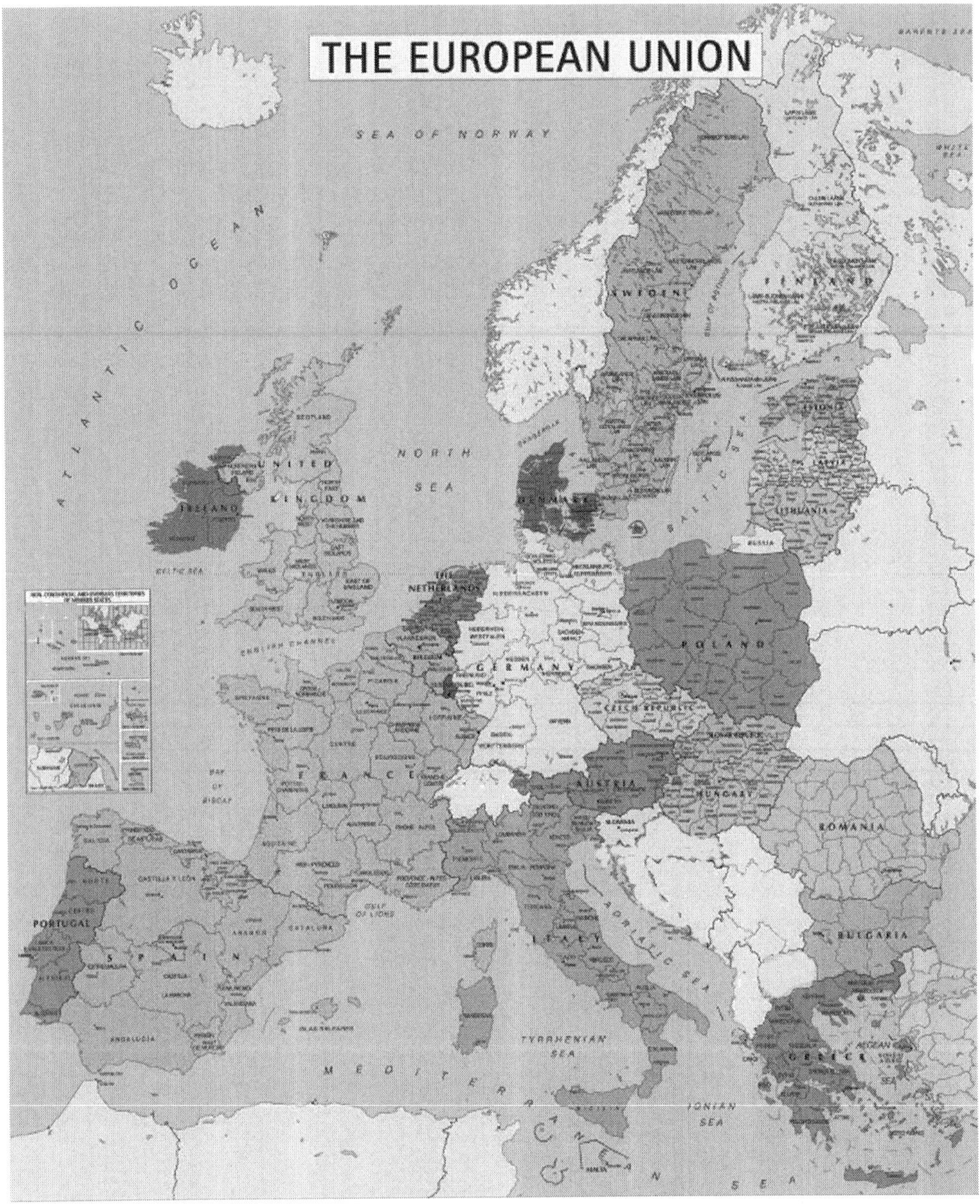

Table 48: Map of the European Union (2007)

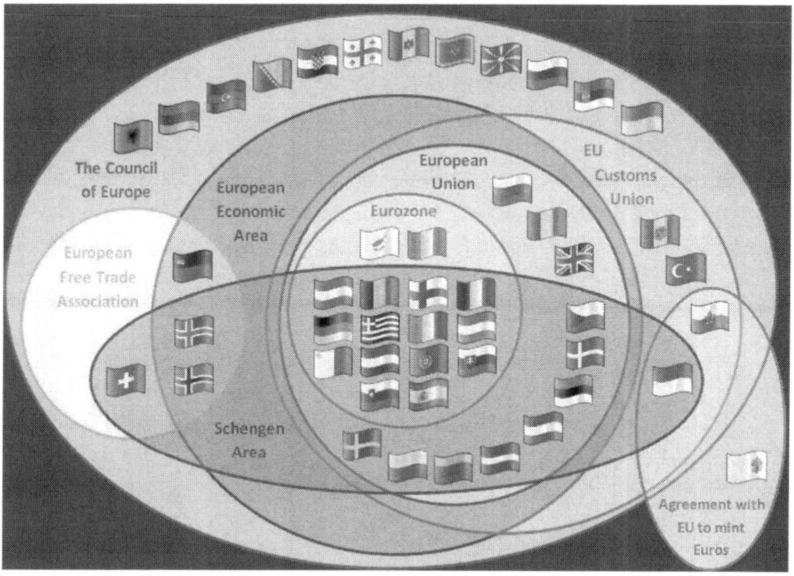

Table 49: Supranational European Bodies[121]

9.3. Sources of E.U. law

9.3.1. Hard and soft Law in E.U.

Research Tip #9.4

As for E.U. avoid using (U.S.) terms as Primary and Secondary sources, but use the Civil Law terms "hard" and "soft" law" – and as for E.U. "law"[122] the latter is very hard to find/nearly non-existent.

Especially after the Treaty of Lisbon it is vital to look at national parliaments' contributions to/legislative history on E.U. "law."

[121] Source: <http://en.wikipedia.org/wiki/File:Supranational_European_Bodies.png> - an interactive map with links to each country and more.

[122] The Treaty of Lisbon has turned down the suggestion in the draft to a E.U. Constitution to use the term "law" (or code/act), see article I-6 of (the draft to the) Treaty establishing a Constitution for Europe, OJ C310, 16.12.2004 p. 0012.

In the European Community, the term "soft law" is also often used to describe various kinds of quasi-legal instruments of the European Communities: "codes of conduct," "guidelines,' "communications," etc. In the area of law of the European Communities, soft law instruments are often used to indicate how the European Commission intends to use its powers and perform its tasks within its area of competence.[123] See, for example, "COM-documents."[124] The gradual process of codification beginning with soft law, that being non-mandatory or advisory principles, has been termed "creeping codification.[125]

The division of law-sources in European Union law is (as Table 4 above):

Hard Law	Treaty of European Union (TEU) & Treaty on the Functioning of the European Union (FTEU)		
(Ranked)	Regulations (general application & binding in all Member States)	Directives (Implementation into national laws – not necessary all Member States)	Decisions (binding upon those to whom decision is addressed)
Soft law	White & Green Papers	Law commentaries	Statements by Ombudsman
(No ranking) (Some claim there does exists no "secondary sources" in the E.U.)	Reports from Commission	E.U. Parliament documents/journals	Member States' Parliament documents/journals

[123] Michael G. Egge, Matteo F. Bay & Janier Ruiz Calzado, *The New EC Merger Regulation: A Move to Convergence, Status of Soft Law In international Law, Antitrust Magazine, Section of Antitrust Law*, AMERICAN BAR ASSOCIATION, Fall 2004 at <www.lw.com/upload/pubContent/_pdf/pub1167_1.pdf>. The European Union may be somewhat ahead of the United States in recognizing the importance of these "soft law" regimes. Jerry L. Mashaw, *Reasoned Administration: The European Union, the United States, and the Project of Democratic Governance*, 122 THE GEORGE WASHINGTON LAW REVIEW, VOl. 76 p. 99, 122 (Nov 2007) at <http://docs.law.gwu.edu/stdg/gwlr/issues/pdf/76_1_Mashaw.pdf>.

[124] COM documents: proposed legislation and other Commission communications to the Council and/or the other institutions, and their preparatory papers. Search in Eur-Lex → Preparatory acts → Commission proposals and opinions at <http://ec.europa.eu/transparency/regdoc/registre.cfm?CL=en>.

[125] Klaus Peter Berger, The Principles of European Contract Law and the Concept of the "Creeping Codification" of Law, 9 EUROPEAN REVIEW OF PRIVATE LAW 21, 21 (2001).

9.3.2. E.U. "law" and Language

Research Tip #9.5

When one does research on the European Union, the primary sources are two treaties,[126] namely on establishing the European Community (TEC (previous EC[127] or TEC or (now) FTEU[128]) and on the European Union (TEU).

On 18 and 19 of October 2007, documents to a so-called "Reform Treaty" or Treaty of Lisbon[129] was approved at an informal meeting of the Heads of State and Government.[130] The treaty[131] was signed by the Council of the European Union in Lisbon on 13 December 2007.[132] It is not as far reaching as a previous draft, the so-called "Constitution Treaty".[133] The Treaty of Lisbon will came into force on 1 December 2009, but large parts of treaty will

[126] See <www.europe.eu/abc/treaties/index_en.htm>.

[127] Originally, the European Community (EC) dealt mainly with economic, social and trade matters.

[128] The Treaty of Lisbon of 2007 renames the treaty once again, now to be named the Treaty on the Functioning of the European Union (TFEU). See Presidency Conclusion's on the Brussels European Council meeting 21-22 June 2007 at <www.consilium.europa.eu/ueDocs/cms_Data/docs/pressData/en/ec/94932.pdf>.

[129] Table of Content on the treaty and "Information and Notices" are printed in the OJ C306, 17.12.2007 p. 0001. Also available at <http://eur-lex.europa.eu/JOHtml.do?uri=OJ:C:2007:306:SOM:EN:HTML>.

[130] See Documents approved at the Intergovernmental Conference, at the level of Heads of State and Government, of 18 October 2007 in Lisbon at <www.consilium.europa.eu/cms3_fo/showPage.asp?id=1317&lang=en&mode=g>. In December 2007 issued as Final Act, Doc. 2007/C 306/02, OJ C306, 17.12.2007 pp. 0231-0271.

[131] Table of Content on the treaty and "Information and Notices" are printed in the OJ C310, 16.12.2004. Also available at <http://eur-lex.europa.eu/JOHtml.do?uri=OJ:C:2004:310:SOM:EN:HTML>.

[132] Treaty of Lisbon amending the Treaty on European Union and the Treaty establishing the European Community of 13 December 2007, OJ C 307, 15.12.2007 pp. 0001—0271. Consolidated versions with Treaty of Lisbon amendments of the Treaty on European Union and the Treaty on the functioning of the European Union are published in OJ C115, 9.5.2008 pp. 0001-0388. Table of Content available at <http://eur-lex.europa.eu/JOHtml.do?uri=OJ:C:2008:115:SOM:EN:HTML>.

[133] Treaty establishing a Constitution for Europe of 29 October 2004, OJ C310, 16.12.2004 pp. 0001-0474. The treaty repealed the Treaty establishing the European Community, the Treaty of European Union, and their supplements and amendments, Art. IV-437.

first take effect in 2014.[134] Its purpose is to make the E.U. work more efficiently, including merging/eliminating the pillar system.[135] As with the nature of most amending treaties, the Treaty of Lisbon is not intended to be read as an autonomous text.

From a researcher's/scholar's point of view, the new treaty expands the area or scope of research, including the number of sources on E.U. "law" and the history behind it, as Member States' national parliaments will be more involved. The Treaty of Lisbon does not - as in the draft to a E.U. Constitution – use of the term "law" (or code/act).[136]

The Treaty of Lisbon (also known as the Reform Treaty) to a large extent replicates the earlier draft to a E.U. "constitutional" treaty. However, some vital parts are not replicated in the Treaty of Lisbon, such as an official E.U. anthem, motto and an official E.U. flag.[137] Thus, politicians have had to desist from attempts at making a "federal union" and accept the facts that citizens in each European country demand preservation of their own culture and (most of their) historical inheritance and desire to remain citizens of their native countries.

As for the "languages" of the Treaty of Lisbon, Article 7 states that it is "drawn up in a single original in the [23 official] languages, [and] the texts in each of these languages being equally authentic, shall be deposited in the archives of the Government of the Italian Republic, which will transmit a certified copy to each of the governments of the other signatory States."[138]

The Treaty of Lisbon once again renames what originally was called the "Treaty establishing the European Economic Community" (EEC into force on 1 January 1958)(= "Treaty of Rome" of 25 March 1957), which in 1993[139]

[134] See Final Act, Doc. 2007/C 306/02, OJ C306, 17.12.2007 pp. 0231-0271.

[135] The Flexibility Clause within the Treaty of Lisbon allows for adjustments of E.U. competence within the defined parameters of the E.U. The existing clause can only be used in connection with the area of the common market. Art 352 (ex Article 308 TEC) of Consolidated TFEU, OJ C115, 9.5.2008 p. 0196.

[136] See article I-6 of (the draft to the) Treaty establishing a Constitution for Europe, OJ C310, 16.12.2004 p. 0012.

[137] Even though a flag with a yellow star for each member state on blue background has been used publicly for years.

[138] OJ C306, 17.12.2007 p. 0135. Art. 55 in of consolidated TEU, OJ C115, 9.5.2008 p. 0045.

[139] By the Maastricht Treaty, also called the "Treaty on European Union" (TEU).

was renamed the "Treaty establishing the European Community" (TEC or EC) to the "Treaty on the Functioning of the European Union" (TFEU).[140]

Thus, after the Treaty of Lisbon the two remaining major treaties are:

- the Treaty on European Union (TEU)[141]
- the Treaty on the Functioning of the European Union (TFEU)[142]

Other parts of the Treaty of Lisbon are:

- Final Provisions[143]
- Protocols[144]
- Annex with Table of Equivalences,[145] and
- Final Act of the Intergovernmental Conference,[146] including
- Declarations[147]

Main Sections in the Treaty of Lisbon[148]		
Article 1(1)-(60)	changes to TEU	OJ p 0010-0042
Article 2 (1)-(295)	changes to TEC	OJ p 0042-0133
Article 3	Final Provisions: Unlimited Period	OJ p 0134
Article 4	Final Provisions: About protocol no. 1 and no. 2	OJ p 0134
Article 5	Final Provisions: Renumbering of TEU and TEC	OJ p 0134
Article 6	Final Provisions: Ratification and time for coming into force	OJ p 0135
Article 7	Final Provisions: Languages and Deposit	OJ p 0135
Protocols		OJ p 0147-201
Annex	tables of equivalences	OJ p 0202-229
Final Act	of the Intergovernmental Conference (+ index for declarations)	OJ p 0231-0327
Declarations		OJ p 0249-271

[140] Presidency Conclusion's on the Brussels European Council meeting 21-22 June 2007 at <www.consilium.europa.eu/ueDocs/cms_Data/docs/pressData/en/ec/94932.pdf>.
[141] OJ C306, 17.12.2007 p. 0010-41.
[142] OJ C306, 17.12.2007 p. 0042-0133.
[143] OJ C306, 17.12.2007 p. 0134-0145.
[144] OJ C306, 17.12.2007 p. 0147-0202.
[145] OJ C306, 17.12.2007 p. 0202-0229.
[146] OJ C306, 17.12.2007 p. 0231-0271
[147] OJ C306, 17.12.2007 p. 0249-0271.
[148] OJ C306, 17.12.2007 p 0001-0271.

The two remaining major treaties after Lisbon have the following structures:

Treaty of European Union (TEU)	
Title I	Common Provisions
Title II	Democratic Principles
Title III	Institutions
Title IV	Enhanced Cooperation
Title V	External Actions and Common Foreign and Security Policy
Title VI	Final Provisions

Table 50: Structure in Treaty of European Union

Treaty on the Functioning of the European Union (TFEU)	
Part 1	Principles
Part 2	Non-discrimination and Citizenship of the Union
Part 3	Union Policies and Internal Actions
Part 4	Overseas Countries and Territories
Part 5	External Action by the Union
Part 6	Institutional and Budgetary Provisions
Part 7	General and Final Provisions

Table 51: Structure in the Treaty on the Functioning of the European Union

On the book's corresponding website[149] are available tables of equivalences of articles in the treaties.[150] Note, that these tables indicates more than just a renumbering of articles.

The full text of the relevant treaty versions can be found in the Official Journal of the European Union as follows:

[149] <http://hssph.net/legalrm/index.html>.

[150] In previous editions printed as Appendix 4, <http://hssph.net/legalrm/Research_book_2-Edition_Appendix_4.pdf>.

E.U.-treaties Versions in Official Journal			
Before Lisbon[151]	**Lisbon Original**[152]	**After Lisbon**[153]	
C321 E, 29.12.2006 p. 5-36	C306, 17.12.2007 p. 10-41	C115, 9.5.2008 p. 13-45	**TEU**
C321 E, 29.12.2006 p. 37-186	C306, 17.12.2007 p. 42-133	C115, 9.5.2008 p. 47-199	**TEC / TFEU**
C321 E, 29.12.2006 p. 187-331	C306, 17.12.2007 p. 134-271	C115, 9.5.2008 p. 201-388	**Addendums**

Table 52: E.U. Treaties Versions in Official Journal (Lisbon)

The two now working treaties consist in turn of the following:[154]

- European Atomic Energy Community Treaty (EURATOM)
- European Coal and Steel Community Treaty (ECSC – Expired in 2002)
- Treaty establishing the European (Economic) Community (EEC, EC or TEC)[155]
- Treaty on European Union (TEU)[156] (originally also called the Maastricht Treaty)
- Treaty of Nice - Amending the Treaty on European Union, the Treaties Establishing the European Communities and certain related acts of 26 February 2001.[157]

****

[151] Index-website at <http://eur-lex.europa.eu/JOHtml.do?uri=OJ:C:2006:321E:SOM:EN:HTML> or <http://eur-lex.europa.eu/LexUriServ/LexUriServ.do?uri=OJ:C:2006:321E:0001:0331:EN:PDF>.

[152] Index-website at <http://eur-lex.europa.eu/JOHtml.do?uri=OJ:C:2007:306:SOM:EN:HTML>.

[153] Index-website at <http://eur-lex.europa.eu/LexUriServ/LexUriServ.do?uri=OJ:C:2008:115:SOM:EN:HTML>.

[154] Another significant document is also the Charter of Fundamental Rights of the European Union, OJ C364, 18/12/2000 p. 0001-0022.

[155] Nice consolidated version in O.J C 325, 24.12.2002 p. 0033-0184.

[156] Nice consolidated version in OJ C325, 24.12.2002 p. 0005-0032.

[157] OJ C80, 10.3.2001 p. 0001-0087. Consolidated version in OJ C325, 24.12.2002 p. 0001-0184. Information on the Nice Treaty can be found in "A Comprehensive Guide" at <http://europa.eu/legislation_summaries/institutional_affairs/treaties/nice_treaty/index_en.htm>.

It should be noted, that the politicians of the E.U. previous had proposed a treaty establishing a "Constitution"[158] for Europe (TCE),[159] but it was rejected in elections or referendums in several member-states by their citizens.

To a certain extent it is also necessary for the scholar to be aware of the founding treaties (original versions with later updating), the amending Treaties, and the accession treaties for each of the five enlargements of the E.U. that have accurred. The main history of what is now the European Union is as follows:

- 1952, 23 July – European Coal and Steel Community (ECSC) ("Treaty of Paris" of 1951)[160] came into force (Expired in 2002)[161]
- 1958, 1 January – Treaty establishing the European Economic Community[162] (EEC)[163] ("Treaty of Rome of 1957") & the European Atomic Energy Community Treaty (EURATOM of 1957)[164] comes into force
- 1967, 1 July - Treaty Establishing a Single Council and a Single Commission of the European Communities of 1965 (also called the "Merger Treaty")[165] comes into force[166]
- 1979 – Direct elections to European Parliament
- 1987, 1 July – Single European Act of 1986[167] (SEA) (amending the Treaty of Rome to a initiate campaign for a Community without in-

[158] In reality, a treaty compiled of previous EU treaties with amendments.

[159] Official Journal C 310 of 16 December 2004 [not in force].

[160] 261 U.N.T.S. 140.

[161] It expired on 23 July 2002. All assets and liabilities of the ECSC was transferred to the European Community on 24 July 2002. Article 1 of Protocol to the Nice Treaty, OJ C325. 24.12.2002 p. 0182.

[162] With the aim to create a common market, eliminate internal trade barriers and allow free movement of factors of production.

[163] Of 25 March 1957, 298 U.N.T.S. 11. By the Maastricht Treaty of 1993, the treaty was renamed the Treaty establishing the European Community (TEC). The Treaty of Lisbon of 2007 renames the treaty once again, now to be named the Treaty on the Functioning of the European Union (TFEU), see Presidency Conclusion's on the Brussels European Council meeting 21-22 June 2007 at <www.consilium.europa.eu/ueDocs/cms_Data/docs/pressData/en/ec/94932.pdf>.

[164] 261 U.N.T.S. 167.

[165] OJ 152, 13.07.1967, p 0002. Reprinted in 4 ILM 776.

[166] Provided for a Single Commission and a Single Council of the then three European Communities.

[167] OJ L169, 29.6.1987 p. 0001. Reprinted in 25 ILM 506.

ternal frontiers by 1993)[168]

- 1993, 1 November – Maastricht Treaty on European Union of 1992[169] (TEU which changed the "European Economic Community" (EEC) to the "European Community" (EC) and includes the so-called Three Pillar structure[170]) becomes operational[171]
- 1994 – Establishment of the European Monetary Institute.
- 1995 – The Schengen Agreement of 1985[172] (creating of open borders without passport controls between most member-states and some non-member-states) come graduately from March 1995 into force in certain signatory states
- 1999, 1 May – Treaty of Amsterdam[173] of 1997 becomes operational & 11 Member States join using a new common currency called the EURO (€)[174]

168 With the aim to remove all frontier controls, principle of mutual recognition to product standards, open public barriers of competition to banks and insurance, remove restrictions on foreign exchange transactions and abolish restriction on cabotage (trucking). It provided for the adaptations required for the achievement of the Internal Market.

169 OJ C 191 , 29.7.1992 p. 0001 – 0110. Reprinted in 31 ILM 247.

170 Creating the EURO currency, common foreign and defense policy, a common citizenship and giving the European Parliament genuine power. Three pillars of the European Union: (a) the European Communities pillar; (b) the Common Foreign and Security Policy (CFSP) pillar; and (c) the Justice and Home Affairs (JHA) pillar (later named the Police and Judicial Co-operation in Criminal Matters (PJC) pillar).

171 The Maastricht Treaty introduced new forms of co-operation between the Member State governments - for example on defence, and in the area of "justice and home affairs". By adding this inter-governmental co-operation to the existing "Community" system, the Maastricht Treaty created a new structure with three "pillars" which is political as well economic. This is the European Union (EU).

172 The *Schengen acquis* - Agreement between the Governments of the States of the Benelux Economic Union, the Federal Republic of Germany and the French Republic on the gradual abolition of checks at their common borders, OJ L 239, 22.9.2000, p. 0013–18 & Convention implementing the Schengen Agreement of 14 June 1985 between the Governments of the States of the Benelux Economic Union, the Federal Republic of Germany and the French Republic on the gradual abolition of checks at their common borders, OJ L 239, 22.9.2000, p. 0019–0062.

173 The Treaty of Amsterdam made substantial changes to the Treaty on European Union, which had been signed at Maastricht in 1992. The Amsterdam Treaty meant a greater emphasis on citizenship and the rights of individuals, more democracy in the shape of increased powers for the European Parliament, a new title on employment, a Community area of freedom, security and justice, the beginnings of a common foreign and security policy (CFSP) and the reform of the institutions in the run-up to enlargement.

174 As of January 2011, the following had shifted to the EURO (€): Andorra, Austria, Belgium, Cyprus, Estonia, Finland, France (including Guadeloupe, French Guiana, Réun-

- 2002 – Euro notes and coins replace national currencies in 12 member states.
- 2003, 1 February – Treaty of Nice[175] of 2001 becomes operational[176]
- 2005 – Dutch and French voters reject the "Treaty establishing a Constitution for Europe" of 2004 (TCE).[177]
- 2007 March - Berlin Declaration (officially the Declaration on the occasion of the 50th anniversary of the signature of the Treaty of Rome) is a non-binding European Union text signed on 25 March 2007 in Berlin (Germany)[178]
- 2009, 1 December - Treaty of Lisbon (also known as the Reform Treaty) of 13 December 2007[179] becomes operational (merging the 3 EU pillars) .
- 2010, March 31 – The Western European Union Treaty of (WEU) is terminated (WEU's activities are due to cease by July 2011).[180]

ion, Saint-Pierre et Miquelon, Mayotte and Martinique), Germany, Greece, Ireland, Italy, Kosovo, Luxembourg, Malta, Monaco, Montenegro, Netherlands, Portugal (including Azores, Madeira), San Marino, Slovakia Slovenia, Spain, and Vatican City. The Eurozone (Euro Area or Euroland) is the largest economy in the world with over 320 million people and a GDP over 2007. - Outside: Until Jan. 2011: Estonia; Until Jan 2012: Lithuania; Until Jan 2014: Bulgaria, Czech Republic, Hungary, Latvia, Poland, Romania, Sweden. No deadline: Denmark and the U.K.

175 It dealt mostly with reforming the institutions so that the E.U. could function efficiently after its enlargement to 25 Member States. OJ C80, 10.3.2001 p. 0001-0087. Consolidated version in OJ C325, 24.12.2002 p. 0001-0184. Information on the Nice Treaty can be found in "A Comprehensive Guide" at <http://europa.eu/legislation_summaries/institutional_affairs/treaties/nice_treaty/index_en.htm>.

176 OJ C80, 10.3.2001 p. 0001-0087. First Consolidated version in OJ C325, 24.12.2002 p. 0001-0184. Latest Consolidated version at <http://eur-lex.europa.eu/JOHtml.do?uri=OJ:C:2006:321E:SOM:EN:HTML>.

177 OJ C310, 16.12.2004 p. 0001-0474. Index at < http://eur-lex.europa.eu/JOHtml.do?uri=OJ:C:2004:310:SOM:EN:HTML>.

178 <www.consilium.europa.eu/ueDocs/cms_Data/docs/pressData/en/misc/93282.pdf> or <http://europa.eu/50/docs/berlin_declaration_en.pdf>.

179 Index for Consolidated (unofficial) version of EU-treaties published in OJ C115, 9.52008 at <http://eur-lex.europa.eu/JOHtml.do?uri=OJ:C:2008:115:SOM:EN:HTML>. The text of the draft to the treaty can be found at <www.consilium.europa.eu/uedocs/cmsUpload/cg00001re01en.pdf>.

180 The Western European Union (WEU or UEO) was an international organisation tasked with implementing the Treaty of Brussels (1948), a defense agreement among Western European nations during the Cold War. In 2009, the Treaty of Lisbon took over the

These treaties, normal ones in the public international law sense, are the basis for relations between the present 27[181] E.U. Member States.[182]

On the book's corresponding website at

<http://hssph.net/legalrm/Research_book_2-Edition_Appendix_4.pdf>

(In previous book-editions printed as Appendix 4) are available tables of equivalences of articles in the different treaties. Note, that these tables indicates more than just a renumbering of articles.

The scholar also has to be aware of the following "opt-outs" of some part of the treaties of:

United Kingdom – Social Protocol (later repealed)
Single Currency
Schengen Accord (Internal border controls over people)

Ireland - Schengen Accord

Denmark - Schengen Accord & Union Citizenship[183]
The Economic and Monetary Union (EMU - Single Currency)
Defense Policy – European Secutiry and Defence Policy (ESDP)
Justice and Home Affairs (JHA)[184]

WEU's mutual defense clause and as a result, as of 31 March 2010, the treaty was terminated.

181 On January 1, 2007, Bulgaria and Romania joined the European Union.

182 Consisting of more than 4,324,782 square kilometres/1,707,642 square miles, with more than 494 million people; and a GDP (nominal) 2007 (IMF) estimate of a total US$15,849 billion.

183 As for the later, the reservation has no practical impact today, *idem*.

184 Denmark later repealed its reservation on the E.U. Regulation 44/2001 of 22/12 2000 on jurisdiction and the recognition and enforcements in civil and commercial matters. OJ L 012 , 16/01/2001 P. 0001 – 0023. Denmark and the E.U. have concluded a so-called parallel treaty that causes the rules of the E.U. Regulation 44/2001 of 22/12 2000 to be used between Denmark and the other E.U. Member States. The Agreement (parallel treaty) came into force on 1 July 2007(OJ L 94, 4 April 2007, p. 70) after decision of 27 April 2006 by the Council of the European Union (OJ L120, 5 May 2006, p. 22) and decree no. 415 of 8 May 2007 from the Minister of Justice pursuant to mandate given in § 10 of Law no. 1563 of 20 December 2006 on the Brussels I Regulation ("Bruxelles I-forordning m.v.") - with the exception of the law's § 13, nr. 1 og 2. See Council Decision 2005/790/EC of 20 September 2005 on the signing, on behalf of the Community, OJ L 299, 16/11/2005 p. 0061-069, and the Agreement between the European Community and the Kingdom of Denmark on jurisdiction and the recogni-

European citizenship

The researcher also may find valuable information on E.U. legislation in the E.U. Parliament Documents, for example, in any question and answer sections.

Since January 1, 2007, the E.U. has had 23 official languages.[185] This fact is reason for great delays in getting new legislation into force, as new legislation cannot be published in the Official Journal before it has been translated into all languages. Due to lack of sufficient numbers of translators of some languages, it can take many months before a new piece of legislation can come into force. Thus, when searching for background material, one often has to go back from the time of the legislation's publication half a year or even more to find the history behind it.

When doing research on E.U. law, one must regard the law from the perspective of a Civil Law area, that is, there is no judge made law as in the U.S. (a Common Law country).

The legislation in the E.U. is made by the Council of the European Union and the Parliament in cooperation. Furthermore, the E.U. Commission does have certain rights pursuant to the treaties to make legislation and thus overrule a national Parliament-issued statute or administrative practice. All institutions and E.U. Member States are obliged to follow the judgments from the ECJ, which has the power to invalidate legislation, but not make new law even though the Court to some extent has developed general principles of law.[186]

There are different types of legislation in the E.U., among which the researcher must distinguish:[187]

- Treaties – made after negations between the E.U. Member States and only binding on a state if ratified by it.
- Regulations – which have general application, are binding in their entirety and are directly applicable in all E.U. Member States. They

tion and enforcement of judgments in civil and commercial matters, OJ L 299, 16/11/2005, p. 0062-0067.

[185] Decision of the Council of 18 December 2006, 2006/955/EC, amending the Rules of Procedure of the Court of Justice of the European Communities as regards the language arrangements, OJ L 386, 29.12.2006, p. 0044.

[186] Like the International Court of Justice, the European Court of Justice applies public international law. See *Opel Austria GmbH v. Council of the European Union* (E.C.J. T-115/94 1997), 1997 E.C.R. II-39 no. 90 (customary international law whose existence is recognized by the International Court of Justice is binding on the Community).

[187] Article 288 of consolidated TFEU, OJ C115, 9.5.2008 p. 0172-173 (ex ante TEC Article 249 (ex ante EC art. 189)).

must be published in the Official Journal before they can come into force.

- Directives – which do not necessarily apply to all E.U. Member States. Rather than being directly applicable in those states, there is a choice of forms and methods of implementing directives into national laws. However, directives are binding on the E.U. Member States to which they are addressed as to the result to be achieved. If a directive applies to all E.U. Member States, it must be published in the Official Journal before it can come into force.
- Decisions – which are binding in their entirety upon those to whom they are addressed. Some decisions need to be published in the Official Journal before they can come into force.
- Recommendations and opinions – which have no binding force.

When reading texts of the treaties and court judgments, pre- and post-Amsterdam of 1996, one must bear in mind the following:

- In the text of the Treaty on European Union of 1992 (Maastricht):
    - provisions were identified by the letters A-S
    - The numbers were preserved for the other three treaties
- Treaty of Amsterdam of 1996:
    - EC Treaty (TEC) renumbered/equivalences from start to finish to eliminate awkward numerical oddities (e.g., Articles 104b and 130t)
    - Switch from letters to numbers in the E.U. Treaty (TEU)

9.3.3. Interpretation of E.U. Statutory law

As mentioned aboves, there are 23 official language in the European Union,[188] of which English, French and German are "working" languages. Thus, the E.U. has 23 authoritative original versions of law,[189] as recorded in article

[188] On interpretation in the E.U., see Stephen Weatherill & Paul Beaumont, E.U. LAW 184-5, 190-92,316-17 (3rd ed.) (1999 Penguin Books); Stehephen Weatherill, CASES AND MATERIALS ON EU LAW (8th ed.)(2007 Oxford Press); Paul Craig & Grainne de Burca, EU LAW – TEXT, CASES AND MATERIALS (4th ed.)(2007, Oxford Press).

[189] However, some treaties have a different regime, e.g., the European Coal and Steel Treaty is only authentic in French. See Article 100. Nevertheless, agreement has been made that German, French, Italian and Dutch are the official and working languages. The EC and Euratom Treaties are authentic in twelve languages. See EC articles 217 & 248 and Euratom articles 190 & 225.

29 of the Rules of Procedure for the E.U. courts (as of 15 January 2008).[190] Article 31 states "[t]he text of documents drawn up in the language of the case or in any other language authorized by the Court pursuant to Article 29 of these Rules shall be authentic."[191]

As for the "languages" of the Treaty of Lisbon, Article 7 states that it is "drawn up in a single original in the [23 official] languages, [and] the texts in each of these languages being equally authentic, shall be deposited in the archives of the Government of the Italian Republic, which will transmit a certified copy to each of the governments of the other signatory States."[192]

In the Simutenkov case, the Advocate General before the ECJ argued that the starting point is the wording of a statute, but "[i]n so doing it must be borne in mind that Community legislation is drafted in various languages and that the different language versions are all equally authentic. An interpretation of a provision of Community law thus involves a comparison of the different language versions."[193]

Research Tip #9.6

Statutory interpretation in the E.U. is statutory interpretation without a single, authoritative text and one cannot expect different language versions of the same act or treaty always to say exactly the same thing.[194]

The goal for the E.U. courts is to capture the essence of E.U. legislation.

[190] Decision of the Council of 18 December 2006, 2006/955/EC, amending the Rules of Procedure of the Court of Justice of the European Communities as regards the language arrangements, OJ L 386, 29.12.2006, p. 0044.

[191] Rules of Procedure of the Courts can be found at the courts website under "Texts governing procedure" at <http://curia.europa.eu/jcms/jcms/Jo2_7003/#B>. Consolidated version of 2 July 2010, O.J. C 177 p. 0001-0036 at < http://curia.europa.eu/jcms/upload/docs/application/pdf/2010-04/rp.en.pdf>.

[192] OJ C306, 17.12.2007 p. 0135. Art. 55 in of consolidated TEU, OJ C115, 9.5.2008 p. 0045.

[193] *Simutenkov v. Ministerio de Educación Y Cultura, Real Federación Española de Futbol*, [2005] 2 C.M.L.R. 11 at AG 14, [2005] ECR I-2579 at 14, 2005 WL 840128 (ECJ), [2006] All E.R. (EC) 42 (European Court of Justice (Grand Chamber) Case C-265/03 of 12 April 2005). See also, Geert Van Calster, *The EU's Tower of Babel – The Interpretation of the European Court of Justice of Equally Authentic Texts Drafted in More Than One Official Language*, 17 (1997) YEARBOOK OF EUROPEAN LAW 363-92 (Oxford Press 1998) [hereinafter VAN CALSTER].

[194] VAN CALSTER *supra* note 192 at 369.

As the E.U. is a multilanguage legal regime, translation is more than a metaphor – it is a basic fact about the entire structure of the law.

Research Tip #9.7

While the ECJ does not use the translation history, E.U. courts use comparison of the various versions of the law as an important tool.[195]

The E.U. courts looks not only at the versions written in the languages of the parties to the particular dispute before the court, but also at other versions. When a dispute is over which of two fully authentic versions of a law should prevail, the status of the statutory language is itself contested. E.U. courts will typically not determine whether some versions reflect an error in translation. Thus, the courts will not make reference to the translation history.

The language of a statute provides privileged evidence of what the legislature intended.

Research Tip #9.8

European courts are more comfortable than American courts in putting the purpose of a statute ahead of the language in the service of effectuating the legislature's will.[196]

In the Schulte case, the Advocate General before the ECJ argued that "[w]here it is difficult to interpret legislation from its wording alone, an interpretation based on purpose becomes fundamental.[197] That is the case where the provision in dispute is ambiguous."[198] Thus, the courts investigate the

[195] *Meico-Fell v Hauptzollamt Darmstadt*, [1991] ECR I-5569 at paras 9-10 (European Court of Justice (Sixth Chamber) Case C-273/90 of 27 November 1991 (it appears from the context in which that provision was adopted that the expression...means...that interpretation is confirmed by an examination of the other language versions, which have a clear meaning).

[196] Lawrence M. Solan, *Statutory Interpretation in the EU: The Augustinian Approach*, Brooklyn Law School, Legal Studies Paper No. 78 page 10 (July 2007) - Available at SSRN: <http://ssrn.com/abstract=998167>.

[197] *Posthumus v Oosterwoud*, [1991] ECR I-5833 at paras 9-10 (European Court of Justice (Third Chamber) Case C-121/90 of 6 December 1991 (a comparison of the various language versions...show...that interpretation, based on the wording of the provision in question, is in conformity with its purpose).

[198] *Schulte v. Deutsche Bausparkasse Badenia AG*, [2006] 1 C.M.L.R. 11 at AG87 (Advocate General), [2005] ECR I-9215, [2006] C.E.C. 115, [2006] All E.R. (EC) 420 (European Court of Justice (Grand Chamber) Case C-350/03 of 25 October 2005).

motivation for the legislation, including founding documents that set forth overarching legal goals, and resolve disputes in a manner that will further those goals.

In the Promusicae case, the Court stated that E.U. community law requires as for E.U. directives that, "the Member States take care to rely on an interpretation of [directives] which allows a fair balance to be struck between the various fundamental rights protected by the Community legal order. Further, when implementing the measures transposing...directives, the authorities and courts of the Member States must not only interpret their national law in a manner consistent with those directives but also make sure that they do not rely on an interpretation of them which would be in conflict with those fundamental rights or with the other general principles of Community law, such as the principle of proportionality."[199]

9.4. Where to find E.U. material

For scholars[200] who are citizens of a E.U. Member State, the following should be noted as far as access to documentation: Article 255 of the Treaty establishing the European Community states that citizens and residents of the European Union have a right of access to European Parliament, Council and Commission documents.[201]

A wealth of information about the history of Europe and its institutions since 1945 is available from European NAvigator (ENA) - an educational platform that focuses particularly on the development of a united Europe. ENA is available in English, French, German and Spanish, though some

199 *Productores de Música de España (Promusicae) v Telefónica de España SAU* - (Reference for a preliminary ruling from the Juzgado de lo Mercantil No 5 de Madrid - Spain), OJ C 64, 8.3.2008, p. 0009 (E.C.J. C-275/06 (Grand Chamber), 29 January 2008).

200 The Delegation of the European Commission to the U.S., Washington, DC, in the spring of 2007, decided to divulge itself of its entire depository collection and awarded it to the University Library System, University of Pittsburgh, currently the home of the Archive of European Integration (AEI). This depository collection begins in the early 1950s and is easily the largest EU collection in the Western Hemisphere. Over the next several years, the AEI will digitize many documents from this collection and post them on the World Wide Web. Archive of European Integration at <http://aei.pitt.edu>.

201 <www.europarl.europa.eu/parliament/public/staticDisplay.do?language=EN&id=151>.

documents are available in other languages at <www.ena.lu>.[202]

Any student or scholar in the world can, from

<http://eur-lex.europa.eu/en/treaties/index.htm>,

access the basic legal texts on which the European Union and the European Communities are founded, plus other essential documents.[203]

From January 1, 2007, all official valid European Union websites were moved to <europa.eu>.

It should be noted that not all pages exist in the online version of the Official Journal, but only in the hardcover printed volumes.[204]

The E.U. uses the following abbreviations in a consolidated versions:

- B = basic act
- M = modifier
- A = Accession Treaty
- C = corrigendum

The CELEX database was closed by the end of 2006 and the information transferred to the European Union Law website, EUR-lex at

<http://eur-lex.europa.eu>.

[202] Using the site is free, although the documents are protected by copyright. ENA is developed by the CVCE (Centre Virtuel de la Connaissance sur l'Europe - Virtual Resource Centre for Knowledge about Europe), a Luxembourg-based public undertaking that is actively supported by the Ministry of Culture, Higher Education and Research.

[203] However, the Commission has proposed changes in Regulation (EC) No 1049/2001 of the European Parliament and of the Council of 30 May 2001 regarding public access to European Parliament, Council and Commission documents, OJ L145, 31.5.2001 p. 0043-0048, which pursuant to the E.U. Ombudsman would decrease access for the public, see Contribution of 2 June 2008 from the European Ombudsman to the public hearing on the revision of Regulation 1049/2001,
<www.europarl.europa.eu/parliament/public/staticDisplay.do?language=EN&id=151>
and Proposal for a Regulation of the European Parliament and of the Council regarding public access to European Parliament, Council and Commission documents, COM/2008/0229 final at
<http://eur-lex.europa.eu/LexUriServ/LexUriServ.do?uri=CELEX:52008PC0229:EN:HTML>.

[204] E.g., the vital reports related to the Brussels Convention, the Lugano Convention and the E.U. Regulation 44/2001 of 22/12 2000 on jurisdiction and the recognition and enforcements in civil and commercial matters can better be found at <http://aei.pitt.edu>. For example Jenard Report no. 1 (1979), OJ C59, 5/3/1979, p. 0001-0065 at <http://aei.pitt.edu/1465/01/commercial_report_jenard_C59_79.pdf>.

However, the E.U. still used CELEX numbers for documents. The Celex number is the unique identifier of each document in EUR-Lex, regardless of language.

It is composed as follows: SyyyyT(T)nnn(n)

- S - 1 character for the sector (see list below)
- yyyy - 4 digits for the year (usually the year of adoption)
- T(T) -- 1 or 2 characters for the document type (see list below)
- nnn(n) - 4 digits (usually) for the document number

> For example, document 32008R1338 is:
>
> a sector 3 document (secondary legislation): 32008R1338
> from 2008: 32008R1338
> a regulation: 32008R1338
> published in the OJ under number 1338: 32008R1338

Document sectors are:

- Sector 1 Treaties
- Sector 2 – International agreements
- Sector 3 – Secondary legislation
- Sector 4 – Complementary legislation
- Sector 5 – Preparatory acts
- Sector 6 – Case law
- Sector 7 – National implementing measures
- Sector 8 – National case law (Nov 2010: under construction)
- Sector 8 – Parliamentary questions
- Sector 0 – Consolidated versions of sector 3 documents
- Sector E – EFTA documents
- Sector C – Other documents published in the O.J. C

Main types of document in each sector[205]		
Sector 3	**Sector 5**	**Sector 6**
L = directives	PC = legislative proposals by the Commission (COM documents)	C = conclusions of the advocate-general
R = regulations	DC = other COM documents	J = judgment by Court of Justice
D = decisions	SC = SEC documents	O = order of the Court of Justice

[205] Full list of sectors and document types (PDF) at <http://eur-lex.europa.eu/en/tools/TABLE_OF_SECTORS_20100521.pdf>.

To monitor the decision-making process between the E.U. institutions, use PreLex at <http://ec.europa.eu/prelex/apcnet.cfm?CL=en>.

Summaries of E.U. legislation can be found through ScadPlus at

<http://europa.eu/legislation_summaries/index_en.htm>.

The EUR-lex Guidelines for good results in Search by Official Journal publication[206] reference are as follows:

- The year field takes 4 characters; the month and day fields take 2 (Example: Year 1999 Month 09 Day 12)
- Always enter the year (month and day fields are optional)
- To get the annexes to the OJ C series, enter A or E after the OJ number (Example: select the C series, then enter 123A to get an OJ with the reference C 123 A).
- The Supplement S to the OJ (calls for tenders) is published in the TED database (choose English in the right upper box).[207]

EUR-Lex at <http://eur-lex.europa.eu/RECH_menu.do?ihmlang=en> allows the following search:

- General search by:
    - Search terms
    - Date or time span
    - Author
    - Classification headings
    - Keyword
- Search by file category:
    - Treaties
    - Legislation
    - Preparatory acts
    - Case-law

[206] The Official Journal (OJ), published daily in 23 languages, consists of the L series (legislation) and the C series (information, preparatory acts and notices). The documents included in the C series are partly published only electronically. The L and C series were introduced in 1968, before which year there was a single series. Some databases used the letters B or P to distinguish this single series from series L and C. The letters B and P do not form part of the official publication reference. The Supplement S to the OJ (calls for tenders) is published in the TED database.

[207] TED (Tenders Electronic Daily) is the Supplement to the Official Journal of the European Union. It contains all active notices published in the Supplement to the Official Journal (OJ S) <http://ted.europa.eu> or <http://ted.europa.eu/TED/main/HomePage.do>.

  - Parliamentary questions
- Search by document number:
  - Natural number
  - Celex number
  - Consolidated text
- Search by publication reference;
  - Official Journal (OJ)
  - European Court Report (E.C.R.)

9.4.1. Treaties

Text of the treaties can be found at <http://eur-lex.europa.eu/RECH_traites.do>.

When reading texts of treaties and court judgments, pre- and post-Amsterdam, bear in mind the following:[208]

- In the text of the Treaty on European Union (TEU) in 1992:
  - provisions were identified by the letters A-S
  - The numbers were preserved for the other three treaties
- Treaty of Amsterdam:
  - EC Treaty (TEC) renumbered/equivalences from start to finish to eliminate awkward numerical oddities (e.g., Articles 104b and 130t)
  - Switch from letters to numbers in the E.U. Treaty

Explanatory texts to the Amsterdam Treaty can be found at:

- A comprehensive Guide - <http://europa.eu/legislation_summaries/institutional_affairs/treaties/amsterdam_treaty/index_en.htm>

Explanatory texts to the Nice Treaty can be found at:

- A comprehensive Guide – <http://europa.eu/legislation_summaries/institutional_affairs/treaties/nice_treaty/nice_treaty_introduction_en.htm>

9.4.2. Regulations, Directives & Decisions:

Regulations, Directives & Decisions:

- Using the Directory of Community Legislation in Force and other

[208] On the book's corresponding website at <http://hssph.net/legalrm/Research_book_2-Edition_Appendix_4.pdf> (In previous book-editions printed as Appendix 4) are available tables of equivalences of articles in the different treaties. Note, that these tables indicates more than just a renumbering of articles.

acts of the Community Institutions:
  - Vol I - Analytical Index
  - Vol II - Chronological index and Alphabethical index
- Using the EUR-Lex database
- Community legislation in force can be found:
  - Analytical structure (after subject matter) – <http://eur-lex.europa.eu/en/legis/latest/index.htm> and archives at <www.eur-lex.europa.eu/en/legis/legis_archives.htm>
- Consolidated Community legislation in force (unofficial versions):
  - Search-website for consolidated legislation <http://eur-lex.europa.eu/RECH_consolidated.do>

9.4.3. Preparatory Documents (COMDocs)

Preparatory Documents (COMDocs) consist of:

- Broad policy consultative documents called "Communications", "Green Paper" and "White Paper"
- Proposals for legislation
- Reports on the implementation of policy

COMDocs can be found in:

- Paper format or on microfiche
- EUR-Lex database <http://eur-lex.europa.eu>.
- European Documents at <http://europa.eu/documentation/official-docs/index_en.htm>.

9.4.4. Official Journal

The “Official Journal” or gazette (OJ – seldom OJE) is divided into the following four parts as illustrated in the table below (next page).

The Supplement S to the OJ is published in the TED database (Tenders Electronic Daily)).[209]

9.4.5. E.U. Case law

European Union Court decisions are available from:

- European Court Reports (ECR): the authoritative texts of ECJ opinions and judgments

[209] It contains all active notices published in the Supplement to the Official Journal (OJ S) <http://ted.europa.eu>.

- Common Market Law Reports (CMLR).

Series	Content	Comment	Citation
L	Agreed legislation	The most important part of this goes to Official Journal	OJ L 213, 7.9.1995, p 0001–0031 or OJ L213 1995 p 1 or OJ L 213, 7/9/1995 p 0001–0031
C[210]	Proposed legislation, notes of ECJ judgments, information notices from the EC, EP resolutions, questions and answers	The contents of this series are varied. Information considered of public interest, but which does not fall into the categories covered by the other series, is dealt with here	OJ C 187, 24.07.1989 p 0001 or OJ C187 1989 p 1 or OJ C 187, 24/07/1989 p 0001
S	Invitations to tender for public contracts	Sometimes referred to as the "supplement"	OJ S118 1995 p 0001
Annex	Debates of the EP	Unlike the other series, the issue number is continuous	OJ Annex no 4-455 p 0032

Table 53: E.U. Official Journal Parts

There are several types of case indexes:

- Numerical access to the case-law at <http://curia.europa.eu/jcms/jcms/Jo2_7045/>. Access to the case-law by case number makes it possible to find information relating to every case brought before the Court of Justice, the Court of First Instance (now the General Court) or the Civil Service Tribunal between 1953 and the present day. Cases are listed by number in the order in which they were lodged at the relevant Registry. Cases may also be located by party names using the "find (Ctrl+F)" function on the toolbar. Cases may be consulted by clicking on the case number.
    - The texts of judgments and orders in cases lodged up to and including 1997 that have been published in the European Court Reports may be consulted by clicking on the case number and following the link to EUR-Lex, the interinstitutional database.

210 In EUR-Lex search: To get the annexes to the OJ C series, enter A or E after the OJ number. Example: select the C series, then enter 123A to get an OJ with the reference C 123 A.

  - Cases lodged since 1998 may be consulted by clicking on the case number and following that link to all the texts relating to the case in question, which are contained in the case-law database of this site.
  - Cases lodged before the Court of Justice from 1953 to 1988 and since 1989.
  - Cases lodged before the Court of First Instance (now the General Court0: since 1989.
  - Cases lodged before the Civil Service Tribunal : since 2005.
- Digest of Community case-law - The Répertoire de jurisprudence communautaire (only in French) at <http://curia.europa.eu/jcms/jcms/Jo2_7046/>. It is a systematic collection of the summaries of the judgments and orders of the Court of Justice and of the Court of First Instance (now the General Court) of the European Communities and the Civil Service Tribunal of the European Union delivered since their inception, presented following a layout subdivided into seven parts:
  - the Community legal order
  - the European Community (EC)
  - the European Coal and Steel Community (ECSC/CS)
  - the European Atomic Energy Community (EAEC/AE)
  - the Brussels Convention
  - the European Civil Service
  - the European Union (E.U.)
- Alphabetical Table of Subject-matter - The Table alphabétique des matières (only in French) at <http://curia.europa.eu/jcms/jcms/Jo2_7047/>. It lists the legal questions dealt with in the decisions of the Court of Justice and the Court of First Instance (now the General Court) of the European Communities and the Civil Service Tribunal of the European Union and in the Opinions of the Advocates General, presented in alphabetical order.
- Annotation of judgments - The Notes de doctrine aux arrêts (only in French) at <http://curia.europa.eu/jcms/jcms/Jo2_7083/>. It gives the references to published legal literature relating to the judgments of the Court of Justice and of the Court of First Instance (now the General Court) of the European Communities and the Civil Service Tribunal of the European Union.
  - Preface
  - Vol. 1 : 1954 - 1988
  - Vol. 2 : 1989 - 2005
- Index A-Z (from 2000) contains:

    - Numeric List of Cases
    - Alphabetic List of Parties
    - Vol. I: Court of Justice (1953 - 1988)
    - Vol. II: Court of Justice and Court of First Instance (now the General Court) (since 1989)
- Notes de References des Notes de Doctrine.
    - The Notes de doctrine aux arrêts gives the references to published legal literature relating to the judgments of the Court of Justice and of the Court of First Instance (now the General Court) of the European Communities and the Civil Service Tribunal of the European Union (only in French). Index by case number to all court reports, including details of case notes in legal journals (available also online from <http://curia.europa.eu/common/recdoc/notes/index.htm>.
    - Preface
    - Vol. 1 : 1954 - 1988
    - Vol. 2 : 1989 - 2005
    - A chronological list
- Index in the final part of each years's ECR
- Index in each volume of CMLR (not annual) contains:
    - Alphabetical table of cases
    - Index of subject matter and community legislative provisions
    - Treaties and regulations referred to
    - Index of cases judicially considered
    - Statutes cited

One can trace a court report in hardcopy in the following manner:

- If one knows the date of judgment, use the index at the back of the ECR (chronological index)
- If one only knows the case reference or the name, use the Index A-Z
- If one wants a topic search, use the annual index to ECR or the volume index to CMLR

The are several electronic sources for E.U. court decisions. Among others:

- EUR-Lex at <http;//eur-lex.europa.eu>
- Court of Justice & Court of First Instance (now the General Court) online at <http://curia.europa.eu/jcms/jcms/j_6/>
- LexisNexis
- Westlaw

9.4.6. Advocate-General's documentation

Opinions from the Advocate-General can be found at <http://eur-lex.europa.eu/RECH_jurisprudence.do>.[211]

9.4.7. E.U. Ombudsman's documentation

The E.U. Ombudsman's Reports, draft recommendations and decisions can be found at <www.ombudsman.europa.eu/home.faces>.

9.4.8. Parliamentary documentation

Parliamentary documentation, can be found at <www.europarl.europa.eu/>[212] or as follows:

<www.europarl.europa.eu/guide/search/docsearch_en.htm>

- Committee Reports are available in hard copy (documents) or microfiche or online from the European Parliament's website at <www.europarl.europa.eu/RegWeb/application/registre/simpleSearch.faces?language=EN> or <www.europarl.europa.eu/RegWeb/application/registre/advancedSearch.faces>.
- Resolutions can be found through the European Parliament's website, in the C series of the OJ, in EUR-Lex
- Debates (verbatim texts) are published in Annex of the OJ, which is indexed by name of MEP, subject and session.
- Parliament's questions (written questions & answers) are published in series C of the OJ and indexed in the Official Journal Index.

The European Parliament Register[213] gives access to the following official documents:

- Draft reports and opinions. Prior to the meetings of Parliament's committees, all documents on the agenda are published on Europarl. One can find them under the heading 'Meeting documents' for each committee. Access to these documents is at present possible only by

[211] Or <http://eur-lex.europa.eu/SuiteJurisprudence.do?T1=V114&T3=V1&RechType=RECH_jurisprudence&Submit=Search>.

[212] Or <www.europarl.europa.eu/news/public/default_en.htm>. The European Parliament United Kingdom Office (in English) at <www.europarl.org.uk>.

[213] <www.europarl.europa.eu/guide/search/docsearch_en.htm>.

date of committee meeting at
<www.europarl.europa.eu/ committees/home_en.htm.>.

- Reports adopted in committee. Search by:
    - list of new reports
    - rapporteur
    - committee responsible
    - report number
    - PE number
    - type of legislative procedure
    - keywords in title or text
- Part-session minutes at <www.europarl.europa.eu/activities/introduction/home.do?language=en>. A provisional version of the minutes is published prior to their approval in plenary, and is later replaced by the final version as published in the Official Journal, C series. Search by: date of sitting, or keywords(s) in title.
- Parliament by document type at <www.europarl.europa.eu/RegWeb/application/registre/listParlDoc.faces>. Opinions of Parliament, legislative resolutions, resolutions, decisions on common positions and joint texts, own-initiative resolutions, budgetary resolutions, etc. Texts published in the provisional version as approved in plenary and subsequently published in the Official Journal, C series, in their final form. Search by: date of adoption in plenary, source referred to in report, or keyword(s) in title.
- Resolutions (all resolutions since July 1994)(Rule 113 of Parliament's Rules of Procedure) and resolutions on cases of breaches of human rights, democracy and the rule of law (Rule 115). Texts published in the provisional version of 'texts adopted' as approved in plenary, and subsequently published in the Official Journal, C series, in their final form. Search by: date of adoption in plenary, reference for motion for a resolution (B6-xxxx) or keyword(s) in title..
- Debates in plenary or verbatim report of proceedings and final text of debates (all debates since April 1996) at <www.europarl.europa.eu/search/simple/perform.do?language=EN&sortBy=relevance&page=1&query=debates&inArchives=false&collection=sides_debats#>. The verbatim record of proceedings of Parliament's debates in plenary is available in the original language of the speakers and, after translation, in all the E.U.'s working languages. The original-language texts are generally published the day after the debate. Provisional translations are published at the same location ap-

proximately four weeks later. These translations are subsequently replaced by the final version, which is also published in an Annex to the Official Journal. Search by: date of sitting, speaker, or keywords(s) in heading of debate.

- Bulletins <www.europarl.europa.eu/bulletins/default.htm> or <www.europarl.europa.eu/references/bull/default_en.htm>. Presentation of the current work of Parliament and its bodies: appears monthly (except in August). A special edition is produced immediately after an E.U. summit, containing both the EP President's address to the European Council and the Presidency Conclusions.
- Parliamentary questions (since 1994/99) at <http://eur-lex.europa.eu/en/questions/questions.htm> OR <www.europarl.europa.eu/QP-WEB/home.jsp?&language=EN>.

Search by Member's name, political group, Member State of origin, question number, Official Journal number, institution to which the question is addressed, or keyword(s) in title or text..

- Rules of Procedure of the European Parliament with Index at <www.europarl.europa.eu/sides/getLastRules.do?language=EN&reference=TOC>.
- Public register of the European Parliament at <www.europarl.europa.eu/RegWeb/application/registre/advancedSearch.faces>
- Legislative Observatory (OEIL): European Parliament data base at <www.europarl.europa.eu/oeil/index.jsp>.

9.4.9. Commission documentation

The Registers of Commission Documents (only documents produced since January 1, 2001) at <http://ec.europa.eu/transparency/index_en.htm> help to identify categories of document, related to various activities of the Commission,[214] namely:

- Green papers are discussion papers published by the Commission on a specific policy area. In some cases, they provide an impetus for subsequent legislation, at <http://europa.eu/documentation/official-docs/green-papers/index_en.htm>.
- White papers are documents containing proposals for Community ac-

[214] The European Commission Representation in the United Kingdom (in English) at <www.cec.org.uk>.

tion in a specific area. They sometimes follow a green paper. White papers contain an official set of proposals in specific policy areas and are used as vehicles for their development at <http://europa.eu/documentation/official-docs/white-papers/index_en.htm>.

- Commission meeting at <http://ec.europa.eu/transparency/access_documents/index_en.htm>
- Register of COM, SEC and C documents at <http://ec.europa.eu/transparency/regdoc/recherche.cfm?CL=en> :[215]
    - COM documents: proposed legislation and other Commission communications to the Council and/or the other institutions, and their preparatory papers;
    - SEC documents: internal documents associated with the decision-making process and the general operation of Commission departments;
    - C documents: legal acts adopted by the Commission in the exercise of its own or delegated powers.
- Application of Community law <http://ec.europa.eu/community_law/index_en.htm>;
- Codecision <http://ec.europa.eu/codecision/index_en.htm>.

This register supplements the PreLex database of interinstitutional procedures <http://ec.europa.eu/prelex/apcnet.cfm?CL=en>, which can be used to search for documents produced by the institutions in drafting Community legislation.

Commission decisions and adopted measures country by country at

<http://ec.europa.eu/information_society/policy/ecomm/implementation_enforcement/eu_consultation_procedures/index_en.htm>.

9.4.10. Consilium (Council of the European Union)

The website for the Consilium (Council of the European Union) is <www.consilium.europa.eu/showPage.aspx?lang=EN>. The register of the Council of the European Union has a search screen at <www.consilium.europa.eu/showPage.aspx?id=1279&lang=EN>. The register contains references for documents produced by the Council since January 1, 1999.

[215] Help on document types can be found at <http://ec.europe.eu/transparancy/regdoc/aidetypesdoc.cfm?CL=en>.

9.4.11. European Council documentation

The website of the European Council, which by the Lisbon Treaty has become an official institution of the E.U. is <www.european-council.europa.eu/home-page.aspx?lang=EN>.

9.4.12. E.U. President documentation

The website for the President of the European Council is <www.european-council.europa.eu/the-president.aspx>.

9.4.13. E.U. Foreign Minister documentation

The High Representative of the Union for Foreign Affairs and Security Policyhas two websites. One related to the Consilium at <www.consilium.europa.eu/showPage.aspx?id=1847&lang=en> and one related to the Commisison at E.U.Foreign Minister <http://ec.europa.eu/archives/commission_2004-2009/ashton/index_en.htm>.

9.4.14. Implementing national laws

One can track the implementation and enforcement of E.U. legislation into national law at the Commissions' website at <http://ec.europa.eu/community_law/index_en.htm>.

9.4.15. EUR-Lex

Full text of the OJ L and C series, Treaties (primary sources), Case-law, Legislation (preparatory and in force), Parliamentary Questions and Documents of public interest at <http://eur-lex.europa.eu/en/index.htm>.[216]

Detailed explanation for EUR-Lex documents and numbering at

<http://eur-lex.europa.eu/en/legis/avis.htm>.

"About EUR-Lex" at <http://eur-lex.europa.eu/en/tools/about.htm> explains and have several links:

EUR-Lex provides free access to European Union law and other docu-

[216] Joint Practical Guide of the European Parliament, the Council and the Commission for persons involved in the drafting of legislation (European Communities, 2003) within the Community institutions at <http://eur-lex.europa.eu/en/techleg/pdf/en.pdf> & Updating of April 2009 at <http://eur-lex.europa.eu/en/techleg/pdf/EN-corrections-clean.pdf>.

ments considered to be public. The website is available in 23 official languages of the European Union; choose your preferred language from the language bar at the top of the homepage. The contents of the site amount to some 2 815 000 documents with texts dating back to 1951. The database is updated daily and every year around 12 000 documents are added.

EUR-Lex offers: daily editions of the Official Journal of the European Union online, simple search, advanced search and browsing options, the possibility to display and/or download documents (PDF, HTML, DOC, TIFF), analytical metadata for each document.

I would like to access the Official Journal of the European Union: The Official Journal of the European Union is the principal source of EUR-Lex content and it is published in the early morning after every working day. It consists of two series: L (Legislation) and C (Information and Notices). E and A are Official Journals published as annexes to the C series (e.g. C 307 A, C 309 E). Latest issues are accessible from the homepage; click on the links in the upper right-hand corner, just under the language bar. Previous issues can be found by clicking on the OFFICIAL JOURNAL link on top of the left-hand menu. You can find an issue of the Official Journal by browsing or by searching. All issues from 1998 onwards are available in PDF. To access texts published before 1998, use the SIMPLE SEARCH - Search by publication reference (Official Journal). The S series is the supplement to the Official Journal of the European Union containing invitations to tender. It is accessible on the TED website (Tenders Electronic Daily) .

I would like to search for a document: There are two search interfaces in EUR-Lex; SIMPLE SEARCH and ADVANCED SEARCH. While advanced search provides a fuller range of search and display features, simple search will accommodate most users' requirements. You have a wide range of search options; search by search terms, search by date, search by author, search by natural number, etc. Another option is to browse our collections and directories; choose from treaties, international agreements, legislation in force, preparatory acts, case-law and parliamentary questions. Each of the aforementioned sectors offers a browsing feature, such as the Directory of European Union legislation in force.

What do I do with my search result? You have direct access to all the documents in your list of search results; just click on your preferred format. You can also check which languages and formats are available, display complementary data, sort or refine your search result to get more relevant documents (find these options on the yellow bar and/or the search box). You can review and/or combine the queries made in one session by clicking on Search history. To get more information on a document follow the link 'bibliographic notice' (example). The notice is a display of metadata (author, dates, indexes, form, related documents, etc.) which provides insight into each document and shows relationships between documents. For bilingual display of a document follow the link Bibliographic notice + Text (bilingual display). EUR-Lex also offers consolidated versions of documents (where available). These versions are intended for documentation purposes only and have no legal value. Find them in the bibliographic notice or by browsing the Directory of European Union legislation in force.

What else can I do? You can read about EU law, the legislative procedures and EU institutions. You can consult the selection of new documents on the homepage or consult our thematic files. EUR-Lex also offers links to the budget of the European Union, the institutions' registers and other documentation and information sources. New developments are announced in our Newsletter.

9.4.16. Miscellaneous

- News: <http://europa.eu/press_room/index_en.htm>
- Statistic from Eurostat at <http://epp.eurostat.ec.europa.eu/portal/page/portal/eurostat/home/>
- EUR-Lex has:
- SCADplus
    - Contains “Summaries of legislation.” Here there are clear and concise summaries of E.U. legislation in all policy areas. Simply click on the subject of choice and access user-friendly explanations of legislation concerning that subject at <http://europa.eu/legislation_summaries/index_en.htm>.
- ECLAS - European Commission Library Catalogue
    - Provides bibliographical references for publications, but no document delivery or copy service.
    - In the standard version of ECLAS or in ECLAS Pro, electronic resources can be found at <http://ec.europa.eu/eclas/>
- The European Union’s publisher
    - Site of the official publications office of the E.U. <http://publications.europa.eu/index_en.htm>.
- The Citizens Signpost Service (CSS)
    - Aimed at E.U. citizens who encounter problems with mobility in the European Internal Market. It has an advisory service, which gives guidance and practical advice to citizens on specific problems they encounter in the E.U. and its Internal

Market. The service is free. Replies are given by phone or e-mail in the language requested by the citizen (one of the 23 official languages) at <http://ec.europa.eu/citizensrights/signpost/front_end/index_en.htm>.

Many resources on the E.U. can also be found in Westlaw and LexisNexis under "European Union" material. In Westlaw, Quick Search allows one to easily retrieve material when one knows a key word, the name, the citation or the reference number.

In Westlaw:

- All European Union Materials (EU-ALL)
- European Union Legislation (EU-LEG)
- European Union Cases All (EU-CS-ALL)
- Common Market Law Reports (CML-RPTS)
- European Union Case Law (EU-CS)
- European Union Preparatory Acts (EU-ACTS)
- European Union Treaties (EU-TREATIES)
- European Union OJC Series (EU-OJCSERIES)
- European Union Parliamentary Questions (EU-QUESTIONS)
- Legal Journals Index (LJI)

In LexisNexis:

- E.U. Commission Decisions on Competition (COMDEC)
- ECJ cases (ECJ)
- E.U. Community Trademar4ks (ECTM)
- E.U. treaties (TREATY)
- E.C. Preparatory Acts; Parliamentary resolutions (PREP)
- E.U. National provisions implementing directives (NATPRV)
- E.U. Parliamentary questions (PARLQ)
- E.U. Commission legislation (LEGSIS)
- E.U. law (ECLAW)
- E.U. News sources combined (ECNEWS)
- Business Guide to EU initiatives (EUINIT)
- E.U. Observer.com (EUOBSV)
- Europe Informatino Service (E.U. stories) (EISENG)
- INFO-92 (INFO92)
- RAPID (E.U. Press Releass) (RAPID)
- Tenders Electronic Daily (TED)

Westlaw's special overview site for European Union material is actually quite good and searching - when available - through Westlaw is often easier than through the E.U.'s own website.

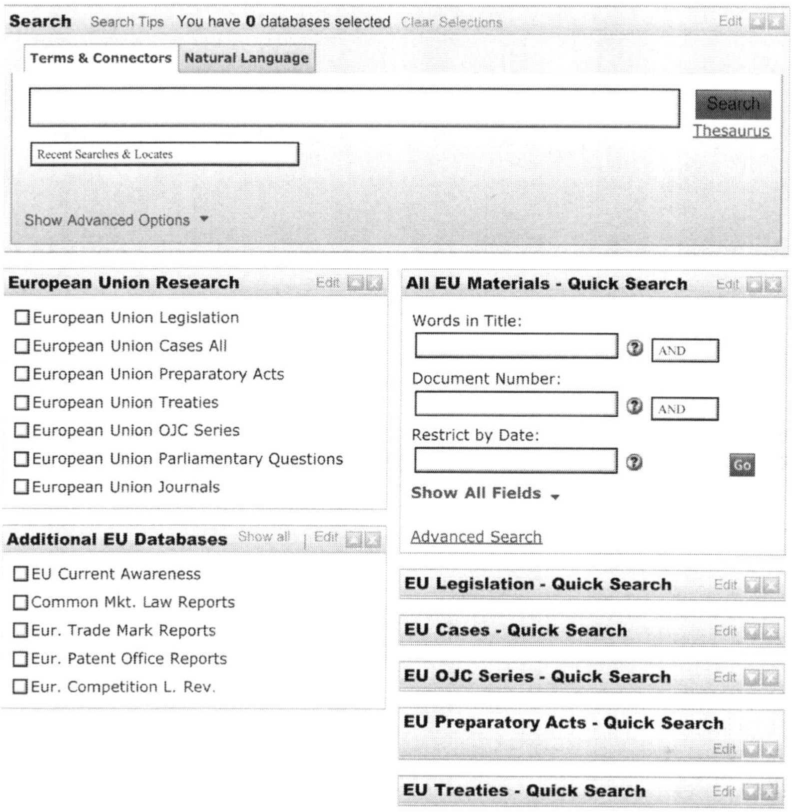

Table 54: Westlaw's European Union Research

E.U. teaching material[217] can be found at

[217] On the Treaty of Lisbon see also E.U. PARL. REPORT ON LISBON *supra* note 39; Treaty of Lisbon at a glance at <http://europa.eu/lisbon_treaty/glance/index_en.htm>; Treaty of Lisbon – Questions and answers at <http://europa.eu/lisbon_treaty/faq/index_en.htm>.

<http://europa.eu/geninfo/info/guide/index_en.htm>,

which site, among others, gives a link to audiovisual material

<http://ec.europa.eu/avservices/home/index_en.cfm> and EUtube
<http://youtube.com/eutube>.

See also E.U. television news service on the Internet at

<http://ec.europa.eu/avservices/ebs/schedule.cfm>.[218]

9.5. Citations

From January 1, 2007, all official European Union websites moved to <europa.eu>.

Example in footnote:[219]
Proposal for a Council Framework Decision on attacks against information systems COM/2002/0173 final – CNS 2002/0086 */, OJ C 203 E, 27.08.2002 p. 109 – 113.

As the E.U. has changed the numbering of several treaty articles over the last few decades, it can be a good idea to also add an older citation in brackets.

Example in footnote:
TEC Article 252 (ex ante EC art. 189c).
TEU Article 4 (ex ante art. D).

9.5.1. Official Journal

Citations for the Official Journal are:

- L, C, S: OJ <series> <issue number> <date.month.year>[220] p. <first

[218] Material for beginners: How the European Union Works: Your Guide to the EU Institutions (European Commission, 2007 - ISBN 92-79-03653-X) at <ec.europa.eu/publications/booklets/eu_glance/68/en.pdf> and Europe in 12 Lessons at <http://europa.eu/abc/12lessons/>. The EU in Power Points at <http://europa.eu/abc/euslides/index_en.htm>

[219] See remark below in footnote 215.

[220] In some E.U. publications is not used periods in the date but slash: <date/month/year>

page (four digits – fill out with zeros[221])> - <last page (four digits)>

- Annex: OJ Annex no<period-number><issue number>p<page number>

See Table 31 above in section 4.3.4.

9.5.2. E.U. Ombudsman

As for the E.U. Ombudsman's decisions, which can be found at <www.europa.eu/documents/ombudsman/index_en.htm>, it should be noted that the citation of documents has changed as follows:

- Until 1996 - <number/dd.mm.yy>, where date is the date when the Ombudsman received the complaint.
- 1997-99 - <number/yy>, where year is only the last 2 figures of the year, and where year is the year when the Ombudsman received the complaint.
- From 2000 - <number/yyyy>, where year is the year when the Ombudsman received the complaint.

9.5.3. Regulations

Citation for a Regulation is:

<institution>Regulations<number>/<year enacted>/<treaty as basic>of<date passed>

Note: Only for/in Regulations does the number precede the number of the act for the year of enactment. Prior to 1990, acts had a unique number. Now it is possible for a decision to have the same number as a directive.

> Example in footnotes:
> Council Regulation No 44/2001 of 22 December 2000 on jurisdiction and the recognition and enforcement of judgments in civil and commercial matters (entry into force 1 March 2002), OJ L 012, 16.1.2001 p 0001 – 0023.

9.5.4. Directive

Citation for Directive is:

<institution>Directive<year enacted>/<number>/<treaty as basic>of<date passed>

[221] In some E.U. publications is used a period after "p" and some do not fill out with zeros.

Note: Prior to 1990, acts had a unique number. Now it is possible for a decision to have the same number as a directive.

9.5.5. Court Decisions

Decisions rendered by the ECJ are numbered with a "C" for court and the CFI with a "T" for tribunal. In the official European Court Reports, ECJ judgments page numbers are preceded by "I-" and CFI judgments by "II-". Citations for case decisions from the E.U. courts:

- Court of Justice - Citation: Case C-<number>/year <plaintiff>v<defendant>[<year>] ECR-I <page>

- Court of First Instance – now the General Court - - Citation: Case T-<number>/year <plaintiff>v<defendant>[<year>] ECR-II <page>

> Example:
> *A. De Bloss Sprl. v. Bouyer*, 1976 E.C.R. 1497 (ECJ 14/76, 1976)
> *Ahlstrom Osakeyhtio v Commission of the European Communities* (Woodpulp case), (E.C.J. C89/85 1988), [1988] 4 C.M.L.R. 901, 1988 E.C.R. 5193

9.6. Reader information for Directory of Community Legislation

The preface on "Information for readers on The Directory of Community Legislation"[222] states that the directory includes not only current Community legislation, but also other instruments reflecting the activities of the European Union (E.U., ECSC, EEC, EC and Euratom), such as policy instruments and decisions taken in individual cases – but of more general interest. It therefore covers:

- agreements and conventions concluded by the Communities in connection with their external relations;
- binding secondary legislation (regulations, decisions, ECSC general decisions and recommendations, and EEC/EC/Euratom directives) under the Treaties establishing the European Union and the European Communities, with the exception of day-to-day administrative acts[223];

[222] <www.eur-lex.europa.eu/en/legis/avis.htm>.

[223] These are mainly acts arising from the day-to-day management of the common agricultural policy or the customs union and having a very limited period of validity, such as

- supplementary legislation, in particular decisions of representatives of the governments of the E.U. Member States meeting within the Council;
- certain non-binding acts considered by the institutions to be important.

The Directory exists in the official languages of the European Union.

The Directory is intended purely for use as a documentation tool and the institutions do not assume any liability for its contents.

9.6.1. Presentation of documents

Each entry comprises: the document number of the act, its title, its bibliographical reference (in most cases the Official Journal of the European Union) and, if applicable, the document number of any amendments, with their publication references in brackets. It also includes available consolidated versions of the basic act and its successive amendments.

> Example:
> 31977L0311
> Council Directive 77/311/EEC of 29 March 1977 on the approximation of the laws of the Member States relating to the driver-perceived noise level of wheeled agricultural or forestry tractors
> (Official Journal L 105 , 28/04/1977 P. 0001 - 0009)
>
> html
>
> Amended by 31982L0890 Replacement Article 1.2 from 21/12/1982
> Consolidated text 01977L0311-19821221
> Incorporated by 21994A0103(52)
> Implemented by 31996D0627 Implementation Article 2
> Amended by 31997L0054 Amendment Article 1.2 from 30/10/1997
> Consolidated text 01977L0311-19971030

9.6.2. The document number

The document number, shown in bold type above the title of the act, consists of a combination of figures and letters, the position of each having a particular meaning (see below 'Explanation of codes').

The document number enables all acts to be identified in the body of the

acts temporarily fixing various rates or amounts. For the most part, they correspond to the titles printed in light type on the contents page of the Official Journal of the European Union.

Directory.

The example given below is a simple, but by far the most frequent, form using 10 positions. Although the document number may theoretically extend to as many as 18 positions, there is no need for the reader to know precisely how document numbers are made up.

Example of document number:
3 1977 R 0311

3 - Documentary sector of the system (sector 3 = secondary legislation)
1977 - Year of adoption or publication of act (1977)
L - Legal form (L = directive)
0311 - Serial or other identifying number of legal act (Regulation No 0311 of the year in question)

The first number (the number 3 in the example just above) indicates the sector in the system under which the act is classified.

Also, in the example shown above, the act forms part of Community secondary legislation (sector 3).

The letter, which is always in the sixth position (the letter L in the example) denotes the legal form of the act (e.g., R for regulation, D for decision, L for directive, etc.).

9.6.3. Title

The document number is followed by the full title of the legal act.

9.6.4. The publication reference

The title of the act is followed by the publication reference of the Official Journal of the European Union.

This reference consists of:

- the number of the Official Journal, preceded in the case of post-1967 instruments (when the Official Journal was divided into an 'L' and a 'C' series) by the letter for the series,
- the date of publication,
- the page number.

Example:
OJ L 105, 28.04.1977 p. 1, is interpreted as follows:

OJ - Official Journal of the European Union
L 105 - L series, No 105

28.04.1977 - date of publication
p. 1 - OJ page (page on which the text of the act begins)

9.6.5. References to amending acts

The publication reference of the act is followed, where appropriate, by references to subsequent acts affecting it (amending, replacing, etc.).

The act referred to is identified by its document number followed by its publication reference in brackets.

Example:
Amended by 31997L0054 (OJ L 277 10.10.1997 p. 24)

Amended by
31997L0054 - Document number of amending act
(OJ L 277 10.10.1997 p. 24) - Publication reference of amending act

9.6.6. References to consolidated texts

If an act and its amendments have been subject to consolidation, the Directory offers links to successive consolidated texts. The consolidated text is identified by its document number. The first part of this number is built from the document number of the basic act and identifies the consolidated family (that is, the basic act and its amendments); the second part refers to the date of effect of the last amending act.

Example:
Consolidated text 01997L0311- 19971030

Consolidated text
01977L0311 - Number of the consolidated family
19971030 - Date of effect of the last amending act

9.6.7. Document retrieval

A document may be retrieved using the analytical structure.

Example:
Retrieval of a decision on the Combined Nomenclature.
The relevant section entitled 'Customs tariffs', is to be found in the chapter entitled 'Customs union and free movement of goods' in the analytical structure:
02. Customs union and free movement of goods
02.20 Basic customs instruments
02.20.20 Customs tariffs

Acts listed in each section are arranged in ascending order of their document numbers: by sector (first figure), year, legal form (indicated by a letter) and serial or other identifying number (e.g., regulation number).

The entry for the decision in question, 597/87, is set out in the section Customs tariffs as follows:

> 41987D0597
> 87/597/ECSC: Decision of the representatives of the Governments of the Member States, meeting within the Council of 18 December 1987 on the nomenclature and rates of conventional duty for certain products and the general rules for interpreting and applying the said nomenclature and duties
> (OJ L 363 23.12.1987 p. 67)

9.6.8. Explanation of codes

Number codes used in the document reference number, by CELEX (the database that ceased at the end of 2006) documentary sector:

1. 1 - Treaty on European Union, Treaties establishing the European Communities and Treaties amending or supplementing them.
2. 2 - External relations of the European Communities (or of the Member States).
3. 3 - Secondary legislation.
4. 4 - Supplementary legislation (decisions of representatives of the Member States meeting within the Council, international conventions concluded between Member States in accordance with Treaty provisions, etc.).
5. 5 - Consolidated documents
6. Sector 1 acts are not included in the Directory. However, the Accession Treaties of Denmark, Ireland and the United Kingdom of 1972, of Greece of 1979, of Spain and Portugal of 1985, of Austria, Finland and Sweden of 1994 and of the Czech Republic, Estonia, Cyprus, Latvia, Lithuania, Hungary, Malta, Poland, Slovenia and Slovakia of 2003[224] are sometimes referred to in amendment references (document numbers '11972B', '11979H', '11985I', '11994N' or '12003T').

Letter codes used in the document reference number indicate the legal form of the act:

[224] Treaty of Athens 2003 - E.U. Treaty of Accession 2003.

A - Agreement, opinion
B - Budget
C - Declaration
D - Decision
E - Common foreign and security policy (CFSP) - common position, joint action, common strategy
F - Justice and home affairs (JHA) - common position, framework decision
G - Resolution
H - Recommendation
J - Non-opposition to a notified joint venture
K - ECSC Recommendation
L - Directive
M - Non-opposition to a notified concentration
O - ECB Guidelines
Q - Institutional arrangement - rules of procedure - internal agreement
R - Regulation
S - ECSC decision of general interest
X - Other document
Y - Other act (published in the 'C' series of the Official Journal)

Codes used for references to other acts

- Adopted by
- Amended by
- Completed by
- Confirmed by
- Consolidated
- Consolidated text
- Application delayed by
- Derogation in
- Application extended by
- Implemented by
- Incorporated in
- Interpreted by
- Partly suspen. by
- Partly re-est. by
- Replaced by
- See
- Suspended by

9.7. Further Reading (updates at corresponding website)

The URL for the corresponding website is <www.hssph.net/legalrm> with a full alphabetic bibliography.

Alford, Duncan E., *European Union Legal Materials: An Infrequent User's Guide* (October 2008) at <http://www.nyulawglobal.org/Globalex/European_Union1.htm>

Berger, Klaus Peter, *The Principles of European Contract Law and the Concept of the "Creeping Codification" of Law*, 9 EUROPEAN REVIEW OF PRIVATE LAW 21 (2001).

CHALMERS, DAMIAN, GARETH DAVIS & GIORGIO MONTI, EUROPEAN LAW (2nd ed.)(Cambridge University Press, 2010)

CRAIG, PAUL & GRAINNE DE BURCA, EU LAW: TEXT, CASES AND MATERIALS (4th ed)(Publisher: Oxford University Press, 2007)

EUROPEAN COMMISSION, YOUR GUIDE TO THE LISBON TREATY (EUROPEAN COMMUNITIES, 2009) at <http://ec.europa.eu/publications/booklets/others/84/en.pdf>

PIRIS, JEAN-CLAUDE, THE LISBON TREATY: A LEGAL AND POLITICAL ANALYSIS (Cambridge University Press, 2010)

Raisch, Marylin J., *European Union*, ASIL Guide to Electronic Resources for International Law at <http://www.asil.org/eu1.cfm>

REINISCH, AUGUST, ESSENTIAL QUESTIONS IN EU LAW (Cambridge University Press, 2009)

REPORT ON THE TREATY OF LISBON (2007/2286(INI)) from the European Parliament's Committee on Constitutional Affairs (Rapporteurs: Richard Corbett & Íñigo Méndez de Vigo), A6-0013/2008, 29 January 2008 at

<www.europarl.europa.eu/sides/getDoc.do?pubRef=-//EP//NONSGML+REPORT+A6-2008-0013+0+DOC+PDF+V0//EN&language=EN>

STEINER, JOSEPHINE & LORNA WOODS, EU LAW (10 ed.)(2009 England: Oxford University Press)

The European Union: A Guide for Americans at

<http://eurunion.org/eu/images/PDF/euguide2009.pdf>

WATT & DASHWOOD'S EUROPEAN UNION LAW (5th ed)(2006 London: Thompson)

9.8. Various Exercises (updates at corresponding website)

9.8.1. Exercise 1

In the European Union regime:

Discuss the differences between:

- Council Regulation EC/44/2001 of 22 December 2000 on Jurisdiction and the recognition and enforcement of judgments in civil and commercial matters, published in O.J. L 012 – 16/01/2001 P.0001-0023

  and

- Brussels Convention on Jurisdiction and Enforcement of Judgments in Civil and Commercial Matters of 27 September 1968, published in O.J. L 299, 31/12/1972 p. 0032-0042

(Students should, of course, by themselves find these instruments online in the European Union Official Journal.)

Which of the two above instruments is the valid one?

What does "Curia" (CVRIA) stand for? (What E.U. institution does the term cover?)

Who publish documents with the term "COM" in the journal number / record number?

What is EUR-Lex?

What is the difference between the Council of Europe and the Council of the European Union - and what are their respective homepages?

9.8.2. Exercise 2 - Terminology exercises

- Explore what terms a foreign country in Europe uses as compared to U.S. terms like “act,” “section,” “paragraph,” and “subsection.”
- What does “litra” or “litera” mean in a European statute?
- Try to find words/terms that differ from U.S. legal terms (for example, from Black's Law Dictionary) on the E.U. Glossary (<http://europa.eu/scadplus/glossary/index_en.htm>)
- Find a Legal Research Guide for a chosen country and present highlights on that country’s law to others.
- In the E.U., what is a “Statement of reasons”? [Use: Codecision Glossary at <http://ec.europa.eu/codecision/stepbystep/glossary_en.htm>].
- In the E.U., what does “Adoption and implementation of the acquis” mean? [Use: Enlargement Glossary at <http://ec.europa.eu/enlargement/glossary/index_en.htm>].
- In the E.U., is the “Exequatur” procedure used between the E.U. Member States? [Use: European Judicial Network in Civil and Commercial Matters Glossary at <http://ec.europa.eu/civiljustice/glossary/glossary_en.htm>]
- In the E.U., what does “GFP” stand for and mean? [Use: Environmental Glossary at <http://glossary.eea.europa.eu/EEAGlossary/>].
- In the E.U., what does “COM” mean? [Use: Information Society Glossary at <http://ec.europa.eu/information_society/tl/help/glossary/index_en.htm>].
- In the E.U., what does “Copenhagen criteria” mean? [Use: Enlargement website at <http://europa.eu/pol/enlarg/index_en.htm>].

CHAPTER 10

China Resources - Law of the Far East

10.1. China – Short Overview

Chinese law belongs to the family of the legal systems in the Far East.[1]

The development of modern law (*fa lü*) in China is based on Civil Law with a pronounced influence of Common Law in the last several decades.[2] However, the Western principle of checks and balances is not used in the People's Republic of China (PRC). Thus, there is no division between the legislative, executive and judicial branches. All power is vested in and controlled by the National People's Congress (NPC).[3]

The NPC is the highest state body and the only legislative chamber in the PRC. The Constitution (*xianfa*)[4] and the Law of Legislation do not provide for a relationship between treaties and domestic law.

The Standing Committee of the NPC (NPCSC) consists of about 150 members of the NPC and is convened between plenary sessions of the NPC. The NPCSC has the constitutional authority to modify legislation within limits set by the NPC, and thus acts as a de facto legislative body. It is led by a Chairman - China's top legislator - who is conventionally ranked third in China's political ranking system, after the General Secretary and President (the latter two positions usually being occupied by the same person).

The NPCSC also has the power to interpret the laws of the PRC, including its constitution. In the PRC, constitutional and legal interpretation are considered to constitute a legislative activity rather than a judicial one, and the functions are split so that the NPCSC provides legal interpretations and the Su-

[1] See above Chapter 2, subsection 2.2.

[2] For example, Hong Kong/England, USA, Canada, and Australia. JONAS BERING LIISBERG, KINAS RETSSYSTEM OG RETSREFORMER 24-25 [China's System of Justice and Judicial Reform] (DJØF Publishing, 1999 – ISBN 87-574-0186-1

[3] *Idem* page 27.

[4] Constitution of 1982 with later amendments.

preme People's Court and the Court of Final Appeal of the Hong Kong Special Administrative Region actually decide cases. Because an interpretation of the NPCSC is legislative in nature and not judicial, it does not affect cases, which have already been decided. Thus, the stare decisis doctrine is not used in China. However, the Supreme People's Court (SPC) has the authority to issue Judicial Interpretations (*sifa jieshi*) as guidelines to the trials, which are then nationally enforceable.

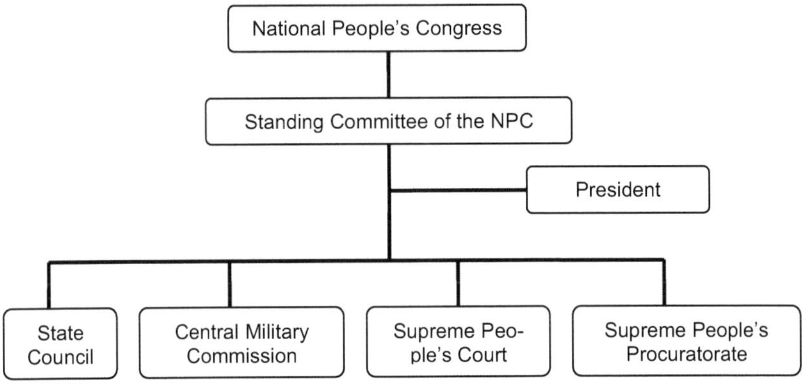

Table 55: State organs of the People's Republic of China[5]

The Chinese court system can be divided into regular and special courts as follows:

[5] Source: Communist Party of Hong Kong.

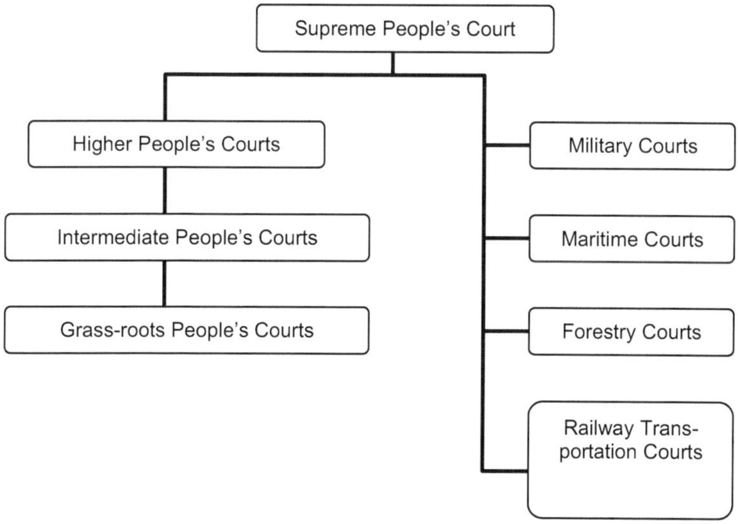

Table 56: China's court system

The Chinese judicial system can be outlined as follows and illustrating the double leadership of the courts, the people's procuratorate (*quisu / renmin jianchayuan*) and the police.[6]

[6] This table is the author's translation into English of "Figur 2" page 54 in Jonas Bering Liisberg, KINAS RETSSYSTEM OG RETSREFORMER [China's System of Justice and Judicial Reform] (DJØF Publishing, 1999). See also Lee F. Peoples, Chinese Legal System (PowerPoint Presentation) at <https://docs.google.com/fileview?id=0B2fXsdh6lT31ZGNmMzg4YWQtNjU3ZS00ODE1LTk5NGUtZjk5NzMyYTYzZGY3&hl=en&pli=1>.

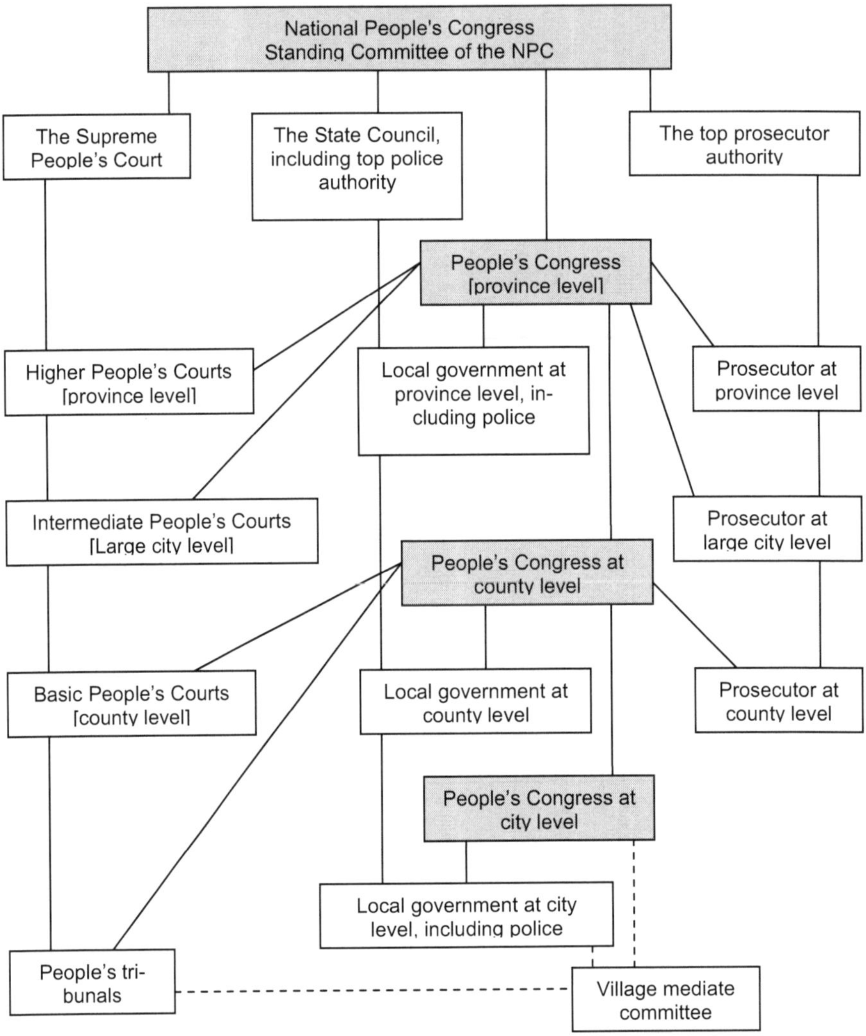

Table 57: Overview of the Chinese judicial system. Broken lines indicate looser principal-subsidiary relationships

The NPC has translated some of China's laws into English and published them as the "Laws of The People's Republic of China." A simplified overview of China's sources of law is as follows:

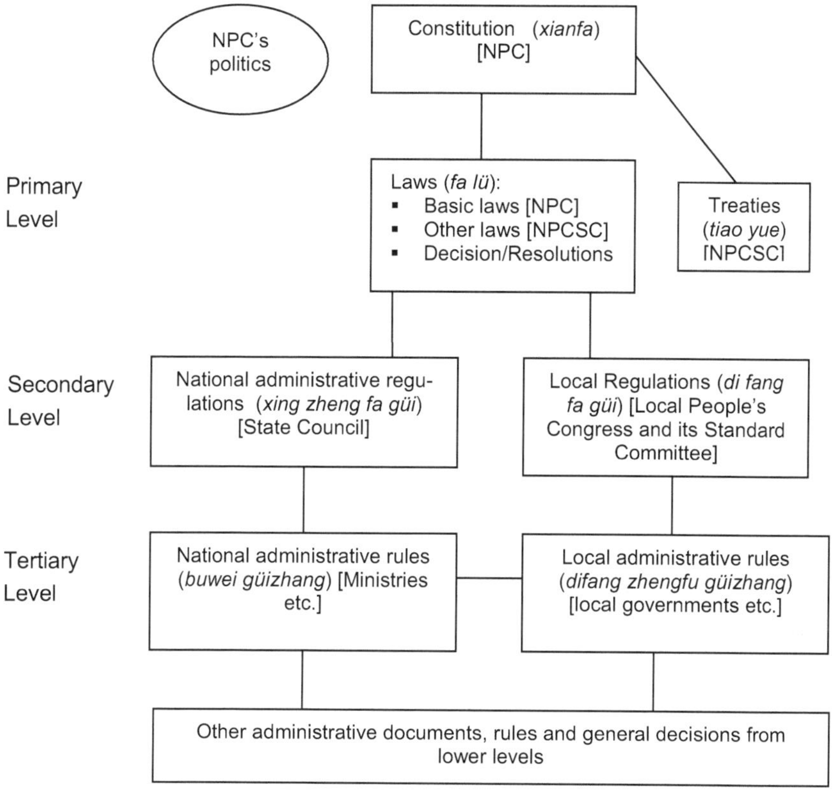

Table 58: Simplified and formalized/stylized overview of Chinese law-sources [7]

10.2. Miscellaneous Chinese material in English

- ChinaLawInfo – online legal database that includes laws, regulations, journal articles, legal news (affiliated with the Beijing University Law School) at <www.lawinfochina.com/index.asp?Succ=1>.
- The Central government's official website at <http://english.gov.cn/>.
- Chinacourt.org offer judicial news and legal information (sponsored by the Supreme People's Court) at <http://en.chinacourt.org/>.

[7] This table is the author's translation into English of "Figur 1" page 38 in Jonas Bering Liisberg, KINAS RETSSYSTEM OG RETSREFORMER [China's System of Justice and Judicial Reform] (DJØF Publishing, 1999).

- Xinhuanet (official government affiliated news agency) at <www.chinaview.cn/china/index.htm>.
- AsianLII contains laws of the PRC at <www.asianlii.org/cn/legis/cen/laws/>.
- SinoLaw contains commercial and business laws, basic laws, major statutes, and regulations (provided by a Chinese information service agency in Beijing) at <www.sinolaw.com.cn/>.
- China Law Digest at <www.chinalawdigest.com/>.
- Chinese Legal Research (University of Washington School of Law, Gallagher Law Library) at <http://lib.law.washington.edu/eald/clr/cres.html>.

10.3. Further Reading (updates at corresponding website)

> The URL for the corresponding website is <www.hssph.net/legalrm> with a full alphabetic bibliography.

China law overview at JURIST: The Legal Education Network, University of Pittsburgh School of Law at <http://jurist.law.pitt.edu/world/china.htm>

CHOW, DANIEL C.K., THE LEGAL SYSTEM OF THE PEOPLE'S REPUBLIC OF CHINA (2. ed)(Thomson/West, 2009)

Free access to Asian Law from The Asian Legal Information Institute (AsianLII)'s website at <www.asianlii.org/>

Greenleaf, Graham, Philip Chung and Andrew Movbray, *Challenges in Improving Access to Asian Laws: The Asian Legal Information Institute* (AsianLII), 9 ASIAN LAW 152-175 (2007)

Research Guides to Chinese Law at <http://docs.law.gwu.edu/facweb/dclarke/public/Research_Guides.html>.

RESEARCH METHODS FOR LAW (Ed. Mike McConville & Wing Hong Chui) (Edinburgh: Edinburgh University Press, 2007)

U.S. Library of Congress Legal Research Guide on China at <www.loc.gov/law/help/china.php>.

CHAPTER 11

Public International Law Resources

11.1. Introduction

As this book's primarily aim is for use in teaching courses on legal research methods in the US and in Continental Europe, this chapter should only be regarded as a very brief introduction to Public International Law.

For Latin phrases consult Appendix 1..

For further reading on Public International Law, consider two famous European books written by Brownlie and Oppenheim.[1]

To understand the history of the sources of international law one has to keep in mind that international law developed over time.[2]

Public International Law[3] is the sum total of legal norms governing rights

[1] Ian Brownlie, PRINCIPLES OF INTERNATIONAL LAW (7th ed.) (Oxford University Press, 2008) & OPPENHEIM'S INTERNATIONAL LAW 23 (9th Ed.)(Eds.: Sir Robert Jennings & Sir Arthur Watts) (London and New York: Longman 1996) [hereinafter OPPENHEIM]. See also, ENCYCLOPEDIA OF PUBLIC INTERNATIONAL LAW, Vol. 1-5 (Edited by Rudolf Bernhardt)(Consolidated library ed.)(Amsterdam; New York: North-Holland, Elsevier Science & Technology, 1992-2003).

[2] The chief reporter of the American RESTATEMENT OF THE LAW (THIRD) - FOREIGN RELATIONS LAW OF THE UNITED STATES (American Law Institute)[hereinafter REST] has found major progress during the 21st century in international law's transition from primitive to modern. Louis Henkin, *Coda: Allegro ma non Troppo*, ASIL NEWSLETTER (Jan.-Feb. 1994), at 1.

[3] Like the International Court of Justice, the European Court of Justice applies public international law, see *Opel Austria GmbH v. Council of the European Union* (E.C.J. T-115/94 1997), 1997 E.C.R. II-39 no. 90 (customary international law whose existence is recognized by the International Court of Justice is binding on the Community), *Ahlstrom Osakeyhtio v Commission of the European Communities* (E.C.J. C89/85 1988),

and duties of the collectivities of the ruling classes[4] - civilized participants in international intercourse in war and peace - without which it would be virtually impossible for the participants to have steady and frequent relations.[5] It is not the rules, but a normative system that operates in a horizontal legal order. Public International Law is a process, a system of authoritative decision-making.[6] It deals with the conduct of nation-States and their relations with other States,[7] and to some extent also with their relations with individuals, business organizations, and other legal entities. In its conceptions, its specific norms and standards, and largely in practice, international law functions between States, as represented by their governments.[8]

Public International Law is to be distinguished from Private International Law or Conflict of Laws,[9] which cover a certain State's rules on judicial jurisdiction and competence, foreign judgments and choice of law.[10] Private

[1988] 4 C.M.L.R. 901, 1988 E.C.R. 5193 no. 22-23 (Commission's decision is not contrary to the rules of public international law), and *Ahlstrom Osakeyhtio v Commission of the European Communities* (E.C.J. C89/85 1993), 1993 E.C.R I-1307 no. 30, *A.Racke GMBH & Co v. Hauptzollamt Mainz* (ECJ 16 June 1998, Case 162/96), 1998 E.C.R.-I-3655, para 45-46.

4 As for international organizations, Judge Gros observed in his separate opinion in the WHO Agreement case that "in the absence of a super-State, each International Organization has only the competence which has been conferred on it by the States which founded it", *Interpretation of the Agreement of 25 March 1951 between WHO and Egypt*, (I.C.J., Dec 20, 1980 (No. 65),), 1980 I.C.J. 73, 103.

5 Thomas Jefferson wrote in support of the 1792 Declaration of the Rights of Nations: "The relationship of one nation with a foreign nation rests on natural law and moral principles as well as on recognized international law. We owe other nations a respect for their chosen form of government as we expect our own form to be respected, and we have no right to interfere in another people's choice of government or internal policy any more than they have to interfere in ours."

6 Rosalyn Higgins, PROBLEMS & PROCESS – INTERNATIONAL LAW AND HOW WE USE IT 1 AND 267 (Clarendon Press, Oxford 1994), Rosalyn Higgins, *International Law and the Avoidance, Containment and Resolution of Disputes – General Course on Public International Law*, RECUEIL DES COURS, Vol. 230 (1991-V) page 23.

7 In this Chapter the term "State" (that is, a nation or country or nation-state) is spelled with a capital "S" to signal the difference between a state or a region of a federal State. This pattern is also used by REST *supra* note 2.

8 Henrik Spang-Hanssen, PUBLIC INTERNATIONAL COMPUTER NETWORK LAW ISSUES 99 (DJØF Publishing Copenhagen 2006) [hereinafter SPANG-HANSSEN-2] and Henrik Spang-Hanssen, CYBERSPACE & INTERNATIONAL LAW ON JURISDICTION 300 (DJØF Publishing, Copenhagen, 2004) [hereinafter SPANG-HANSSEN-1].

9 SPANG-HANSSEN-1 *supra* note 8, at 206.

10 Municipal law governs the domestic aspects of government and deals with issues between individuals, and between individuals and the administrative apparatus. The In-

International Law is law directed to resolving controversies between private persons, natural as well as juridical, primarily in domestic litigation, arising out of situations having a significant relationship to more than one State.[11]

11.2. Monists versus Dualists

Research Tip #11.1

When studying Public International Law one must keep in mind from what country's perspective one is doing the research.

This is due to the existence of two different approaches among scholars and authorities as to whether international law is superior or not to national law.

Pursuant to a pure monistic idea, the national and international systems make up one single legal system. Some monists claim international law supercedes national law. Others think the opposite.

Dualists on the other hand, hold that the national and the international legal systems are different systems, and exist in their own separate spheres. International law has no independent status in national law. It only becomes relevant if and when the national authorities decide to create national law on the basis of the international system.

11.3. Sources of Public International Law

The Internet has had a dramatic impact on international legal research. In the past international law sources were difficult to identify and locate, but now many are available through websites of the United Nations, other international organizations and law schools' and university websites.

The sources of international law must not be confused with the basis of international law; the latter is to be found in the common consent of the international community. The sources of law concern the particular rules that constitute the system, and the processes by which those rules become identifiable as rules of law.[12]

ternational Court of Justice, in the Case of *Barcelona Traction, Light, and Power Co, Limited* (Belgium v. Spain) (Second Phase) of February 5, 1970, 1970 I.C.J. 3, referred to the rules generally accepted by municipal legal systems, not the municipal law of a particular state.

[11] "Foreign law" is the domestic law of another national jurisdiction.

[12] OPPENHEIM *supra* note 1 at 23.

The Statute for the International Court of Justice[13] (ICJ[14]) lists in Article 38 the following sources for international law:

a) International conventions,[15] whether general or particular, establishing rules expressly recognized by the contesting States;
b) International custom, as evidence of a general practice accepted as law;
c) The general principles of law recognized by civilized nations;
d) Subject to the provisions of Article 59 [no Stare Decisis Doctrine], juridical decisions and the teaching of the most highly qualified publicists[16] of the various nations, as subsidiary means for the determinations of rules of law.

The ICJ is the "Highest Court on Earth, a Bench from which there is no appeal."[17] The Court has a dual role: (A) to settle in accordance with international law the legal disputes submitted to it by States, and (B) to give advisory opinions on legal questions referred to it by duly authorized international organs and agencies. Pursuant to Article 59 of the ICJ Statute, a "decision of the Court has no binding force except between the parties and in respect of that particular case."

Treaties and custom are the most important "law-sources"[18] in public international law.[19]

Under article 38(1)(d) of the ICJ Statute - the subsidiary category of international sources - has in recent years evolved was is called "soft law,"[20] that

[13] Statute of the International Court of Justice of 26 June 1945, 156 U.N.T.S. 77, 59 Stat. 1055, T.I.A.S. No. 993 [hereinafter ICJ Statute].

[14] Homepage <www.icj-cij.org>.

[15] On interpretations of treaties, see especially Article 26-33 of the Vienna Convention on the Law of Treaties of 23 May 1969 (into force 27 January 1980), U.N.T.S. Vol. 1155 p. 331, also at <http://untreaty.un.org/ilc/texts/instruments/english/conventions /1_1_1969.pdf>.

[16] See below section 11.5.5.

[17] Arthur Eyffinger, THE INTERNATIONAL COURT OF JUSTICE, 1946-1996 (Kluwer Law International, the Netherlands 1996).

[18] The Danish term is "retskilder".

[19] Peter Blume, JURIDISK METODELÆRE [Legal Methodology] 201 (Fifth Edition, Copenhagen: Jurist- og Økonomforbundets Forlag [DJØF Publishing] 2009).

[20] "For example, there may be an [non-binding] agreement that requests the participants harmonize their domestic laws as much as possible but does not require them to do so. There may be a provision within that requests each party to supply evidence to the other and exchange information with regard to the enforcement of competition laws, and yet leaves the ultimate implementation to the discretion of each party. In international law, this type of agreement may be referred to as a "soft law," as opposed to a

is, actually not law but rather agreed guidelines, commitments, joint statements, or intentions of common policies, for example resolutions adopted by the United Nations General Assembly or other multilateral bodies.[21]

Thus, the division of law-sources in pubic international is as follows (see, Table 1 above in Chapter 1 with footnotes):

Primary Sources (Ranked)	Jus Cogens[22]			
	International Treaties – establishing rule expressly recognized by the [involved] States	International Custom - as evidence of a general practice accepted as law	The General Principles of law recognized by civilized nations	The practice of international organizations, most notably that of the United Nations, as it appears in the resolutions of the Security Council and the General Assembly
Soft law[23]	Judicial decisions	The most highly qualified juristic writings		

"hard law," which requires contracting parties to observe the terms of an agreement," *International Cooperation in the Enforcement Of Competition Policy* by Mitsuo Matsushita, 468 WASHINGTON UNIVERSITY GLOBAL STUDIES LAW REVIEW 463 at <http://law.wustl.edu/wugslr/issues/volume1/p463Matsushit a.pdf>. The terminology of "soft law" remains relatively controversial because there are some international practitioners who will not even deign to accept its existence and for others, there is quite some confusion as to its status in the realm of law. However, for most international practitioners, development of soft law instruments is an accepted part of the compromises required when undertaking daily work within the international legal system, where states are often reluctant to sign up to too many commitments that might result in national resentment at over-committing to an international goal, Michael G. Egge, Matteo F. Bay & Janier Ruiz Calzado, *The New EC Merger Regulation: A Move to Convergence, Status of Soft Law In international Law*, ANTITRUST MAGAZINE, Section of Antitrust Law, American Bar Association, Fall 2004 at <www.lw.com/upload/pubContent/_pdf/pub1167_1.pdf >.

21 SPANG-HANSSEN-1 *supra* note 8 at 229, Malcolm N.Shaw, INTERNATIONAL LAW 92 (4th ed.)(Cambridge, England: University Press 1997), Antonio Cassese, INTERNATIONAL LAW 160 (Oxford, England: Oxford University Press 2001); §103(2)(d) of REST *supra* note 2.

22 AKEHURST'S MODERN INTRODUCTION TO INTERNATIONAL LAW 56-60 (8th ed.) (by Peter Malanczuk)(New York ; London : Routledge, 2002) [hereinafter AKEHURST].

23 *Idem*, at 54.

11.4. Interpretation of international instruments & Travaux Préparatoires

The main task for any of tribunal,[24] which is asked to apply or construe or interpret[25] a treaty, can be described in a single sentence: "the duty of giving effect to the expressed intention of the parties, that is, their intention as expressed in the words used by them in the light of the surrounding circumstances".[26]

Part III of the Convention on the Law of Treaties[27] contains specific rules for interpretation[28] (the rules are not regarded as codification of any customary law rule, but they are rules in practice used in diplomatic circles). A

[24] Whether an international court is obliged to fill in gaps, and to avoid pronouncing a *non liquet* ("[I]s a competent legal tribunal in the position to refuse a definite answer to a legal question (in terms of rights and duties of the parties concerned) on the basis of material gaps" in international law), is a matter of dispute. See AKEHURST'S MODERN INTRODUCTION TO INTERNATIONAL LAW 50 & 349 (8th ed.) (by Peter Malanczuk)(New York ; London : Routledge, 2002); Ige F. Dekker & Harry H.G. Post, *The Completeness of International Law and Hamlet's Dilemma, in* ON THE FOUNDATIONS AND SOURCES OF INTERNATIONAL LAW 8-30(2003, T.M.C. Asser Press, The Hague, Netherlands); Judge Rosalyn Higgin's separate opinion in *Advisory Opinion on the Legality of the Threat or Use of Nuclear Weapons* (United Nations)(International Court of Justice, Advisory opinion of 8 July 1996), 1996 I.C.J. 226, 934.

[25] On interpretation. See OPPENHEIM *supra* note 1, at 1266-1284; Ian Brownlie, PRINCIPLES OF INTERNATIONAL LAW 631-638 (5th ed.)(Oxford Press, 2002).

[26] Lord Arnold Duncan McNair, THE LAW OF TREATIES 365 (Oxford Clarendon Press 1961). See also, Rudolf Bernhardt, *Interpretation in International Law, in* ENCYCLOPEDIA OF PUBLIC INTERNATIONAL LAW 1416-1426 (Rudolf Bernhardt (Ed.), Elsevier 1995) & OPPENHEIM *supra* note 1, at 1266-128 & 423.

[27] Articles 26-38 in the Vienna Convention on the Law of Treaties of 23 May 1969 (into force 27 January 1980), U.N.T.S. Vol. 1155 p. 331, also at <http://untreaty.un.org /ilc/texts/instruments/english/conventions/1_1_1969.pdf>. As of April 2007, the convention has been ratified by 108 States. The U.S. is not a party, but it signed the Convention on 24 April 1970.

[28] Treaty law is the daughter of customary international law. The interpretation of treaties takes place on the basis of customary international law and the validity of treaties is determined by customary law. Treaties per se are ineffective without the support of customary international law. There is the difference that the treaty norm remains in the form in which it is frozen into the treaty (until such time as the treaty is changed), whereas the customary norm having an independent existence of its own, can continue to develop. It is a critical advance in a situation when fast moving changes require more adaptability and flexibility in a rule of law, I.C.J. Judge C.G. Weeramantry, UNIVERSALISING INTERNATIONAL LAW 233 & 239 (Boston: Martinus Nijhoff Publishers, 2004).

"General Rule of Interpretation" is given in Article 31:

> 1. A treaty shall be interpreted in good faith in accordance with the ordinary meaning to be given to the terms of the treaty in their context and in the light of its object and purpose.
> 2. The context for the purpose of the interpretation of a treaty shall comprise, in addition to the text, including its preamble and annexes: (a) any agreement relating to the treaty which was made between all the parties in connection with the conclusion of the treaty; (b) any instrument which was made by one or more parties in connection with the conclusion of the treaty and accepted by the other parties as an instrument related to the treaty.
> 3. There shall be taken into account, together with the context: (a) any subsequent agreement between the parties regarding the interpretation of the treaty or the application of its provisions; (b) any subsequent practice in the application of the treaty which establishes the agreement of the parties regarding its interpretation; (c) any relevant rules of international law applicable in the relations between the parties.
> 4. A special meaning shall be given to a term if it is established that the parties so intended.

Articles 32 gives supplementary means of interpretation, including using preparatory works[29] as supplementary sources:

> Recourse may be had to supplementary means of interpretation, including the preparatory work of the treaty and the circumstances of its conclusion, in order to confirm the meaning resulting from the application of article 31, or to determine the meaning when the interpretation according to article 31: (a) leaves the meaning ambiguous or obscure; or (b) leads to a result which is manifestly absurd or unreasonable.

The last the rule given in Section 3 of the Convention on the Law of Treaties, "Interpretation of Treaties," Article 33, deals with interpretation of treaties authenticated in two or more languages, Article 33:

> 1. When a treaty has been authenticated in two or more languages, the text is equally authoritative in each language, unless the treaty provides or the parties agree that, in case of divergence, a particular text shall prevail.
> 2. A version of the treaty in a language other than one of those in which the text was authenticated shall be considered an authentic text only if the treaty so provides or the parties so agree.
> 3. The terms of the treaty are presumed to have the same meaning in each authentic text.

[29] "Travaux Préparatoires," see further below.

4. Except where a particular text prevails in accordance with paragraph 1, when a comparison of the authentic texts discloses a difference of meaning which the application of articles 31 and 32 does not remove, the meaning which best reconciles the texts, having regard to the object and purpose of the treaty, shall be adopted.

Black's Law Dictionary defines *Travaux Préparatoires* as: "materials used in preparing the ultimate form of an agreement or statute, and especially of an international treaty; the draft history of a treaty." The material must have been known to all parties comprehended by the main international instrument[30] (e.g., a treaty).[31] "Travaux Préparatoires" is not restricted to material set down in writing;[32] compare sections 3-4 of article 31 of the Law of Treaties.[33] However, information can only be regarded as "Travaux Préparatoires" if it has been put forward by a person who officially, in negotiations, represented a State or international organization, which later is a party to the final instrument (e.g., treaty), and – of course – this was known to the other parties.[34]

[30] Terms used for international agreements are: treaty, convention, agreement, protocol, covenant, charter, statute, act, declaration, concordat, exchange of notes, agreed minute, memorandum of agreement, memorandum of understanding and modus vivendi. Whatever their designation, all international agreements have the same legal status, except as their provisions or the circumstances of their conclusion indicate otherwise. Comment to §301 of REST *supra* note 2.

[31] Compare the main principles for all interpretations of international instruments in Part III of the Vienna Convention on Law of Treaties, *supra* note 15, and in *Young Loan Arbitration (Belgium vs. France*), 59 INTERNATIONAL LAW REVIEW 495, 544 (1980).

[32] "The term must *normally* be restricted to material set down in writing" [authors emphasis added]. *Young Loan Arbitration (Belgium vs. France*), 59 INTERNATIONAL LAW REVIEW 495, 544 (1980).

[33] *Supra* note 15.

[34] Four Models of Publication of Travaux Preparatoires has been proposed by Jonathan Pratter, *An Approach to Researching the Drafting History of International Agreements* (December 2005) at <www.nyulawglobal.org/globalex/travaux_preparatoires.htm>. However, only model III ("treaty-specific conference records") refers to the fact that legally binding international instruments are always done through a conference between states or international organizations representatives. This means that although"Travaux Préparatoires" material under models I, II & IV can be found through one of the parties' archives or websites, these models do not illustrate how international instruments are made or how the "Travaux Préparatoires" come into being or are produced – thus they cannot be relied upon.

11.5. Where to find public international law?

11.5.1. Customary Rules of International Law

When searching to find international custom[35] as evidence of a general practice accepted as law, what is sought for, is a general recognition among States of a certain practice as *obligatory*.

Usage versus Custom: When a custom or usage is generally established, either between all the civilized nations in the world, or only between those of a certain continent, as of Europe, for example, or between those who have more frequent intercourse with each other; if that custom is in its own nature indifferent, and further, if it be useful and reasonable, it becomes obligatory on all the nations in question - who are considered as having given their consent to it, and are bound to observe it towards each other, as long as they have not expressly isused a resolution that it will not be observed in the future.

But if that custom contains any thing unjust or unlawful, it is not obligatory; on the contrary, every nation is bound to relinquish it, since nothing can oblige or authorize a State to violate the laws of nature.

The American Restatement of the Foreign Relations Law of the United States at Section 102(2), reads "Customary international law results from a general and consistent practice of States followed by them from a sense of legal obligation." The notes to the section go on to explain that "Subsection (2), includes diplomatic acts and instructions as well as public measures and other governmental acts and official statements of policy, whether they are unilateral or undertaken in cooperation with other States ... [and for] a practice of States to become a rule of customary international law it must appear that the States follow the practice from a sense of legal obligation (opinio juris sive necessitatis); a practice that is generally followed but which States feel legally free to disregard does not contribute to customary law."

This idea is reinforced in Section 103(2)(d), discussing the evidence of a rule, and accepting as evidence "pronouncements by States that undertake to State a rule of international law, when such pronouncements are not seriously challenged by other States."

[35] See art. 38(b) of ICJ Statute *supra* note 13; SPANG-HANSSEN-1 *supra* note 8 at 215; §102(1)(a) & (2) of REST *supra* note 2; STATEMENT OF PRINCIPLES APPLICABLE TO THE FORMATION OF GENERAL CUSTOMARY INTERNATIONAL LAW as amended at the 2000 London conference (International Law Association), at <www.ila-hq.org/pdf/CustomaryLaw.pdf>.

There are two Elements of Custom:

1. Objective Element: General Practice
2. Subjective Element: *Opinio Juris*

It is important to stress, that all elements are dependent on the circumstances of each case and situation. In the latter instance, obviously a value judgment is made by the competent decision-maker.

Opinio juris sive necessitates means "of the opinion that it is a necessary law." This maxim implies that an observing State must perceive a customary practice as one that it is obligated by international law to observe.

As for the objective versus subjective element, some authors have denied the importance of this psychological element. It is regarding the subjective element, again, that the ICJ has obviously had to appraise the relevant practice.

Only in exceptional cases and situations will there be created "instant" customary law. If, say, the community of all States unequivocally and without any dissent considers certain acts, which have not been known before, to be illegal, the *opinio juris* might suffice even if no practice could have yet evolved.[36]

11.5.1.1. Customary Norms of Different "Sanctity"

One has to distinguish between fundamental norms versus technical and less important norms. Among fundamental norms are principles of sovereign equality of States, *pacta sunt servanda*,[37] good faith, equity.

The following are two fundamental norms in public international law:

- Ius/Jus Cogens:[38] "ones from which there can be no retreat."
- Erga Omnes:[39] "in relation to all".

11.5.1.1.1. Ius/Jus Cogens

There are certain norms or rules of public international law from which there can be no derogation. These are known as *jus cogens*,[40] are *peremptory* norms that cannot be negotiated in any way, including via treaty.

[36] Other examples: acts respecting the Continental Shelf, or Economic Zones, or a multilateral treaty provision that is so general that it can gain the character of an international customary rule.

[37] See Appendix 1, Glossary.

[38] See below section 11.5.1.1.1.

[39] See below section 11.5.1.1.2.

[40] SPANG-HANSSEN-1 *supra* note 8 at 223.

Article 53 of the Vienna Convention on Treaties states, as to treaties conflicting with a peremptory norm of general international law (*ius cogens*): "A treaty is void if, at the time of its conclusion, it conflicts with a peremptory norm of general international law. For the purposes of the present Convention, a peremptory norm of general international law is a norm accepted and recognized by the international community of States as a whole as a norm from which no derogation is permitted and which can be modified only by a subsequent norm of general international law having the same character."

11.5.1.1.2. Erga Omnes

Obligations erga omnes pertain to the enforceability of norms of international law; the idea appears to be that certain violations of the norms of international law are so significant that they harm the international community as a whole.

The concept is controversial because it implies that individual States and the international community may be legally responsible for what occurs in the affairs of independent States.

There are two fundamental characteristics of *erga omnes*:

- Universality, in the sense that obligations erga omnes are binding on all States without exception;
- Solidarity, in the sense that every State is deemed to have a legal interest in their protection.

11.5.1.1.3. Differences between Jus Cogens and Erga Omnes

While *jus cogens* is a category of norm from which no derogation is permitted, *erga omnes* is but a related concept that pertains more to the rights and obligations on the part of States in the event certain rules are violated.

The *jus cogens* norms and the obligations *erga omnes* arise out of the belief that some rules or norms are so essential for the protection of fundamental interests of the international community that any breach thereof is considered to affect the international community as a whole.

The following list of differences between *erga omnes* and *jus cogens* can be set forth:

- Jus cogens develops over time;
- Erga omnes is more variable.
- Jus cogens is a rule of substance; these rules are so fundamental, that one cannot derogate from them.
- Structurally, jus cogens is a subset of erga omnes.
- Jus cogens trumps erga omnes.

Some rules identified as *erga omnes* may also be considered *ius cogens*. In brief, the relationship between the two concepts are:

- Ius Cogens: Relates to derogability
- Erga Omnes: Generality of standing

Unlike *ius cogens*, *erga omnes* rules may be limited to a group of States.

11.5.2. Treaties

A treaty[41] is a binding agreement under public international law concluded by subjects of international law, namely States and international organizations.

Treaties can be called by many names: treaties, international agreements, protocols, covenants, conventions, exchanges of letters, exchanges of notes, etc. However, all of these instruments are equally treaties, and the rules are the same, regardless of what they are called.

Treaties can be loosely compared to contracts.[42] Both are means by which willing parties assume obligations among themselves, and a party to either who fails to live up to the imposed obligations can be held legally liable for such breach.

The central principle of treaty law is expressed in the maxim *pacta sunt servanda* - "pacts must be respected".

The Vienna Convention on the Law of Treaties, article 2(1)(a), defines a treaty as: "an international agreement concluded between States in written form and governed by international law." This provision authoritatively defines "treaty" for public international law purposes.

The American Restatement (Third) of the Foreign Relations Law of the United States provides in § 301: "under customary international law oral agreements are no less binding although their terms may not be readily susceptible of proof." Comment b points out that, by any widely accepted definition, treaties are binding internationally.

In the international law hierarchy, custom has priority over treaties, but treaties may prevail over general law. The governing principles are:

- When not specified, treaty and custom have equal weight.
- General presumption: treaties are not intended to derogate from general custom.
- Lex specialis derogat generalis (specific prevails over general).

[41] See Article 38(a) ICJ Statute *supra* note 13.

[42] Judge Sir Gerald Fitzmaurice, Legal Adviser of the British Foreign Office and later Judge of the ICJ: "Treaties are not more a source of law than an ordinary private law contract."

In exceptional cases, a treaty may give rise to new customary rules (or assist in their creation) "of its own impact," if it is widely adopted by States and the clear intention of the parties is to create new customary law, e.g., as in The North Sea case.[43]

Treaties can be divided into the following categories, which will be of value for the researcher:

- Law-Making Treaties (Traités-lois)
    - Treaties which act as contracts yet resemble national statutes in content.
    - They impose obligations on all parties to the treaty and seek to regulate the parties' behavior over a long period of time.
    - They create law by forming an agreement upon general universal legal principles.
    - Such treaties usually have numerous parties.
    - Law-making treaties are often used to create general norms of conduct, and tend to be broadly applicable.
    - However, even "law making" treaties are not enforceable against any party that does not wish to abide by the law.
- Contract Treaties (Traités-contrats)
    - Treaties which resemble contracts - they regulate or manage a specific area of activity.
    - These are not sources of law but merely legal transactions only applicable to the States which make the treaties and not a whole host of nations.
- Bilateral treaty
    - A bilateral treaty is a treaty between two parties.
- Multilateral treaty
    - A multilateral treaty is a treaty among more than two parties.
- Copies of the Bilateral and Multilateral Treaties:
    - Bilateral treaties are usually written in two original copies and exchanged;
    - Multilateral treaties are written in a single original copy, which is given to a depository and then copies are distributed to the signatories;
    - Even a bilateral treaty may permit accession by other parties, and thus become a multilateral treaty after the first accession.

The dichotomy between "law-making treaties" and "contract-treaties"

[43] *North Sea Continental Shelf Cases* (Federal Republic of Germany vs. Denmark; Federal Republic of Germany vs. Netherlands), (International Court of Justice, Judgment of 20 February 1969), 1969 I.C.J. 3.

might not always be clear and useful from a general point of view, but the contract treaty is more likely to be nullified by war than a law-making treaty.

The background for treaties can be illustrated as in the table below.

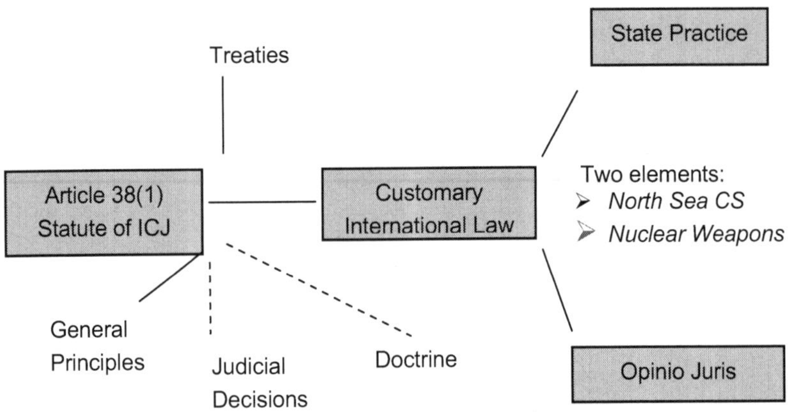

Table 59: The background for treaties[44]

When a treaty "codifies" international law, it means that it collects rules and customs of international law regarding a certain topic and lists them clearly. Thus, the implication is that it is not making new law but is merely making existing customary international law into conventional international law. However, this is not entirely accurate, since codifications often will slightly modify and clarify existing customary law. The Statute of the U.N. International Law Commission defines codification as: "The more precise formulation and systematization of rules of international law in fields where there already has been extensive State practice, precedent and doctrine."

The United Nations' International Law Commission[45] was established by the U.N. General Assembly in 1947 to promote the progressive development of international law and its codification. In doing so, the U.N. fulfilled one of

[44] *North Sea Continental Shelf Cases* (Federal Republic of Germany vs. Denmark; Federal Republic of Germany vs. Netherlands), (International Court of Justice, Judgment of 20 February 1969), 1969 I.C.J. 3, 57 & *Legality of the Threat or Use of Nuclear Weapons* (United Nations), (International Court of Justice, Advisory opinion of 8 July 1996), 1996 I.C.J. 226, 267.

[45] International Law Commission <www.un.org/law/ilc/index.htm>.

the purposes in Article 13 of the U.N. Charter, which states:

1. The General Assembly shall initiate studies and make recommendations for the purpose of:
    a) promoting international co-operation in the political field and encouraging the progressive development of international law and its codification;
    b) promoting international co-operation in the economic, social, cultural, educational, and health fields, an assisting in the realization of human rights and fundamental freedoms for all without distinction as to race, sex, language, or religion.
2. The further responsibilities, functions and powers of the General Assembly with respect to matters mentioned in paragraph 1(b) above are set forth in Chapters IX and X of the U.N. Charter.

The idea is to develop international law through the restatement of existing rules or through the formulation of new rules. The U.N.'s International Law Commission's work can be valuable for legal researchers because the Commission is composed of 34 members who are elected by the General Assembly for five-year terms and who serve in their individual capacities, not as representatives of their governments. Most of the Commission's work involves the preparation of drafts on topics of international law. Some topics are chosen by the Commission and others are referred to it by the General Assembly or the Economic and Social Council.

Since 1949 the U.N.'s International Law Commission has submitted final drafts or reports with respect to eleven of topics or sub-topics, as follows:

- Regime of the High Seas
- Regime of territorial Waters
- Nationality, including statelessness
- Law of treaties
- Diplomatic intercourse and immunities
- Consular intercourse and immunities
- Arbitral procedure
- Succession of States in respect of treaties
- Succession of States in respect of matters other than treaties
- Jurisdictional immunities of States and their property
- State responsibility

For an example of the Commission's breadth of work on its agenda, for its fifty-fifth session in the summer of 2003, the topics were:

- Diplomatic protection
- Reservations to treaties

- Unilateral acts of States
- International liability for injurious consequences arising out of acts not prohibited by international law (international liability in case of loss from trans-boundary harm arising out of hazardous activities)
- Responsibility of international organizations
- Fragmentation of international law: difficulties arising from the diversification and expansion of international law
- Shared natural resources.

The 59th session agenda included:

- Shared Natural resources
- Respect of international organizations
- Reservations to treaties
- Effects of armed conflicts on treaties
- Obligations to extradite – expulsion of aliens.

The reports from the Commission may contain value for the researcher for interpretation of an article in a treaty, especially if the formulation of an article has not been changed subsequent to the commission's report in the final treaty text.

11.5.3. General Principles of Law

Article 38 (1)(c) of the Statute of the International Court of Justice[46] states the Court shall apply the general principles of law recognized by civilized nations.[47] The American Restatement[48] rightly points out that general principles, even if not incorporated or reflected in customary law or international agreement, may be invoked as supplementary rules of international law where appropriate. To avoid confusion, the researcher must make a distinction between the following principles:

- Principles generally recognized in national law
- Principles of international law
- Principles applicable in legal relations and legal logic

General principles of municipal law are seldom used by the International Court of Justice (ICJ).

A principle of law is a general one, if it is being applied by most representative systems of municipal law. The municipal law must be internationalized. The principles must be similar, though not necessarily identical.

[46] See above footnote 13.
[47] SPANG-HANSSEN-1 *supra* note 8 at 226; REST *supra* note 2 at §102(1)(c) & (3).
[48] REST *supra* note 2 at § 102 (4) (on sources of international law).

When a legal researcher wants to determine the content of a general principle of law he/she must use comparative law (methods).[49] Roscoe Pound, once Dean of Harvard Law School, stated: "If we…compare the authoritative techniques received in different bodies of law and the modes of applying them, this along with the established comparison of authoritative precepts and doctrines as it has gone in the past, will yield a complete, well-rounded comparative method well worthy of a place among the received methods of the science of law. Such a method is needed in the economically unifying world of today and will be needed even more as we achieve the more complete unification that will overcome the nationalism we have inherited from the sixteenth century."

11.5.4. Decisions of the Tribunals

Under article 38(d) of the Statute[50] of the ICJ,[51] juridical decisions of tribunals, - that is, of the ICJ itself, of arbitrations and of other tribunals and municipal courts – are only to be regarded as a subsidiary means for determinations of the rules of law. Thus, the ICJ cannot use the principle of *stare decisis*. ICJ article 59 states: "The decision of the Court has no binding force except between the parties and in respect of that particular case." However, the ICJ does refer in its decisions to its former jurisprudence in the interest of judicial constancy. Also, the ICJ has no legislative power.

The limitations in article 38 as to listed sources for the ICJ does not mean that the legal scholar should not use the international case law as a source in dissertations and theses. For example, the ICJ Fisheries and North Sea cases[52] contain important considerations from different judges that, to a certain extent, reflect the evolution of international law. There are numerous collections of decisions of the international courts and arbitrate tribunals.

[49] See this book's Chapter 4.

[50] See above footnote 13.

[51] ICJ decisions are at <www.icj-cij.org/homepage/index.php>.

[52] *Fisheries Jurisdiction* (Federal Republic of Germany v. Iceland) of July 25, 1974, 1974 I.C.J. 175; *Fisheries Jurisdiction* (United Kingdom of Great Britain and Northern Ireland v. Iceland) of February 2, 1973, 1973 I.C.J. 3; *Fisheries Jurisdiction* (United Kingdom of Great Britain and Northern Ireland v. Iceland) of July 25, 1974, 1974 I.C.J. 3; *North Sea Continental Shelf Cases* (Federal Republic of Germany vs. Denmark; Federal Republic of Germany vs. Netherlands) of 20 February 1969, 1969 I.C.J. 3.

11.5.4.1. International Tribunals

The following should be regarded as international tribunals as their statute are aimed to cover the whole world / Earth:[53]

- The International Court of Justice in The Hague (ICJ)[54]
- The International Criminal Court in The Hague (ICC)[55]
- International Tribunal for the Law of the Sea in Hamburg (ITLOS)[56]

11.5.4.2. Regional Tribunals

Of tribunals covering regional areas can be mentioned:

- The European Court of Human Rights (ECHR)[57]
- The Court of Justice of the European Union (ECJ)[58]
- The Inter-American Court of Human Rights (IACHR)[59] – website in English at <www.corteidh.or.cr/index.cfm?CFID=663160&CFTOKEN=89912718>.
- Court of Justice of the African Union [not yet established] – website <www.africa-union.org/root/au/organs/Court_of_Justice_en.htm>. It will include what was intended to be The African Court on Human and Peoples' Rights (ACHPR)[60] [not yet operational] – website in English <www.aict-ctia.org/courts_conti/achpr/achpr_home.html>.

11.5.4.3. Certain National Tribunals with larger impact

Certain national tribunals have been made due to international involvement and their decisions can thus have some larger impact. For example:

[53] See also, Stefania Bondurant, *A Practitioner's Guide: An Overview Of The Major International Arbitration Tribunals*, 3 SOUTH CAROLINA JOURNAL OF INTERNATIONAL LAW & BUSINESS 21 (2006).

[54] Website <www.icj-cij.org>.

[55] Website <www.icc-cpi.int>.

[56] Website <www.itlos.org>.

[57] The ECHR has jurisdiction to deal with cases brought by individuals (rather than states). Website <www.echr.coe.int/echr/>.

[58] The ECJ has jurisdiction to deal with cases brought by individuals. Website <http://curia.europa.eu/>.

[59] Makes up the human rights protection system of the Organization of American States (OAS), which serves to uphold and promote basic rights and freedoms in the Americas.

[60] In a July 2004 decision, the Africa Union Assembly resolved that the future Court on Human and Peoples' Rights would be integrated with the African Court of Justice.

- International Criminal Tribunal for the Former Yugoslavia (ICTY) - website <www.icty.org>
- International Criminal Tribunal for Rwanda (ICTR) – website <www.unictr.org>

11.5.5. Writings of Publicists and Authors

Pursuant to article 38(d) of the Statute[61] of the ICJ, the teaching of the most highly qualified publicists of the various nations is to be regarded as a subsidiary means for determinations of the rules of law. However, this source is not used by the ICJ in its decisions; yet, it may be referred to in separate and dissenting ICJ opinions.

In this category of source should also be mentioned various legal research institutions:

- International Law Commission
- Institut de droit International
- International Law Association
- Hague Academy of International Law
- International Law Institute
- Restatement of the Law (Third) of the Foreign Relations Law of the United States (by the American Law Institute), especially those sections that are not stated as part of U.S. domestic law.

Among the list of persons acknowledged to belong to this source are:

- Ian Brownlie, Principles of Public International Law
- M. Bedjaoui, Droit international – Bilan et perspectives
- Antonio Cassese, International Criminal Law
- Patrick Dailliere et Alain Pellet, Droit International Public
- T.O. Elias, New Horizons in International Law
- J.L. Fernandès-Flores, Derecho internacional público
- E. Jimenez de Arechaga, El derecho intercional público
- Louis Henkin (Ed.), Restatement of the Law (Third) of the Foreign Relations Law of the United States (by the American Law Institute); & Foreign Affairs and the United States Constitution
- Oppenheim's International Law
- Malcolm N. Shaw, International Law
- G.I. Tunkin ed., International Law – A Textbook
- W. von Vitzthum et M. Bothe, Völkerrecht

[61] See above footnote 13.

11.5.6. Resolutions and declarations of International Organizations

Resolutions and declarations of international organizations (see further below Chapter 12) are not mentioned as sources in Article 38 of the ICJ. However, it appears they should be considered within the scope of the traditional sources of international law. In the future, they may be designated as a separate source category.[62]

The researcher has to be aware that different types of resolutions exist:

- Political issues
- Economic and social issues
- Legal issues
- Administrative and internal matters, like measures concerning the staff of the organization

11.6. Where to find material

The United Nations treaty series collection is available on online at <http://untreaty.un.org>. From 1962 onward, these have also been published in International Legal Materials (I.L.M.) by the American Society of International Law (ASIL). See also ASIL's Electronic Information System for International Law (EISIL) at <www.eisil.org>.[63]

General information on Public International Law can be found above in section 5.3.5. Writings of Publicists and Authors.

The leading law journals in the field of public international law are:

- American Journal on International Law (1907-)
- European Journal of international Law (1990-)
- International and Comparative Law Quarterly (1952-)
- Leiden Journal of International Law (1988-)
- Recueil des Cours (1924-) (reprints (in French and English) lectures offered each summer at the Hague Academy of International Law by leading international lawyers)
- Revue Générale de Droit Internationale Public (1984-)(in French)
- Zeitschrift für Ausländishes Öffentliches Recht und Völkerrecht (Heidelberg Journal of International Law) (1924-) (in German and English)

[62] Ricardo Monaco, *Sources of International Law in* R. Bernhardt, ENCYCLOPEDIA OF PUBLIC INTERNATIONAL LAW, Volume Four p. 476 (2003) (Max Planck Institute for Comparative Public Law, Elsevier 2003).

[63] See also, Guide to International Legal Research (LexisNexis, June 2010).

- British Yearbook of International Law (1921-)
- German Yearbook of International Law – Jahrbuch für Internationales Recht (1957-)
- Max Planck Yearbook of United Nations Law (1997-)
- Annuaire Français de Droit International (1955-)
- African Yearbook of International Law – Annuaire Africain de Droit International (1993-)

Various international organizations' websites that should be mentioned include:

- United Nations <www.un.org>
- International Court of Justice <www.icj-cij.org>
- International Criminal Court <www.un.org/law/icc/index.html>
- International Law Commission <www.un.org/law/ilc/index.htm>
- International Committee of the Red Cross <www.icrc.org>
- Council of Europe <www.coe.int/portalT.asp>
- European Court of Human Rights <www.echr.coe.int>
- Inter-American Court of Human Rights <www1.umn.edu/humanrts/ iachr/iachr.html>
- Inter-American Commission on Human Rights <www.cidh.oas.org>
- Inter-American Court of Human Rights <www.corteidh.or.cr/ index_ing.html>.

United Nations material can be found on its website <www.un.org> and legal relevant practice of the UN can be found in the official Repertory of Practice of United Nations Organs (1958-), United Nations Judicial Yearbook (1962-) and Yearbook of the United Nations (-1947-).

Material from the U.N.'s International Law Commission (ILC) can be found in the Yearbook of the International Law Commission (1949-) and at

<www. un.org/law/ilc/index.html>.

The Max Planck Institute for Comparative Public Law and International Law in Heidelberg has a very well organized web site that gives web links in a thematic order <www.mpil.de/en/LINK/epilvr.cfm>.

Yale Law School - The Avalon Project - has diplomatic documents, treaties and other documents relating to U.S. practice at <www.yale.edu/ lawweb/avalon/avalon.htm>.

Fletcher Multilaterals Project has texts of numerous international conventions - organized chronologically and thematically - as well as web links to other useful research tools at <fletcher.tufts.edu/multilaterals.html>

New York University Law Library Guide to Foreign and International Legal Databases has, under the section "Foreign databases for Jurisdiction," various web links to the national legislation and case law of many countries at <www.law.nyu.edu/library/foreign_intl/index.html>.

Antonio Cassese has published *International Law* and *International Criminal Law* at Oxford University, which publisher has created an Online Resource Centre with links to materials related to these two books. These links provide a structured way to find links to material; see

<www.oup.com/uk/orc/bin/9780199259397/> and
<www.oup.com/uk/orc/bin/ 9780199259113/>.

Useful online catalogs can be found at these libraries:

- Peace Palace Library, whose catalog lists the monographs owned by the library and references every article published within one of the specialized journals that the library holds <www.ppl.nl>
- Max Planck Institute (Heidelberg) <aleph.mpg.de/aleph/fjec225vvft1q9sfvglk7g1qfrepbnsp2uak1majxues9gvexe-02830/file/start-0>
- Max-Planck Institute - Library Catalog <www.virtual-institute.de/eindex.cfm>
- European University Institute - Library <biblio.iue.it>
- Université Paris 1 - Bibliothèque de Cujas <www-cujas.univ-paris1.fr>
- USA - Library of Congress <www.loc.gov>
- Yale Law School - Avalon Project <www.yale.edu/lawweb/avalon /avalon.htm>
- Fletcher School of Law and Diplomacy <fletcher.tufts.edu/ multilaterals.html>
- University of Chicago - International Law Database <www. lib.uchicago.edu/~llou/forintlaw.html>
- Italian National Librarian Service <opac.sbn.it>
- University of Minnesota - Human Rights Library <www1.umn.edu/ humanrts/index.html>
- Peace Palace Library Catalogue <www.ppl.nl/catalogue>
- New York University Law Library Guide to Foreign and International Legal Database <www.law.nyu.edu/library/foreign_intl/index.html>
- T.M.C. Asser Instituut <www.asser.nl/vr/indxvr.htm>.

Finally, it should be noted that a great deal of material can be found in Westlaw and LexisNexis under the heading "International:"

In Westlaw:

- International law, Law reviews, Texts, and Bar Journals (INT-TP)
- International Court of Justice (INT-ICJ)
- Intenrational Criminal Tribunal for Rwanda (INT-ICTR)
- International Criminal Tribual for the Former Yougoslavia (INT-ICTY-ALL)
- International HR journal (INTLHRJ)
- International Leal Materials (ILM)
- International Commercial Arbitration (ICA-ALL)
- International Legal Material Cumulative Index (ILM-INDEX)
- International Trade Commission (FINT-ITC)
- International Trade Law and Regulation (INTTLR)
- International Treaties and Forms (INF-TF)
- International Commercial Treaties (ICA-TREATIES)
- Internet and Online Law (IOLAW)
- United Nations Commission on International Trade Law (UN-CITRAL-MODL)
- American Journal of International Law (AMJIL)
- American Society of International Law (ASIL)
- ILSA Journal of International and Comparative Law (ILSAJICL
- Index to Foreign Legal Periodicals (IFLP)
- International and Comparative Law Quarterly (ICLQ)
- Journal of International Criminal Justice (JINTCRJ)
- Journal of International Legal Studies (JILS)
- ALR International (ALRINTL)
- International Legal Materails Comulative Index (ILM-INDEX)
- Restatement of the Foreign Relations Law of the United States (REST-FOREL)

In LexisNexis:

- American Journal of International Law (AJIL)
- Internatioanl Law Review Articles (INTLR)
- International Legal Materials (ILM)
- International Trade Commission Materials (ALLITC)
- International Trade Commission Decisions (ITC)
- American Society of International Law (ASIL)
- Forcign Affairs (FORAFR)

11.7. Citations

As for the correct setup of citations, The New York University Journal of International Law and Politics in 2006 published a valuable Guide to Foreign and International Legal Citation (GFILC) with help from scholars in different countries,[64] which is available for free download at <www.law.nyu.edu /journals/jilp/Final%20GFILC%20pdf.pdf>. Given gaps in the information included in this first edition, one must expect it to be updated.[65]

Another source for citations has been made by the Faculty at Oxford University, England,[66] which guide in the back lists citations guides for other jurisdictions.

Yet, another source for citations is the American legal citation guide known as the *Bluebook*.[67]

> Example of citation in footnotes of cases from the International Court of Justice:
> Adv. Op. Application for Review of Judgment No 158, 1973 I.C.J. 166
> *Legality of the Threat or Use of Nuclear Weapons*, Advisory Opinion, 1996 I.C.J., pp. 241-242 para 29
>
> *Nottebohm case (Liechtenstein v. Guatemala)*(Second Phase) of April 6, 1955, 1955 I.C.J. 4.
>
> *Case concerning Military and Paramilitary Activities in and against Nicaragua (Nicaragua v. United States of America)* of June 27, 1986, 1986 I.C.J. 14, 106 para. 202
>
> Example of citation in footnote of General Assembly resolution:
> Universal Declaration of Human Rights, G.A. Res. 217A, U.N. Doc. A/810 (1948)
>
> Example of citation in footnote of a Treaty:

[64] The GFILC is also available in spiral-bound, paperback form by sending US$ 20 payable to "Journal of International Law and Politics" at: Circulation Department, Journal of International Law and Politics,110 West Third Street, New York NY 10012, USA. Also available for free download from <www.law.nyu.edu/journals/jilp/gfilc.html >.

[65] See also, MANUAL OF INTERNATIONAL AND FOREIGN LEGAL CITATION: THE GREENBOOK (Ed. Shepard Broad Law Center) (William S. Hein & Company, January 2007).

[66] Standard for Citation of Legal Authorities (University of Oxford, 2006) at <www.competition-law.ox.ac.uk/published/oscola_2006.pdf>.

[67] A UNIFORM SYSTEM OF CITATIONS ("the Bluebook"), published by the universities of Columbia, Harvard, Pennsylvania and Yale.

Convention on the High Seas, Apr. 29, 1958, 13 U.S.T. 2312, T.I.A.S. 5200, 450 U.N.T.S. 82.
Charter of Fundamental Rights of the European Union, OJ C 364, 18/12/2000 pp. 0001-0022.

11.8. Further Reading (updates at corresponding website)

The URL for the corresponding website is <www.hssph.net/legalrm> with a full alphabetic bibliography.

AKEHURST'S MODERN INTRODUCTION TO INTERNATIONAL LAW (8th ed.) (by Peter Malanczuk)(New York ; London : Routledge, 2002)

American Society of International Law Electronic Research Guides at <www.asil.org/resource/home.htm>

Bernhardt, Rudolf, *Interpretation in International Law*, in ENCYCLOPEDIA OF PUBLIC INTERNATIONAL LAW (Rudolf Bernhardt (Ed.), Elsevier 1995)

Bondurant, Stefania, *A Practitioner's Guide: An Overview of the Major international Arbitration Tribunals*, 3 SOUTH CAROLINA JOURNAL OF INTERNATIONAL LAW AND BUSINESS 21 (2006)

BROWNLIE, IAN, PRINCIPLES OF INTERNATIONAL LAW (7th ed.) (Oxford University Press, 2008)

Canick, Simon, & Beth Williams, *Guide to Treaty Research, Columbia Law Library* (2010) at <www.law.columbia.edu/library/Research_Guides/internat_law/treaty_research>

CASSESE, ANTONIO, INTERNATIONAL LAW (Oxford, England: Oxford University Press 2001);

COHEN, MORRIS L., ROBERT C. BERRING & KENT C. OLSON, HOW TO FIND THE LAW (Chapter 15 - International law)(9. ed.)(St. Paul, Minn.: West, 1989)

Dekker, Ige F., & Harry H.G. Post, *The Completeness of International Law and Hamlet's Dilemma* in ON THE FOUNDATIONS AND SOURCES OF INTERNATIONAL LAW (2003, T.M.C. Asser Press, The Hague, Netherlands);

Egge, Michael G., & Matteo F. Bay & Janier Ruiz Calzado, *The New EC Merger Regulation: A Move to Convergence, Status of Soft Law in International Law*, Antitrust Magazine, Section of Antitrust Law, American Bar Association, Fall 2004 at <www.lw.com/upload/pubContent/_pdf/pub1167_1.pdf>.

ENCYCLOPEDIA OF PUBLIC INTERNATIONAL LAW, Vol. 1-5 (Edited by Rudolf Bernhardt)(Consolidated library ed.)(Amsterdam; New York: North-Holland, Elsevier Science & Technology, 1992-2003)

EYFFINGER, ARTHUR , THE INTERNATIONAL COURT OF JUSTICE, 1946-1996 (Kluwer Law International, the Netherlands 1996)

Gaebler, Ralph F., *Conducting Research in Customary International Law* in CONTEMPORARY PRACTICE OF PUBLIC INTERNATIONAL LAW (Ed. Ellen Schaffer & Randall Synder)(Dobbs Ferry, New York: Oceana Publications, 1997)

GlobaLex International Law Research Guides at <www.nyulawglobal.org/globalex/index.html>

Guide to International Legal Research (The George Washington International Law Review) (Newark, NJ : LexisNexis Matthew Bender, 2010)

Hague Conference of Private International Law at <www.hcch.net/index_en.php>

Higgins, Rosalyn, *International Law and the Avoidance, Containment and Resolution of Disputes – General Course on Public International Law*, RECUEIL DES COURS, Vol. 230 (1991-V) page 23

HIGGINS, ROSALYN, PROBLEMS & PROCESS – INTERNATIONAL LAW AND HOW WE USE IT (Clarendon Press, Oxford 1994)

Hoffman, Marcy, *Features - Researching U.S. Treaties and Agreements* at <www.llrx.com/features/ustreaty.htm>

International Cooperation in the Enforcement Of Competition Policy by Mitsuo Matsushita, 468 Washington University Global Studies Law Review 463 at <http://law.wustl.edu/wugslr/issues/volume1/p463Matsushit a.pdf>.

International Law Research at GlobaLex at <www.nyulawglobal.org/globalex/index.html#>

International Legal Research Tutorial, Duke Law School at <www.law.duke.edu/ilrt/>

International Legal Search Tutorials – Customary International Law at <www.law.duke.edu/ilrt/cust_law_1.htm>

International Legal Search Tutorials – Treaties at <www.law.duke.edu/ilrt/treaties_1.htm>

JANIS, MARK W., AN INTRODUCTION TO INTERNATIONAL LAW (Chapter 2 - Treaties) (4. ed.)(New York: Aspen Publishers, 2003)

LOWE, VAUGHAN, INTERNATIONAL LAW (England: Oxford University Press, 2007)(an update of James Brierly's Law of Nations)

MCNAIR, LORD ARNOLD DUNCAN, THE LAW OF TREATIES (Oxford Clarendon Press 1961)

Monaco, Ricardo, *Sources of International Law* in in ENCYCLOPEDIA OF PUBLIC INTERNATIONAL LAW (Rudolf Bernhardt (Ed.), Elsevier 1995)

OPPENHEIM'S INTERNATIONAL LAW (9th Ed.)(Eds.: Sir Robert Jennings & Sir Arthur Watts)

(London and New York: Longman 1996)

Rehberg, Jeanne, *Finding Treaties and Other International Agreements* (Chapter 6) in ACCIDENTAL TOURIST ON THE NEW FRONTIER: AN INTRODUCTORY GUIDE TO GLOBAL LEGAL RESEARCH (Ed. Jeanne Rehberg & Radu D. Popa)(Littleton, Colo. : F.B. Rothman, 1998)

RESTATEMENT OF THE LAW (THIRD) - FOREIGN RELATIONS LAW OF THE UNITED STATES (American Law Institute)

SHAW, MALCOLM N., INTERNATIONAL LAW (4th ed.)(Cambridge, England: University Press 1997)

Shelton, Dinah, *Normative Hierarchy in International Law*, 100 AMERICAN JOURNAL ON INTERNATIONAL LAW 291 (2006)

SPANG-HANSSEN, HENRIK, CYBERSPACE & INTERNATIONAL LAW ON JURISDICTION (Chapters 24-26) (DJØF Publishing, Copenhagen, 2004)

STATEMENT OF PRINCIPLES APPLICABLE TO THE FORMATION OF GENERAL CUSTOMARY INTERNATIONAL LAW as amended at the 2000 London conference (International Law Association), at <www.ila-hq.org/pdf/CustomaryLaw.pdf>.

Vienna Convention on the Law of Treaties of 23 May 1969 (into force 27 January 1980), U.N.T.S. Vol. 1155 p. 331, also at

<http://untreaty.un.org /ilc/texts/instruments/english/conventions/1_1_1969.pdf>.

WEERAMANTRY, C.G., UNIVERSALISING INTERNATIONAL LAW (Boston: Martinus Nijhoff Publishers, 2004).

CHAPTER 12

International Organizations' Resources

12.1. International Organizations – Short Overview

An international organization is an organization with an international membership, scope, or presence. The main types are:

- International nongovernmental organizations (INGOs)
- Intergovernmental organizations or international governmental organizations (IGOs)
- Global Public Policy Networks (GPPNs).

INGOs are non-governmental organizations (NGOs) that operate internationally. These can be divided into:

- International non-profit organizations, for example the International Committee of the Red Cross and the World Organization of the Scout Movement
- International companies / multinational corporations, like Coca-Cola and Toyota.

IGOs are organizations that are made up primarily of sovereign states ("member states"). These include the United Nations (UN), Council of Europe[1] (CoE) ,[2] and World Trade Organization (WTO).

GPPNs take various forms and may be made up of states and non-state actors. Non-state actors involved in GPPNs may include: intergovernmental or-

[1] Consisting of 47 European states, including Russia and Turkey. Its institutions are: (A) Committee of Ministers, (B) Parliamentary Assembly, (C) Secretary General, (D) Commissioner for Human Rights, (E) European Court of Human Rights. It was founded on 5 May 1949 by the Treaty of London. Member States are all the central and eastern European states, except Belarus, Kazakhstan, Kosovo and the Holy See (Vatican).

[2] Note: This is not the same as the "European Council" - in short: "the Council" - also named the "Council of Ministers" or "Consilium", which is an institution in the European Union, see Chapter 7 at footnote 16.

ganizations, states, state agencies, regional or municipal governments, in partnerships with non-governmental organizations, private companies, etc. Example are the Internet Governance Forum (IGF)[3] and Global Internet Governance Academic Network (GigaNet - A global network for scholars of Internet governance).[4]

It should be noted here that the European Union is unique in that it is much more than an international organization. It is not a federation like the United States. Nevertheless, to a certain extent, the E.U. has similarities in function and organization to the United States.

As mentioned above in subsection 11.5.6. on the subject of international law resources, resolutions and declarations of international organizations are not mentioned as sources in Article 38 of the ICJ. However, it appears they should be considered within the scope of the traditional sources of international law. In the future, they may be designated as a separate source category.[5]

12.2 Further Reading (updates at corresponding website)

The URL for the corresponding website is <www.hssph.net/legalrm> with a full alphabetic bibliography.

Andersen, Maureen Ratynski, *Where to Begin...When you Don't Know How to Start: Tips for Researching UN Legal Materials*, 31 INTERNATIONAL JOURNAL OF LEGAL INFORMATION 264 (2003)

Burnett, Anne, *International Organizations*, ASIL Guide to Electronic Resources for International Law at <www.asil.org/resource/intorg1.htm>

COHEN, MORRIS L., ROBERT C. BERRING & KENT C. OLSON, HOW TO FIND THE LAW (Chapter 15 - International law - International Organizations)(9. ed.)(St. Paul, Minn.: West, 1989)

Hague Conference of Private International Law at <www.hcch.net/index_en.php>

International Committee of the Red Cross at <www.icrc.org/Eng/ihl>

International Legal Research Tutorials – International Organizations at

[3] <http://intgovforum.org>.

[4] <http://giga-net.org/>.

[5] Ricardo Monaco, *Sources of International Law in* R. Bernhardt, ENCYCLOPEDIA OF PUBLIC INTERNATIONAL LAW, Volume Four p. 476 (2003) (Max Planck Institute for Comparative Public Law, Elsevier 2003).

<www.law.duke.edu/ilrt/int_orgs_1.htm>

Ochoa, Christina, *The Individual and Customary International Law Formation*, 48 VIRGINIA JOURNAL OF INTERNATIONAL LAW 119 (2007)

United Nations at <www.un.org>.

United Nations Documentation Research Guide at <www.un.org/depts/dhl/resguide/>

War and International Humanitarian Law, International Committee of the Red Cross at <www.icrc.org/eng/war-and-law>

APPENDIX

1. Glossary: Terms & Abbreviations

See also Index below.

a fortiori - By a stronger reason. A term used in logic to denote an argument that a fact must exist because another fact exists which includes or is analogous to the first fact.

a mensa et thoro - From bed and board. Refers to a qualified divorce by which the parties are separated or live apart without affecting the marriage itself. Compare a vinculo matrimonii.

a posteriori - From the effect to the cause. A term used in logic to denote an argument which takes ascertained facts and reasons backward or inductively to show their cause.

a priori - From the cause to the effect. A term used in logic to denote an argument that takes a principle as a cause and proceeds to deduce the effects that necessarily follow.

A Uniform System of Citation, see Bluebook

a vinculo matrimonii - From the bond of matrimony. Refers to a complete and unqualified divorce. Compare a mensa et thoro.

AALL – American Association of Law Librarians.

AALS – Association of American Law Schools.

ab antique - Of an ancient date; from antiquity.

ab initi - From the beginning or inception.

accomplice - Partner in crime.

actio criminalis - Criminal act.

actor sequitur forum rei - The rule of the plaintiff having to submit to the defendant's court - plaintiff must choose the jurisdiction in which the alien is located.

actus non facit reum nisi mens sit rea - The intent and the act must both concur to constitute the crime.

actus reus - Guilty act. A wrongful deed; generally coupled with mens rea to establish criminal liability.

ad damnum - To the damage. In a complaint, the name of a clause containing a statement of a plaintiff's money loss or other damage suffered.

ad hoc - Pertaining to a particular purpose only.

ad idem - To the same effect.

ad iterim - In the meantime.

ad litem—While the lawsuit is pending.

ad satisfaciendum - To satisfy.

ad valorem - According to value.

ad vitam - For life.

addendum - Something that is added or to be added; a list or section of added material.

adjudication - A formal decree or pronouncement of judgment by a court.

ADR - Alternative Dispute Resolution

advance sheets - Paperbound pamphlets containing the most recent court decisions published in a given case reporter series. Periodically, several advance sheets are collected and published in a hard-bound version as a new case reporter volume, at which time the old advance sheets are no longer needed. The term can also apply to recent statutes or regulations. Advance sheets occur after slip laws or slip opinions but before the laws or opinions are bound in final hard copy volumes.

affidavit - A written statement of facts made under oath before someone authorized by law to administer oaths. The person making the statement is called an "affiant."

AG – Advocate-General (in the European Court of Justice).

ALA - American Library Association.

aliunde - From another place; from outside.

allegation - What a party to an action states, in a pleading, that he or she intends to prove.

amicus curiae - Friend of the court. An individual or organization who has no absolute right to appear in a lawsuit, but who is allowed by the court to offer argument to protect his or her interest or requested by the court to file a brief in the action because of a strong interest in the subject matter.

amicus curiae brief – Friend of the court brief – a brief written by an individual or group not a party to the litigation. Non parties must first ask the court for permission to file an amicus brief. Some United States Supreme Court cases will have dozens of amicus briefs submitted

Amsterdam Treaty – The Treaty on European Union of October 1997.

Amsterdam Treaty of 1996 – A treaty under the European Union.

animus - An intention; a state of mind; design; will.

animus furandi - Intention to steal.

animus testandi—Intention to make a will.

annotations - (1) The full text of a demonstrative / representative case, followed by a discussion of a significant legal trend or issue it represents; (2) In statutory research, the term is used to refer to brief summaries of court decisions interpreting and applying statutes. These summaries appear in annotated statutory compilations, after the reprinted text of individual statutes to which they relate; (3) "Annotations" is also used to refer to detailed articles, prepared and published by Lawyers Cooperative Publishing Company in its American Law Reports Annotated ("A.L.R.") series, analyzing points of law raised in selected court decisions, statutes, and administrative regulations.

answer - The pleading by which a defendant responds to a plaintiff's complaint. See complaint, pleading.

appellant - The party in an action who appeals a court's decision or judgment to a higher court. Some courts use the term "petitioner" instead of "appellant." See petitioner. Compare appellee.

appellee - The party in an action against whom an appeal is taken. The appellee is usually but not always the winner in the lower court. Further, because an appeal may involve multiple issues decided by the lower court, a given party may be an appellant with respect to some issues and an appellee with respect to others. A party's status as appellant or appellee has no necessary correlation to his or her original status as a plaintiff or defendant in the lower court. Finally, some courts use the term "respondent" instead of "appellee." Compare appellant.

assumpsit - A promise to pay to or do something for another.

aut dedere aut judicare - dedere aut judicare - The principle of "aut dedere aut judicare" is the duty of the state to extradite or to prosecute the accused; while universal jurisdiction only refers to a right of the state to prosecute the accused

automatic appeal - A criminal appeal by operation of law, directly from a trial court to the state supreme court, upon imposition of a death penalty sentence.

black letter law—A colloquial term for summary statements of fundamental and widely accepted principles of law.

BLAW - Bloomberg Law.

Blog – web-log – essentially a journal, maintained on an Internet Website, that is periodically updated and is meant for public consumption. Typically consisting of short posts arranged in reverse chronological order. Blogs enable people to publish comments and ideas instantly for others to read.

blue book – (1) The informal designation "Bluebook" of A Uniform System of Citation, a joint publication of the law reviews of Columbia Law School, Harvard Law School, the University of Pennsylvania Law School, and Yale Law School, explaining proper citation format; (2) A book that describes the organization of federal or state government. Sometimes called black book, green book, red book or government manual.

blurb – A brief promotional notice or statement. A case blurb is a one-paragraph note for a particular legal point decided by the court.

bona fide - In good faith. (1) Made in good faith, without fraud or deceit (e.g., bona fide offer); (2) Compliant with the law (e.g., bona fide pension plan); (3) Sincere or genuine (e.g., bona fide signature). Compare mala fide.

boolean logic - A system of logic based on operators such as AND, OR, and NOT. In many search engines, search terms are linked with these Boolean operators to formulate more precise queries.

brevet - A privilege, such as a patent, granted to a private citizen by a government. In military law, a commission promoting an officer to a higher rank but without a corresponding pay increase.

brief - (1) a written document prepared by counsel to file in a legal proceeding, setting forth the pertinent facts, the applicable law, and an argument supporting counsel's position and challenging the opponent's position; (2) a summary or abstract of a court decision, usually prepared by a law student to assist in understanding the decision's significance.

briefing - A technique which serves both as an efficient means of recording notes and as an additional analytical tool.

bulletin board - A computer system used as an information source and forum for a particular interest group. The bulletin board typically holds postings made by various participants and replies to those postings from other participants, thus centrally stored

BVerfGE - Bundesverfassungsgericht (German Federal Constitutional Court).

C., see Command papers.

CALR - computer-assisted legal research.

canons – Formalized rules for construction of statutes.

capias ad satisfaciendum - A writ commanding a person to be taken and kept, so that he will appear in court on a certain day to satisfy damages or a debt.

Cartwheel – a word association technique designed to assist the creative use of indexes in law books, that is, to develop the habit of phrasing every word involved in the problem fifteen to twenty different ways.

case – (1) see action, cause of action, lawsuit; (2) a court's decision.

casebook - A compilation of extracts from instructive cases on a particular subject, usually with commentary and questions about the cases, designed as a teaching aid.

Casebook Method – An inductive system of teaching law in which students study specific cases to learn general legal principles. Professor Christopher C. Langdell introduced the technique at Harvard Law School in 1869. The casebook method is now the most widely used form of instruction in American law schools. Also termed case method; case system; Langdell method. Cf. Hornbook method.

causa mortis - In contemplation of approaching death.

cause of action - Any civil or criminal question litigated or contested before a court of justice; the basis for a lawsuit, e.g., breach of contract, trespass, assault. See also action, case, lawsuit.

caveat - Caution; warning; notice to beware.

caveat emptor - Buyer beware. A doctrine holding that purchasers buy at their own risk.

Cd., see Command papers.

cert. – see certiorari.

certiorari - To be more fully informed - An extraordinary writ (often abbreviated as "cert.") issued by an appellate court, at its discretion, directing a lower court to deliver the record in the case for review. In the United States most commonly used to refer to information (writ of certiorari) from the Supreme Court as its discretionary device to choose the cases it wishes to hear.

cestui que trust - A person who has a beneficial or equitable interest (e.g., the right to receive rents or profits) in property whose legal title is held by someone else.

cestui que vie - A person the length of whose life measures the duration of another person's estate.

cf. – "conferre" - meaning "to compare." A signal, used in connection with a citation, directing the reader's attention to an authority containing a point analogous to the point made by the person citing the authority.

CFSP – see Common Foreign and Security Policy

chattel - Movable or transferable property; especially personal property.

chose - A thing; an item of personal property.

chose in action - An item of personal property not presently in an individual's possession, but whose possession the individual has a right to recover through a legal proceeding; also refers to the right itself to bring an action for the recovery of the personal property or for some other remedy (e.g., damages for loss) with respect to the property.

citation - The title or other identification of a primary or secondary legal authority, such as a constitution, statute, court decision, or treatise. Lawyers use citations to establish or support propositions they assert in their oral and written legal arguments.

citator - A reference work used in legal research to update certain legal authorities by tracing their subsequent history and treatment, e.g., later judicial history and interpretation of reported court decisions and later judicial and legislative treatment of statutes. The title of the preeminent citator used in American legal re-search is Shepard's Citations.

cite - In legal research, argumentation, and writing, the term means to provide a citation; also frequently used as a shortened form of "citation." See citation.

civil - Pertaining to an appeal or original proceeding in a case that is neither criminal nor a juvenile delinquency case.

civil action - Every action other than a criminal action; an action based on a private wrong, as opposed to a crime, which is considered a wrong to the public in general. Compare criminal action.

claim - A statement or declaration of a legal right. Often used interchangeably with the term allegation. See allegation.

clean bill – a new bill, incorporating amendments to an earlier bill, which is then submitted for the earlier bill. Clean bills will be assigned a new bill number.

Cmd., see Command papers.

Cmnd., see Command papers.

code - A compilation of statutes or administrative regulations arranged by subject matter or topic.

Co-decision (E.U.) - The procedure through which the Council and the European Parliament enact most E.U. legislation. Under the Lisbon Treaty, it will form part of the Ordinary Legislative Procedure.

codicil - A supplement or addition to a will modifying, explaining, or otherwise qualifying the will in some way.

Command papers - papers submitted by the Governmental agencies to the British Parliament - are numbered and prefixed with an abbreviation of 'command' which has changed over time to allow for new sequences, as follows: C. 1870-1899; Cd. 1900-1918; Cmd. 1919-1956: Cmnd. 1956-1986; Cm. 1986- . Command Papers often cover topics on which the government intends to act, but also can include Treaties, State Papers, Policy Papers, Annual Reports, Reports of Royal Commissions, Reports of Departmental Committees, Reports of Tribunals and Commissions of Inquiry, etc. Command Papers are published by TSO (The Stationery Office - <www.tso.org.uk/) for OPSI (The Office of Public Sector Information - <www.opsi.gov.uk/). See guilde on British Documents at <http://guides.library.fullerton.edu/docslinks/britparlpapers.htm#COMMPAPFINDINGAIDS>.

commissioner - A substitute judicial officer, employed by the court, who performs judicial or quasi-judicial duties assigned to him or her. A commissioner may be authorized to decide only limited pretrial issues of fact and law or to conduct complete trails. Commissioners frequently act as temporary judges.

Common Foreign and Security Policy (CFSP) (E.U.) - Following on from earlier efforts, since the early 1970s, at cooperation in the area of foreign policy, the Common Foreign and Security Policy was established as the "second pillar" in the Maastricht

Treaty (1992) and developed under the Amsterdam Treaty (1997) and the Treaty of Nice (2001). The common policy exists in parallel to the separate foreign and security policies of the E.U. Member States. The Lisbon Treaty contains extensive provisions on Common Foreign and Security Policy.

common law - Principles and rules of law developed, modified, and applied by courts rather than by legislatures (which create statutory law). Common law is sometimes referred to as "judge-made law" or "case law."

Common Security and Defence Policy, see European Security and Defence Policy.

companion bill – a bill introduced in one house of Congress that is identical or very similar to a bill introduced in the other house of Congress. Since a bill must pass both houses of Congress, the introduction of companion bills can expedite the process.

complainant - The person who files a complaint; another term for "plaintiff" or "petitioner." See complaint, petitioner, plaintiff.

complaint - The pleading with which a plaintiff starts an action. In a criminal action, the complaint is called an "indictment" or "information." See pleading.

compromis - A special agreement between states to submit a particular issue either to an arbitral tribunal or to the International Court.

concurring opinion - When a court has a panel of judges ruling on a single case, a judge agreeing with the conclusions, result, or outcome stated in the opinion of the court, but disagreeing with the court's rationale, may write a separate opinion (called a "concurring opinion") agreeing with the result but stating different reasons for reaching it. Concurring opinions are not the law of the case nor binding as precedent, but they may provide a legal researcher with useful insight into the manner in which a court might interpret or apply the case in the future.

conflict of laws - see private international law.

consuetudo est servanda – All international subjects must comply with customary rules.

coram nobis - Before us. A writ of error directed to another branch of the same court.

coram non judice - A court without jurisdiction to make a particular determination.

corpus delicti - The body of a crime; the physical thing upon which a crime has been committed, e.g., the corpse of a murdered person, the burned out shell of a stolen automobile. The fact of a transgression.

corpus juris - The body of the law.

correlation table – A common characteristic of law treatises or digest is that they are occasionally revised. After revision, a correlation table will help the user find where subject matter from the older table is found in the revised edition.

Council of Europe - The Council of Europe is an intergovernmental organization, set up in

1948, which includes in its aims the protection of human rights and the promotion and awareness of Europe's cultural identity and diversity. It has a wider membership than the E.U. . Though all Member States of the E.U. are also members of the Council of Europe, the latter is a distinct organisation in its own right.

Council of Ministers / Council (E.U.) - The Council of Ministers (formally named simply the Council) is the E.U. institution in which the governments of the Member States are represented. The Council consists of one representative of each Member State at Ministerial level. The Council meets in a whole range of formations, mainly sectoral (e.g. the Ministers for Agriculture when the Council takes decisions on the Common Agricultural Policy). The President (or chair) of the Council is the Minister of the Member State currently holding the E.U. Presidency. Up to now, this was for a six-month term according to an agreed and equal rotation. The Treaty of Lisbon contains some changes in regard to the Council of Ministers. Compare with the European Council.

cour de cassation - In various countries, exist courts of cassation [court of cassation], which review and overturn previous rulings made by lower courts. They are roughly equivalent to the Supreme Court of the United States.

count - A statement or declaration of a legal right. Often used interchange-ably with the terms "allegation," "claim," and "cause of action." See allegation, claim, and cause of action.

Court of Appeal - The California court that hears (1) appeals in all noncapital cases in which a superior court has original jurisdiction and (2) appeals under other special circumstances, as prescribed by law.

criminal - pertaining to an appeal or original proceeding charging the violation of criminal law.

criminal action - A lawsuit in which the government, as prosecutor, tries to persuade a judge or jury to punish a person for violating a criminal statute.

culpa - The civil law or Roman law term employed by lawyers from non-common law countries to refer to civil fault, neglect, or negligence or lack of reasonable care.

d.b.e. - Abbreviation for de bene esse.

damages – A financial award given to a person in a lawsuit because of someone else's unlawful conduct. There are two broad categories of damages: (a) compensatory damages are awarded to repay a person for an injury or loss he or she has suffered, and (b) punitive (or exemplary) damages are imposed solely to punish someone for an injury or loss he or she inflicted on another person.

damnum absque injuria - Damage or loss that cannot be redressed by a proceeding in law.

database - A collection of information organized in such a way that users (often both people and computer programs) can quickly select desired pieces of data.

de bene esse - Conditionally; provisionally. Refers to proceedings that are allowed to stand in the interim, but which are subject to future modification, e.g., allowing a witness who may not be available for trial to testify immediately, subject to possible future re-examination and exclusion of the earlier testimony at trial if the witness becomes available.

de facto - Actually; in fact. Compare de jure.

de jure - By operation of law. Compare de facto.

de lege ferenda - Relating to the law as it should be if the rules were changed to accord with good policy.

de minimis - Minimal; trivial; so trifling as to be of no consequence in the law.

de minimis non curat lex - The law does not concern itself with trifles.

de novo - Anew; from the start.

decision - A court's or other tribunal's disposition (e.g., affirmance or reversal) of a case. Although technically different from an opinion, the two terms are often loosely used as synonyms. See and compare opinion.

dedere aut judicare – see aut dedere aut judicare.

defendant - The person defending against or denying the allegations in a complaint, indictment, or information. There can be more than one defendant in a lawsuit.

defendant in error - Another term for an appellee. See appellee.

delegated act (E.U.) - Under the proposals in the LisbonTreaty, where there are non-essential elements to a legislative measure, these laws may delegate to the European Commission the power to enact detailed measures to supplement or amend these elements. The objective, content, scope and duration of these delegations has to be defined in the original legislative measure. The Council of Ministers and the European Parliament are to supervise the use of this power and may also revoke any such delegation.

delict - A wrongful act; tort.

demurrer - A pleading stating that although the facts alleged in a complaint may be true, they are insufficient for the plaintiff to state a claim for relief and for the defendant to frame an answer.

depublished opinion - Unique to California. A Court of Appeal opinion that the Court of Appeal has certified for publication but that the California Supreme Court, acting under its constitutional power over opinion publication, directs the Reporter of Decisions not to publish in the Official Reports and that may be cited or replied upon only in limited circumstances.

détournement de pouvoir - a term of French administrative law originally, meaning abuse of administrative powers by public officials.

dicta - Plural of dictum.

dictum – see obiter dictum.

digest - An essential case-finding tool. Legal research reference works containing very brief summaries of reported court decisions, with the summaries arranged by subject matter so that all case summaries on a single point of law are collected together, regardless of the date of issuance of the individual court decisions. It is a multivolume index to the law consisting of major topic headings, thousands of subheadings, and headnotes (short summaries of legal propositions stated in published court case.

Digressively Proportional (E.U.) - This refers to a system of representation of E.U. Member States in the European Parliament, whereby the number of seats a country has is broadly proportional to the size of its population but with the ratio between the number of seats and the population size being progressively more favourable the smaller the size of a country's population.

diligentia quam in suis - The standard of care normally exercised by a particular person in the conduct of his affairs.

disposition - Termination of a proceeding. Civil dispositions before trial include transfers to another trial court, dismissals, summary judgment, and other judgments before trial. Criminal dispositions before trial include transfers to another trial court, sentences after pleas of guilty or no contest, and dismissals. Civil dispositions after trial include entry of judgment after jury trial and court trial. Criminal dispositions after trial include acquittals, grants of probation, and sentences after conviction.

dissent - When a court has a panel of judges ruling on a single case, judges disagreeing with the majority's decision may express their views in dissenting opinions, which may disagree with all or only part of the majority opinion. Dissents are not the law of the case nor binding as precedent, but they may provide legal researchers with useful summaries of competing interpretations of specific legal principles or doctrines, and help them in doing their analyses of the strengths and weaknesses of the majority decision.

dolus - The intention to inflict some harm, together with the foreseeable consequences of the intended harm.

donatio mortis causa - Gift made upon contemplation of death, and conditioned upon the occurrence of the donor's death.

double jeopardy - The principle of "ne bis in idem" (non bis in idem or non bis idem or double jeopardy)(Not twice for the same thing) - forbidding more than one trial for the same offense.

duces tecum - Bring with you. Refers to a directive instructing a person who has been summoned to appear to bring with him or her some document, piece of evidence, or other thing to be inspected. See subpoena duces tecum.

due process clause - The constitutional provision that prohibits the government from unfairly or arbitrarily depriving a person of life, liberty, or property. (There are two Due Process Clauses in the U.S. Constitution, in the 5th and 14th Amendments.)

duty - A legal obligation.

E.C. - European Community.

E.C. Treaty – The Treaty establishing the European Union (the EEC treaty with amendments of 1991).

ECHR - The European Convention on Human Rights and Fundamental Freedoms, signed in 1950 under the aegis of the Council of Europe, sets out a list of human rights, which the participating countries guarantee to respect and uphold. The Convention established, for the first time, a system of international protection for human rights offering individuals the possibility of applying to a dedicated international court – the European Court of Human Rights – for the enforcement of their rights. All Member States of the E.U. have ratified the Convention. The E.U. Lisbon Treaty envisages that the E.U., as such, would seek to join the Convention.

e.g. - Exempli gratia - meaning for example.

easement - An interest in land owned by another person, consisting of the right to use or control the land, or an area above or below it, for a specific limited purpose.

ECB – European Central Bank.

ECF - Electronic Court Filing (U.S.)

eCFR - Electronic Code of Federal Regulations (U.S.)

ECHR – European Court of Human Rights.

ECJ – European Court of Justice.

ECSC – European Coal and Steel Community.

ECU – European Currency Unit.

EDI – Electronic data interchange.

EEA – European Economic Area - consisting of Norway, Iceland and Liechtenstein, which participate in the E.U.'s internal market while not assuming the full responsibilities of E.U. membership. Cf. EFTA.

EEC – European Economic Community, now EC.

EFTA – European Free Trade Association (consisting of Norway, Iceland, Liechtenstein and Switzerland). Also, compare EEA.

ejusdem generic - Of the same kind, class, or nature. A rule that is some-times followed in construing the words of written documents: where general words are linked with enumerated examples of persons or things, the general words are not construed in their broadest meaning, but are construed as applying only to persons or things of the same kind, class, or nature as those specifically enumerated.

electronic agent - Computer program designed, selected, or programmed to initiate or respond to electronic messages or performances without review by an individual

e-mail - Electronic mail - the transmission of messages over networks.

EMI – European Monetary Institute.

EMS – European Monetary System.

EMU – European Monetary Union.

en banc - On the bench. Descriptive of a court session in which all judges of the court are present and participating. Refers to a session of court in which all the judges of the court (rather than a smaller panel of selected judges) participate in deciding a case.

Enjoin - To require or command someone to do, or not to do, some act. See injunction.

erga omnes – Obligations owed to the entire international community, irrespective of consent on the part of those thus affected.

ergo - Therefore.

ESCB – see European System of Central Banks.

ESDP, see European Security and Defence Policy.

et al. – “et alii” ," meaning "and others."

et seq. - Abbreviation for "et sequentia," meaning "and the following."

et ux. - Abbreviation for "et uxor." See below.

et uxor - And wife..

EURATOM – European Atomic Energy Community.

EURECA – (1) European Retrievable Carrier; (2) An early subset of the California’s Registry System.

Eurojust (E.U.) - The European Judicial Co-operation Unit. A body of national prosecutors, magistrates or police officers from the Member States, established in 2002 under the Treaty of Nice to coordinate the fight against crime. The Treaty of Lisbon contains some changes in respect of Eurojust and its work.

European Council (E.U.) - The European Council is the term used to describe the institution within which the Heads of State or Government of the E.U. Member States meet regularly. It meets at least twice a year – more recently, about four times – and the President of the European Commission attends as a full member. Its functions are to give the E.U. the impetus it needs in order to develop and to define general policy guidelines and priorities. The Lisbon Treaty contains changes in regard to the European Council.

European Court of Auditors (E.U.) - The Court of Auditors is an institution that acts like the auditors of a business or other organisation. It monitors the E.U. 's accounts, examining the legality and regularity of the revenue and expenditure in the budget and ensuring sound financial management.

European Defence Agency (E.U.) - The European Defence Agency was established in 2004 to support the E.U. Member States and the E.U. Council in their effort to improve European defence capabilities in the field of crisis management, to monitor the capability commitments of Member States, and to promote harmonisation of procurement and support defence technology research.

European Security and Defence Policy (ESDP) (E.U.) - Established in 1999 at the Cologne European Council, the ESDP aims to allow the E.U. to develop its civilian and military capacities for crisis management and conflict prevention at international level, thus helping to maintain peace and international security, in accordance with the United Nations Charter. It will be renamed the Common Security and Defence Policy under the Treaty of Lisbon.

European System of Central Banks (ESCB) is made up by the European Central Bank (E.U.) and the national central banks of all E.U. Member States.

Europol - European Police Office, established under an agreement reached in 1995 and which entered into force on 1 October 1998, but only became fully operational on 1 July 1999. Europol's headquarters are in The Hague and it coordinates police cooperation throughout the E.U. in particular, agreed areas, for example in the areas of drug trafficking, clandestine immigration networks, trafficking in stolen vehicles, trafficking in human beings (including child pornography), counterfeiting currency and falsification of other means of payment, trafficking in radioactive and nuclear substances, terrorism and money-laundering. The Treaty contains some changes in respect of Europol and its work which are summarised in this document.

ex curia - Out of court.

ex injuria non oritur jus - The principle that no benefit can be received from an illegal act.

ex officio - By virtue of an office or official position.

ex parte - From the part. On or from one party only, usually without notice to or argument from the adverse party; pertaining to one party only.

ex post facto—After the fact.

ex rel.—Abbreviation for "ex relatione," meaning "upon relation of." Refers to legal proceedings commenced on behalf of the United States or an individual state, but on the instigation of an individual who has a private interest in the matter (for example, "United States ex rel. Smith v. Jones").

exempla gratia - For example (typically abbreviated as "e.g.").

expressio unius est exclusio aiterlus - A rule that is sometimes followed in construing the words of written documents: the express mention of one thing implies the exclusion of others.

expressio unius est exclusio alterius - Also termed inclusio unius est exclusio alterius; expressum facit cessare tacitum - a canon of construction holding that to express or include one thing implies the exclusion of the other, or of the alternative.

exterritorial jurisdiction - A court's ability to exercise power beyond its territorial limits.

falsus in uno, falsus in omnibus - False in one thing, false in every-thing.

FDsys - Federal Digital System (US).

federal question - In litigation, a legal issue involving the interpretation and application of the U.S. Constitution, an act of Congress, or a treaty. Jurisdiction over federal questions rests with the federal courts. 28 USCA § 1331.

felony - A criminal case alleging an offense punishable by imprisonment in a state prison or by death.

ferae naturae - Of a wild nature

fiat -Let it be done. An official proclamation.

flagrante delicto - In the very act of committing the wrong.

Flexibility Clause (E.U.) - The flexibility clause within the Lisbon Treaty, the antecedents of which go back to the Treaty of Rome, allows flexible adjustments of E.U. competence within the defined remit of the E.U. The existing clause can only be used in connection with the common market. The new clause will allow flexibility in all areas of the E.U.

fructus industriales - Fruits of one's industry or labor, e.g., cash crops produced through cultivation, such as tobacco. Compare fructus naturales.

fructus naturales—Products produced by nature alone, e.g., milk, ore. Compare fructus industriales.

fully briefed appeal - A pending appeal in which all briefs have been filed.

G.A. - General Assembly of United Nations.

GATS - General Agreement on Trade in Services.

GATT – General Agreement of Tariffs and Trade.

GPO - United States Government Printing Office.

green paper - an "official," heavily researched report on a topic, or a government document that proposes and invites discussion on approaches to a problem (and may lead to issuance of a "white paper', see below).

habeas corpus – “You have the body.” A writ employed to bring a person before a court, most frequently to ensure that the party's imprisonment or detention is not illegal; refers to various writs whose object is to bring a person before a court, most commonly directing the release of a person from illegal confinement.

haec verba—See in haec verba.

headnote - A one-paragraph summary of a specific point of law decided in a case. Headnotes appear at the beginning of a case, and are usually written by the editors of the publisher of the case reporter in which the decision appears. Some times, however, the judges themselves or other court personnel will prepare these summaries.

heriditaments—Inheritable property.

hornbook – (1) A book explaining the basics of a given subject; (2) A textbook containing the rudimentary principles of an area of law. Cf. Casebook.

hornbook method – A method of legal instruction characterized by a straightforward presentation of legal doctrine, occasionally interspersed with questions. It predominates in the U.S. in certain fields of law, such as procedure and evidence. Cf. Socratic and Casebook methods.

i.e. – “Id est.” - that is.

ibid. – see ibidem.

ibidem - At the same place, e.g., in the same book (typically abbreviated as "ibid."). See also idem.

ICC – International Criminal Court OR international chamber of commerce.

ICJ – International Court of Justice.

ICT – Information and Communication Technologies.

id est - that is (typically abbreviated as "i.e.").

id. “idem.” - See below; at the same place, e.g., in the same book (typically abbreviated as "id."). In legal writing, the abbreviation for “idem” is preferred to “ibid.” for referring to a previously cited reference.

IGC - Intergovernmental Conference (E.U.) - A conference composed of representatives from each E.U. Member State in which amendments to the treaties can be agreed through negotiations.

ILC – UN’s International Law Commission.

in camera - In a chamber. (1) In the judge's private chambers; (2) In the courtroom with all spectators excluded.

in custodia aegis - In legal custody; in the keeping of the law.

in forma pauperis - As a pauper. Refers to permission given to a poor person to sue without paying his or her own court costs.

in haec verba - In these precise words; in the same words.

in limine - At the beginning; preliminarily.

in loco parentis - In the place of a parent.

in pals - Refers to proceedings conducted outside of court; commonly used in contradistinction to written matters or matters of record.

in pari delicto - Equally at fault.

in pari materia - Pertaining to the same subject. A rule that is sometimes followed in construing statutes: statutes dealing with the same subject matter are construed together, that is, in relation to one another, or as a whole.

in personam - Against a person. Descriptive of court actions involving or determining the rights, interests, and obligations of a person. Compare in rem.

in re - In the matter of; concerning; in regard to. The phrase is commonly used in the title of non-adversary judicial proceedings that revolve around a particular thing or person, such as a bankruptcy or guardianship proceeding (for example, "in re John Doe").

in rem - Against a thing. Descriptive of court actions involving or determining the status of a thing, and therefore the rights of persons generally with respect to that thing, such as a right to property. Commonly used to describe legal proceedings taken against a thing or piece of property (for example, a property foreclosure action), as opposed to personal actions. Compare in personam.

in rem jurisdiction (in rem) - A court's power to adjudicate the rights to a given piece of property, including the power to seize and hold it. Also termed jurisdiction in rem. Cf. personal jurisdiction; subject-matter jurisdiction.

in situ - In the original place.

in toto - Completely.

indebitatus assumpsit - An action to recover on a debt. See assumpsit.

indexable web - The publicly indexable Web is limited to those pages that are accessible by following a link from another Web page that is recognized by a search engine

indicia—Signs or indications.

indictment - A criminal complaint issued by a grand jury at the request of a prosecutor and charging a person with a crime. See complaint. Compare information.

information - A criminal complaint issued by a prosecutor (e.g., a district attorney) rather than by a grand jury, and charging a person with a crime. See complaint. Compare indictment.

information retrieval - The processes, methods, and procedures used to selectively recall recorded data from a database.

infra - Below; appearing below. Compare supra.

injunction - An order from a court requiring or commanding someone to do, or not to do, some act. See enjoin, relief, remedy.

intelligent agents – work as personal assistants in the same computer environment as the user. The object of these agents is to act in a way geared towards one certain persona and, in a manner of speaking, independently and intelligently. E.g., they sort through electronic mail according to the respective user's preferences, point out news and offers that could be of interest to the user or come up with suggestions for shopping.

inter alia - Among other things.

inter alios - Among other persons; among those who are strangers to the proceedings.

inter partes - Between or among the parties.

inter se - Among themselves.

inter vivos - Between the living. Frequently used to describe a transaction by which property is passed from one living person to another, as opposed to a transfer by will from a deceased person.

internet - a decentralized global communications network connecting millions of individual users and machines.

Internet protocol (IP) - a part of the TCP/IP suite of protocols that allows the various machines that make up the Internet to communicate with each other.

internet service provider (ISP) - an organization or company that provides access to the Internet. Examples of national-level ISPs include America Online (AOL), Earthlink, and Microsoft Network (MSN).

intra vires - Within the scope of one's powers or authority. Compare ultra vires.

intranet – A private network, within a company or organization, that serves shared applications intended for internal use only – although some may be found on the public Internet.

Ioannina Compromise of 29 March 1994 (E.U.) states that if members of the E.U. Council representing between 23 votes and 26 votes express their intention of opposing the taking of a decision by the Council by qualified majority, the Council will do all within its power, within a reasonable space of time, to reach a satisfactory solution that can be adopted by at least 68 votes out of 87. The Treaty of Nice puts an end to the Ioannina compromise. E.U. Glossary at <http://europa.eu/scadplus/glossary/ioannina_compromise_en.htm>.

IP - see Internet Protocol

IP-address - An identifier for a computer or device on a TCP/IP network. Networks using the TCP/IP protocol route messages based on the IP address of the destination. The format of an IP address is a 32-bit numeric address written as four numbers separated by periods. Each number can be zero to 255 (e.g., "1.160.10.240" could be an IP address).

ipse dixit - A bare assertion that is made, but not proved.

ipso facto - In itself; by virtue of the fact itself.

IRAC – A system used by some U.S. law students to organize their answers to exam questions and to write appellate briefs. I = Issue (question), R = Rule (facts & rules), A= Application (analysis), and C = Conclusion.

ISP – see Internet Service Provider.

IT - Information technology.

ITU - International Telecommunication Union.

ius cogens – see jus cogens

ius commune Europaeum - European "common law". The phrase "the common law of the civil law systems" means those underlying laws that create a distinct legal system and are common to all its elements.

IW - Information Warfare.

j.n.o.v. - Abbreviation for "judgment non obstante veredicto," meaning "judgment notwithstanding the verdict." See non obstante veredicto.

jurisdiction - This term has two different meanings: (1) the authority of a court or other tribunal to take cognizance of a case and to render a decision in it that is legally binding on certain persons or property; and (2) a geographical territory (e.g., a state) in which a particular body of law applies.

jurisprudence – (1) The study of the fundamental elements of a legal system; (2) A system, body, or division of law.

jus cogens – or ius cogens - Peremptory norms of general international law.

key number - The name given by West Publishing Company to its digest system of indexing court decisions. West identifies thousands of narrow, separate points of law discussed in court decisions, designates those points as "sub-topics" under its broader digest topics, and then assigns a permanent "Key Number" to each subtopic. These topics, subtopics, and Key Numbers comprise the digest system West uses for indexing its case reporters. Key Numbers remain constant throughout all West digests and reporters, that is, all cases dealing with a given point of law will be summarized in West's digests under the same topic, subtopic, and Key Number. Publishers of non-West case reporters and digests use similar indexing systems, but there the functional equivalent of a Key Number is called a "section number," or occasionally a "paragraph number."

KeyCite - Westlaw's equivalent to Shepard's/shepardize, that is a citator to determine whether a case or statute is good law and to retrieve citing references.

L.S. - See Locus Sigilli.

Langdell method – see Casebook Method.

Languages of the Treaty of Lisbon (E.U.) - This refers to the languages in which the Treaty is to be drawn up, each version being equally authentic, as set out in Article IV-10, the last article of the Lisbon Treaty.

law-foundation-sources (only with a plural "s") [our reformulation of "sources of law"] - the science / knowledge on/of jurisprudence / origins of legal concepts and ideas. This a highly particular, scientific term, for what a jurist considers regarding what should and what should not be allowed to be a source of law. For example, should "custom" or "legal cultural tradition" be allowed to be a "source of law"? This subject matter is covered in a basic, first-year university course in Civil Law countries. The concept is sometimes even in the U.S. called "sources of law" and deals with what a source of law is, what it should be, and how it arises; how to make interpretations of legal texts; how to use a source or sources of law; and whether there exists any governing hierarchy.

law-source(s) [our reformulation of "sources of law"] - something (such as a constitution, treaty, statute, or custom) that provides authority for legislation and for judicial decisions. This is the normal American understanding in a legal research course. The term is used in this book, except in Chapter 5 (on US legal research methods). Thus, it deals with the concepts of governmental institutions that formulate legal rules and the published manifestations of the law.

lawsuit - A legal proceeding brought in a court in which one or more persons tries to make one or more other persons do something or stop doing something, and/or to pay damages. Other terms sometimes used interchangeably with "lawsuit" are "action," "case," and "cause of action."

Legal Base (E.U.) - In order for the E.U. to have power to act in any area, that area must have what is known as a "legal base" in the treaty structure. Any areas where the E.U. is to have such power must be recognized formally and explicitly in the legal structure of the treaties. The Treaty of Lisbon maintains all areas where there were legal bases previously and creates legal bases in some further, limited areas.

Legitimacy - This is a political concept, relating to whether, or how far, a political system or a set of political arrangements or institutions is regarded as being valid and worthy of acceptance or support by the people who are governed under such arrangements or whose lives are affected by what is done by the institutions.

Lisbon Process or Strategy (E.U.) - Launched at an E.U. summit in Lisbon, Portugal in 2000, the Lisbon Process or Strategy is a voluntary co-ordination (often referred to as the Open Method of Co-ordination) of a whole range of economic, social and sectoral policies among E.U. Member States. It aims to make the E.U. the most competitive and knowledge-based economy in the world by 2010. (Not to be confused with the

Treaty of Lisbon).

lex causa – that nation's law that is used in the case at issue (Private International Law or Conflicts of Law).

lex domicilii - The law of the domicile.

lex ferenda - see de lege ferenda.

lex fori – The law of the nation in which the court dealing with the case at issue is located (Private International Law or Conflicts of Law), that is, where the suit is brought.

lex loci - The law of the place.

lex loci contractus - Either the law of the place where the contract was made, or the law by which the contract is to be governed (which may or may not be the same place) (Private International Law or Conflicts of Law).

lex loci delicti – The law in the nation, where the injury or harm has occurred or where the act has been done (Private International Law or Conflicts of Law).

lex loci solutionis – The law at the place of performance of the contract at issue (Private International Law or Conflicts of Law).

lex posterior derogate priori - A later law repeals an earlier one.

lex posterior generalis non derogate priori speciali - A later law, general in character, does not derogate from an earlier on, which is special in character.

lex rei sitae – see lex situs.

lex situs – lex rei sitae – The law in the nation where the an object or subject in the case at issue is located (Private International Law or Conflicts of Law).

lex specialis derogate generali - A special law prevails over a general law.

liability - Legally enforceable responsibility of one person to pay damages as a result of committing an injurious act or of owing an obligation or debt. See damages.

Lisbon Treaty of December 2007 (E.U.)

lis pendens - A pending lawsuit.

locus delicti - The place or, more usually, the particular state or jurisdiction in which a wrong or offense was committed.

locus sigilli—The place of the seal. The place for the seal on a written document (usually abbreviated as "LS.").

locus standi - The power to apply to a tribunal for a particular remedy; more specifically, the existence of a sufficient legal interest in the matter in issue.

logit regit actum – The law at the place determines the formality (Private International Law or Conflicts of Law).

long-arm statutes – Laws describing exterritorial jurisdiction for each state in United

States.

looseleaf reporter (services) – (1) Fill a gap in the reporting of primary legal authorities by giving the most up-to-date information on case law, statutes, administrative regulations, and developing trends in the law; (2) Treatises that prove the most up-to-date information on case law, statutes, administrative regulations, and developing trends in the law.

Maastricht Treaty = The Treaty on European Union (TEU) of December 1991 [amended by the Amsterdam Treaty].

mala fide - In bad faith. Compare bona fide..

mala in se - Describes acts wrongful in themselves; unconscionable or morally wrong acts. Compare mala prohibita.

mala prohibita - Describes acts that are wrongful because prohibited by law. Compare mala in se.

malum in se - Evil in itself. A crime or act that is inherently immoral, such as murder, arson, or rape. Also termed malum per se.

malum prohibitum - Prohibited evil. An act that is a crime because it is prohibited by statute; the act itself is not necessarily immoral.

mandatory authority - See authority.

Mastricht Treaty – nick-name for the Treaty on European Union of 1992.

mens rea - Guilty mind. Criminal intent; generally coupled with actus reus to establish criminal liability.

MEP – Member of the European Parliament.

mesne - Intermediate; intervening; the middle between two extremes.

model act – Proposed laws written by the Commissioners of United State Laws and the American Law Institute, for example Model Penal Code.

modus operandi - Method of operating.

Mootness Doctrine - The principle that American courts will not decide cases in which there is no longer any actual controversy.

moral turpitude - Conduct that is contrary to justice, honesty, or morality, or that violates accepted community standards.

motion - A request made to a court asking that it do something in a lawsuit. In making a motion, a person is said to "move" the court to do something. Example: "Plaintiff moves the court to have the defendant held in contempt for refusing to answer the question."

municipal law - Municipal law governs the domestic aspects of government and deals with issues between individuals, and between individuals and the administrative apparatus.

mutatis mutandis - With the necessary changes in detail.

N.B. – see nota bene.

NCCUSL - National Conference of Commissioners on Uniform State Laws (in U.S.).

NCCUSL – National Conference of Commissioners on Uniform State Laws.

Ne bis in idem (ne bis idem) - No person should be proceeded against twice over the same matter.

ne exeat - A writ prohibiting a person from leaving the jurisdiction of the court or some other specified place.

NGO - Non-governmental organization.

Nice Treaty of 2001 - A treaty under the European Union.

nisi prius - Denotes a court of first instance; a trial court, as opposed to an appellate court.

nolle prosequi - A declaration that one is unwilling further to prosecute part or all of a case against a defendant.

nolo contendere – "I will not contend." - A plea in which a defendant in a criminal prosecution neither admits nor denies the charges, but agrees to accept punishment determined by the court. No contest.

non compos mentis - Not of sound mind or memory.

non constat – "It does not follow." - Commonly used to refer to conclusions that, although they may appear to follow, do not necessarily follow.

non obstante veredicto - Notwithstanding the verdict. Refers to a judgment entered by court order for a plaintiff or defendant, even though the jury has returned a verdict against that party.

non sequitur - Something that does not follow.

nota bene - An instruction to "note well" (frequently abbreviated as "N.B.").

nudum pactum - A promise made without legal consideration, such as a promise supported by mere good will or affection.

nulla crimen sine lege - There is no crime in the absence of (applicable) law when and where an act is committed.

nulla poena sine lege - An individual may be considered criminally responsible only for conduct which was unambiguously criminal at the time of its commission and must be sentenced in accordance with law.

nunc pro tunc - Now for then. Refers to an action having retroactive effect.

OJ – Official Journal of European Union.

obiter dicta - see obiter dictum.

obiter dictum – (1) Statements by a court in an opinion that are not necessary to the decision of the case; gratuitous or incidental commentary by a judge; (2) A statement of opinion or belief considered authoritative due to the dignity of the person making it; (3) A familiar rule; a maxim.

ODR - Online Dispute Resolutions.

OECD - Organization for Economic Cooperation and Development.

OEEC – Organization of European Economic Cooperation.

Opinion - A statement by a judge or court or other tribunal of the rationale followed in reaching the result (e.g., reversal or affirmance) in a particular case. See also concurring opinion, dissent, per curiam and plurality opinion.

original proceedings - Cases commenced in an appellate court, commonly called writ proceedings. The most common are writs of mandamus and prohibition, usually seeking an order addressed to lower court, and writs of habeas corpus, usually addressed to a person holding another in official custody.

original proceedings - Petitions for writs within the state supreme court's original jurisdiction. The most common types are mandamus and prohibition, which may relate to either civil or criminal matters, and habeas corpus.

pacta sunt servanda - The principle that agreements are binding (and are to be implemented in good faith).

parallel citation – (1) The additional, equivalent title or identification (see citation) of a single court decision's verbatim; (2) Citations to additional reporters where the text or an opinion can be found.

part material - See in pari materia.

part passu - On equal footing.

particeps criminis - A criminal accomplice; partner in crime.

party - A participant in a transaction or proceeding, e.g., party to a contract, party to a lawsuit. In a lawsuit, the most common parties are plaintiffs and defendants, although there are also other kinds of parties, such as third-party plaintiffs, third-party defendants, and intervenors.

PCIJ – Permanent Court of International Justice.

pendente lite - During the progress of a lawsuit.

per curiam - By the court. When a court sits by a panel of judges, this term is used to designate an opinion written by the whole court, rather than by one particular judge.

per diem - By the day. A charge, fee, or allowance calculated by the day.

per se - In and of itself; inherently.

persona non grata - A person who is considered unacceptable.

personal jurisdiction – A court's power to bring a person into its adjudicative process.

persuasive authority, see authority. A court's power to bring a person into its adjudicative process; jurisdiction over a defendant's personal rights, rather than merely over property interests. -- Also termed in personam jurisdiction; jurisdiction in personam; jurisdiction of the person; jurisdiction over the person. Cf. in rem jurisdiction.

Petersberg Tasks (E.U.) - In the Maastricht Treaty of 1992, the Member States of the E.U. undertook to enhance co-operation on international affairs through the Common Foreign and Security Policy. The Treaty of Amsterdam, 1997 reflects new priorities of humanitarian, rescue, peacekeeping and crisis management tasks – the Petersberg tasks (called after the venue in Germany where agreement on them was reached) – by incorporating these tasks into the European E.U.'s Common Foreign and Security Policy. The Lisbon Treaty extends the tasks to cover joint disarmament operations, military advice and post-conflict stabilisation.

petition - A formal written application to a government body requesting that the tribunal exercise its authority to achieve a particular effect; a complaint is an example of one kind of petition.

petition for review - A request for state supreme court review of a state court of appeal decision.

petition for review denied - An order by the state supreme court declining review of a state court of appeal decision.

petition for review granted and held - An order by the state supreme court granting review of a state court of appeal decision that will be held until a lead case addressing a related issue has been decided by the state supreme court.

petition for review granted and transferred - Any order by the state supreme court granting review of a state Court of Appeal decision but transferring review of the case to a state court of appeal without additional action by the state supreme court.

petitioner - The person who files a petition. See petition. See also appellant.

plaintiff - The person who brings a civil action by filing a complaint in a court. There can be more than one plaintiff in a lawsuit. In a criminal action, the plaintiff is called the "prosecution" or "the government."

plaintiff in error - Another term for an appellant. See appellant.

pleading - The written statement containing a party's allegations about each point or issue involved in the lawsuit. In civil actions, the principal pleadings are the complaint, filed by the plaintiff, and the answer, which is filed by the defendant and which responds to the complaint. See allegation, answer, complaint.

plurality opinion - When a court has a panel of judges ruling on a single case and no opinion of any one judge in the case obtains the agreement of the majority of judges participating, the plurality opinion is the opinion with which most of the judges on the panel agree.

pocket-parts – publishers' updating pamphlets to be inserted in a slot (a "pocket") in the cover of the hardbound volume of case digests, annotated statutes, treatises, legal encyclopediea, and ALR.

posse comitatus - The power or force of the county; the populace of a county that a sheriff may summon in certain cases to help keep the peace, make arrests, etc.

POTUS – President of the Unites States.

presentment—A statement issued by a grand jury without a prosecutor's participation and charging that a crime has been committed.

prima facie - On the face of it; at first blush. Refers to something initially presumed to be true until the appearance of some evidence to the contrary.

primary authority - See authority.

principle of conferral (E.U.) - The principle of conferral means that the E.U. does not have general competences in its own right, but only those that are specifically conferred upon it by the Member States in the founding treaties and their subsequent modifications. The E.U. can only act on the basis of a provision of the treaties that authorises it to do so. In treaty terms, competence means the legal capacity or ability to legislate or to take other action.

Principle of Loyal Cooperation (E.U.) - The principle which commits the E.U. and its individual Member States to assist each other in carrying out tasks, common or coordinated, which flow from the obligations they have assumed and refrain from acting in ways that would block or impede discharge of those tasks.

pro bono - For the good. Descriptive of legal services provided free of charge, especially legal services provided for the public good.

pro bono publico - For the public good.

pro forma - As a matter of form.

pro hac vice - For this one particular occasion.

proportionality (E.U.) - The principle that E.U. action must not exceed what is necessary to achieve the objectives of the Treaties.

pro se - For oneself. Descriptive of one who represents oneself in court, without the assistance of legal counsel.

pro tanto - To that extent; as far as it goes.

pro tempore - For the time being; temporarily.

profit a prendre - The right to take the fruits, or profits, from the land of another, such as the right to cut and remove timber from another's land.

pur autre vie - For or during the life of another. Denotes an estate in land which a person holds during the life-time of another designated person.

q.c.f. - Abbreviation for "quare clausum fregit." See below.

QMV, see Qualified Majority Voting.

quaere - A query; question; doubt. Frequently used to indicate that the point or statement that follows is open to question.

qualified majority voting (QMV) (E.U.) - QMV is the form of decisionmaking used for most Council of Ministers decisions. Currently, each E.U. Member State is assigned a number of votes weighted according to a scale which groups together E.U. Member States of similar population size. Under the Lisbon Treaty a new system of QMV will apply, based on a “Double Majority”.

quantum meruit - The amount a person deserves as compensation for services rendered.

quare clausum fregit - Because he broke the close. Refers to a type of legal proceeding for trespass—specifically, "breaking a close," meaning unlawfully entering upon another person's land.

quasi-in-rem jurisdiction - Jurisdiction over a person but based on that person's interest in property located within the court's territory. Also termed jurisdiction quasi in rem.

quid pro quo - Something for something. Refers to the giving of one thing of value for another thing of value.

quo warranto - By what authority? Refers to legal proceedings undertaken to ascertain whether an officer is acting within the scope of the authority granted him by law.

ratio - ratio decidendi - The principal proposition or propositions of law determining the outcome of a case; or, the only legal consideration necessary for the decision of a particular case.

ratione materiae - By reason of the subject-matter.

ratione personae - Determined by the status and dignity of the person or entity as such.

ratione temporis - Conditioned by reference to time.

re - In regard to. Commonly used to designate legal proceedings in which there is only one party. See in re.

real property - Land and anything permanently attached to it.

real-time audio/video - Communication of either sound or images over the Internet that occurs without delay in real time, much like a telephone conversation.

reasoned opinion E.U.) - (1) The European Commission scrutinises steps taken by each Member State to implement E.U. law and, if dissatisfied, may issue what is known as a “reasoned opinion” to Member States governments. This is a sort of “early warning system” within which the Commission outlines the measures that will need to be taken in order for the E.U. Member State (s) to fully implement the E.U. law in question.

Should these measures not be taken, then the Commission refers the matter to the European Court of Justice; (2) A second meaning of the term arises in the protocol of the Lisbon Treaty on applying the principles of proportionality. There, the term refers to an opinion with reasons, put forward by a national parliament (or one of its Houses) that a proposal for a law, made by the Commission, is in breach of the principle of subsidiarity. In this case, a reasoned opinion is part of an "early warning system", to be operated by national parliaments.

rebus sic stantibus - The implication of a term that the obligations of an agreement come to an end with a change of circumstances.

recall - A measure of the effectiveness of document retrieval expressed as a ratio of the total number of relevant documents in a given database (or on the Web) to the number of relevant entries or documents retrieved in response to a specific search. However, determining a search's recall can be problematic because it is often very difficult to determine the total number of relevant entries in all but very small databases. Contrast with precision.

RECOP - Report of Current Opinions (US).

record filed - The filing of the trial court clerk's transcripts (copies of documents filed in the case) and the reporter's transcript (the typed version of oral proceedings).

reduced to misdemeanor - Cases in which a charge original filed as a felony is disposed of as a misdemeanor.

Reform Treaty – see Lisbon Treaty

regulation - A directive issued by a government agency, pursuant to statutory authority, to implement and carry out a governmental policy or program. Unless invalidated by a court or rescinded by the agency, a regulation has the effect of law and binds those over whom the agency has regulatory power. Regulations are also referred to as "rules."

rehearing en banc – All the judges of a court sitting together to rehear a case in a panel (or more precisely, the number of judges required by local court rules "to make a full bench")

relief - Assistance or redress given to a party in a civil or criminal action when the court determines the party has a right to it. A temporary injunction is an example of the kind of relief a court has the power to grant. See, and compare with, remedy.

remand - To send back, as when an appellate court returns a case to a trial court for further proceedings.

remedy - Something that corrects a violation of civil or criminal law. Unlike relief, which can be given before, during, or after trial, a remedy is given only after an injury has been fully proved to a court. In short, a remedy is always relief, but relief is not always a remedy). Damages and permanent injunctions are two kinds of remedies in civil cases. Imprisonment, restitution, and fines are types of remedies available in criminal cases. See, and compare with, relief.

remote viewing - the capability of system administrators (whether they be IT "helpdesk" personnel or teachers in a classroom) to view what is being displayed on a given workstation or computer from their own location.

reply - A pleading sometimes made by a plaintiff in response to a defendant's answer. See pleading, answer.

reporters - Published volumes containing court decisions arranged chronologically by date of decision.

request for publication or depublication - A case in which the sole relief requested is for the state supreme court to order that a state court of appeal decision be either published or depublished.

res – Resolution; thing; object; property.

res adjudicate - A common but less preferred spelling of 'res judicata." See res judicata.

res gestae - The whole of a transaction, including all its incidental circumstances. In the law of evidence, the phrase is often used to denote one exception to the hearsay rule allowing the admission of evidence about acts and declarations surrounding the event under investigation.

res inter alios acta - A matter affecting third parties and not opposable to the legal persons between whom there is an issue.

res ipsa loquitur—The thing speaks for itself. Refers to the rebuttable presumption that a defendant who had the injury-causing instrumentality in his exclusive control must have been negligent because the accident in question would not normally have occurred without negligence in connection with the instrumentality. A tort law doctrine permitting the presumption of negligence if an accident is of a kind that ordinarily would not occur without the defendant's negligence.

res judicata - A thing adjudicated. A claim, issue, or cause of action conclusively settled by a judgment and no longer open to litigation. The principle that an issue decided by a court should not be reopened. A doctrine in civil law to the general effect that matters fully and finally adjudicated on their merits between or among parties to a lawsuit may not subsequently be re-litigated by or among those same parties, or their privies.

res nullius - An asset susceptible of acquisition but presently under the ownership or sovereignty of no legal person.

respondeat superior - Let the master answer. A doctrine in civil law by which a master (or principal) generally is liable or answerable for the wrongful acts of his servant (or agent).

respondent - A term sometimes used interchangeably with "appellee." See appellee.

restatement – Overview of law published by the American Law Institute. A leading scholar – selected as "reporter" for each legal topic – has the task to absorb all the existing case-law and extract general rules, after where a group of advisers and the reporter will formulate a text to be published as a "restatement." The task of the reporter is to lay down the law in its present positive form – not to improve or modernize it.

ripeness - (1) The circumstance existing when a case has reached, but has not passed, the point when the facts have developed sufficiently to permit an intelligent and useful decision to be made. (2) The requirement that this circumstance must exist before a court will decide a controversy. The opposite of the Mootness Doctrine.

rubric – (1) A title, category, or designation; (2) An established rule, tradition, or custom.

rule - see regulation.

sanction – 1) Official authorization; 2) A punitive or coercive measure resulting from a failure to comply with a law, rule, or court order.

scienter - To know. Guilty knowledge of the criminal, misleading, or manipulative nature of one's act or omission.

SCOTUS – Supreme court of the United States.

SEA - E.U. Single European Act of 1986

seriatim—One at a time; serially.

services of general interest (E.U.) - This is an expression in the E.U. treaties to describe telecommunications, water, postal, transport services and other infrastructure in the E.U. Member States, as well as education, health, that are widely regarded as basic necessities for a satisfactory life under modern conditions in Europe.

Session Laws – The compiled slip laws of a designated legislative session, bound together in chronological, pre-code form.

Seville Declaration (E.U.) - Solemn declarations by the Irish Government and the European Council in 2002 relating to Ireland's participation in the Common Security and Defence Policy.

Schengen Acquis - The body of legal provisions now incorporated into E.U. law and originally being two agreements concluded among European states in 1985 and 1990, which deal with the abolition of systematic border controls among the participating countries. Also termed the Schengen Agreement.

Shepard's – see shepardize.

shepardize – or Shepard's or KeyCite - To determine the subsequent history of a case, that is, has a case been overruled, modified, followed, criticized, distinguished etc., or has a statute been overruled by case law. In the early 1870's, Frank Shepard realized the necessity for tracking the discussion of principles of law in court opinions, and also tracking the history of these opinions. Thus, he devised a method for extracting this information and indexing it for the benefit of legal researchers. Today, the system is owned by LexisNexis. See also KeyCite (Westlaw)

sic - Thus; in this manner. Frequently used to indicate a mistake in an original writing being quoted.

sine die - Without assigning a date for a further meeting or hearing. Frequently used to refer to a final adjournment.

slip law – Legislative, at state and federal levels, in its first printed form; the first official text or enacted statutes. A statute published in pamphlet or single sheet form soon after its passage.

slip opinion - An individual court decision published separately from other opinions, and soon after it is rendered.

Socratic Method – A technique of philosophical discussion – and of U.S. law-school instruction – by which the questioner (a law professor) questions one or more followers (the law students), building on each answer with another question, especially an analogy incorporating the answer. The method forces law students to think through issues rationally and deductively – a skill required in the practice of common law. Also termed question-an-answer.

soft law - Refers to quasi-legal instruments which do not have any legally binding force, or whose binding force is somewhat "weaker' than the binding force of traditional law. Also, it is associated with international law. See also the book's index.

solidarity clause (E.U.) - A clause contained in the Lisbon Treaty committing the E.U. and its Member States to aid another Member State(s) if that Member State(s) is/are the victim of either a terrorist attack or natural or man-made disaster.

solvitur ambulando - "It is solved by walking," that is, the problem is solved by a practical experiment.

sources of law – see law-foundation-sources and law-source(s)

special legislative procedure (E.U.) - A number of areas outlined in the Lisbon Treaty lie outside the remit of the Ordinary Legislative Procedure and fall under what is described as a "Special Legislative Procedure". Decision-making procedures vary and may allow for a dominant role for either the Council of Ministers or the European Parliament. In some cases, proposals may come from sources other than the Commission. Unanimity is also allowed for in some cases.

stare decisis - To stand by things decided. The doctrine of precedent, under which a court or tribunal should follow its own previous decisions and those of other tribunals of equal or greater authority when the similar facts, regardless of whether the parties are the same, arise again in litigation - unless there is a compelling reason not to.

status quo—The existing state of things.

Stability and Growth Pact (E.U.) - An agreement introduced in the lead-up to monetary E.U. , the aim of the Stability and Growth Pact is to ensure that the E.U. Member States continued their budgetary discipline efforts once the single currency was introduced. The pact details technical arrangements on surveillance of budgetary positions as well as co-ordination of economic policies and implementation of an excessive deficit procedure, allowing the Council to penalise any participating Member State which fails to take appropriate measures to end an excessive budget deficit. In the medium term, the Member States have undertaken to pursue the objective of a balanced or nearly balanced budget.

sua sponte - On a person's or court's own motion; voluntarily; without prompting.

subpoena - Under penalty. A writ commanding a person's presence before a court or other tribunal, under threat of penalty. A court order compelling a person to appear and give testimony on a certain matter. See "subpoena duces tecum."

subpoena duces tecum - A writ, process, or order directing a person to produce or deliver certain papers or things in his possession or control.

subsidiarity (E.U.) - The principle that the European E.U. does not take action (in areas of shared competence) unless it is more effective than action taken at national, regional or local level.

sui generis - In a class by itself; the only one of its kind.

suit - See lawsuit. Also called "action."

summons - A notice delivered by a sheriff or other officer informing someone that a civil action has been commenced against him or her, and that he or she is required to appear as a defendant in court on a certain date to answer the complaint.

supranational (E.U.) - In the context of the E.U., the term usually refers to the institutions that exist to pursue the common E.U. interests, shared by the E.U. Member States. It also refers to the discharge of functions and exercise of powers by those institutions, transcending national boundaries, in the domains where the E.U. Member States, in the treaties, have conferred those functions and powers on them. The supranational approach is often contrasted with the intergovernmental approach that involves keeping supranational institutions, and their role, to a minimum.

supersedeas - Name of a writ ordering a stay in legal proceedings, such as the suspension of enforcement of a lower court judgment pending an appeal.

supra - Above; appearing above. Compare infra.

syllabus - (1) An abstract or outline of a topic or course of study. (2) a headnote. The syllabus constitutes no part of the opinion of the court but has been prepared by the reporter of decisions for the convenience of the reader.

syllogism - (1) A deductive scheme of a formal argument consisting of a major and a minor premise and a conclusion (as in "every virtue is laudable; kindness is a virtue; therefore kindness is laudable"); (2) a subtle, specious, or crafty argument; (3) deductive reasoning (Merriam-Webster Dictionary).

TCE - Treaty establishing a Constitution for Europe (not in force).

TEC – Treaty establishing the European Community.

TED (Tenders Electronic Daily) - Supplement to the Official Journal of the European Union (OJ S).

TEU – Treaty on European Union = Maastricht Treaty.

TFEU –see Treaty on the Functioning of the European Union

Thomas - Legislative information from the Library of U.S. Congress (named after Thomas Jefferson), available at <Thomas.loc.gov>.

Treaty of Athens 2003 - E.U. Treaty of Accession 2003 - Agreement between the European Union and ten countries (Czech Republic, Estonia, Cyprus, Latvia, Lithuania, Hungary, Malta, Poland, Slovenia, Slovakia), concerning these countries' accession into the E.U.

Treaty of Luxembourg 2005 - Treaty of Accession 2005 - Agreement between the member states of European Union and Bulgaria and Romania, concerning these countries' accession into the E.U.

Treaty on the Functioning of the European Union (TFEU) - The Lisbon Treaty of 2007's rename of The Treaty of Rome of 25 March 1957 = Treaty establishing the European Economic Community (EEC into force on 1 January 1958), which by the Maastricht Treaty of 1993 was renamed the Treaty establishing the European Community (TEC).

Three Pillars (of the European Union) – A categorization of the subject matters dealt with in the treaties creating the E.U.

Three Strike rule - A minimum sentence of imprisonment in a state prison for 25 years if a defendant has three or more prior felony convictions (including from another state), e.g. California Penal Code §§ 667 and 1170.12.

tort - A civil wrong for which a remedy (usually damages) may be obtained. A civil (that is, private) injury other than a breach of contract. It is different from a crime, which is considered an injury to the public even though just one person may be directly injured. A tort has three elements: (1) a legal duty that the defendant owes to the plaintiff; (2) a violation of that duty; and (3) an injury to the plaintiff resulting from that violation. Often, the same act that constitutes a tort is also a crime, and the person who commits it can be prosecuted both criminally by the government and civilly by or on behalf of the individual directly harmed. For example, if Doe deliberately shoots Roe, Doe has committed a battery that is both a tort and a crime. The government can prosecute Doe criminally, and Roe can sue Doe civilly to try to get money (that is, damages) for his injuries

tortfeasor - One who commits a tort; a wrongdoer.

travaux préparatoires - Preparatory work; preliminary drafts, minutes of conferences, and the like, relating to the conclusion of a treaty.

trial de novo - A new trial in which all the issues of fact and law are reconsidered, as if no previous trial had taken place.

U.S.C. - United States Code.

U.S.C.A. - United States Code Annotated.

U.S.C.S. – United States Code Service.

UfR – Danish case repoter using the following citation form: <"UfR" "year.page" "abbreviation in court hierarchy">: H = Supreme Court of Denmark – Højesteret - Information in English at <www.hoejesteret.dk/?id=303>; Ø = Easter Appeal Court - Østre Landsret; V = Western Appeal Court - Vestre Landsret; SH = The Maritime and Commercial Court - Sø- og Handelsretten i København; No letter = lowest Danish court (but not necessary being first instance court).

UKSC – United Kingdom Supreme Court

ultra vires - In excess of one's powers. Compare intra vires.

UN – United Nations.

UNCITRAL - United Nations Commission on International Trade Law.

UNCTAD - United Nations Conference on Trade and Development.

UNECE - United Nations Economic Commission for Europe.

Uniform Acts – Drafts for desirable areas for intra-American unification of law made by National Conference of Commissioners on Uniform State Laws (NCCUSL).

Uniform System of Citation, see Bluebook

USCCAN - United States Code Congressional and Administrative News - is a West Group publication that collects selected Congressional and administrative materials for publication in a single resource. USCCAN is published in monthly pamphlets that contain a cumulative subject index and cumulative Table of Laws Enacted in addition to the selected documents. Among other documents, USCCAN. publishes the full text of new federal laws, selected committee reports from thc House and Senate, signing statements, presidential proclamations, executive orders, reorganization plans, President's messages, Federal Regulations, proposed constitutional amendments, Federal court rules, and sentencing guidelines all arranged in chronological order. When published in bound volumes, the legislative history documents are placed in separate volumes apart from the rest of the materials published by USCCAN.

Uxor - Wife.

vel non - Or not; whether or not.

Vendor-neutral citation – a movement in the United States away from citing cases to bound, often commercial, reporters to citing by more a universal means (such as, for example, to title of case, docket number assigned by the court and specific paragraph number – all which remain constant regardless of publication format).

venire – To appear in court. The name of a writ summoning a jury (also called a "venire facias"). "Venire" is also used to refer to the list of names of jurors thus summoned.

venue - The proper or a possible place for the trial of a lawsuit, usually because the place has a connection with the events that have given rise to the lawsuit.

vi et armis - By force and arms.

viz. - To wit; that is to say.

voir dire—To speak the truth. A preliminary examination by a judge or lawyer to test the suitability of witnesses or prospective jurors, conducted to explore competency, conflict of interest, etc., which may be grounds for objection to their qualifications either to serve as jurors or give testimony as witnesses.

volenti non fit injuria - One who consents to injury cannot sue for damage suffered.

white paper - an official report setting out government policy on an issue to be voted on by the country's parliament (compare with “green paper”).

WIPO - World Intellectual Property organization.

writ - A written court order commanding the addressee to perform or refrain from performing a specified act, or giving authority to have it done.

WTO - World Trade Organization.

2. Citations and Signals for U.S. material

CITATIONS

Citation identifies a legal authority or reference work.

The universities of Columbia, Harvard, Pennsylvania and Yale together publish the "Bluebook" ("A Uniform System of Citations"), which contains technical rules about citation form in, e.g., citing cases, statutes, administrative rules, books, legal encyclopedias and law reviews.

The Association of Legal Writing Directors has created an alternative, the ALWD Citation Manual, which contains one system for all legal documents, making no distinction between law review articles and other types of writing. The Manual has been adopted by professors at more than ninety law schools, many paralegal programs, and a number of law reviews, moot court competitions, and courts.[1]

The New York University, Journal of International Law and Politics published in 2006 a Guide to Foreign and International Legal Citation (GFILC).[2]

If one has access to Westcheck this feature should be used to check citations before delivering a dissertation (start the computer process and take a long coffee-break – if the paper is too long, divide it into parts and check each part).

The following subsections will give the most normal and relevant rules for citation in the U.S.

[1] <www.alwd.org/cm/>, The ALWD Citation Manual: A Professional System of Citation (Third Edition by Darby Dickerson).

[2] The GFILC is available for free download at <www.law.nyu.edu/journals/jilp/gfilc.html >. The GFILC is also available in spiral-bound, paperback form by sending U.S.$ 20 payable to "Journal of International Law and Politics" to: Circulation Department, Journal of International Law and Politics, 110 West Third Street, New York NY 10012, USA.

Research Tip #Appendix 2

REMEMBER: Under the U.S. citations system to ALSO pin-point the page referring to the quotation one makes. Thus, giving only the first page of the source is not enough.

Cases

The standard case citation contains:

1. Name of the case
2. Published sources in which one can find the case
3. Information in parentheses indicating:
   - the year the decision was issued, and
   - when not apparent from the name of the cited reporter volume,
   - the court which issued the decision; and
4. Prior or subsequent history, if any, of the case

Example for footnotes:
Adam v. Saenger, 303 U.S. 59, 62 (US 1938)
United States v. Layton, 509 F.Supp 212, 216 (N.D.Cal., 1981), appeal dismissed, 645 F.2d 681 (9th Cir. 1981), cert. denied, 452 U.S. 972 (US 1981).

The Bluebook specifies for each case reporter when a parallel citation should be provided as part of a standard citation. There are several ways to find a parallel citation if one only knows the citation of one reprint of a case:

- Check the decision. If a parallel citation exists, the case caption may list it.
- Check the Table of Cases found in the case digest that summarizes decisions of the court that issued the decision in which one is interested. If there is a parallel citation for the decision, one will find it listed with the title of the decision in this table
- Check the Shepard's Citations that treat the decision in which one is interested. In the Shepard's table for the decision, one will normally find the parallel citation in parentheses as the first entry. If one does not find this parenthetical citation, it means (a) the parallel citation is contained in another volume of the same Shepard's set; (b) the parallel reprint has not been published yet; or (c) there is not / and will not be – a parallel reprint of the decision
- Check West's National Reporter Blue Book or (for selected states) West's Blue and White Books. These series of charts provide parallel West reporter citations for state decisions also published in official

non-West reporters. The national edition's charts also cross-reference parallel citations between the official U.S. Reports and West's Supreme Court Reporter.

Statutes

Federal statutes are cited to either:

- the United States Code (U.S.C.), which is the preferred source, or to
- the Statutes of Large (Stat.)

<u>Citation of the United States Code</u>

1. Number of the Code title (each title dealing with a particular subject matter)
2. Abbreviation ("U.S.C.")
3. Statutory section number within the title
4. Date of the edition or supplement

<u>Citation of the Statutes of Large</u>

1. Name of the act
2. Public law or chapter number
3. Volume number of the Statutes at Large
4. Abbreviation ("Stat.")
5. Page on which the cited statute begins
6. Year the statute was enacted

Administrative Law

A citation to the Code of Federal Regulations ("C.F.R.) include:

1. Number of the C.F.R. title (each title dealing with a particular subject matter)
2. Abbreviation ("C.F.R.")
3. Section number
4. Year of publication

A citation to the Federal Register ("Fed.Reg.") includes:

1. Volume number (a volume runs for the calendar year)
2. Abbreviation ("Fed.Reg.")
3. Page number on which the cited material begins
4. Year of publication

Books

Book citations include:

1. Volume number
2. First initial and last name of each author

3. Full main title as it appears on the title page (but not any subtitle)
4. Particular page, section, or paragraph the reader should look at (where appropriate)
5. Edition of the book (if there has been more than one edition)
6. Publication date

The Bluebook has a number of rules for citing books when the general rule does not cover the situation, such as when the book:

- is a translation
- has several editors
- has several authors

Examples for footnotes:
Rosalyn Higgins, PROBLEMS & PROCESS – INTERNATIONAL LAW AND HOW WE USE IT (Clarendon Press, Oxford 1994 – ISBN 0-19-876410-3)

Henrik Spang-Hanssen, Cybercrime and Jurisdiction in Denmark in CYBER-CRIME AND JURISDICTION - A GLOBAL SURVEY (Ed. Bert-Jaap Koops & and Susan W. Brenner, 2006 T.M.C. Asser Press, The Hague – ISBN 9067042218)

K. Zweigert & H.Kötz, INTRODUCTION TO COMPARATIVE LAW (3rd ed.)(Tony Weir trans., Clarendon Press, Oxford 1998)

Legal Encyclopedias

Citations to the two leading U.S. national legal encyclopedias – Corpus Juris Secundum ("C.J.S.") and American Jurisprudence 2d ("Am.Jur.2d") – have the following common elements:

1. Volume number of the encyclopedia
2. Abbreviated name of the encyclopedia ("C.J.S." or "Am.Jur.2d")
3. Title of the topic in the encyclopedia
4. Section number within the topic
5. Specific page (if any) being cited within the section
6. Date of publication of the volume, as well as any pocket part for the encyclopedia if the reader is being specially referred to material in it

Law Reviews

The usual citation to a law review article includes:

1. Last name of the author of the article
2. Title of the article
3. Volume number of the law review (if there is no volume number, then year of publication)

4. Abbreviated name of the law review (see the Bluebook's abbreviations list)
5. Page on which the article begins
6. Year of publication in parentheses (if not already included elsewhere in the citation)

> Examples for footnotes:
> Lawrence Lessig, Legal Issues in Cyberspace: Hazards on the Information Superhigh-way: Reading the Constitution in Cyberspace, 45 EMORY.L.J. 869, 899 (1996)
>
> Examples of articles on the www:
> Henrik Spang-Hanssen, The earthly chaos in websites - question of jurisdiction and net-censorship (2001) at <www.hssph.net/Article1.html>

SIGNALS

Citations are frequently introduced by words called "signals." These words indicate how the writer wants one to view the cited authority in connection with the principle that the citation relates to. The signal provides a concise shorthand context for the citation.
The most common signals are:

- See generally - Indicates the cited authority provides useful background information about a given point.
- See, e.g. - Indicates that the cited authority directly supports a proposition. It further indicates that other authorities also could have been cited for the same proposition, but that no purpose would be served by citing them all because their citation would be merely duplicative.
- Cf. - Indicates that the cited authority states a proposition. Different from that stated by the person citing to the authority, but that the cited authority's proposition is sufficiently analogous to lend support.
- Contra - Indicates that the cited authority contradicts a given point.
- Id. – idem – same as just before.
- Supra – (superus) above (mentioned).
- Cert. Denied – Supreme Court denied certiorari.
- Cert. Dismissed – Supreme Court dismissed certiorari.
- Aff'd – affirmed.
- Reh'g – rehearing.
- Rev. – revised / revised.

3. Courts in U.S. Federal Circuits[1]

State	No	Abbrev	1	2	3	4	5	6	7	8	9	10	11
Alabama	22	Ala											11*
Alaska	49	Alaska									9		
Arizona	48	Ariz.									9		
Arkansas	25	Ark.								8			
California	31	Cal.									9		
Colorado	38	Colo.										10	
Connecticut	5	Conn.		2									
Delaware	1	Del.			3								
District of Columbia		D.C.											
Florida	27	Fla.											11*
Georgia	4	Ga.											11*
Guam		Guam									9		
Hawaii	50	Haw.									9		
Idaho	43	Idaho									9		
Illinois	21	Ill.							7				
Indiana	19	Ind.							7				
Iowa	29	Iowa								8			
Kansas	34	Kan.										10	
Kentucky	15	Ky.						6					
Louisiana	18	La.					5						
Maine	23	Me.	1										
Maryland	7	Md.				4							
Massachusetts	6	Mass.	1										
Michigan	26	Mich.						6					
Minnesota	32	Minn.								8			
Mississippi	20	Miss.					5						
Missouri	24	Mo.								8			
Montana	41	Mont.									9		
Nebraska	42	Neb.								8			
Nevada	36	Nev.									9		
New Hampshire	9	N.H.	1										
New Jersey	3	N.J.			3								
New Mexico	47	N.M.										10	
New York	11	N.Y.		2									

[1] Source: Henrik Spang-Hanssen, CYBERSPACE JURISDICTION IN THE U.S: THE INTERNATIONAL DIMENSION OF DUE PROCESS Appendix C (Complex 5/01, Norwegian Research Center For Computers and Law, Oslo University 2001). Also free downloading from website <www.hssph.net/legalrm>.

North Carolina	12	N.C.				4							
North Dakota	39	N.D.								8			
North Mariana Islands		N.Mar.I.									9		
Ohio	17	Ohio						6					
Oklahoma	46	Okla.										10	
Oregon	33	Or.									9		
Pennsylvania	2	Pa.			3								
Porto Rico		P.R.	1										
Rhode Island	13	R.I.	1										
South Carolina	8	S.C.				4							
South Dakota	40	S.D.								8			
Tennessee	16	Tenn.						6					
Texas	28	Tex.					5						
Utah	45	Utah										10	
Vermont	14	Vt.		2									
Virginia	10	Va.				4							
Virgin Islands		V.I.			3								
Washington	42	Wash.									9		
West Virginia	35	W.Va.											
Wisconsin	30	Wis.							7				
Wyoming	44	Wyo.										10	

* Until October 1, 1981 part of the 5th Circuit

4. U.S. Library of Congress Classification System

A General works
- AC Collections
- AE Encyclopedias
- AG Dictionaries
- AI Indexes
- AM Museums
- AN Newspapers
- AP Periodicals
- AS Academies and learned societies
- AY Yearbooks. Almanacs. Directories
- AZ History of scholarship. The humanities

B Philosophy. Psychology. Religion
- B Philosophy. (General)
- BC Logic
- BD Speculative philosophy
- BF Psychology
- BH Aesthetics
- BJ Ethics
- BL Religion. Mythology. Rationism
- BM Judaism
- BP Islam. Bahaism. Theosophy, etc.
- BQ Buddhism
- BR Christianity
- BS The Bible
- BT Doctrinal theology
- BV Practical theology
- BX Christian denominations

C Auxiliary sciences of history (General)
- CB History of civilization
- CC Archaeology
- CD Diplomatics. Archives. Seals
- CE Technical chronology. Calendar
- CJ Numismatics
- CN Inscriptions. Epigraphy
- CR Heraldry
- CS Genealogy
- CT Biography (General)

D History (General) Europe (General)
- DA Great Britain
- DAW Central Europe
- DB Austria. Hungary. Czechoslovakia
- DC France
- DD Germany
- DE The Greco-Roman World
- DF Greece
- DG Italy
- DH Low Countries. Benelux Countries
- DJ Netherlands (Holland)
- DJK Eastern Europe (General)
- DK Russia. Soviet Union. Former Soviet Republics. Poland
- DL Northern Europe. Scandinavia
- DP Spain. Portugal
- DQ Switzerland
- DR Balkan Peninsula. Turkey
- DS Asia
- DT Africa
- DU Oceania (South Seas)
- DX Gypsies

E-F History: America
- E United States (General)
- F United States local history. Canada. Latin America

G Geography. Anthropology. Recreation
- G Geography. (General). Atlases. Maps
- GA Mathematical geography. Cartography
- GB Physical geography
- GC Oceanography
- GE Environmental sciences
- GF Human ecology. Anthropogeography
- GN Anthropology
- GR Folklore
- GT Manners and customs (General)
- GV Recreation. Leisure

H Social Sciences
- H Social Sciences (General)
- HA Statistics
- HB Economic theory. Demography
- HC Economic history and conditions
- HD Industries. Land Use. Labor
- HE Transportation and communications
- HF Commerce
- HG Finance
- HJ Public finance
- HM Sociology (General)
- HN Social history and conditions. Social problems. Social reform
- HQ The family. Marriage. Women
- HS Societies: secret, benevolent, etc.
- HT Communities. Classes. Races
- HV Social pathology. Social and public welfare
- HX Socialism. Communism. Anarchism

J Political Science
- J General legislative and executive papers
- JA Political science (General)
- JC Political theory
- JF Political institutions and public administration — General
- JK Political institutions and public administration — United States
- JL Political institutions and public administration — Canada. Latin America
- JN Political institutions and public administration — Europe
- JQ Political institutions and public administration — Asia. Africa. Australia. Pacific area
- JS Local government. Municipal government
- JV Colonies and colonization. Emigration and immigration. International migration
- JZ International relations

K Law
- K General. Comparative and uniform law. Jurisprudence
- KBR-KBU Canon Law and Law of the Roman Catholic Church. The Holy See
- KD United Kingdom and Ireland
- KDZ America. North America
- KE Canada
- KF United States
- KG Latin America. Central America. West Indies
- KH South America
- KJ-KK Europe
- KL-KW Asia. Africa. Pacific Area. Antarctica
- KZ Law of nations

L Education
- L Education (General)
- LA History of education
- LB Theory and practice of education
- LC Special aspects of education
- LD Individual institutions — United States
- LE Individual institutions — America (except United States)
- LF Individual institutions — Europe
- LG Individual institutions — Asia. Africa. Oceania
- LH College and school magazines and papers
- LJ Student fraternities and societies, United States
- LT Textbooks

M Music
- M Musical works
- ML Literature on music
- MT Musical instruction and study

N Fine Arts
- N Visual Arts (General)
- NA Architecture
- NB Sculpture
- NC Drawing. Design. Illustration
- ND Painting
- NE Print media
- NK Decorative arts. Applied arts.
- NX Arts in general

P Language and Literature
- P Philology. Linguistics
- PA Greek and Latin languages and literatures
- PB Modern languages (General). Celtic languages
- PC Romance languages
- PD Germanic languages (General). Scandinavian languages
- PE English language
- PF West Germanic languages
- PG Slavic, Baltic, Albanian languages and literature
- PH Uralic, Basque languages and literatures
- PJ Oriental philology and literature (General). Semitic languages and literature

PK Indo-Iranian languages and literatures
PL Languages and literatures of Eastern Asia, Africa, Oceania
PM Hyperborean, Indian, and Artificial languages
PN Literature (General)
PQ French, Italian, Spanish and Portuguese literatures
PR English literature
PS American literature
PT Germanic literatures
PZ Fiction and Juvenile belles lettres

Q Science

Q Science (General)
QA Mathematics
QB Astronomy
QC Physics
QD Chemistry
QE Geology
QH Natural History. Biology
QK Botany
QL Zoology
QM Human anatomy
QP Physiology
QR Microbiology

R Medicine

R Medicine (General)
RA Public aspects of medicine
RB Pathology
RC Internal medicine
RD Surgery
RE Ophthalmology
RF Otorhinolaryngology
RG Gynecology and obstetrics
RJ Pediatrics
RK Dentistry
RL Dermatology
RM Therapeutics. Pharmacology
RS Pharmacy and materia medica
RT Nursing
RV Botanic, Thomsonian, and eclectic medicine
RX Homeopathy
RZ Other systems of medicine

S Agriculture

S Agriculture (General)
SB Plant culture
SD Forestry
SF Animal culture
SH Aquaculture. Fisheries. Angling
SK Hunting sports

T Technology

T Technology (General)
TA Engineering (General) Civil engineering
TC Hydraulic engineering. Ocean engineering
TD Environmental technology. Sanitary engineering
TE Highway engineering. Roads and pavements
TF Railroad engineering and operation
TG Bridge engineering
TH Building construction
TJ Mechanical engineering and machinery
TK Electrical engineering. Electronics. Nuclear engineering
TL Motor vehicles. Aeronautics. Astronautics
TN Mining engineering. Metallurgy
TP Chemical technology
TR Photography
TS Manufactures
TT Handicrafts. Arts and crafts
TX Home economics. Hospitality industry

U Military Science

U Military science (General)
UA Armies: Organization, distribution, military situation
UB Military administration
UC Maintenance and transportation
UD Infantry
UE Cavalry. Armor
UF Artillery
UG Military engineering. Air forces
UH Other services

V Naval Science

(For naval history, see D-F)

V Naval science (General)
VA Navies: Organization, distribution, naval situation
VB Naval administration
VC Naval maintenance
VD Naval seamen
VE Marines
VF Naval ordnance
VG Minor services of navies
VK Navigation. Merchant marine
VM Naval architecture. Shipbuilding. Marine engineering

Z Bibliography and Library Science

Z Books Writing. Paleography. Books Industries. Trade. Libraries. Bibliography
ZA Information resources (General)

LIBRARY OF CONGRESS
www.loc.gov

CATALOGING DISTRIBUTION SERVICE
101 Independence Ave., S.E.
Washington, DC
20541-4912
www.loc.gov/cds

2/02

5. Some Popular Databases in Westlaw

In Westlaw, the main division of categories is into the following, from choosing online the menu View Westlaw Directory:

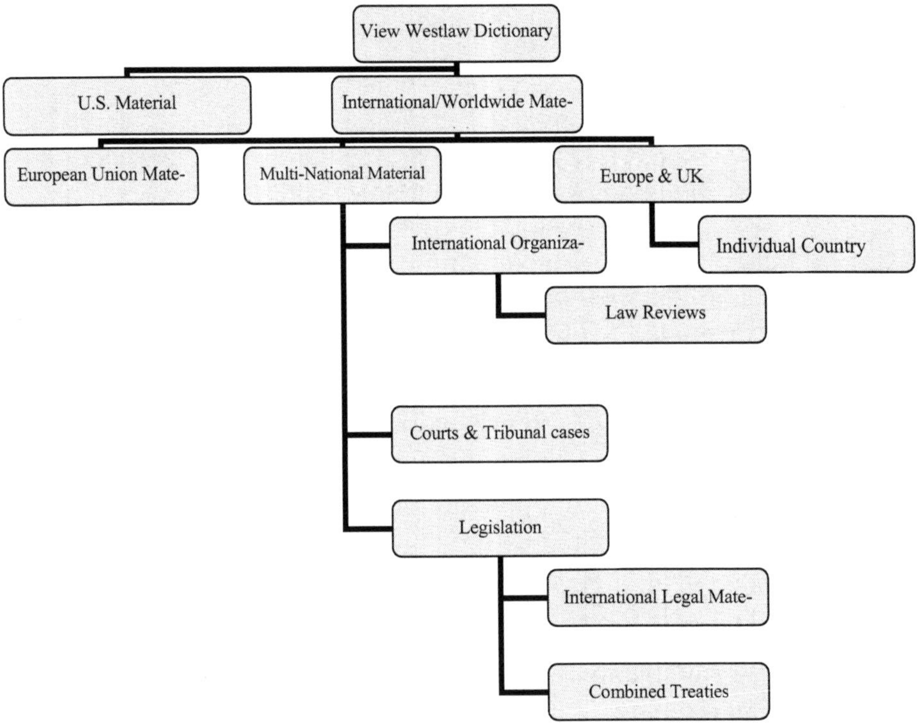

Table 60: Westlaw Database Overview

Subject	Database Identifier
All Federal & State cases (U.S.)	ALLCASES
UK-cases	UK-CASELOC
European Reports All	EU-RPTS-ALL
European Union Cases All	EU-CS-ALL
Common Market Law Reports (EU)	CML-RPTS
Federal Communications – Cases (U.S.)	FCOM-CS
Intellectual Property cases	FIP-CS
All Law Reports (U.S.)	All-RPTS
International Court of Justice	INT-ICJ
International Criminal Tribunal for Rwanda	INT-ICTR
International Criminal Tribunal for the Former Yugoslavia	INT-ICTY-ALL
International Commercial Arbitration	ICA-ALL
WTO & GATT Panel decisions	WTO-DEC
Text & Periodicals (U.S.)	TP-ALL
Journal & Law Review (U.S.)	JLR
Text & Treatises (U.S.)	TEXTS
American Law Reports (U.S.)	ALR
American Jurisprudence 2d (U.S.)	AMJUR
Restatement (U.S.)	REST
American Journal of Comparative Law (U.S.)	AMJCL
Communications Law Reviews, Texts & Bar Journals (U.S.)	COM-TP
Intellectual Property - Reviews, Texts & Bar Journals (U.S.)	IP-TP
Legislation cases (Text & Periodicals) (U.S.)	LTG-TP
American Journal of Comparative Law (U.S.)	AMJCL
Communications Law Reviews, Texts & Bar Journals (U.S.)	COM-TP
Intellectual Property - Reviews, Texts & Bar Journals (U.S.)	IP-TP

Legislation cases (Text & Periodicals) (U.S.)	LTG-TP
World Journals and Law Review	WORLD-JLR
International Law, Law reviews, Texts, and Bar journals	INT-TP
International HR journal	INTLHRJ
International Legal Material	ILM
International Legal Material Cumulative Index	ILM-INDX
International Trade Commission	FINT-ITC
International Trade Law and Regulation	INTTLR
U.N. Commission on International Trade Law – Model laws	UNITRAL-MODL
American Journal of International Law	AMJIL
American Society of International Law	ASIL
ILSA Journal of International and Comparative Law	ILSAJICL
International and Comparative Law Quarterly	ICLQ
Journal of International Criminal Justice	JINTCRJ
Journal of International Legal Studies	JILS
ALR International	ALRINTL
Restatement of the Foreign Relations Law of the United States	REST-FOREL
Index to Foreign Legal Periodicals	IFLP
United Kingdom law Reviews	UK-JLR
European Law Review	EURLR
Columbia Journal of European Law	CLMJEURL
European Competition Law Review	ECLR
European Intellectual Property Review	EIPR
All European Union Materials	EU-ALL
European Union Commission legislation	EU-LEG

European Union Treaties	EU-TREATIES
European Union Preparatory Acts	EU-ACTS
European Parliamentary questions	EU-QUESTIONS
European Union OJC Series	EU-OJCSERIES
Tenders Electronic Daily	TENDERDLY
European Union Community Trademark	EC-TM
Legal Journals Index	LJI
State Statutes Annotated (U.S.)	ST-ANN-ALL
Combined Treaties	CMB-TREATIES
International Treaties and Forms	INT-TF
International Commercial Arbitration Treaties	ICA-TREATIES
Internet and Online Law	IOLAW

6. Sample Syllabus – U.S. Legal Research

Class	Topic	Reading Assignment	Other Assignments
1	Basic differences between common law and Civil Law	Book Chapter 1 except section 1.4 Book Chapter 5, section 5.1. Book section 5.1.0 Exercise: book section 5.11.4	
2	New sources and non law research databases	Book sections 5.3. and 5.4.	Patrick, *Beyond Case Reporters: Using Newspapers to Supplement the Legal-Historical Record* (June 16, 2010). Available at SSRN: <http://ssrn.com/abstract=1625978>.
3	Secondary sources in law	Book section 5.2.1	Osbeck, Impeccable Research[1], Part III
4	Legislation in the United States and legislative histories	Book section 5.2.3.3	McDade, *Legislative history is easy to find with various databases*, STUDENT LAWYER, December 2006, p. 10.
5	Statutory research	Book sections 5.2.2. and 5.2.3.	Whisner, *The United States Code, Prima Facie Evidence, and Positive Law*, 101 LAW LIBRARY JOURNAL 545 (2009).

[1] Osbeck, Mark K., IMPECCABLE RESEARCH : A CONCISE GUIDE TO MASTERING LEGAL RESEARCH SKILLS (St. Paul, MN : West, 2010).

6	Regulatory research	Book section 5.2.4.	Federal Regulatory Directory, 14th Edition, pp 1-21.
7	Case law research	Book section 5.2.5.	Abramson, Kennedy and Pollock, *Inside the West Empire*, THE AMERICAN LAWYER, October 1983, p. 90.
8	Using citators	Book section 5.6	Lee, *Introducing and Integrating Free Internet Legal Research into the Classroom* (June 10, 2009). UNIVERSITY OF MIAMI LEGAL STUDIES RESEARCH PAPER No. 2010-05. Available at SSRN: <http://ssrn.com/abstract=1509673>. & SURRENCY, ERWIN C. A HISTORY OF AMERICAN LAW PUBLISHING (New York: Oceana Publications, 1990) chapter 14.
9	Research process – putting it all together	Book sections 5, 5.7, 5.8 and 5.9.	Osbeck, Impeccable Research,[1] Part I.
10	Future directions and review of student exercises	Book sections 5.5, 5.11.1, 5.11.2 and 5.11.3	Ehrlich, *Westlaw's new upgrade – WestlawNext*, PLAINTIFF, May 2010, p. 30, and <http://www.public.resource.org/law.gov/>.

7. Sample Syllabus – European Union

Class	Topic	Reading Assignment	Other Assignments
1	Basic differences between common law and Civil Law Legal families	Book Chapter 1 except section 1.4 Book chapter 2	Consider the reading with the country wizard given in Charter 3 section 3.7.1.1 and prepare for discussion on the differences between the U.S. and a country in continental Europe
2	Requirement for studying foreign law & interpretation Comparative Law Method – not only comparison	Book chapter 3 Chapter 1, section 1.4 Chapter 4	Exercises in 3.11.1 & 2
3	Civil Law basics for Americans Legal science and legal philosophy in Civil Law countries	Book Chapter 7, section 7.1 until subsection 7.1.6.1 Book subsection 7.1.7	
4	Citations Introduction to legal research in Civil Law countries Legal methodology The legal method in principle	Book subsection 7.1.8. Book subsection 7.2.1. Book subsection 7.2.2. Book subsection 7.2.3	
5	The method in detail	Book section 3.3 until subsection 7.3.2	
6	Use of the source of law Interpretation of the law-sources	Book subsection 7.3.2. Book subsection 7.3.3.	

7	Relations between national law and International / E.U. law	Book subsection 7.3.4	
8	European Union[1] Sources of E.U. law	Book Chapter 9 sections 9.1 & 9.2 Book section 9.3	Exercise section 9.8.1
9	Where to find E.U. material, inclusive online websites Reader information for directory of Community legislation Citations	Book section 9.4 Book section 9.6 Book section 9.5	Exercise section 9.8.2
10	Student presentations		For example over legislation that a Member State has not implemented and therefore been reprimanded by the E.U. Commission

[1] Some E.U. secondary education teaching material can be found at <www.eurunion.org/infores/teaching/secondary.htm>.

8. Sample Syllabus – Non-US & E.U.-Law Material

Class	Topic	Reading Assignment	Other Assignments
1	Basic differences between common law and Civil Law Legal families	Book Chapter 1 except section 1.4 Book chapter 2	Consider the reading with the country wizard given in Charter 3 section 3.7.1.1 and prepare for discussion on the differences between the U.S. and a country in continental Europe
2	Requirement for studying foreign law & interpretation Comparative Law Method – not only comparison	Book chapter 3 Chapter 1, section 1.4 Chapter 4	Exercises in 3.11.1 & 2
3	Civil Law basics for Americans Legal science and legal philosophy in Civil Law countries	Book Chapter 7, section 7.1 until subsection 7.1.6.1 Book subsection 7.1.7	
4	Citations Introduction to legal research in Civil Law countries Legal methodology The legal method in principle	Book subsection 7.1.8. Book subsection 7.2.1. Book subsection 7.2.2. Book subsection 7.2.3	
5	The method in detail	Book section 3.3 until subsection 7.3.2	
6	Use of the source of law Interpretation of the law-sources	Book subsection 7.3.2. Book subsection 7.3.3.	
7	Relations between national law and International / E.U. law Russian Resources - Civil Law	Book subsection 7.3.4 Chapter 8	

8	England Resources – Common Law China Resources – Law of the Far East	Book Chapter 6 Book Chapter 10	
9	Public International Law Resources	Book Chapter 11	
10	International Organization's Resources	Book Chapter 12	
11	Student presentations		Presentation of where to find law of a specific country and how it is governed

9. Tables

10. Index

Also look above in Appendix 1 "Glossary: Terms & Abbreviations" which also contain important information.

§

A

B

D

E

F

G

J

K

L

S

T

U

Backlist

DJØF Publishing
www.djoef-forlag.dk

Abnormally Low Tenders
With an Emphais on Public Tenderes
By Grith Skovgaard Ølykke – 1. ed. 2010
ISBN 978-87-574-2359-4

Art and Law
The copyright Debat
By Morten Rosenmeier & Stina Theilmann (eds.) – 1. ed. 2005
ISBN 978-87-574-1298-7

Assistance to Victims of Descrimination by Eyuality Bodies of the EU-Member States
-A Scandinavian Perspective
By Bjørn Dilou Jacobsen – 1. ed. 2010
ISBN 978-87-574-1298-7

Changing international Law to Meet New Challenges
Interpretation, Modification and the Use of Force
By Andreas Laursen – 1. ed. 2006
ISBN 978-87-574-1529-2

Conflict Management in the Family Field
– and other Intimate and Close Relations
By Pia Deleuran (ed.) – 1. ed. 2011
ISBN 978-87-574-2303-7

Copenhagen Competition 2010
On Access to Medicines
By Laura Nielsen (ed.), 1. ed. 2010
ISBN 978-87-574-2254-2

The Copenhagen Competition on Climate Change
By Anita rønne, Peter Pagh & Laura Nielsen (eds.), 1. ed. 2009
ISBN 978-87-574-2096-8

Crime, Punishment and Justice
Selected articles from a Scholarly Career
By Ulla V. Bondesen – 1. ed. 2007
ISBN 978-87-574-1763-0

Custum
The Development and Use of a Legal concept in the Middle Ages
Proceedings of the Fifth Carlsberg Academy Conference on Medieval Legal history
By Per Andersen, Mia Münster-Swendsen & Helle Vogt (eds.) – 1. ed. 2009
ISBN 978-87-574-2017-3

Cyberspace & International Law on Jurisdiction
By Henrik Spang-Hanssen – 1. ed. 2004
ISBN 978-87-574-0890-4

Danish Arbitration Act 2005
By Ketilbjørn Hertz – 1. ed. 2005
ISBN 978-87-574-1427-1

Danish Buiness Law
By Bent Iversen, Lars Lindencrone Petersen & Morten Wegener (eds.)
4. ed. 2010
ISBN 978-87-574-2132-8

Embedding Mahr in the European Legal System
By Rubya Mehdi & Jørgen S. Nielsen (eds.) – 1. ed. 2011
ISBN 978-87-574-2475-8

Enforcement of the EU Public Procurement Rules
By Roberto Caranta & Steen Treumer (eds.) – 1. ed. 2011
ISBN 978-87-574-2328-0

Europe
The New Legal Realism
Essays in Honour of Hjalte Rasmussen
By Henning Koch, Karsten Hagel-Sørensen, Ulrich Haltern & Joseph H.h: Weiler (eds.) – 1. ed. 2010
ISBN 978-87-574-2282-9

European Legal Method
By Ulla Neergaard, Ruth Nielsen & Lynn Rosberry (eds.) – 1. ed. 2011
ISBN 978-87-574-2377-8

Free Movement in the European Union
By Morten Broberg & Nina Holst-Christensen – 4. ed. 2010
ISBN 978-87-574-2044-9

Gender Equality in European Contract Law
By Ruth Nielsen – 1. ed. 2004
ISBN 978-87-574-0687-0

The IN-House Providing in European Law
By Mario Comba & Steen Treumer (eds.) – 1. ed. 2010
ISBN 978-87-574-2168-2

Integrating Welfare Functions into EU Law
From Rome to Lisbon
By Ulla Neergaard, Ruth Nielsen & Lynn Roseberry – 1. ed. 2009
ISBN 978-87-574-1898-8

Is the Sui Generis Rights a Failed Experiment?
A legal and Theoretical Exploration of How to Regulate Unoriginal Database Contents
By Robin Elisabeth Herr – 1. ed. 2008
ISBN 978-87-574-1881-1

Judicial Accommodation of Human Rights in the European Union
By Ane Maria Røddik Christensen – 1. ed. 2007
ISBN 978-87-574-1689-3

Law and Learning in the Middle Ages
Proceedings of the Second Carlsberg Academy Conference on Medieval Legal history
By Mia Münster-Swendsen & Helle Vogt (eds.) – 1. ed. 2006
ISBN 978-87-574-1437-0

Law and Literature
Interdisciplinary Methods of Reading
By Karen-Margrethe Simonsen & Ditlev Tamm (eds.) – 1. ed. 2010
ISBN 978-87-574-1878-1

Law and Power in the Middle Ages
Proceedings of the Fourth Carlsberg Academy Conference of Medieval Legal history.
By Per Andersen, Mia Münster-Swendsen & Helle Vogts (eds.) – 1. ed. 2008
ISBN 978-87-574-1884-2

Law and Private Life in the Middle Ages
Proceedings of the Sixth Carlsberg Academy Conference of Medieval Legal history.
By Per Andersen, Mia Münster-Swendsen & Helle Vogts (eds.) – 1. ed. 2011
ISBN 978-87-574-2159-0

Law and Religion in Multicultural Societies
By Rubya Mehdi, Hanne Petersen, Erik Reenberg Sand & Gordon R. Woodman (eds.), 1. ed. 2008
ISBN 978-87-574-1843-9

Law and Religion in the 21st Century
Nordic Perspectives
By Lisbet Christoffersen, Svend Andersen & Kjell Å Modéer (eds.),
1. ed. 2010
ISBN 978-87-574-2368-6

Law before Gratian
Law in Western Europe c. 500-1100
Proceedings of the third Carlsberg Academy Conference on Medieval Legal history
By Per Andersen, Mia Münster-Swendsen & Helle Vogt (eds.) – 1. ed. 2007
ISBN 978-87-574-1647-3

The Law of Green and Social Procurement in Europe
By Roberto Caranta & Steen Martin Trybus (eds.) – 1. ed. 2010
ISBN 978-87-574-2325-9

Mediation
– a non-model
By Vibeke Vindeløv – 1. ed. 2007
ISBN 978-87-574-1479-3

Mediation
Six ways in seven days
By Hans Boserup – 1. ed. 2007
ISBN 978-87-574-1755-5

Regulating competition in the EU
By Bent Iversen, Pernille Wegener Jessen. Bent Ole Gram Mortensen, Michael Steinicke & Karsten Engsig Sørensen (eds.) – 1. ed. 2008
ISBN 978-87-574-1697-8

The Principal Danish Criminal Act
The criminal Code, The Corrections Act, The Administration of Justice Act
By Vagn Greve, Gitte Høyer, Malene Freese Jensen & Martin Spencer – 3. ed. 2006
ISBN 978-87-574-1334-2

The New EU Public Procurement Directive
By Ruth Nielsen & Steen Treumer (eds.) – 1. ed. 2005
ISBN 978-87-574-1244-4

Public international Computer Network Law Issues
By Henrik Spang-Hanssen – 1. ed. 2006
ISBN 978-87-574-1486-8

Public Procurement Law
– the EU directive on public contracts
By Simon Evers Hjelmborg, Peter Stig Jakobsen & Sune Troels Poulsen – 1. ed. 2006
ISBN 978-87-574-1408-0

The Role of Courts in Developing a European Social Model
– Theoretical and Metodological Perspectives
By Ulla Neergaard, Ruth Nielsen & Lynn Rosberry (eds.) – 1. ed. 2010
ISBN 978-87-574-2172-0

The Services Directive
– Consequences for the Welfare State and the European Social Model
By Ulla Neergaard, Ruth Nielsen & Lynn Rosberry (eds.) – 1. ed. 2008
ISBN 978-87-574-1806-4

Yearbook for Nordic Tax Research 2007
Taxation of Pensions
By Robert Påhlsson (ed.) – 1. ed. 2007
ISBN 978-87-574-1774-6

Yearbook of Nordic Tax Research 2008 Taxcation of Capital and wage Income: Towards separated or more Integrated Personal Tax Systems?
By Robert Påhlsson (ed.) – 1. ed. 2008
ISBN 978-87-574-1872-9

Yearbook of Nordic Tax Research 2009
The Non-Fiscal Purposes on Taxation
By Jane Bolander (ed.) – 1. ed. 2009
ISBN 978-87-574-2077-7

Yearbook of Nordic Tax Research 2010
Taxation on Individuals and Goods in the Nordic Countries upon Cross Border Mobility
By Jane Bolander (ed.) – 1. ed. 2010
ISBN 978-87-574-2276-4